L. RON HUBBARD

Messiah or Madman?

L. RON HUBBARD

Messiah or Madman?

by BENT CORYDON

Barricade Books Inc., Fort Lee, N.J.

Published by Barricade Books Inc., 1530 Palisade Avenue, Fort Lee, NJ 07024
Distributed by Publishers Group West, 4065 Hollis, Emeryville, CA 94608

Copyright © 1987, 1992 by Bent Corydon

Revised, expanded and updated edition.

Printed in the United States of America.

Library of Congress Cataloging-in-Publication Data
Corydon, Bent.
    L. Ron Hubbard : messiah or madman? / Bent Corydon. —Rev.,
updated, and expanded ed.
      p.   cm.
    ISBN 0-942637-57-7 (pbk.) : $12.95
    1. Hubbard, L. Ron (La Fayette Ron), 1911–   . 2. Scientologists—
United States—Biography.   3. Church of Scientology—History.
I. Title.
[BP605.S2C67   1992]
299′.936′092—dc20
[B]   91-39368
                                                 CIP

Acknowledgement

Brian Ambry organized and wrote the update sections and reorganized and improved the book for this paperback edition. His work on research and writing for the original book was substantial and without him this book would not have been possible.

Contents

7

PART TWO

"Unscrupulous Womanizer" to "Ascended Messiah"

PART TWO UPDATE

ADDENDUM
—For The Second Edition—

Preface

In 1970 Paulette Cooper wrote, and had published, a book called *The Scandal of Scientology* containing some biographical matter on Hubbard. She was hounded by Church of Scientology agents for a decade, and at one point was almost convicted on Federal felony charges, having been framed by Church agents.

Documents obtained by the FBI in 1977 revealed an elaborate plan to have her incarcerated, or have her driven to suicide. She finally received a large cash settlement from the Church, with the understanding that she would not press criminal charges against Scientology, and also would stop the publication of her new book on the subject.

In 1979 Omar Garrison, a professional writer who had previously written three books at the request of L. Ron Hubbard's agents, was commissioned by him to write his biography. He was given access to thousands of private documents, many of which Hubbard erroneously believed no longer existed. Garrison spent 18 months pouring over them and interviewing people from Hubbard's past. As he gained more and more information, he came to a decision that he could not, in good conscience, write the "PR" biography that had been intended.

In early 1984, disgusted by the entire affair, Garrison accepted a large cash sum by Hubbard's agents not to write the biography which he was then planning. This one would have given what was, in his own estimation, a truthful account of Hubbard's life.

The majority of the documents and information, on which Garrison was to have based the biography, were revealed in a trial in a Los Angeles Courtroom in mid 1984. Gerry Armstrong assisted Garrison by locating thousands of Hubbard's documents, and was the key subject of this trial.

These revelations backed up many of the stories told to me by Hubbard's first son, Ron Jr.

In 1986, after the "Church" discovered that the book you are reading was being written, a roughly 6'4" 250 lb man in a black leather jacket and gloves arrived at my workplace asking for me.

11

Failing to locate me, he told one of my assistants, "Since Corydon's not here, you'll do." He then yelled, "You are standing in the way of Ron's bridge!" and proceeded to punch him in the face, and knock him around.*

Obscene and threatening phone calls to my home became commonplace, often occurring while I was out and directed at my wife, telling her, "We know you're alone!"

****

L. Ron Hubbard Jr. was contracted as co-author of this book and co-operated for more than half of its writing, providing information. He was then offered an undisclosed amount of money by Church of Scientology representatives to cease any assistance on the book and remove his name from it.

He took the money and signed papers to that effect. Lyle Stuart, the publisher, having in hand a prior signed contract, decided to go ahead regardless.

In 1972, Ron Jr. had signed affidavits saying that statements he had made about his father were false. He later claimed he did so after much harassment.

Less than a year after Ron Jr. left his father's organization in 1960 he was talking openly about his experiences. That was when his father wrote an official Church policy stating:

"If attacked on some vulnerable point by anyone or anything or any organization, always find OR MANUFACTURE enough threat against them to cause them to sue for peace." (emphasis added)

Whenever Ron Jr. has spoken publicly, the Church has trotted out his "signed retraction."

Unfortunately for them, many other documents have surfaced in court that have backed up the majority of what Hubbard's son had been saying. And nothing he has said about his father has, to my knowledge, been proved incorrect.

During my visits to his home in Carson City, Nevada, I found Ron Hubbard Jr. a gentle man who showed enormous affection for his wife and now grown children.

He claimed that the well-being of his then young family was the chief consideration in signing these specious affidavits.

Testifying under oath in 1982, Ron Jr. stated:

---

*This person's name is Dennis Clarke. He has since been promoted to the position of "Director" of **The Citizen's Commission on Human Rights,** one of Scientology's "front groups." He now wears a suit and tie, and eye-glasses.

"They [the Church] were very upset that I had appeared in public and started spilling the beans . . . Bob Thomas [head of the intelligence wing of Scientology in the U.S. at the time] showed me pictures of my children going to and from school. We got calls in the night. My wife was scared to death with calls. People were looking through the windows of our little house . . .

"I didn't have any money . . . What happened was that they wanted me to recant and—I was under duress at the time—and because I was scared stiff. . . And I didn't know what the legal ramifications were . . . occurred in 1972 . . . In order to protect my wife and children I signed the recant."

I felt this had a ring of truth. Especially when added to what I knew of the sinister ability of Hubbard's agents to "persuade" others into complying with his intentions.

Ron Jr. accepted money from the Church in May of 1986 (partly to cease co-operation with this book), while he was in a severely weakened physical condition. Ron Jr. is a diabetic. During the prior six months, he had part of his foot amputated and hovered near death for three days during a subsequent operation on his abdomen. These events had, besides the physical and emotional trauma, left him in a financially devastated condition.

****

Concurrent with "the Church making peace" with Hubbard's eldest son in 1986, a woman—now in her mid thirties with red hair and unmistakable features distinguishing her as a Hubbard—who's first name is Alexis, was paid a sum of money to settle her claim to part of Hubbard's estate.

She refused, however, to sign a document presented to her as part of the agreement by Church of Scientology representatives. It spelled out a bizarre claim that L. Ron Hubbard JUNIOR is her real father. (The probate case being settled was based on the fact that the deceased L. Ron Hubbard SENIOR is her real father. His name is on her birth certificate.)

This attempt to get L. Ron Hubbard's daughter by his second marriage to attest that Hubbard's son is her real father, was another in a long series of often shockingly successful cover-ups.

****

As of the Spring of 1991, I have been a regular target for Scientology harassment—both "legal" and otherwise—for over a decade. I have been sued six times. I have counter-sued twice.

I have had to struggle within a court system which does not recognize as meaningful the long-standing Scientology policy of using frivolous lawsuits for purposes of harassment.

It's been very hard work. Yet I've been amazingly successful—or lucky. There **are** good judges, and even some honest lawyers. Unfortunately, over-all, the "legal system" works in favor of the rich: competent lawyers are **expensive.** And the system of near endless "appeals" often can bring the average person to his knees financially—and sometimes, emotionally.

I've watched many fall by the way-side. Silenced in various ways: by threats, harassment of family members, litigation induced financial problems, stress related illnesses, and—perhaps most insidiously— so-called "legal settlements" arrived at under these—and other— conditions of **duress.**

In light of all this, it occurred to me that there is no absolute guarantee that I will always be able to withstand the Machiavellian-like machinations of this big sticky trap called the Church of Scientology. I have a family to support. It is feasible that I may collapse financially before the legal process is complete, and also feasible that I may have to "settle" on less than ideal terms.

With this in mind, I wish to state that no matter what my fate may be, that one thing is absolutely true: I whole-heartedly support all of those who are working to make known the many hidden facts about this amoral and exploitive organization, and expose the truth about its founder, L. Ron Hubbard.

I unequivocally stand by the contents of **L. Ron Hubbard, Messiah or Madman?** This book has helped many to think through, and sort out, their disturbing experiences with Scientology. It has also helped to "inoculate" those who might otherwise be vulnerable to Scientology.

I look forward to seeing a Second Edition in paperback.

****

Who was Hubbard? What are the many secrets he worked (and now his Church works) so hard to keep concealed?

The story of L. Ron Hubbard is a study of the bizarre. The more one knows about him, the more one feels he should have been impossible. It just could not happen. But there he was: A chain-smoking enigmatic bundle of contradictions.

Introduction:
Scientology Celebrates
L. Ron Hubbard's
"Spiritual Ascension"

"Best-selling author, Founder of Scientology, friend to millions," proclaims the headline of a full-page paid announcement in the *Los Angeles Times* and other major newspapers across the planet.

Under a photograph of the Founder the text continues:

> L. Ron Hubbard . . . a man whose tremendous contributions to virtually all walks of life have made him the greatest humanitarian in history.
>
> Indeed, few men have achieved so much in so many different fields. Author, philosopher, educator, research pioneer, musician, photographer, cinematographer, horticulturalist, navigator, explorer and humanitarian—Mr. Hubbard has been widely recognized for his contributions in all of these fields. . . .

Presented are many eulogies, including:

> "My only sorrow is that L. Ron Hubbard left before I could thank him for my new life."—SONNY BONO.

> "Dynamic, dramatic, dynamitic—this was the red-headed ball of fire I first met in 1937. Ten years later I became his agent. He gave the world of science fiction and fantasy two acknowledged masterpieces: *Final Blackout* and *Fear*. In both the literary world and the mundane he left a mark on humankind that will be felt in the 21st century, a century about which he frequently wrote and which in 'real' life he attempted to influence for the better. I see him now, blazing away on

that Typewriter in the Sky."—FORREST J. ACKERMAN, Renowned Science Fiction Agent and Author.

"L. Ron Hubbard set a star-high goal for us. He documented it with pure science. He taught it with pure love. He's left nothing but pure inspiration."—CHICK COREA, award-winning Jazz Composer and Musician.

A subsequent glossy memorial booklet was included as a supplement in issues of the *Los Angeles Times* and *New York Times*.

****

A few days prior to the first advertised collection of eulogies . . .

27 January 1986:
Scientology Churches and Missions all over the planet are ordered by International Management to close their doors. Their staff and public are instructed to proceed to specified locations where they will view a special event broadcast via satellite. Those Scientologists from the Los Angeles area are told to proceed directly to the Hollywood Palladium. The event is to start at seven P.M. sharp. Every seat is filled well before then.

Large speakers above the stage blast forth stirring music. The stage is decorated with giant Scientology symbols and huge photographs of the Founder. The music and setting have an obvious impact on the audience, representing the reach of Scientologists for ultimate spiritual freedom and ability.

As the music reaches its finale, 24-year-old "Commander" David Miscavige appears. He is a tiny man and his flim frame cuts a small figure on the large stage. Wearing a dress naval uniform of the elite Sea Organization, he is resplendent with gold braid and shoulder lanyard. Miscavage, the de facto third most powerful executive of the Church of Scientology, now that Hubbard is gone, begins to speak. (None of the people in the audience is yet aware that Hubbard is dead).

MISCAVIGE:

I've very happy that you could all make it to this important briefing this evening.
In 1980 LRH moved off the lines so that he could continue his writings and research without any distractions. For many years Ron had

said that if he was given the time, and if others wore their hats* and did their jobs in expanding the Church, he would be able to concentrate on and complete all of his researches into the upper OT** levels, so that the bridge*** would be laid out in full for all of us.

Over the past six years LRH has been intensively researching the upper bands of OT. . . .

Approximately two weeks ago, he completed all of his researches he set out to do.

The crowd, awed and delighted, responds with oohs and aahs and abundant applause.

Commander Miscavige continues:

He has now moved on to the next level of OT research. It's a level beyond anything any of us ever imagined.

This level is in fact done in an exterior state. Meaning that it is done completely exterior from the body. At this level of OT, the body is nothing more than in impediment and encumberance to any further gain as an OT.

Thus at 2000 hours, the 24th of January, AD36,† L. Ron Hubbard discarded the body he had used in this life time for 74 years 10 months and 11 days.

. . . He thought it was important that Scientologists be the first to become aware of this fact.

. . . The body is a physical object. It is not the being himself. The being we know as L. Ron Hubbard still exists; however, the body could no longer serve his purposes. His decision was made at complete cause. . . . He has simply moved on to his next step.

. . . LRH, in fact, used this lifetime in the body we knew, to accomplish what no man has ever accomplished. He unlocked the mysteries of life, and gave us the tools so we could free ourselves and our fellow man. L. Ron Hubbard completed everything he set out to do and more. The fact that he causatively, willingly discarded the body, after it was no longer useful to him, signifies his *ultimate* success: the conquest of life that he embarked upon half a century ago.

Miscavige begins to clap, slowly almost mechanically. His ever-

*Did their jobs.
**Operating Thetan. A spiritual being restored to his "native state" of godlike abilities.
***A gradient series of steps leading, supposedly, to O.T.
†After Dianetics (Hubbard's book *Dianetics, the Modern Science of Mental Health* was published in 1950).

present fierce stare becoming even more intense. The packed Palladium bursts into applause during which the crowd is led in a series of Hip-hip hoorays! The applause lasts for some twenty minutes until Miscavige finally stops, permitting the rest to do the same.

Commander David Miscavige is obviously pleased and, perhaps, a little relieved.*

Miscavige introduces Earle Cooley, Boston lawyer and recently proclaimed "Scientologist." He is a large man with a face reminiscent of a well-fed, aging Irish boxer. Cooley announces that he has seen to the execution of the wishes expressed by Hubbard in his will; that he has contacted the coroner's office and the funeral parlor, and that the body was cremated the next day at three P.M. (less than 24 hours after his death).

COOLEY:

There are several very important matters that I wish to bring to your attention.

First, the body of L. Ron Hubbard was sound and strong and fully capable of serving this Mighty Thetan [Scientology word for Spiritual Being] for many years, had that suited his purpose.

. . . Thus, by the decision to continue his work outside the confines of his body, and by the decision to do it now, L. Ron Hubbard has given the ultimate expression of his love for you.

He has, in effect, told us the Church is in good hands: "You can do it all. Your future is assured. Secure in this knowledge I go about my work elsewhere. You have all of the tools. You have all of the resources to take this planet and to save Mankind.

"Support and rally behind your leaders. Together you will win the total victory and achieve the ultimate goals of Scientology. Take what I have given you with my love."

****

In 1949 a broke middle-aged science fiction writer authored a book which became a best seller: *Dianetics, the Modern Science of Mental Health*. Mail arrived at his doorstep by the sack-load, and the money rolled in.

In 1952 that author, L. Ron Hubbard, unveiled a more spiritually oriented subject, Scientology.

One year later, he founded the Church of Scientology, using his

*Miscavige has since become Scientology's absolute dictator. See 'Updates'.

Dianetic following as a base. Over the years it grew, becoming a multi-million dollar operation.

The *Encyclopedia Brittanica Yearbook* states: "According to a study by Peter Rowley [author of] *New Gods in America* . . . largest of the new religions is Scientology."

Werner Erhard, of EST fame, called L. Ron Hubbard the "greatest philosopher of the twentieth Century."

Researchers in the field of para-psychology at Stanford Research Institute went so far as to have many of the various Scientology counseling techniques applied to themselves.

For over a quarter of a century Hubbard lectured to audiences all over the world. He was exciting, witty, charming and brilliant.

Celebrities arrived seeking enlightenment. John Travolta, Karen Black, Chick Corea, Stephen Boyd, Gloria Swanson, William Burroughs . . . the list goes on.

There are even those who claim to have witnessed him change his body's size, read minds, move objects telekinetically, or zoom up ladders defying gravity.

To his followers he is the reincarnation of the Buddha: The much-prophesied Messiah awaited by untold millions in the Far East and throughout the world. The Meitreya; "He whose name is kindness"; the one with the golden hair. It had been prophesied he would appear in the West, some two and a half thousand years after Buddha's death.

Wrote Hubbard:

> Everywhere you are
> I can be addressed
> But in your temples best
> Address me and you address
> Lord Buddha
> Address Lord Buddha
> And you then address
> Meitreya.

PART I
(1967–1984)

THE ADVENTURES
OF THE
COMMODORE
AND
PART ONE UPDATE

1

A Seafaring Messiah with a "Mission to Save the Planet"

In the fifties, when L. Ron Hubbard established himself as the "lighthearted" leader of what was presented as an anti-authoritarian "scientific religion," it never occurred to anyone that he would, eventually, become the Commodore of his own private navy, and absolute dictator of an enormous authoritarian bureaucracy.

Scientology was a roaring financial success in the sixties, and purchasing a ship was well within his means. So, late in 1966, he bought a yacht and two ships in England, and another ship for crew-training purposes in the States: a small flotilla. The largest of these was the 342-foot ship *Royal Scotsman* (later renamed the *Apollo*), which had been used, during the Second World War, as transport for Winston Churchill.

These years, and into the late seventies, marked the peak of Hubbard's drama, and are noteworthy for, among other things, his defiance of the powers that be—including the United States government.

It was during this time that the bulk of the Church's assets (said by Church President Heber Jenzsch to be a billion dollars) were accumulated, and during which he built the Sea Organization.

It was also during this period that Scientology completed its transition into a militant cult; a transition that took a decade and a half.

Hubbard did all this while claiming that he had resigned from the Church management in 1966 (an announcement which was carried by most of the major media at the time). He was merely a writer in seclusion, he said.

23

But as "Commodore" of the "Sea Org," he remained in control of the movement.

****

In the 1960s Scientology boomed. On five continents students of Scientology studied intently in "academies" at their "local Churches."

People arrived in droves to take courses. Counseling techniques—directed toward resolving such things as learning disabilities, psychosomatic ills, unwanted fears and compulsions, drug and alcohol dependency, communication problems, upsets in life, and many other areas—were studied, practiced and applied.

At L. Ron Hubbard's home, a large Georgian manor on a 40-acre estate in the rolling green countryside of Sussex, England, hundreds of eager students were attending the Saint Hill Special Briefing Course. This course featured live lectures by L. Ron Hubbard until his departure in December 1966, when he began his "Sea Project."

By this time there were also two other "advanced organizations" where "upper level" counseling and training were done (in Scotland, soon to be moved to Copenhagen, Denmark, and in Los Angeles).

****

I had become involved in Scientology at the age of 19 in 1961, having been impressed with Hubbard's books and the theory and practice of Scientology's counseling methods.

"Man is basically good," Hubbard had explained. And now with a truly workable science of the mind and spirit, that basic goodness could be freed of aberrations—the dark impulses, pain, and confusions—that had enveloped it.

Punishment and duress were now no longer necessary to maintain order and so allow society to operate. Besides, punishment "didn't work," and was only a short-term solution, making matters worse in the long run. With the know-how contained in Scientology, Hubbard explained, Mankind could finally attain to a high level of rationality. Mutual understanding and freedom were now possible.

"Ron," as we referred to him (he had encouraged us to feel that he was our personal friend), had spoken to us in books and on tape about our unrealized mental and spiritual abilities, of the state of "clear," where an individual is not held down by negative or traumatic experiences of the past, is fully alive in the "here and now," able to enjoy life fully. A "clear" would operate at full mental capacity, and have the ability to recall anything that has ever happened to him. He would be free of psychosomatic ills. These ills, Hubbard had asserted, comprise 75 percent of all man's ailments.

We, like most Scientologists, believed we were on our way to creating a new civilization—a truly sane planet. Personal "success stories" abounded. Anyone listening to these stories and watching the faces of the people could not but be impressed with their personal gains and genuine enthusiasm. "Scientology Works" was the message.

Hubbard had told Scientologists to be great. Greatness meant that one continued to love others despite all invitations to hate. He had said that the essential self, the soul or "thetan," never dies; but simply "drops" one body and then goes off in search of another, to be born once more and start another round.

He had, we believed, mapped out and "built a bridge" (a system of counseling techniques that progressively get more advanced) which would increase a person's awareness of himself and others, and increase his abilities—even beyond "clear"—to where one could move around, perceive, manipulate objects and communicate without need of a body. One would then be able to leave his body and, as a spirit, go off to smell the sea breezes or soar among the mountain tops. This was called the state of "OT," meaning "operating thetan."

The spirit or "thetan" could return to its "native state," a state wherein compulsive and artificial reliance on a body has been overcome.

Hubbard was fond of relating the aims of Scientology, as it applies to the individual, to the Buddhist goal of freeing oneself from the continuing cycle of birth and death.

At the highest state of "OT" one would have "Total Freedom." This state was defined as "the ability to be at cause knowingly and at will over thought, life, form, matter, energy, space and time, subjective and objective."

The discoveries that would enable people to ultimately achieve this, he said, had come partly from his study of nuclear physics, a subject he claimed to know a lot about, since he "had attended the first class in nuclear phenomena taught at George Washington University." A book by him called *All About Radiation* introduced him as a nuclear physicist and an engineer; so, to many, he appeared to speak with considerable authority.

His claimed credentials made him credible to a generation taught to admire the wonders of modern science.

Besides, he had stressed that no one needed to believe what he said; they should check it out for themselves. "What is true for you is what you have observed for yourself. Nothing in Dianetics and Scientology is true for you unless you have observed it." This principle came from Buddhism, another subject he apparently knew a lot about. He had, he said, traveled extensively in the Far East and had drunk deeply of the wisdom contained in the lamaseries and other centers of wisdom there. And—although not much publicized to outsiders—Scientologists knew him as the reincarnation of the Buddha himself.

****

Mary, my wife, and I had arrived in England from New Zealand in August of 1967. We had mortgaged our home and had hoped to meet Ron at his home, Saint Hill Manor. All this to discover that, months earlier, he had left for places unknown, and was embarking on the Sea Project. This was promoted as an all-out project to "Clear the Planet." The Sea Project soon became the "Sea Organization."

To qualify for Hubbard's elite Sea Organization, referred to as the "Sea Org," recruits were (and still are) required to sign a billion-year contract. Most of them fully expected to serve the full billion years; after all, a thetan (spirit) never dies and, after the inhabitants of this planet had achieved the state of clear, there would be other planets out there in the universe that also needed to be "cleared."

There were wonderful, late-night conversations about the Space Org. This would be set up after Earth had been made a "Scientology Planet." Artists painted space ships soaring through the universe, with the Sea Org emblem on their bows. These paintings were reproduced on the walls of the Scientology organizations throughout the world.

Many of these "orgs" had Hubbard's bronze bust in their front lobbies. His pictures were everywhere: classrooms, halls, and offices. Per policy, an office was also set up for him, usually impeccably decorated and furnished and awaiting his chance visit, even in orgs that were desperately short of floorspace.

****

After 1967, the hub around which all Scientology revolved was the flagship *Apollo*, an immaculately scrubbed white ship cruising majestically through the blue waters of the Mediterranean Sea. Here lived and worked the elite of Scientology in what was billed as the sanest and safest space on earth.

Here also worked L. Ron Hubbard, in a plush oak-panelled office.

He was in touch with all Scientology activities around the world by a modern telex system that rivalled those of major corporations. Of the 300 to 400 crew members, some 20 worked long hours just manning the telexes and other communications systems between Hubbard and his world-wide organizations.

****

The four-year-old boy could no longer cry. He had been nearly 48 hours in the chain locker of the flagship *Apollo* and his entire body was aching from his efforts to chip off rust. His knees and hands were raw with cuts and bruises. His voice was raspy from crying, and he was desperately afraid. He was constantly making resolutions to never, never again eat the Commodore's telexes—the most recent crime of which he had been accused.

Little Tony had entered the chain locker through the tiny manhole that led to it. The metallic sound as the lid slammed shut sounded final somehow. The space was cramped for even his small body, and he was enveloped by darkness. It was wet in there and very, very scary. The chains of the ship's anchor took on the dimensions of a monster. At one point a rat scuttled by him squealing. He was sure he was going to die.

The thin strips of yellow paper coming from the telex machines, like streamers of birthday party confetti, had been just too tempting. It had been so boring and serious, with everyone working constantly; but these strips of paper seemed to be enticing Tony to play. He put them in his mouth and pretended they tasted sweet, like chewing gum.

The Commodore had been outraged, and just the fact that this person had a young body was in no way going to prevent him from administering the appropriate penalty.*

Little Tony was "out ethics," a "down stat" (someone who didn't produce adequately for the group—or who produced bad products—and, thus, had "down statistics").

****

In 1965 Hubbard had redefined the term "ethics." Being "ethical" now meant, essentially, being "upstat."

---

*This scene is reconstructed based on conversations with Tony's mother, and with others on the ship at the time.

"We award production and up statistics and penalize non-production and down statistics. Always," wrote Hubbard, "reward the up statistic and penalize the down . . ." (In Scientology, a "down stat" has no rights.)

According to their statistic each individual was assigned an "ethics condition." Those assigned a low "condition" (below "normal") had to work their way up through all those above.

These conditions are from the highest to the lowest:

> Power
> Affluence
> Normal Operation
> Emergency
> Danger
> Non-Existence
> Liability
> Doubt
> Enemy
> Treason
> Confusion

With the advent of the Sea Org era, Hubbard further redefined the term "ethics." Having one's "ethics in," for all intents and purposes, now equated to aiding or obeying HIS intentions; and removing any distractions and opposition to those intentions.

"The purpose of ethics," Hubbard wrote in 1968, "is to remove counter intentions from the environment. And having accomplished that the purpose becomes to remove other intentionedness from the environment." ("Intentionedness" is another bit of Scientologese hopefully never to be incorporated into the English language.)

In the fifties, Hubbard had defined "ethics" or "being ethical" as "rationality toward the highest level of survival for the individual, the future race, the group, and Mankind." In the eyes of a good Sea Org member there was no problem in harmonizing both definitions. Hubbard was, after all, the infallible Messiah, here to save Mankind. Any command he gave was thus to be unquestionably obeyed.

"Command Intention!"

This was Org-speak for "what Ron wants." Command Intention was expected to be uppermost in the minds of all loyal staff members, indeed all Scientologists.*

*The manipulative aspects of "org-speak" are examined in 'The Dark Side of Scientology-Speak: Manipulation Through Language.' See 'Addendum'.

****

The chain locker was dangerous. Located at the very bow of the ship under the water-line. It was the place where the section of the chain not in the water was stored. When the entire chain was brought up it filled most of this comparatively small, wet, dark, and sometimes rat-infested locker.

The only thing that was holding the chain in the locker was what is called a devil's claw, which was located well above the locker on the deck of the ship. If someone were to kick the claw, the entire chain would be pulled at high speed out of the locker by the weight of the anchor, and anyone down in the locker could very easily get caught in the outgoing chain and be yanked to his death.

One crew member told of the devil's claw being loosened by accident while he was in the chain locker. He expressed his terror at coming so close to dying. The chain "came alive" and gyrated around as it was being pulled out at high speed while he crouched, frozen by fear, as tightly as he could against the side of the locker. By some miracle he was unhurt.

Sometimes children would peer down into the chain locker where some other child had been assigned and teasingly threaten, "We're going to kick the devil's claw!"

****

Tony's mother had left him in the care of another Sea Org woman while she was gone on a "mission" to "raise the stats" of an ailing land organization. When she returned she was shocked to discover that her son had been placed in the chain locker.

She was "handled," however, with explanations about how "out ethics" and "down stat" Tony had been. "He is really a very old thetan [spirit] with a young body," she was told. "He should not be permitted to use that young body to stir up sympathy." (Interviewed in 1986, five years after leaving the Church, she expressed bewilderment as to how she could have accepted such explanations.)

Prominent ex-Scientologist John McMaster, the "World's First Real Clear," was a major factor in the huge financial success of Scientology during the sixties.

According to McMaster:

> Hubbard had ordered a little girl who was a deaf mute down into the chain locker sometime in 1968. Hubbard was going to cure her deafness by shoving her down there!

This came to my attention after she'd been there for about a week because the Master at Arms at the time, a beautiful girl, came to me and said, "John, I've got to have you come and see what's going on." I had just come back from a world tour promoting Scientology.

And I said, "What is it?" And she told me about this little girl. Her parents were from London. Her father and mother had separated, and the mother had brought three or four of her children onto the ship.

I went down there and released her out of it. I pulled out the door pegs that were put down to make sure this poor little thing couldn't get out.

Then I went to Hubbard and said, "What the hell are you doing?"
And he said, "John, what the hell are you talking about?"
And I said, "What are you *really doing!*" I was screaming at him.
And he said, "Oh God, release her. I didn't know she was in there."

Shortly thereafter, McMaster was made a galley hand and subjected to extreme physical labor, lack of sleep, and other hardships.

"Hubbard wanted to break me," he said.*

After he resigned from the Church of Scientology in late 1969, he was officially "declared" a "suppressive person" or "S.P." (evil psychotic) by Hubbard.

****

Talking about the inception of "heavy ethics" into the world of Scientology, John Ausley (a feisty Floridian who joined the Sea Org in 1968 and quickly rose to a top position) says:

John McMaster seriously bottom lined on the chain locker. Kids would get locked up in there. To John's mind you don't take a four-year-old and put him down in a hatch, and batten the hatch so he can't get out. You don't terrorize a kid. . . .

Hubbard used a "shotgun" (right-hand man who did his bidding) called Otto Roos. Otto and McMaster were very different. . . .

There was a dude who had been slowly working out of "doubt." He was a mellow, friendly, shy guy.

This was 1968.

You had to do 48 hours of non-stop amends in "doubt," at which point you were upgraded to "liability." Then you'd have to do another

*A common practice of groups using destructive forms of "mind-control" is the sudden demoting of executives to menial positions. (See 'Terms Applicable to Scientology' in 'Addendum'.

24 hours of non-stop amends—I'm talking about hard physical labor—at which point you're upgraded to "non-existence."

You then have to do 12 more hours: with people all over your physical ass and your mental faculties. And as the person winds down, he becomes more and more vulnerable. So it's a WILL trip.

Anyway this was a kid who stuttered. Otto didn't like him.

I think he was about up to "non-existence" when he couldn't take it any more. So he went to bed after three days. This isn't a guy's average going to bed; when you hit horizontal you go out like a light!

Along about the second or third day, if you didn't continue in steady physical motion, you pass out on your feet.

Anyway, Otto grabbed this kid out of an upper bunk in the middle of a deep sleep, and body slammed him from five or six feet onto the floor. He put a knife blade to his throat and started screaming he was gonna kill him since he was a "down stat"!

Otto seriously freaked this kid out for life right there. I mean it didn't help his stuttering at all! Some maniac with "upstat" braid, who is Hubbard's right-hand shotgun, is going to slit your throat for being a "downstat"—and all this instantly after having already been body slammed from six feet up in the middle of a dead sleep.

Otto Roos wrote about his experiences in 1984 when no longer a member of the Church:

> I believe I was the only one who would just walk into LRH's office with information when I was not able to get through to him any other way.
>
> At times he called me into his office and even his bedroom to talk. This was when he wanted to sort something out, and needed someone to talk to. This went on all night sometimes, and I would just listen and acknowledge. He always thanked me very graciously. "Thank you for listening, Otto," and, unless upset, he was extremely courteous.

Otto Roos gave some of the rationalization behind the position he held and the way he had conducted himself:

> Having myself experienced the atrocities of war, unlike many of my friends, I swore I wasn't going down into those rusty old tanks, for up to a week without sleep, chipping rust, while Masters at Arms checked outside to ensure the chipping didn't stop. This was too much like the concentration camps from my childhood days.
>
> I determined that I would not also go through anything like one of our "S.P.s" [John O'Keefe], who had a fear of heights and had to be

virtually winched up to the crow's nest (a little bucket at the top of the mast, too small to sit or lie in). This ritual, of winching him up and down from there, was repeated every alternative four hours for some 84 hours.

It must seem incredible that anyone would put up with such treatment. John O'Keefe, whose experience while aboard is very briefly glimpsed in Chapter 4, is still a loyal Church member. Prior to his joining the Sea Org, while at Saint Hill in England in 1966 he wrote a poem which later appeared in *Advance!*, an official Scientology magazine. It focused on the "wins" he was having in his counseling:

> . . . And as the world outside
> Unheeding, blindly reels along
> I clear away the chains
> Upon my being
> As men have dreamed of doing
> Through unrecorded time
> And each night I grow
> In understanding
> And potential
> And soon now
> The job will all be done
> And I will fly
> Higher and brighter
> Than any bird or sun.

John O'Keefe could never have guessed the form in which he was destined to "fly higher."

Otto Roos continues:

> This severe discipline started in earnest in September of 1967 when the condition of non-existence was accompanied by the penalty of no right to food. Ray Thacker [a woman in her fifties, at the time] was the first to have this condition assigned. Huddled in a corner, she was avoided by all, in compliance with the order. Occasionally she was thrown a crust of bread.

JOHN AUSLEY:

> Hubbard had this big muster. We all lined up by division and stood at attention while he talked and his messengers recorded it all on tape.

He made everyone stand at attention while he talked. He was running a General Patton flow rather than an enlightenment flow.

I leaned out of line and just stared at him. And he was this physical predator: like, "I'm making all these people stand at attention and I'm proud of it."

He was using the idea that the world was about to blow up, and he had the only solution, as a recruiting method for slave labor.

****

In the early 1970s, Hubbard began surrounding himself with nubile teenage girls. These became his "messengers."

These young people had received no other education, since coming aboard, than their Sea Organization training, and had no real experience of anything outside of the world of the ship and Scientology.

Hubbard seemed to trust his teenage messengers more than he did anyone. He was, however, also served by the teenagers' parents, as well as teachers, laborers, architects, doctors, lawyers and businessmen. These people also endured the rigors of Sea Org discipline, and they served him along with the youngsters, for room and board and a pittance of pocket money.

Tonja Burden, a 13-year-old daughter of Sea Org parents, who had proudly sent her to the *Apollo* to work for Ron (while they remained at a Sea Org installation in Los Angeles), was a Commodore's messenger in training. She claims that she saw people placed in the chain lockers on a number of occasions at the direct orders of Hubbard.

Tonja wrote, in a legal affidavit, years after leaving the Sea Org:

> I saw one boy held in there for thirty nights crying and begging to be released. He was only allowed out to clean the bilges, where the sewerage and refuse of the ship collected.

Tonja joined the ship in 1974. "She was about thirteen or fourteen," says Hana Eltringham, who was a top Scientology Executive working with Hubbard since before the inception of the Sea Org.

HANA (ELTRINGHAM) WHITFIELD:

> Tonja was a little kid; a little blond-haired, child-faced girl. She joined the ship with the idea of becoming a Commodore's messenger.
>
> The main Commodore's Messenger duties at the time were to walk around with LRH, carry his ashtray and light his cigarettes (LRH smoked three to four packs of filterless Kools a day), and carry mes-

sages for him and bring answers back to him.

The messengers were extremely competitive, I mean they would vie for his attention.

The "qualified" messengers wore little white boots up to their knees with high heels on them. They had short mini-skirts with close to bikini halter tops tied in a knot between their breasts.

Tonja was a "trainee," so, for most of the time that I saw her in '74–'75, she was in a subordinate position. (She had not yet achieved messenger status.)

She was either washing his clothes or ironing them as well as doing the other messengers' clothes. She did his household work. Other times I saw her working in the galley (possibly for punishment). She was up to her elbows in soap suds in one of those washing troughs.

Perspiration was just dripping and her blond hair was plastered down to her scalp. She was looking very flushed and hot, with all these pans and things around; just a very unhappy face!

She slept below decks with the other trainees in conditions that were not good at all. You see, the *Apollo* was all metal. The areas that we mainly sailed in '74–'75, which was Portugal and Spain, then across the Atlantic into the Caribbean, are near equatorial and so are very hot and humid. In the summer time (and in the winter time to only a slightly lesser degree), when the sun is beating on the ship's metal decks and hull, the areas below decks get absolutely *unbearable*.

I can only liken it to some of those metal punishment tanks and boxes that the prisoners of war were put into by the Japanese. That's what it was like.

So Tonja lived below decks in a dorm, with maybe 12 to 16 people. And those dorms below decks smelled bad of body odor. No matter how much we cleaned, they stank.

A more complete story of Tonja Burden is told in Chapter 10.

****

The more "productive" or "up-stat" crew members would be rewarded with one day off every two weeks, and counseling (usually called "auditing," derived from the Latin word "audire," meaning "to hear or listen"). This auditing often took on the aura of a Catholic confessional. However, in this case, the "sins" were searched out with the help of an "E-Meter" (short for "electrometer"), which is an electronic measuring device with a dial and a needle that reacts to thoughts a person has which he feels uncomfortable about, or mental pictures that he flinches from looking at.

The E-Meter is functionally similar to what most people think of as a lie detector, and is a variation of the psycho-galvanometer, long used by psychologists. It is a small portable instrument, some 13 inches by 10 inches by about 2 inches deep. A pair of electrical wires and two ordinary soup cans extend from it. These cans are held loosely in the hands and act as electrodes.

Everything of note that a person says while on this meter is written down by the auditor. Thoughts of the most intimate nature are recorded on paper; and the folder, containing all this material, is sent to a "case supervisor," for study and further instructions as to the next areas to be probed by the auditor.

On the ship the case supervisor was often Hubbard himself. Thus he knew his crew in a way that even their mothers and fathers had never known them.

This situation could obviously give him enormous power over the minds of those receiving the auditing. His motives were rarely under suspicion of course; but if suspicion were ever to arise, it would be quickly "cleaned up" with an "ethics handling." (In this case a talking to in the first instance, and sterner measures as required.)

****

The practice of "handling down stats" by placing them in the chain locker, of hard physical labor used as punishment, of sleep deprivation, of throwing them overboard while the ship was at dock, and the other novel "ethics handlings" continued while the Commodore, and therefore most of the crew, turned his attention to more important matters. There was, after all, "a planet to take."

"The planet is ours!" Hubbard had proclaimed.

"A Scientology planet!" was the rallying cry.

Just as Hubbard had put "ethics in" on the "down stats" aboard the *Apollo*, so "ethics" had to be "put in" on Earth itself. "Ethics" had to be "put in" so that "tech" could then be "put in."

The "tech" was contained in Hubbard's voluminous writings and numerous taped lectures, and included the counseling or "auditing" techniques that he claimed would bring about the ideal state for an individual, and eventually for mankind as a whole.

The 300 to 400 on board, and the multitude of his adherents around the world, believed Hubbard when he claimed that he had, by himself, researched and written the "technology"; a task "comparable to the discovery of fire and greater than the invention of the wheel."

To them he was not just the Commodore, he was Source!*

---

*A capital "S" is used when referring to Hubbard as source, in the same manner as a capital "G" is used for God.

Hubbard had emphasized repeatedly that the technology had to be kept "100 percent standard," meaning that it was to be done exactly as he intended it be done. Anything considered to fall short of this standard, was called "out tech." This applied both to the auditing tech and what he called "Admin Tech"—administrative technology—used to manage his organizations.

In 1972 he decided that the Scientology organizations around the world were to be shocked out of what he considered their lethargic state. (They weren't producing enough income.) They therefore must have "out tech and out admin" (i.e., be violating his rules of auditing and administration).

He had been trying to make enough money for him to buy or influence a country, somewhat as Robert Vesco did in the Caribbean. This was to be the first step in "taking the Planet."

He determined that the orgs would have to become big money makers. In order to achieve that, he decided, they would have to come out of their three or four thousand.dollar a week mentalities and start acting like multinational corporations.

This would require "ruthless managers," he concluded. So he directed his executives to become "unreasonable," meaning that they would henceforth accept no reason for low statistics. (In other words, dollars or else!)

The "Class Eight" course, run by Hubbard aboard the ship in 1968, had introduced the overboarding* of public and crew in order to induce the "unreasonable attitude" which he wanted instilled, and exported via them, into *auditors* throughout his worldwide organizations.**

Now he needed similar "instant ethics" for *executives*.

Towards this end, the "Flag Executive Briefing Course" was initiated and, during training of Sea Org personnel on this course, he was busy figuring out how to create the impact he wanted.

Hubbard used the idea of a pagan ceremony in order to instil the correct attitude into Laurel Sullivan and a friend who were called to his office to be "handled" regarding flubs they had made in auditing.

---

*The ceremony where someone was tossed off the side of the ship while at anchor.
**According to John McMaster, this course was part of a project which "was intended to give Hubbard a telepathic control of Earth."

HANA ELTRINGHAM:

The ceremonies were done below deck in a section of the ship that had been used as a classroom for crew study.

There a large idol, Kali, had been erected of papier mâché. It looked very solid and real and was painted in gold.

The only light in this huge otherwise empty training room, down in the bowels of the ship, was the flickering of a few candles.

Sandra Wilson was one of those who went through the ceremony. She was brought forward and led up to Kali.

In front of Kali had been erected a cardboard representation of an organization, a shoe box with painted-on windows and so on. Some of the crew filed in ceremoniously, dressed in monks' cloaks and carrying burning torches which left a strong smell permeating the room.

She was handed a hammer and commanded: "Your proposed plan for your organization would have destroyed it. You are a student of Kali, the goddess of Destruction.

"Destroy this organization!"

She solemnly smashed the mocked-up organization with the hammer.

(Since the crime of destruction of a Scientology organization is indoctrinated heavily into Scientologists as the most evil act imaginable, to do so—even in effigy—was an excrutiatingly painful experience for most.)

Then, following the orders relayed from LRH, she bowed down and chanted to the idol, admitting her "evil intention" to destroy her local organization, and dipped her hands in blood (or a solution which was a very good imitation), and smeared it onto the idol, after which chicken bones were strung around her neck.

She came out of there in shock and was overcome with grief for some 48 hours.

As I watched her in this terrible state I was quietly outraged by what had happened. But I hid my outrage; even doubted its validity.

I had been thoroughly trained that if I were being critical of LRH or his actions, it must be because of my own hidden misdeeds and crimes.

****

"Man thrives on a challenging environment," Hubbard had written. The ship and its severe system of discipline would seem to have been designed to test this maxim to the limit!

During one phase of the *Apollo*'s voyage in 1968, "offenders" were put into the air ducts below the engine room. In the high humidity, with their own perspiration stinging in their eyes, they would chip rust from the sides of the ducts with heavy short-handled hammers. Enough light bulbs had been strung throughout the ducts so that these inmates could see the rust they were removing.

They would continue at this at times for days, without sleep, while they crouched or sat and took turns keeping each other awake. (Anyone falling asleep—as detected by officers outside noticing the hammering had stopped—would much prolong the ordeal for all.) They sang little songs and told each other stories.

HANA ELTRINGHAM:

> They were treated like criminals—even rats.
> They would get their food delivered by way of buckets, lowered into the ducts. This punishment lasted anywhere from 24 hours to, on a few occasions, a couple of weeks.
> Since they were not allowed out to use toilet facilities, duct inmates had to find some corner to relieve themselves as best they could, creating the stench of human excrement and urine throughout the ducts.

****

The Sea Organization officially came into being in August 1967 while Hubbard was in the Spanish Canary island of Las Palmas (having fled England's tax agencies). He had earlier ordered a ship purchased in England which he called the *Avon River*. (It would later be renamed the *Athena*, during a ceremony attended by Greek military dignitaries, while berthed in Greece in the latter part of 1968.)

This purchase was followed by the acquisition of a larger ship, the *Royal Scotsman* (which was renamed the *Apollo* in the same ceremony).

The *Apollo* had been used as an Irish Channel ferry transporting cattle in its latter years, and the first Scientologists to board her had been treated to 16-hour days, scraping cow manure from the decks. This task was done between stints of seaman's duties such as cooking or manning the helm.

It didn't matter that they had no sea experience or training. A phrase commonly heard those days was: "Make it go right!"

During the winter of late 1967, the *Apollo* set off from

Southhampton in England and plowed through the waters of the East Atlantic to the Mediterranean Sea, where it met up with the *Athena* and a small yacht, *The Enchanter*, which sailed in from the Canaries, a group of Spanish islands off the coast of North Africa, where the "Sea Project" (forerunner of the Sea Org) was begun.

The next several years were packed with adventure, drama and mystery.

While the Apollo was berthed in the Moroccan port of Safi, a young American girl crew member named Susan Meister had been found dead on board, with a bullet hole through her forehead.*

It was reported to be a suicide. Her father, to this day, is convinced that his daughter was murdered.

****

In the late sixties, there were a number of parties aboard, with local dignitaries in attendance.

HANA ELTRINGHAM:

> LRH would attend these, and I watched him drink glass after large glass of rum and Coke: three-quarters rum and one-quarter Coke; some seven or eight in an evening. Yet he never slurred a word and never swayed or in any way acted the slightest bit inebriated.

Despite these displays of cordiality, things invariably turned sour in one port after the other.

Between the years 1967 and late 1974, the ships managed to wear out their welcome in every Mediterranean and North African port, following a different drama in each country.

The ships were initially warmly welcomed in most ports because of the fact that the crew was spending up to 50 thousand dollars a week for supplies. Quite a boost to some local economies.

In an attempt to quiet the bad public relations, a song and dance ensemble had been created, dubbed "The *Apollo* All-Stars," which performed for the locals in each port. They also produced a record album titled "The Power of Source."**

---

*'A Piece of Blue Sky,' by Jon Atack includes an insightful and disturbing chapter on this unsolved sudden death.
**"Source" was, of course, L. Ron Hubbard.

For a while, this seemed to be stemming the tide of bad reviews. In the long run, however, this solution turned out to be a band-aid, rather than a cure, for anti-*Apollo* sentiments.

The ship and its crew, of mostly young Americans, did not harmonize with anything the people of these countries had ever seen before, and in some countries the locals came to the conclusion that they must be a front for the CIA. This was rather ironic, considering that Hubbard was fond of blaming most of his and Scientology's problems on various government agencies such as the CIA, as well as psychiatry and the World Federation of Mental Health.

Amusingly enough, other countries came to the conclusion that they must be Communists since they had so many female crew and over a period of time two female captains (e.g., Mary Sue Hubbard and Hana Eltringham). To them only the Soviets would use women as crew and appoint them to the ranks of high officers.

The Scientologists in turn considered the locals ignorant "wogs." This term was used by the British, during their colonial days, to describe the Arabs of the Middle East. While considering Arabs the scum of the earth, the British sarcastically called them "Worthy Oriental Gentlemen," or wogs.

Hubbard took the term and altered its meaning to include all non-Scientologists. So while the locals viewed the denizens of the *Apollo* as strange, most of the Scientologists viewed them, and treated them largely, as a vastly inferior species.

And all public disclaimers to the contrary, they viewed L. Ron Hubbard as their own, in-residence God.

****

Anyone freshly exposed to this scene, coming out of what passes for normal western society, could well be excused for asking what it all meant? Who was Hubbard? What did he really want? And how had all this come to be? Why was this ship cruising around the Mediterranean? And what were these 300 to 400 people up to, working some 16 hours a day for around $7.00 a week?

Occasionally a reporter would set out in pursuit of the ship to find answers to these questions. One from London's *Daily Mail* actually got himself an interview with Hubbard. The reporter decided that the "chain-smoking, evasive" Mr. Hubbard was a bad fellow, and no further live interviews were ever granted.

Reporters are usually a cynical lot, many Scientologists concluded;

and hadn't Ron often said that all reporters and their editors were interested in was violence, money and sex?

Who could question the sincerity of a man who worked so hard to create a new civilization for mankind? Who except those with evil deeds to hide!

Hubbard had often told them that only those who had *crimes* of magnitude attacked Scientology. And "attacking Scientology" came to mean any probing interest in or critical questioning of the organization or, especially, L. Ron Hubbard himself.

Scientologists were exhorted by him to unearth the lurid sex, violence and other crimes that his critics *must* have committed, and to feed these to the courts or press. People who left or attacked Scientology, were publicly declared "Fair Game" until the end of 1968.

"Fair game" meant that enemies of Scientology, *"may be deprived of property or injured by any means by any Scientologist, without discipline of the Scientologist. May be tricked, sued, lied to or destroyed"* (Hubbard Policy Letter of October 18, 1967). (Emphasis added)

After 1968 Hubbard wrote an ambiguous statement (to appease a British government investigation) purporting to cancel the "fair game" policy. In fact his wording cancelled the term "fair game" in name only. This method of handling enemies remained very much in force. The policy was in fact reaffirmed, but was to be exercised more covertly, in order to circumvent the huge public relations "flaps" it was generating.

****

Since the initial, essentially positive reviews of *Dianetics* by the press in early 1950, the news media had generally ridiculed L. Ron Hubbard and his "Science-Fiction Religion."

In the late sixties through 1975, the ship and its odyssey had fared no better with the "yellow gutter press," as Hubbard had dubbed it. There were regular highly critical articles, especially in the London newspapers.

The press also had a field day when, in July of 1968, the British Minister of Health, Kenneth Robinson, had labeled Scientology "socially harmful," declared its founder an "undesirable alien," and refused him further entry into England.

On the other hand, many Scientologists wondered, where was the press with their big headlines when Sir John Forster, who headed a

government inquiry into Scientology, had recommended lifting the
ban on foreign Scientologists in 1972.

In his report to the House of Lords, Sir John stated:

> I am wholly satisfied that the great majority of the Scientologists are
> wholly sincere in their beliefs, show single minded dedication to the
> subject, spend a great deal of money on it and are deeply convinced
> that it has proved of great benefit to them.

Then Sir John noted dryly:

> But it is only fair also to make the obvious point that none of this
> furnishes evidence of the sincerity of the Scientology leadership,
> whose financial interests are the exact opposite of those of their follow-
> ers.

****

The next seven chapters are an episodic look at the "Commodore's
Time Upon The Waves." Examined also are the origins of his personal
"philosophy," his "methods of operation," and his fundamental motives.

2

Searching for Treasure Stashed in Previous Lives

"I know with certainty where I was and who I was in the last 80 trillion years."—L. RON HUBBARD.

Elena Lorrel, in her early twenties at the time, was as close to being Hubbard's confidante as was possible with him, for over a decade. (She has young children. At her insistence it was agreed not to use her correct name to avoid Church harassment.)

ELENA LORREL:

In early 1968, with the Sea Org still in its infancy, we were just pulling out of Puerto Spain, and LRH came out of a solo auditing session (where he audited himself) with a big all-knowing grin on his face.

He was going "Uh-huh! Uh-huh! Uh-huh!" He was just baiting someone to ask, "What's happening?" and beg him for an explanation.

Someone did, and he revealed that he had actually been the author of *The Prince*. He was the Duke of Medici when he wrote it, he explained, and he had been ripped off posthumously. Machiavelli was a thief, not the author of this classic, having fraudulently published the stolen manuscript over his own name.

On another occasion he let it slip that he had been Robespierre, the famous lawyer during the French revolution.

And he also claimed to have been Cecil Rhodes in Southern Africa up till 1902, and between Rhodes and this life beginning in 1911, a little boy who drowned.

He would talk about the vast level of influence Rhodes had on the

43

British crown. He explained that, as Rhodes, he was the darling of Queen Victoria.

She and the Kaiser of Germany were squabbling monarchs. They argued often about where the boundaries of their colonies were in Africa, and he was very instrumental in helping to cool down the temper tantrums between them.

At the same time Rhodes had hid big gold stashes in the Rhodesian and South African areas.

LRH wanted to recover these while he was there in 1966.

Of course, Scientologists had no inkling of any of this.

****

Another reason Hubbard went off to Rhodesia in 1966 was to make that a Scientology country.

He spent eight million of the Church's money on that venture in order to establish himself as a major entrepreneur and benefactor of that troubled country.

Explains Elena:

> He failed. Then he set up the Sea Org.
>
> While he didn't succeed in his attempt to take over Rhodesia, he made enough political headway there to cause Ian Smith, the Prime Minister, to become concerned about him and, following a speech by LRH on national TV, the government cancelled his visa. (A report by the *Rhodesia Herald,* July 14, 1966, corroborates part of that story.)

Hubbard concluded from the Rhodesian failure that, no matter how super-capable or "OT" any individual is, he will be defeated by an organized group.

In support of this conclusion (which he claimed was the basic idea behind the formation of the Sea Organization), he explained in "Ron's Journal 1967":

> . . .I have already made an experiment. I went off by myself into Southern Africa to see whether or not an OT would make it singly and all alone, without any assistance, against the environment around him. And I found out that he would not do too much good.
>
> But a group of OTs would be entirely irresistible, and necessary to carry off this type of operation.

John McMasters says that in 1969 Hubbard gave secret orders to him (he was Hubbard's emissary to the U.N. at the time), to cultivate a Black African state, with a seaport, and get them interested in

Scientology. He was to persuade them that L. Ron Hubbard had their interests at heart. He was to tell them that this man had been banned from Rhodesia and South Africa, because he had tried to free the Black People.

****

ELENA LORREL:

Another reason we were in that part of the world sailing around on these ships was the fact, LRH explained, that he had been a corsair (pirate), sailing between the Mediterranean and the new world in the 1700s when the rum triangle was going on.

Amongst other things, we were searching for the booty he said he had stashed in different places around the Mediterranean during that lifetime.

Oh yes, we were there searching for gold. The real reason for the Sea Org initially was for him to go back and collect these stashes of gold. And then at the same time to amass a group of people to win him a country.

HANA ELTRINGHAM:

In 1967, when it was still the Sea Project and we were just a small group, and another time in '68 on the Avon River during the whole track (a thetan's entire time span over thousands of lives) mission, LRH mentioned that the intention of the whole track recall mission was to dig up the treasure, secrete it again, possibly in Spanish banks.

He had some idea about Spanish banks, and he wanted to work out a foolproof way that he would be able to identify and pick up the keys and combinations, in his next lifetime, to those same bank accounts. He was very emphatic about having it stashed for a future life. But he had to devise a foolproof way of doing it. Where could he leave keys to a bank vault, he speculated aloud to me, that would be there at hand in the next lifetime, where he could recognize it, come by and pick it up and get the treasure. He had to somehow get that worked out and he hadn't done so fully yet. Because where could he leave keys like that, or something, so that he could get at it again.

This was not the announced reason for the Sea Org. There were a few different "shore stories"* presented over a period of time to explain its purpose.

*A story (lie) told to the "wogs" ashore. This got expanded to mean any lie designed to cover any covert activity.

There was also a "shore story" for the five-week cruise on the *Avon River* (renamed the *Athena*) and the small yacht *Enchanter* (renamed *Diana*) which Hubbard and a small crew embarked on in the beginning of 1968. (Leaving the *Royal Scotsman*—*Apollo*—berthed in the port at Valencia, Spain.)

Wrote L. Ron Hubbard in his book about that adventure, titled *Mission Into Time*:

> The purpose of the cruise was to test whole track recall [memory of past lifetimes].

Without giving away the fact that they were searching for what he believed to be his past-life hidden gold, he does explain in the book some of the methods he used to locate "target areas."

HUBBARD:

> What I would do is write down "so and so and such and such and so and so and there you find the so and so and such and such." Then we would call the object or location of what we were looking for "the target."
>
> With good Sea Org efficiency, we would organize the missions . . . and the boats would go out. They'd check and cross-check to see if they could locate the target and whether or not the whole track recall of the situation was correct.
>
> I would write up an area that I'd never been to this lifetime, describing the area precisely, and then parties would go out and exactly locate the target and ascertain whether or not these recalls were correct. There were four targets in all. . . .
>
> I should be careful about this sort of thing because my reputation is always at stake. There are tremendous numbers of people around who keep saying, "Ron ought to be. . . ." My only answer to them is "Ron is."
>
> Anyway, I was over in Carthage about the second or third century B.C., operating there with the Carthaginian Fleet.
>
> There's a gag about this. Nobody was ever promoted in World War II who was in the battle zone. My crew once presented me, when I'd been passed over for promotion by reason of physical disability, with a commission that said, "Phoenician Navy 1003 B.C." That's funny because it's almost true.
>
> I used to have a nice time around Carthage—nice sailing water and so on. Around 200 B.C., I knew a girl over in Nora (it wasn't called Nora then) who was the current Goddess of Tanit and a good-looking girl.

We had a lot of good-looking girls in Carthage, but they didn't come up
to her.

. . . It was usually a good thing that I called into Nora with a war
vessel because it was almost a matter of war. The girl would say, "Hey,
how are *you?*" and all the other guys didn't have a chance for a while.

The book goes on to detail how the missionaries found a temple
entrance in Nora, and photos are shown of missionaries unearthing
what is said to be this entrance.

And Hana Eltringham is called upon, by Hubbard in his book, to
"tell you whether or not this was a positive result":

. . . it was indeed a positive result. We found the base of the old
temple right at the top of the hill . . . We scraped around the bottom of
the ditch and found it was tiled underneath a thin layer of dust and dirt.

The next mission was South to Tunisia, where the ancient city of
Carthage lies, mainly underwater, off the coast. Here on land they
again found their target area demonstrated by Hubbard in the form of
a clay model and a map drawn by him. Again this is verified by a mis-
sionary.

HUBBARD:

Just as we were leaving, we had asked for some sort of license to lie
off the coast. You always have to have a piece of paper. We sent over an
Arab interpreter of ours by the name of Mestasi. He got confused
about the whole thing and said we were going to go underwater. . . .

These people were very confused and they tried to tell us that we
mustn't go off the coast and do any diving because, if we did any diving, they would have to confiscate the ship.

I thought that was very interesting. They could give us a piece of
paper to permit us to dive but just the thought of us diving made them
very upset. I thought, "What the devil is underwater around here
that's so interesting to dive for?"

According to Hubbard's account, it turned out that the government
had discovered the ancient city of Carthage under there and they
were scared stiff somebody was going to come along and loot the
place.

Hubbard makes no mention of it in his account, but he had divers
go down at night to check it out for treasure.

HANA ELTRINGHAM:

As far as I knew no treasure was found or taken.

However, Larry Reeves (who joined the ship some time after the "Mission Into Time" project and has since left the Church), claims:

Because of legalities all this had to be kept secret, but I personally saw the treasure. It was in a huge wooden crate, built from two-by-sixes, the size of a small room. This carton was kept in the hull of the ship, near where I used to work. I'm a treasure buff, so when I opened up one of the boards and looked through, I knew what I was looking at! There were ancient gold coins, and jewels of all kinds. It was like looking at a huge pirates' chest.

Larry made it plain, when I interviewed him, that he believed it had been seized by divers from the Carthage ruins, during the "Mission Into Time" venture.

HANA ELTRINGHAM:

There was lots of money aboard. We had to courier 7 or 8 million dollars in cash to Switzerland. And on a later trip much more than that was couriered. It was couriered from the Dutch Antilles island of Cura-çao, near Venezuela. LRH was really like a squirrel with nuts, stashing it.
He stashed gold bullion too.

ELENA LORREL:

A mission was sent to a restricted area in Nora in Sardinia where their missionaries were caught in the act of trying to remove the gold. What happened was that they played stupid and got off.

HANA says:

Now LRH did have some special boats built in Valencia, Spain, after the "Mission Into Time" voyage.
Later on in 1968 they were brought onto the *Apollo,* while she was stationed in Greece. They were flat-bottomed great big sled-like craft, about 12 feet long by about 5 and a half to 6 feet wide, about 2 feet deep and sturdily built. Liz Gablehouse had to scout around and find some quiet motors to put on them.

Their purpose was to do some secret missions; to go back to those particular treasure sites and, late at night, land on the beach. They were to pull the vessels up onto the sand, sneak ashore and dig up the treasure, bring it back, load it onto the craft, and return to the *Apollo*.

In all honesty, I think there was something to the Mission Into Time. There were several sites found and witnessed by me that I felt corroborated what he had predicted. Through the use of P and M scopes. These consist of a flat disk, something like a Hoover or a vacuum with dials on the top. You run it across the ground like a Geiger counter. And it measures and detects metallic substances, like gold and silver, down in the earth.

There were a number of sites where we actually did that checking against paper grids, that were a smaller scale of the actual area. We'd run this thing up on the grid, marking where the actual sites were.

We found one such site at Nora in Sardinia. We were investigating the temple of Tanit. On one corner of this temple floor it was definite and, to me, irrefutable evidence.

Where he had predicted there would be some precious metal, the scope went crazy.

At many of the sites we inspected where we were certain there was treasure, it turned out to be some historical site like Carthage and Nora. And, being historical sites, they were guarded.

****

Back in Valencia, the *Apollo* had encountered serious difficulties with the port authorities, due mainly to the incompetence of its crew. Hubbard was furious. This had caused him to cut off his searches for treasure and head the *Athena* back to Spain. There would be hell to pay!

3

L. Ron and the Beast

Science fiction editor and author Sam Moscowitz tells of the occasion when Hubbard spoke before the Eastern Science Fiction Association in Newark, New Jersey in 1947:

> Hubbard spoke . . . I don't recall his exact words; but, in effect, he told us that writing science fiction for about a penny a word was no way to make a living. If you really want to make a million, he said, the quickest way is to start your own religion.

It sure worked for him. Being the commodore of one's own private navy is not exactly the normal, run-of-the-mill hobby of aging science fiction writers.

Decent, often intelligent but somewhat naïve people, whose dreams for a better world sometimes blinded them, were the income producers for this new religion.

Hubbard found such people useful. Having good intentions themselves, they assumed he had the same.

Thousands paid the outrageous prices for the Scientology courses and auditing. To give an idea of how much people are willing to pay in today's money, here is an example of a price charged for auditing, taken from a recent official magazine from one of Hubbard's top organizations: Twelve and a half hour sections of a type of auditing called "Lists 10, 11, and 12" are priced at $13,000.00 per section. In other words, this auditing costs over $1000.00 per hour! And one must buy a minimum of 25 hours!

One organization, the Flag Land Base—which became the senior organization when the ships were sold in 1975—was recently (late

1985) reputedly taking in up to two million dollars a week, and averaging a million. "Flag," operated on 10 percent of its income, with the remainder going to accounts controlled by "upper management."

According to accounts by Hubbard's former personal aides, money—tens of millions—originating from Europe for Flag services were channelled into Hubbard's personal accounts.

And according to the findings of a Federal Court judge, the ships were owned by a Panamanian corporation called Operation Transport Corp. (OTC), a "for profit corporation." Some 82 percent of the shares were owned by L. Ron Hubbard and his wife Mary Sue.

"Non-profit" Scientology organizations around the world were told by the OTC that they owed untold millions for consulting services and training of their executives. They attempted to pay these "bills" as best they could, coming up with as much as 90 percent of their weekly gross income in payments to OTC.

This was quite a setup. The Panamanian corporation was in a position of having multi-millions in payments "owed" to it, while the "non-profit" churches could never fully pay these bills, which just kept mounting. They therefore had absolutely no profits to show the IRS. On the contrary, they were awash in paper "debts" to OTC.

Hubbard had a lot going for him. He had a formula that enabled him to run his own church for huge profits accruing to him. He could write "scriptures" with a guaranteed market, getting for example $20,000.00 for one "Technical Bulletin."

He had money rolling in from his special book publishing and distribution system, a system which netted him much more than mere royalties.

And by 1977 he had an international intelligence operation of proportions comparable to that of some fairly sizeable countries. This kept him informed of the most intimate details of any and all organizations, governments and individuals who might try to spoil his game.

****

It is very easy for a person exposed to this information to jump to the conclusion that all he was interested in was making lots of money. Not so. Hubbard wanted much more than just money; he intended to have personal power on a scale that only a few in history have ever credibly aspired to.

In pursuit of this objective he was a man obsessed, generating an energy that was, at times, seemingly superhuman.

MAGIC

One definition of magic is, "Total commitment to get, to achieve, to win—with such totality that one's life itself becomes the ritual of that commitment." (It has been noted that, when that commitment "is malevolent, the magic is black.")

For Hubbard, morality was a straitjacket worn by fools. Morality was utilized only when it aided him in reaching his objective. (He gave lip service to all sorts of noble humanitarian sentiments, but he also visibly, especially from the mid-sixties on, gave vent to base motives expressed in vindictive policies and writings.)

His WILL was the supreme consideration.

This philosophy has been described as "the ends justify the means." This vaguely says it, but it describes neither the intensity nor the total commitment which appears to have driven him.

His life was indeed a ritual of total commitment to the achievement of power. Power concentrated exclusively under his control.

Hubbard may have had this drive for power—this obsession—all his life. But the point at which it burst into a raging passion was, according to Ron Jr., sometime in his teens when Ron Hubbard and his mother visited the Library of Congress in Washington, D.C. From that time on he was, more and more, able to support his obsession with a detailed, well-developed philosophy.

His mother was at the Library tracing back her family's genealogy, while he was poking around trying to find something that interested him. He did.

It was a tiny volume called *The Book of the Law*. According to its writer, Aleister Crowley, *The Book* was "dictated" to him in Cairo, between noon and one P.M., on three successive days: April 8th, 9th, and 10th, in the year 1904.

The "author" called himself Aiwas, and claimed to be "a messenger from the forces ruling this Earth at present." Aiwas, a spirit "possessing fantastic knowledge and powers," delivered the alleged dictation telepathically. This was Crowley's Bible, and perhaps the most important book in the life of L. Ron Hubbard.

The Book proclaims "The Law of Thelema."* This law consists of a "simple code of conduct":

"DO WHAT THOU WILT."

Of *The Book* Crowley, towards the end of his life, wrote:

*Thelema is the Greek for "will."

. . . it is a sublime synthesis of all science and all ethics. It is by virtue of this Book that Man may attain a degree of freedom hitherto never suspected to be possible, a spiritual development altogether beyond anything hitherto known.

Crowley's writings are impressively prolific. In his *Magick in Theory and Practice* he states:

THE WHOLE AND SOLE OBJECT OF ALL TRUE MAGICKAL TRAINING IS TO BECOME FREE FROM EVERY KIND OF LIMITATION.

(Crowley added a "k" to the word magic to differentiate his subject from that which had attracted "weaklings" and "dilettantes.")

Adopting the same *stated* purpose for Scientology, as Crowley had for his Magick, Hubbard says, in a 1952 taped Scientology lecture:

OUR WHOLE ACTIVITY TENDS TO MAKE AN INDIVIDUAL COMPLETELY INDEPENDENT OF ANY LIMITATION. . . . Old Aleister Crowley had some interesting things to say about this. He wrote the *Book of the Law*.

In the same lecture series, Hubbard also states:

The magical cults of the 8th, 9th, 10th, 11th and 12th centuries in the Middle East were fascinating. The only modern work that has anything to do with them is a trifle wild in spots, but is a fascinating work in itself, and that's the work of Aleister Crowley—the late Aleister Crowley—my very good friend. . . . He signs himself "the Beast," mark of the Beast 666. . . .

Hubbard only mentioned the Crowley connection to his followers during the loose-lipped days of the Philadelphia Doctorate Course lectures in December of 1952. To my knowledge he never said a word about it to anyone, other than his eldest son, after that time.

****

Francois Rabelais (c. 1495–1553) is not mentioned in *The Book of the Law*, but the "Law of Thelema" actually derives from a book penned by him.

Rabelais, a priest and graduate of the Sorbonne Seminary, in Paris, worte a book called *Gargantua*. It was written in the style of a farcical adult fairy tale, since it contained ideas that were greatly at variance to those of the Catholic Church of his day, ideas that could well have been officially labelled heresy (with the resulting death penalty) had they been seriously presented.

Rabelais tells of "how the Thelemites were governed, and of their manner of living":

> All their life was not spent in laws, statutes or rules, but according to their own free will and pleasure. They rose out of their beds when they thought good: They did eat, drink, labor, sleep when they had a mind to it and were disposed for it. None did awake them, none did offer to constrain them to eat, drink, nor any other thing; for so had Gargantua established it. In all their rule, and strictest tie of their order, there was but this one clause to be observed.

> DO WHAT THOU WILT.

> Because men that are free, well born, well bred, and conversant in honest companies have naturally *an instinct and spur that prompteth them unto virtuous actions, and withdraws them from vice, which is called honor* . . . (Emphasis added)

So wrote Rabelais.

Of course there is room for abuse of this injunction. What if "the instinct and spur that prompteth to virtuous actions" is lacking? What if one decides that one's "proper course" involves enslaving or overwhelming others? What if the application of one's "will" results in the denial of another's freedom? Such action would, by definition, be "black."

When viewing the Commodore's ship *Apollo*, the law to be adhered to was more like, "Do What Ron Wilt," the officers and crew being subjected to the strictest of rigors, while Ron did as he pleased. His will was supreme.

Robert Heinlein, a one-time friend of Hubbard's, suggested this well in a recent novel. He referred to his followers as "L. Ronners" and "Hubbardites." Some ex-Scientologists use the term "Rondroids." *The* stable dictum for his followers is his written or spoken intention: "DO WHAT RON SAYS."

****

Crowley's *The Book of the Law* adds a new and fiery twist to the Law of Thelema as described by Rabelais.

In the words of *The Book:*

We have nothing with the outcast and the unfit: let them die in their misery. For they feel not. Compassion is the vice of Kings: stamp down the wretched and the weak: this is the law of the strong: this is our law and the joy of the world.

. . . I am of the snake that giveth Knowledge & Delight, and stir the hearts of men with drunkenness. To worship me take wine and strange drugs . . . They shall not harm ye at all. It is a lie, this folly against self . . . Be strong oh man! lust, enjoy all things of sense and rapture . . .

. . . the kings of the earth shall be kings forever: the slaves shall serve.

Them that seek to entrap thee, to over throw thee, them attack without pity or quarter; and destroy them utterly.

I am unique and conqueror. I am not of the slaves that perish. Be they damned and dead! Amen.

Pity not the fallen! I never knew them. I am not for them. I console not: I hate the consoled and the consoler!

(According to Ron Jr., his father never sincerely felt remorse or sympathy.)

Did the young L. Ron Hubbard take special note, when he read:

. . . in these runes [words and letters of *The Book*] are mysteries that no Beast [Crowley] shall devine [understand]. Let him not seek to try: *But one cometh after him . . . who shall discover the key to it all.* (Emphasis and bracketed words added.)

According to Ron Jr. his father considered himself to be the one "who came after"; that he was Crowley's successor; that he had taken on the mantle of the "Great Beast." He told him that Scientology actually began on December the 1st, 1947. This was the day Aleister Crowley died.*

****

Who was the "Great Beast"? Who was Aleister Crowley?

"THE WICKEDEST MAN IN THE WORLD . . . " was how the contemporary press described him. Raised by parents who belonged to a fundamentalist Christian sect, and who believed that everyone outside of their particular group would be damned eternally in hell fire, he was

---

*Many people interpret *The Book of the Law* and Crowley's overall work in many ways. Here I am only attempting to illustrate what appears to have been Hubbard's interpretation of *The Book*.

forbidden to read any book other the Bible until about the age of twelve. And read it he did.

In his teens he decided that he was none other than THE BEAST of *Revelations*, and proclaimed himself as such. A shocking declaration, especially in the Victorian Age.

But Crowley was also an accomplished poet, chess master, painter, master mountaineer and explorer. He also claimed to have mastered Buddhism, Taoism, Yoga, and, most of all, magick.

Yet he was also a regular user of cocaine, opium, peyote, and hashish.

At the age of forty-five he proclaimed himself a saint of the Gnostic Church, becoming a "god" in his own temple, by which time he was infamous in a number of countries, banned from some and forced to leave others.

His reputation for wild sex and drug orgies, which he combined with the religious rites of his self-instituted order, was a major factor in his difficulties with various governments.

He established "The Abbey of Do What Thou Wilt" on the island of Cefalu, Sicily, where he lived with a collection of mistresses, performing sexual, narcotic, and occult experiments.

It is perhaps co-incidental that Hubbard, in the late fifties, set up his headquarters at Saint Hill Manor in England, less than half an hour's drive from what had been Aleister Crowley's house in Tunbridge Wells. (The house is now owned and occupied by the lead drummer of Led Zeppelin's band—another reputed admirer of Crowley. Certainly Crowley seems to have been popular with the Beatles, who presented his image among a group of "people we like" on their "Sargent Pepper's Lonely Hearts Club Band" album.)

MAGICK AND DRUGS

Was Hubbard's WILL reinforced by the Magick, in which drugs played a major part?

Could it be that Scientology's founder—publicly vehemently anti-drug since the mid-1960s, and having written extensively since that time on the harmful effects of drug use—was himself a heavy drug user? Was Ron Jr. telling the truth when he said that his father began using drugs beginning in his teens, and continued at least until he (Ron Jr.) left the organization in December, 1959?

Comparing the harmful effects of alcohol with various drugs,

Hubbard wrote in the revered "first book" (*Dianetics, the Modern Science of Mental Health*):

> Opium is less harmful [than alcohol], marijuana is not only less physically harmful but also better in the action of keeping a neurotic producing, phenobarbital does not dull the senses nearly as much and produces less after effect. . . .

While few of his followers seem to be aware of the fact, in the same book he recommends the use of Benzedrine in certain cases to overcome the "reactive mind."

Amusingly enough, he states in a policy letter, "Keeping Scientology Working": "We will not speculate here on . . . how I came to rise above the bank."*

RON JR.:

> I need not speculate, I know!

> I remember in 1952 in Philadelphia, while he was taking a needle in the arm, containing cocaine. He grinned at me, winked wryly and said, "Shades of Sherlock Holmes"!
> Dad gave a lot of his lectures on cocaine or stimulants of one kind or another. He could really get brilliant on the stuff.

Hubbard's friend and "magick partner" of the late forties was a chemist named Jack Parsons. Parsons was the head of Crowley's Organization, the "*Ordo Templi Orientis*" in California. He scribed this verse which was printed in the February 21st, 1943 issue of the *Oriflamme, Journal of the O.T.O.*:

> I hight Don Quixote, I live on peyote, Marijuana,
> morphine and cocaine,
> I never know sadness, but only a madness,
> That burns in the heart and the brain.
> I see each charwoman, ecstatic, inhuman, angelic, demonic, divine.
> Each wagon a dragon, each beer mug a flagon
> That brims with ambrosial wine.

Hubbard mentions Jack Parsons in the "Professional Auditor's Bulletin" of 15 April 1957:

---

*"Bank" = "reactive mind." It is similar to the "unconscious mind" that so fascinated Freud.

Now I have been very fortunate in my life to know quite a few real geniuses—fellows that really wrote their name fairly large in the world of literature and science. . . . One chap by the way, who gave us solid fuel rockets and assist take-offs for airplanes too heavily loaded on aircraft carriers, and all the rest of this rocketry panorama, and who formed Aerojet in California and so on. The late Jack Parsons . . .

According to Ron Jr., his father used drugs and self-hypnosis in order to beef up his WILL:

For years he used—even in the thirties—sound scribers. I think you would call it that. . . . The original dictaphones, and IBM had one too . . ., And he would read these—what he called the "Affirmations"— into the dictaphone. This is when they were non-erasable. You know, the old Edison with the wax cylinder.

He would write these up, or he'd take quotes from the *Book of the Law*, and other places; then he'd take whatever he had in the way of drugs and play 'em back. Usually he used headphones.

Hardly anyone believed Ron Jr. when he told this story; but the "Affirmations," in their original hand-written version, were brought into evidence in open court in Los Angeles in mid-1984, and are part of the court record.

One of these "Affirmations" is: "All men shall be my slaves! All women shall succumb to my charms! All mankind shall grovel at my feet and not know why!"

Ron Jr. states in a sworn affidavit:

I have personal knowledge that my father regularly used illegal drugs including amphetamines, barbituates and hallucinogens. He regularly used cocaine, peyote, and mescaline.*

According to statements made by attorney Michael Flynn, Hubbard, until at least February of 1980, filled out fraudulent "doctor's" prescriptions for a large array of medical drugs for himself.

And while the Church has sued attorney Michael Flynn more than a dozen times based on various accusations including libel (all of which suits have been dismissed to date), they have never mentioned

---

*Hubbard recommends as a "good book" Aldous Huxley's *Doors of Perception* in his "Operational Bulletin no. 17" of Feb '56. This work of Huxley's deals with his experiences while experimenting with mescaline.

Flynn's allegations regarding Hubbard's "illegal self-medication" in any of these suits.

Other statements to the effect of massive self-medication are by Gerry Armstrong (who was a witness to Hubbard's diary and other documents), Sara Northrup Hubbard, and John McMaster, all of whom I interviewed.

Sara Hubbard explained that Hubbard was "self-medicated," but that during the five years they were married, she knew of no instances when he used "street drugs."

Armstrong, told me, among other things, of a letter from Hubbard to his third wife Mary Sue when Hubbard was in Las Palmas during 1967 at the inception of the Sea Org. This letter is now in the custody of the court. In it Hubbard tells his wife: "I'm drinking lots of rum and popping pinks and greys."*

John McMasters told me that on the flagship *Apollo* in the late sixties, he witnessed Hubbard's drug supply. "It was the largest drug chest I had ever seen. He had everything!"

It was shown in the Armstrong trial in Los Angeles in 1984 that Hubbard even had blank prescription slips from the U.S. Navy, one of which had a prescription for phenobarbital (a barbituate and hypnotic) written in Hubbard's handwriting.

Also, in the Armstrong trial where the "Affirmations" were introduced, a letter by Hubbard to his first wife was revealed, the last sentence of which declared: "I do love you, even if I used to be an opium addict."

****

If Hubbard was indeed a "druggie," his followers are not. While many Scientologists appear to be nicotine and caffeine addicts, that is as far as it goes.

Scientologists do not use drugs. And there is even a Scientology anti-drug program—Narconon—originally established by an inmate of Arizona State Prison named William Benitez. It has been quite successful at times in getting people off drugs.

In this context, Ron Jr.'s statement that his father *"was not a Scientologist,"* as startling as it may seem to some, begins to make some sense:

> He was not a Scientologist, and even said so publicly on several occasions, but people would just slide over it.

---

*I'm told that "uppers and downers" are sometimes referred to as "pinks and greys."

For example, the wise and humanitarian sentiments expressed in his writings and lectures had nothing to do with him or how he conducted his affairs. His private life was the antithesis of what he wanted his public image to be. He hardly ever took his own advice.*

It is possible, however, that Hubbard did follow the advice he gave during a Philadelphia Doctorate Course lecture in December of 1952,** when he said:

You should be able to drink as much as you want, use the body in any way you want.

In the same lecture series Hubbard said:

Just because I did something like Scientology, people think I'm supposed to be perfectly controlled, and a perfect gentleman. That's a non-sequitur.

Hubbard had a habit of describing himself while pretending to be describing another. This, perhaps, was the case in the following dissertation excerpted from one of his taped lectures. If so, it is revealing:

Looking down the line at the spirit of men of great and murderous deeds . . . and you'll find out they're strange boys; *very* strange boys. They just never, never kind of nailed down in the right place, and did just exactly the right things. You look in vain for the old school tie.

There was a great old fellow in China named Wang the Innovator. And Wang the Innovator practically turned China upside down and right side up again, and upside down, and left it that way. But he organized a lot of systems.. . .He laid down the laws that are going to be this way and that way. He laid 'em all down very nicely and he had

---

*Of course, from the mid-sixties onward what may have been the "true Hubbard" began to show up, to some extent, in such things as the "Fair Game Law" and sadistic "ethics." But such vindictive or destructive sentiments were kept very "low profile."
**"My father was high during most of these lectures," claims Ron Jr., "and he was, on occasion, very frank, revealing his true feelings." Not spotting this material in time to edit it out before it became widely circulated was a major blunder by the Church.

them all patterned out very beautifully. But he himself didn't kind of follow that. He was a wild man. Nobody could ride up along side of him. He had more women than he could count.

It is of particular interest to note that he equates men of *great* deeds with men of *murderous* deeds: ". . . men of great and murderous deeds . . ."

4

"Mankind's Only Hope"

"Your next endless trillions of years and the whole agonized future
of every man, woman, and child on this planet depend on what you do
here and now, with and in Scientology."

—L. RON HUBBARD

The following story, which occurred during the first year of the
Apollo's voyage, is one of adventure and exploited idealism. This is a
brief glimpse of the story of Hana (Eltringham) Whitfield, a young
woman who had worked with Hubbard closely and loyally for many
years.

Her story is representative of thousands of others, during the history of Scientology. She became a zealot for Hubbard's cause: a stoic
true believer. Long-time friendships, and even deep love, were discarded when these conflicted with Command Intention.

****

In Rhodesia in the late fifties, Hana (tall, with fair skin, dark hair
and soft features) was in her late teens when she read one of her
mother's books by Madame Blavatsky. The author, somewhere in its
pages, prophesied that in 1950 a fair-complexioned man in the West
would begin a movement that would lead the planet to enlightenment.

This story appealed greatly to Hana's sense of romance. She
dreamed of playing a part in making a world where peace and happiness was a reality. And where awareness of spiritual phenomena was
the rule rather than the exception.

When she came across Scientology in March of 1965, she felt that she had discovered the man of whom Madame Blavatsky had spoken. After studying to become an auditor in Johannesburg, she decided she would give this man her full devotion, and travelled to England to attend the Saint Hill Special Briefing Course, which was then conducted personally by Hubbard.

She was very impressed by Hubbard when she first saw him. He appeared serene, confident, beneficent, and very, very wise.

For many months she studied under him and his wife Mary Sue; she spent long days immersed in his teachings.

She drilled, for example, the exact series of questions that constituted certain "processes," while facing a large plastic doll.

The doll served as a substitute for an actual person being there to receive the questions. The questions used were considered very powerful and, if directed at a live person, would stir up subconscious emotions and "forces" or "charge" that could cause considerable discomfort, unless "audited" expertly.

She aimed her questions right at the center of the doll's head. Each word was clearly enunciated, and delivered with just the right amount of intention.

Hana was assisted by a "coach" who would answer for the doll and assist her through the drill. In this case it was a "problems process."

She would soon be running this process on a real "preclear," having first enquired as to the people, past and present, in the person's life. She would be looking for "charged terminals," i.e., people the person was upset about (or had "charge" on); the idea being to free up the person from any worry, fixation, or compulsive "figure-figure" on any person or thing.

Based on the reaction of the preclear, and the E-meter, she would select the most "charged" terminal and run the process on it.

While drilling the process, fruits instead of real people are used, however.

> Hana: "Invent a problem that is of comparable magnitude to an apple."
> Coach: "Ah. . . . having a banana on my desk."
> Hana: "Good. How could that be a problem to you?"
> Coach: "It might be too ripe and attracting a lot of fruit flies."
> Hana: "O.K. Can you conceive of yourself figuring on that?"
> Coach: "Mmmm. . . . yes."
> Hana: "Fine. Invent a problem that is of comparable magnitude to an apple. . . .

The same question is asked over and over, usually until the preclear has a "cognition" or realization regarding the area of address.

Hana was fascinated by the hundreds of processes and impressed by their effectiveness.

Listening to Ron's lectures, and reading his many books, was stimulating. Ron had a great sense of humour and he answered complex questions on life and human behaviour in a clear, easy-to-understand manner. She also appreciated the obligatory constant reference to dictionaries, to ensure she understood the exact meanings of the words used.

After graduating from the Saint Hill Special Briefing Course, Hana joined staff. Then in August of 1967 she was on a mission to assist the Los Angeles Organization when she received a special confidential invitation, on behalf of Hubbard, inviting her to join the newly formed Sea Project.

HANA ELTRINGHAM:

I joined the ship in Las Palmas, in the Canary Islands in the Atlantic Ocean off the coast of North Africa.

The *Avon River* was already there up on these stilts, being renovated.

LRH had a villa on the island about six or seven miles from the harbor and he would come to the ship every afternoon and stay, sometimes until quite late, supervising the refit and talking to the crew.

There was a side to him that, around, this time, I was just becoming aware of: the furious screaming—just an amazing outrage that would pour out of him at something that was going wrong.

There was one time when he came walking down from outside through the great big wooden fence that blocked off the beach from the street. It was quite a stretch of beach, maybe a 30–40 yard stretch down to the water. And the ship was up on this great big wooden trellis work.

Even as he was halfway down the beach, I was standing with my clipboard up, because I was the Master at Arms at the time, and I was responsible for making sure everything was going right. And I'd be in absolute fear by the time he was due to come on board, in case he found something that I had missed.

So I was there and I was watching him, and halfway down that beach he knew something was wrong, and I could see his face start to contort and get red.

And I'd start to go, "Oh my God! What have I missed now!"

He started bellowing. His face got this cherry red; all screwed up, and he was just bellowing at the top of his lungs.

He was screaming and shouting at full volume. You could hear that voice everywhere.

And he came *marching* down towards the gangplank. Still screaming and now pointing up to the side of the ship where the Spanish workmen were painting the white paint over the red anti-rust coat. The top coat was being applied over the entire hull of the ship, from the deck all the way down to the bottom of the ship.

He was screaming and gesticulating and pointing up at us. I didn't know what was wrong. I mean the painters had been doing it most of the afternoon before he appeared on the scene. And when I looked down at the side of the ship I could see nothing wrong.

By this time people were stopping their work and looking; fearful, wondering what all this was about—even the workmen.

Then, through his screaming, I heard him say, "Look at the paint! Look at the paint!"

I put my head over the side of the ship and looked along the hull at the paint. And then I saw it! It looked like the paint was growing hundreds and hundreds of hairs! The white coat of paint was actually furry.

I later discovered that the rollers the workmen were using were of an inferior quality. As they were rolling, some fibers were coming off the rollers and sticking to the paint, making the ship look like it was growing hair.

Halfway down the beach he knew something was wrong. Now I have never forgotten that, and I have never gotten over the fact that from that distance—25 or 30 yards away, he could see what was going on.

At times he could be extremely perceptive—astonishingly so—he could also be totally irrational: quite out of it and crazy.

The negatives and abuses that seem so outrageous to me now, were then less than dim shadows. It was just justified away. . . .

In these early days of the Sea Project I felt emotions that you only find in fiction. It was one of those things: here we are braving the seas with this amazing man, you know. It had a kind of mystique that you just don't get in everyday life—the romance and adventure—it was all unbelievably exciting!

John O'Keefe, another dedicated Sea Org member, and Hana Eltringham were deeply in love and had been so for some time. As she tells it:

The whole thing just built up so much more through all this adventure. We were very close.

Hubbard sent John O'Keefe off to pick up the *Avon River* (soon to be renamed the *Athena*), and to captain her to an appointed destination.

HANA:

Now LRH said that John's orders were to leave Gibraltar and sail due East and join us in Cagliari, on the Italian island of Sardinia.

John swore that those orders were not what he received from LRH. John said that his orders were to sail northeast and to join the ship up in Monaco.

So John took the ship out of Gibraltar and sailed northeast. Aboard the *Avon River*, with John there was only a skeleton crew: a dozen to 15 or so, at most.

They all noticed the huge black clouds on the horizon and a storm building, as they were approaching the Balearic islands.

None of the crew, however (having never before been in the Mediterranean), would have been aware that this area, north of the Balearic islands, is a storm center in the Med. That's where a lot of the hurricanes in this area are actually born.

They rode straight into a hurricane. It was one of the worst this area had had for some 15 years. There were something like 17 ships lost.

And this little tub called the *Avon River* sailed slap bang into it. They were caught in that storm for about three days. They were barely making headway.

There were forty-foot waves and this little ship just staggering up through all this. They couldn't see through the screaming of the wind and all the foam and spray that was being blown by the wind across the tops of the waves.

There is nothing you can see when you are out there in that kind of storm. I mean you are blind. All you know is that the ship is going up the next wave and you know its going down into the trough and you've got to keep the ship headed right into the waves, otherwise it will turn over.

Now, throughout that, at one point the hydraulic steering on the bridge broke! (meaning essentially that the power steering broke). The wheel on the bridge was connected with lines down into the motors and the pumps and those lines were filled with oil so that they could maneuver the rudder. And those were the lines that broke.

There was steering oil all over the place; on the bridge and elsewhere.

So they had to connect up the emergency steering in the aft in order to keep the ship headed into the waves. They had some people back aft steering and some on the bridge, connected by walkie-talkies.

The crew didn't sleep for two and a half to three days. They couldn't eat. There was no way they could cook in the galley with this motion going on. People were being sick all over the place.

It is absolutely a wonder that that ship came through that!

Now, John saw, at one point, that they must have been getting somehow close to Ibiza. He happened to see that they were close to an island on the radar. They would come up the crest of a wave and he could "see" the island by a brief blip on the radar. He would "see" the blip of it on the radar and as they went down into the trough they would of course not be able to see anything.

But John was very very clever. He managed somehow to get the ship out. He said the waves had lengthened in distance so they must have been getting out towards the edge of the storm. And he managed to get the ship close enough between the waves to the islands so that, at one strategic point, they were able to veer sharply to starboard and get into the lee of the land, before the next wave hit.

So some two to three days after the *Apollo* got down to Cagliari we got the message from John that he was in Ibiza and that the ship was safe:

"We're all OK, managed to get to port safely, the ship is safe, the crew are safe, we have lost two lifeboats and external refrigerator, the windows up on the bridge are badly damaged, one of the antennas is damaged."

He had, I think, sent a wire to Monaco to ask if the *Apollo* was there and received a reply that she had sailed to Cagliari, so he sent his message there to the Port Captain's Office.

LRH got the message and went berserk!

The ship was not supposed to be anywhere near Ibiza, according to LRH, it was supposed to be on its way directly to Cagliari.

He sent a communication back, and a few other communications ensued and then John had orders to sail for Cagliari.

About a day and a half later they arrived in Cagliari. And by this time the Old Man* had postmortemed the situation sufficiently to arrive at his own conclusions.

By the time John arrived with the ship in Cagliari, I had already heard LRH say that John must have been on drugs when he left the ship in Ibiza to go to Gibraltar because he "had consistently misduplicated the orders."

I asked Hana how she felt about the idea that Hubbard, not John O'Keefe, may have been the one on drugs. She answered, "Now in retrospect, I think that's a very good possibility."

---

*At this time Hubbard still allowed the affectionate title "Old Man" to be used.

****

HANA:

The *Avon River* "limped" into Cagliari. It looked filthy. It *looked* like it had been through a storm.

LRH had messengers running backwards and forwards between the two ships.

In Cagliari LRH demoted John from captain to third engineer and put somebody else in charge of the ship. When she arrived in the middle of the day or in the early afternoon, messenger runs were going back and forth between LRH and John, getting whatever LRH wanted to know.

The *Avon River's* new captain was given orders to sail immediately to Valencia, Spain.

LRH was unwilling to accept somebody's suggestion that they at least be allowed to rest overnight. He said, "No, they don't deserve it. That ship is in disgrace. They are all equally responsible." And he ordered them to turn right around and go straight back.

Those people *were exhausted* and you could see it. They had come through a major hurricane, sailed all the way to Cagliari. Just arrived, they barely had time to take on a few provisions and fuel up and here come the orders to sail again, for some three days, to Valencia!

I barely had time to see John. I was very shook up about the whole deal and about how he looked. Those black rings under his eyes haunted me. He'd lost weight—it looked like some 10 to 15 pounds. They all looked that way.

And then the next day we on the *Apollo* ended our cycles in Cagliari and sailed for Valencia.

By the time we got there the *Avon River* was already in Valencia. That was when LRH convened a Committee of Evidence on John.

Without my being aware of it he appointed me as the chairman.

He was aware that we were lovers and when the messenger brought him the printed page announcing the Committee of Evidence I was standing next to him.

He turned around with this half smile on his face and he said, "Poetic justice, isn't it!"

And I took a look at the Committee announcement and saw my name on it as the chairman. It had all the charges there against John: "Dereliction of duty, non-compliance with orders," etc., one after the other . . . every charge in the book.

It grabbed me in the gut. I was to sit in judgment on the man I loved.

I would no more have thought of questioning LRH . . . I didn't dream of questioning him! He had a way about him. He would get mad and he'd be furious, and he'd vent that fury in all directions. And as that phase passed—it would take half an hour to an hour—and as he started to get "answers" (either his own answers or answers that were brought to him by messengers or whatever) he would come out of that anger and get into this enthusiastic vengefulness.

He would be smiling and, by God, he would be out to *get* someone. He would be so proud of himself for having gotten as far with this thing as he had gotten. And then, gradually over the next day or so, he would calm down.

I knew I had to find John guilty. Absolutely!

There was no way out, even though he had not taken drugs as LRH had accused him.

So since LRH said it was so, *it was true!* Also, since this was already in the bill of particulars of the Committee of Evidence, put there by Ron, it didn't even occur to any of us to question it.

LRH was the guy who had the answers to save Mankind. John was merely the man I loved. I looked at it from the standpoint of "the greatest good for the greatest number." That's how I looked at it, even though I cared for him deeply.

We wrote up our findings saying, "guilty," even though he said he wasn't guilty.

Deep down I knew it was very unfair because I knew the worth of the man. I knew that John had pulled off something pretty damned fantastic. My God, with 17 ships that went down in one of the worst hurricanes that they'd had in the area for 15 years. And the little *Avon River* had come through it with a little amateur crew on board!

And the captain, the person directing the others in this emergency, and saving the ship, was a guy on drugs?

Can you imagine if those people had all been lost! And since they were so untrained, what the hell was LRH even doing sending them out to sea?

We found John guilty and upheld his assignment to a condition of treason.

I now firmly believe that I was selected as chairman of the committee because LRH wanted me to break up with John. This fact completely escaped me at that time.

John claimed he had received verbal orders from LRH to sail past Ibiza to Monaco.

LRH said that, in effect, this was all a delusion of John's. After all, "He was on drugs."

So John finally left the Sea Org.

There were moments where I wondered if I had made the right decision, to let John go and not go with him, but they were so brief, even though coming from the heart. Because the greater glory of the Sea Org and the greater mission that we were on just swept those little doubts away so quickly—so quickly.

Almost anything was excusable as far as we were concerned, because of what we had to achieve. The mission that we were on was so huge that a bit of violence here, a bit of injustice here and a "crucifiction" or two there, was taken for granted.

The breakup of our relationship was taken for granted. These things had to happen—because we had to move so fast, so rapidly, over such a great distance that you might have to bend or break someone and something in order to get there. Above all, we *had to get there*! Anything else was swept away to make room for that greater purpose. This was the over-riding consideration.

****

Bob Ross, who introduced Dianetics into Israel in 1951, was perhaps very much on the mark when, after reading this account, he stated: "It reminds me of S.S. Nazi training where boys are given dogs to train and live with for a year; at which point they are ordered to kill their dogs."

5

The Deceptive and "Schizoid" Nature of the Scientology Movement:

Or How in The World Could Anyone Ever Become Involved In This Thing?

"We own quite a bit of property over the world. We will be acquiring more, as well as some countries."—L. Ron Hubbard, 1971

Throughout the 1950's Hubbard talked a great deal about the "spirit of play," the importance of having a "light heart," of how punishment did not work. He spoke of how groups were composed of individuals, and of the importance of individual freedom. Scientologists to this day read these words and sigh at the wisdom of it all. At the same time they nod their heads agreeably over sentiments by Hubbard—originated mainly from the mid-sixties on—which reflect the opposite viewpoint. Making one's peace with blatant contradictions in the writings of one's beloved Founder is just one small aspect of what it takes to be a happy, well-adjusted Scientologist.

Hubbard Communications Office Bulletin of 7 February 1965, "Keeping Scientology Working":

> If they're going to quit let them quit fast. If they're enrolled, they're aboard, they're here on the same terms as the rest of us—win or die in the attempt. Never let them be half minded about being

Scientologists. The finest organizations in history have been tough, dedicated organizations. Not one namby-pamby bunch of panty-waist dilettantes have ever made anything. It's a tough universe. The social veneer makes it seem mild. But only the tigers survive—and even they have a hard time.

This is a deadly serious activity. And if we miss getting out of the trap now, we may never again have another chance.

When Miss Pattycake comes to us to be taught, turn that wandering doubt in her eye into a fixed, dedicated glare and she'll win and we'll all win. Humor her and we all die a little.

Also in a serious vein, Hubbard claimed to have isolated the enemy of Scientology in 1967. The enemy, he declared, consisted of one small group that had "hammered at Scientology since 1950." He claimed to have isolated a "dozen men at the top," and the organization they used, and all its connections around the world. "They're as red as paint," he said. " 'Psychiatry' and 'mental health' was chosen as a vehicle to undermine the West! And we stood in their way."

****

In the months that followed the departure of her lover, John O'Keefe, Hana found herself becoming a favorite of Hubbard's, who promoted her to high positions of responsibility. And she was falling even more under his spell.

HANA ELTRINGHAM:

We were en route from La Ghoulette (the outer Tunis harbor) back to Valencia, Spain, having ended the "Mission Into Time" project.

R [as Hubbard was sometimes called, mainly for "security reasons"] called me into his office and told me I was henceforth the Captain. Joe Van Staden would be vacating that position, as he was being sent on a mission.

I said "O.K." or something, left the office . . . and freaked!

This lifetime I had not had *any* sea experience, even with small boats. And my sole experience was on the *Avon River (Athena)*—about five months, with none of that in a command position.

I must have sat down at my desk in the 'tween decks, as the next thing I recall is R beckoning me from the door leading into his office.

R had his E-meter in his hand and with the other hand gave me the two cans and told me to hold them.

With no preamble he set up the meter, the two of us standing in the doorway leading from the 'tween decks into his office.

"When were you last a Captain?" he asked me.

I gave him one experience (from a past life) and he acknowledged me.

He asked me to go earlier and find another similar incident. I did so.

I got a pretty major incident and related it to him, while he was nodding his head enthusiastically and encouraging me on and on.

That must have been what he was looking for, I guess. . . .

"Are you a Loyal Officer?"* he then asked me.

That question threw me. I exhilarated on it, and at the same time I felt confused.

R let that go and just sent me on my way.

About fifteen minutes later he came out of his cabin to where I was on the deck.

He peered closely at me—into my eyes.

I smiled at him and told him that all was O.K.

"That last question really indicated," I told him, "although I really haven't put all the pieces of the puzzle together."

He patted me on the back really affectionately.

"That's *my* girl!" he said, beaming. "You'll be finding out more about that quite soon."

At that, he turned and walked back into his office.

THE LIABILITY CRUISE

Valencia, on the south coast of Spain, 1968.

ELENA LORREL:

While we were off on the "Mission Into Time" project, the *Apollo* was left in Port in Valencia, Spain. Among the officers, who included Mary Sue [Hubbard's wife] there were none who knew enough navigation to move the ship.

Even the person who was the captain at the time didn't know how to move it, so it had been moored at a single berth for about two months. One day the Port Captain's office asked them to move it.

So the captain, in order to cover his ass, went ashore and exploded at the Port Captain. He pulled a real Krushchev type incident, almost

---

*Not having done the level of Operating Thetan III yet, Hana would not have been aware of what Hubbard was talking about. The full significance of Hubbard's question will become apparent to the reader in Chapter 11 of the second part of this book, entitled "The Wall of Fire."

like beating his shoe on the table, and they ended up getting kicked out. And we "lost Spain"* as a result of that.

This entire mess caused us to have to end our "Mission Into Time" early. We were in the middle of some digs in Carthage and we were not able to complete them as a result of this situation. So we went storming back to Valencia, to salvage the *Apollo's* crew!

Once we got back, the Old Man [Hubbard] had all of us from the *Athena* put in charge of moving the *Apollo*. (We had by that time been out to sea for three months and had lived in the hardest of weather. The heavy storm season in the Mediterranean, during which we had been at sea constantly, between treasure digs, had made us seasoned sailors.)

Just before we moved it, we were moored right next to the *Apollo* and the Old Man had this incredible shouting match with Mary Sue in his office. You could hear through the wall like it was cardboard.

He really blooped her through the universe saying that he had never really wanted her and the kids to be there, and she should just pack up, take the kids and ship out!

It went on and on: She had let him down by not moving the ship, letting this big port flap happen.

He was just screaming at her at the top of his lungs.

And she begged him to allow her to stay.

Then after a time, responding to her pleas, he said, "Well what are you going to do about this ship of fools?"

She proposed that she be allowed to prove herself.

So we moved the ship out to anchor and the Commodore took away their flag. They only had a gray rag that was flown at half mast and they went on what was called the liability cruise.

****

They were gone for two and a half months and they had a very rigorous schedule. We, the *Athena* crew (it was the flagship at the time because the Commodore was on it) stayed in port for part of this time.

The *Apollo* was on this cruise with the stated reason to train its crew, with Mary Sue as the captain.

You can imagine some 120 crew all having to do their able-bodied-seaman training, and all sorts of other nautical courses and ethics conditions, in order for the ship to be upgraded from liability.

---

*Hubbard "wanted a country," a place where he was safe and could "pull all the strings." "Taking" a single country was to be the first step to "taking" the planet; thus the talk of "losing" countries.

They had to be radarmen, conning officers, and so on.

So it took them two and a half months, and it was during that period that they violated a couple of major international conventions and really got us messed up in a couple of countries.

First of all, they were sent off on the liability cruise with no flag. So they couldn't go into any port. They had no flag to fly (and you can't go into port without flying a flag to identify yourself). Secondly, the fact that they had a female captain in Spanish waters pretty much identified them with Soviet or iron curtain country ships.

They were sent off with charts that were old and not up-dated and they did not know the military zones they started cruising in. And they started cruising in top secret military zones that were categorically forbidden, such as where there were nuclear submarines training.

They went aground a couple of times, and it was just a comedy of errors.

So they were finally stopped at gun point and the ship was taken over and the Spanish navy came aboard and arrested them under cover of machine guns. They interviewed Mary Sue and couldn't believe that it wasn't a spy ship.

They were released from arrest but it was after that that the rumors started about the "spy ship," and it became compared with the American spy ship *Pueblo*.

Reports went up to the ministry of the interior and they thought we were connected to the CIA or KGB, and the *Apollo* was banned from Spain.

****

All three vessels (*Apollo, Athena* and yacht *Diana*) had joined up in Corfu, Greece, during the last months of 1968.

The ships were berthed in Corfu when people were first being tossed into the harbor. The Old Man was just really rabid and yelling and screaming a lot.

For some time throwing violators of Hubbard's rules over the side of the ship ("overboarding" them) became a Sea Org tradition. Usually they were thrown off the 'tween (second) deck, but there were a couple of occasions when they went off the promenade deck (some 25 feet above the water).

There were rules written by Hubbard in a "Flag Order" which listed orders of severity of overboarding, such as: from which deck, should the person be blindfolded, and should his hands or feet be tied.

Every morning a solemn ceremony was performed at dawn, when

offenders of the previous day were listed by the Master at Arms. Then the offender was picked up by two of the MAA's assistants and was heaved out over the sea.

There was "tech" written by Hubbard at the time giving the theory behind this kind of discipline. He wrote about how the reactive mind (subconscious mind) actually exerts a "force" against an individual which propels him towards wrongdoing. It is therefore necessary, he asserted, to apply an even greater force on the individual towards "right doing."

Within a system of due process, that is essentially how penal systems could be said to work. Due process was not usually available, however, as the following example illustrates.

Homer Shomer, a businessman who was aboard the Apollo told me:

> I remember being on the bridge of the flagship. A 19-year old-girl named Marrianne Wicher was the radar plotter. We were on a watch.
>
> LRH came up on the bridge and looked in the radar screen and saw two ships that he considered fairly close. They were about five miles away. And he just really ripped into her.
>
> He called her the foulest names and instantly assigned her to the Rehabilitation Project Force:*
>
> "You mother fuckin' cock suckin' cunt! You're endangering the ship! You're assigned to the RPF!" and he kicked her off the bridge.

BACK AT ST. HILL MANOR

While the early Sea Org adventures were occurring, my wife and I were working long hours at Saint Hill in England. We were studying and auditing for barely enough money to live on. We had signed contracts for two and a half years, in exchange for cut rates on courses and auditing.

Furnace Woods, which surrounded our little rented cottage, was very beautiful in the spring and we went for walks on the rare occasion when we had a little time off.

We heard occasional stories of life at sea on the *Apollo* and *Athena*. We were told there was some fairly severe discipline. But generally we knew little of what was going on. Had I known about the children in the chain locker, for example, I would have been extremely upset

---

*Essentially a Scientology slave labor force.

and confused. After all I planned to have a family, and I dreamed of applying Hubbard's "tech" on raising children to my own kids.

I had read most of Hubbard's writings on "how to live with children" such as:

> You want to raise your child in such a way that you don't have to control him, so that he will be in full possession of himself at all times. Upon that depends his good behavior, his health, his sanity.
>
> Children are not dogs. They can't be trained as dogs are trained. They are not controllable items. They are, and let's not overlook the point, men and women. A child is not a special species of animal distinct from Man. A child is a man or a woman who has not attained full growth.
>
> How would you like to be pulled and hauled and ordered about and restrained from doing whatever you wanted to do? You'd resent it. The only reason a child "doesn't" resent it is because he's small. You'd half murder somebody who treated you, an adult, with the orders, contradiction and disrespect given the average child. The child doesn't strike back because he isn't big enough. He gets your floor muddy, interrupts your nap, destroys the peace of your home instead. If he had equality with you in the matter of rights, he'd not ask this "revenge." This "revenge" is standard child behavior. . . .
>
> The sweetness and love of a child is preserved only so long as he can exert his own self-determinism. You interrupt that and, to a degree, you interrupt his life.
>
> There are only two reasons why a child's right to decide for himself has to be interrupted—the fragility and danger of his environment and you, for you work out on him the things that were done to you, regardless of what you think. . . .

The idea of some discipline was not repugnant to me. After all, rather some discipline for the sailors on a ship, than that they all should lose their lives when the badly run ship sinks.

But wanton punishment? That wouldn't have made any sense. After all, it was Hubbard who wrote:

> Blackmail and punishment are keynotes of all dark operations. . .punishment doesn't cure anything. . . . Man is basically good and is damaged by punishment. . . . Harsh discipline may produce instant compliance but it smothers initiative.

These sentiments very much applied in counseling (auditing). I audited someone with the datum in mind that the force and punishment and trauma experienced by this person was part of what was wrong with him, and needed to be gradiently faced up to, so he or she became free from the negative effects of these things.

The other side of this was the "overt" side. The person also needed to gradiently confront the force, punishment and trauma he had inflicted on others, as these things were a major source of his current problems and irresponsibilities.

As I saw it, the idea in auditing, was to increase one's ability to confront and communicate, to become more alive, more oneself. For me auditing was a wonderfully effective way of unhypnotizing people.

There was an "Auditor's Code," of which the two most important points were: "Do not evaluate for the preclear" (this meant that in no way should the auditor tell the "preclear" what he should or should not think), and "Do not invalidate or correct the preclear's data."

Also very important was the rule: "Always remain in good two-way communication with the preclear during the session." This denotes always letting the preclear know what procedure is being run, always being alert to anything he wishes to say and being willing to hear it fully and with interest, and acknowledging that one has heard what he has said and that one has understood it.

Following these rules appeared to work for me in the most amazing way. Mary and I quickly gained a reputation as very effective auditors. We became highly sought after, and we were very proud indeed of the constant flood of praise and stories of changed lives. The affection showered upon us by those we had helped was a source of enormous gratification.

Auditing was very much the essence of civilized communication. For me, and many others at the time, this was what Scientology was all about.

One of the most publicized of all of Hubbard's writings is a piece called "What is Greatness":

> . . . The hardest task one can have is to continue to love one's fellows despite all reasons he should not.
> And the true sign of sanity and greatness is to so continue.
> For the one who can achieve this, there is abundant hope. . . .
> True greatness merely refuses to change in the face of bad actions against one—and a truly great person loves his fellows because he understands them. . . .
> When cruelty in the name of discipline dominates a race, that race has been taught to hate. And that race is doomed.
> The real lesson is to learn to love.

It would have been inconceivable that L. Ron Hubbard, who had "discovered" all this wisdom, would himself act in complete violation of it.

Possibly there were those around him—people he had not yet detected—who were violating these truths; but he himself? The thought just did not occur.

It would be some time before I'd realize that the civilized communication and counseling I so valued served mainly as the "bait on the hook."

6

Wogs vs. Operating Thetans

"We're in this for blood."—L. RON HUBBARD

In the fall of 1974 the *Apollo* sailed to Lisbon in Portugal, following its most recent sojourn in Tenerife and other Canary islands. (These islands, located off the southern coast of Morocco in the East Atlantic, had taken turn playing host to the *Apollo* throughout most of 1974.)

In Portugal she was allowed access to Lisbon's harbor. Here, prior to their leaving, the crew were witnesses to the leftist coup (dubbed "the flower revolution" by the press). They could see the tanks rolling in the streets.

There was a quiet tension among the crew as the ship steamed away from Lisbon, heading for the Portuguese island of Madeira. Having been repeatedly expelled from ports throughout the Mediterranean and the Eastern Atlantic, along with observing the hostilities in Lisbon, had given them an odd feeling of being cut adrift.

They entered the harbor of Funchal, Madeira, and were granted berthing rights by the harbor authorities. The feeling of relief was palpable.

As was their custom, the crew unloaded their motorcycles and parked them on the dock alongside the *Apollo*. Hubbard had always been a motorcycle buff. At this point in time he owned two, his favorite being a big American-made Harley-Davidson.

Captain Bill Robertson, a man with a personality perhaps every bit as colorful as Hubbard's, and whose loyalty to him bordered on the fanatical, saw to it that Hubbard's steward personally ensured that his machines were well cared for. They were taken off the ship first, and given the best location on the dock. Kept in top running condition, they were washed and polished daily.

Following Hubbard's lead, Captain Bill owned his own motorbike, and so did many others of the higher ranking crew members. Mary Sue Hubbard owned a small car.

None of the crew had much in the way of personal possessions, and those who owned a motorcycle generally showered the same attention on their machine as a doting parent would on an only child.

Besides the pride of possession, the bikes gave their owners a precious taste of independence from the disciplines and confines of the ship. They could go riding off for an hour or so a day. And on their day off, once every two weeks, they could actually forget that the ship existed for an entire 12 hours! (This day off was conditional on their having their "statistics up," meaning that they had produced adequately, according to rigorous and sometimes ridiculous standards which required that every week's production be better than the previous. If this was not so they forfeited their "holiday.")

At Funchal, the routine of unloading the bikes was adhered to in the same manner as at previous ports, and the buying of supplies and the unloading of trash went on with the normal, high energy, hustle and bustle.

Buyers were sent into the township to get fresh produce at the lowest possible prices, and the *Apollo* began its refueling procedure. There were hundreds of locals crowding around the wharf—an unusually large number.

"Hey Americanos!" Portuguese abuses. Something exploded on the main deck. There was the sound of glass shattering, a melee at the head of the gangplank, and the quartermaster was screaming for help.

Cobblestones (ripped from the pavement of the wharf) and bottles were landing on the deck. "There's someone injured on the poop deck!" yelled the bosun, "Get some guys up there to help."

"There are soldiers over there, why the hell don't they fucking give us a hand?" muttered a ship's officer.

Louise Botika (not real name), who was in charge of taking care of the Commodore's safety, says:

> I was awakened by someone yelling that the ship was being attacked. I ran up to his room and he was in a cocky mood. He first of all gave orders that the crew were to mimic everything the crowd was yelling.

They followed his instruction to no avail. Then, in an attempt to drive back the crowd, the sea hoses (those used to pump sea water) were pulled to the front line in order to spray them.

There was inadequate pressure, and the result was only to infuriate the crowd even further.

Kima Douglas' jaw had been broken. Another girl was sobbing from pain and being blinded by the blood flowing into her eyes from a head injury.

Louise continues:

> LRH grabbed a bullhorn and ran out onto the deck, yelling "Communista! Communista!" Just why I'll never know. It certainly didn't work.
>
> Then he ran back in and grabbed a camera with a flash and began photographing the mob. This did have some value later.

"Dammit, they're dumping the bikes into the bloody ocean!" someone yelled. "There's not a thing we can do about it. We'd get bloody killed down there. Oh shit! there goes the Commodore's bike. Jesus, I just don't believe this!"

There were a couple of attempts to loosen the ship from her moorings by the mob. The crew of the *Apollo* fought with bravado, disguising their fear which bordered on terror at times. Some even went down the gangplank in a foolhardy attempt to fight off the attackers who were loosening the ropes.

MIKE GOLDSTEIN:

> I was Captain Bill's yeoman when the thing happened. Initially I was put in charge of putting together and arming a bunch of guys with steel pipes and grouped them at the gangplank to repel any boarders. They never managed to make a real attempt at boarding, however, so we were never tested.
>
> The crowd was yelling "CIA! CIA! CIA!" It's really funny when you come to think about it, here we were with our clever shore story, that we were Operation Transport Corporation, managing businesses around the world. The idea was never to tell them that we were Scientologists because it might bring on an attack. So they didn't know we were Scientologists—something we could have proved. They sure knew that we weren't business management, however. That they were certain of!

Louise continues her story:

The riot lasted a couple of hours and we were finally able to get the militia to move in and help us, partly by offering to give them what they thought was the film from LRH's camera which had the exposures of the riot on it. Madeira is one of Portugal's prime tourist spots and they didn't want the bad publicity. So LRH made a great gesture of exposing the film to the light in front of them. In fact he had previously taken out the roll containing the shots of the rioters and replaced it with another.

The militia had virtually cleared the wharf and everything had calmed down, when the Commodore suddenly yelled *"Duck!"* and everyone jumped for cover.

There was no apparent threat to anyone at the time. "That guy can't be trusted with that gun!" he said, without indicating who he meant.

This apparently paranoid reaction contrasted sharply with his prior reckless behavior of exposing himself to possible blows by rocks and bottles as he strutted on the open deck shouting into a bullhorn and taking photographs.

The ship was taken out into the harbor a way, where she dropped anchor.

The next day divers were sent down who dredged up some motorcycles and Mary Sue Hubbard's little mini-car. Meanwhile other crew members took on supplies while the militia were still there to protect them.

****

James Hare, an auditor on the *Apollo*, had managed to get away from the ship for a time to ride his bike into the township for a visit to a bar.

He was a little bit drunk as he rode back towards the ship. As he approached the wharf he saw the riot in progress and sensed that his life was in extreme danger. Realizing that he would be recognized as "one of them," he swung his bike inland and sped away.

Four locals spotted him, jumped on motorcycles and followed in hot pursuit. The chase lasted for several minutes until Hare took a bend too fast. "My bike ate it, and I ate it," he says. "The lights went out."

Four days later the lights came back on. He was in a hotel. There was dried blood all over his pillow and "a fair sized hole" in the back of his head. He was relieved to see his guitar (James is a highly regarded flamenco musician). It was in good shape and had apparently been thrown clear when he and his bike had hit the pavement.

Someone had taken mercy on him, delivering him to the hotel and taking money from his pocket to pay for his keep.

His bike was totaled, he discovered, but he caught a taxi to the wharf only to discover the ship was no longer there.

He returned to the States and his only subsequent contact with Scientology was when he was visited by Scientology agents warning him to shut up about his experiences. One of the experiences they had in mind was his being party to a rescue of Quentin Hubbard (Hubbard's oldest son by his third wife Mary Sue) from a hillside in Madeira. He was unconscious from an overdose of drugs when they found him. According to James Hare, it was an apparent attempted suicide.

(Hubbard's response to Quentin's behavior was to have him thrown into the Rehabilitation Project Force. See Chapter 8, "Crucifying the Evil Out.")

Quentin was a gentle caring young man in his late teens, who told his close friend Cathy Cariatakis repeatedly, "I don't want to be a Hubbard!" He wanted go off somewhere and become an airline pilot. Instead, he was being trained and apprenticed as a Case Supervisor.

The ship had left Funchal for an offshore location to drop anchor and prepare for a long voyage.

It was ostensibly due to head for Buenos Aires. (Actually, under cover of darkness the blacked-out ship changed direction towards the southern part of North America.)

After the ship left Portugal, the liaison office in Lisbon was raided by the local police, but Scientology agents there had shredded and burned all evidence of their activities.

The events of that day became known among the crew members as the "rock concert."

****

WHY WAS THE APOLLO TURNED AWAY FROM ALMOST ALL MEDITERRANEAN AND EASTERN ATLANTIC PORTS AND THEN ATTACKED IN MADEIRA, PORTUGAL?

The official Scientology story was that there was an international conspiracy by the World Federation of Mental Health being orchestrated against the ship throughout the area using such agencies as the CIA, British Intelligence, Interpol and British consulates.

There is, however, a consistent viewpoint expressed by the ex-Sea Org members interviewed for this book. They share a conviction that the ship's troubles had something to do with how Hubbard and the crew conducted themselves.

ELENA LORREL:

There are some missing chapters in the story of this period that are completely unknown even to many veteran Sea Org members. These missing chapters have enabled lots of myths to develop. They have to do with what the ships were *really doing* as opposed to what we proclaimed to Scientologists we were doing.

What we *were* doing was James Bond stuff in all these different countries.

Some of the missions that we undertook were real intelligence missions: to the U.N., and to the World Federation of Mental Health, for example, as well as to almost every government of the countries we visited.

We were infiltrating these groups. . . . I mean we were finding the people trying to assassinate a king; we were trying to settle between one tribe fighting another tribe; trying to covertly back one political candidate versus another. All kinds of political manipulations like you'd never imagine were going on, and it was all being pulled off by a very few people.

Most Sea Org members were robotic, rigidly following Scientology think. Put under pressure and duress, they would just blab everything. So there was only a very small group of us that had to do it all over a period of 10 or 12 years. We'd been out on scenes where we had to break into presidential palace grounds, con our way past guards, and so on.

What really caused the Rock Festival was typical of what got us in trouble in most ports:

The fact is that *we just didn't add up!*

The *Apollo* would arrive in their quiet harbor and suddenly there were 47 motorcycles and three different bands playing! Here we were at the same time, supposedly, a business management operation . . . Also a shore unit was set up in their town by us that was working on a project we had contracted with the Lisbon government (in an attempt by us to gain influence).

I think the people in Madeira may also have thought we were spying on them (the locals) for the government in Lisbon. . . .

Another reason for our troubles was that we wouldn't observe customs and regulations because we were so damned arrogant.

LRH was creating the problem, more than not. He was getting so excited. Cathy Cariatakis or I would go into some country and ally it and he would be so excited. He was like a child with this whole new playground. He just couldn't contain himself. He would want to get into everything.

What LRH wanted to do would almost invariably involve some violation of an agreement we had made.

INFILTRATING "THE ENEMY"

Elena continues:

LRH sent off a "SMERSH" mission to Switzerland. We were caught red-handed by the Swiss Minister of Health and received a summons to a meeting with him and the Attorney General, surrounded by security police.

We were just caught, hung tied and quartered, until I somehow managed to convince the minister that I truly was a member of the World Federation of Mental Health. I told him that what we were trying to do really was the result of an internal squabble within that organization.

He finally bought this line, dropped the idea that we were impostors, and asked the law enforcement guys to leave.

We had been trying to incorporate as the World Federation of Mental Health. The WFMH had never been incorporated in Switzerland. It was incorporated and started in the U.S. Margaret Mead and Brock Chisholm and some of the old-time shrinks were some of the founding members.

We were going to incorporate in Switzerland and were planning, thereafter, to sabotage the entire mental health movement.

In order to register in Switzerland, they had to have been incorporated first. We discovered they had registered with no prior incorporation, making them illegitimate. So we seized on this situation and decided to incorporate in their place.

We wanted to get member mental health groups all over the world to join us. We were planning to achieve that by bad mouthing the existing heads of the WFMH. One of our key weapons was the fact that we had discovered that the heads of the WFMH were creaming and skimming a lot of money off the top. We had documents to prove this.

We had gotten these documents from two missions prior to mine, sent to Switzerland to ransack a couple of offices and loot the files. Among the files they brought back to the ship were documents which revealed the tracking of money which came in. It showed how it had been skimmed off the top by some of these WFMH executives.

So we went to incorporate and they said, "You can't do that. There is already a corporation of that name." And we said, "No, you'd better check your records, and you'll find they aren't incorporated." And they said, "Well they're registered here," and we said, "Well they're not incorporated." And they said, "Well, they are in Delaware." And we said, "Yes but they're only registered there, they're not incorporated there."

So when it came down to the wire (that they weren't properly incorporated), the Swiss authorities turned it over to the Ministry of Health. This was because, while they knew we were right, they didn't want to stab the WFMH in the back.

So they referred it to the Minister of Health for a ruling.

While we were waiting for the decision, we prepared a letter-head with WFMH markings on it. We established an office and put up large posters and plastered the Federation of Mental Health name all over it. We got the program going. We sent mailings out to all the major drug companies around the world, saying that we really were in favor of euthanasia (in this case "mercy" killing on a broad scale, a euphemism for ridding society of "undesirables") and that we wanted endowments from them to push it through in the United Nations.

We figured that if the drug companies were sleazy enough to back it they would send us money, and if they were pretty cool they would realize that the WFMH were evil SOBs because they were pushing euthanasia.

Either way we came out O.K. We would either make the WFMH look like a bunch of sleazebags, or we would end up with a good amount of money for operating capital.

This project was one of several forerunners of the later "Operation Snow White" conducted by Scientology against agencies in the U.S. and England.

A GREEK TRAGEDY

ELENA:

. . . In 1968, in Corfu, Greece, LRH moved onto the *Royal Scotsman* (soon to be named *Apollo*), making that the flagship.

The ship was in fact getting on very well with the military junta. Cathy Cariatakis, whose native language is Greek, had helped forge friendly relations with the head Colonel of the junta. This relationship was so warm that one of the junta attended the naming service of the *Apollo*, *Athena* and *Diana*.

Things went along splendidly and LRH was having an absolutely marvelous time dreaming up ideas for creating a base there on the island of Corfu. There were plans to establish a Saint Hill Organization and an Advanced Organization to be called the University of Philosophy.

Then LRH had the idea to write an article on Democracy, Greece being the originator of Western Democracy.

He was very proud of the piece and ordered Cathy Cariatakis to have it translated and published in the major Greek newspapers. She did so.

There are many versions as to why things went sour with the Greek government and resulted in Hubbard, the ship and its crew, being ordered to leave. One version, which seems the most credible, was that the military junta (depending for its very survival upon keeping the sentiments for a return to democracy at bay) did not appreciate the ideas expressed in Hubbard's article.*

Being ordered out of Greece in March of 1969, was the second formal expulsion, eventually leading up to the "rock concert" in Madeira.

PLOTS TO KILL THE KING OF MOROCCO

ELENA:

The next major country we lost was Morocco. . . .

The ship's having been kicked out of Corfu, Greece was the last straw for the Old Man. He had already been kicked out of Hull in England, and when they tried to pull into Gibraltar they were denied entry there, and then later there was the *Royal Scotsman* mess in Spain.

So the Old man decided for us to disconnect from land and go out and float for as long as our emergency stores would last and just get our scene together. And we did that for about two months off the coast of Morocco.

---

*It would appear that Hubbard also, in fact, had little appreciation for the idea of democracy. He had written in 1965:

"And I don't see that popular measures, self-abnegation and democracy have done anything for Man but push him further into the mud . . . democracy has given us inflation and income tax."

It was during this "disconnection cruise" that LRH had a heart attack on the bridge. . . .

On this cruise we did a lot of ship's work and eventually we were forced to call into the port of Safi, there in Morocco, to get emergency stores.

Richard Wrigley was the ship's PR man and he went ashore in Safi and met the Pasha (the Mayor) of Safi. The Pasha invited him back and he brought me along as his escort. And I made great friends with the Pasha and his wife.

LRH and MSH had bought a Villa on a beautiful estate in Morocco near Tangiers. During that following year they lived there relatively peacefully, while the ship sailed mainly in the East Atlantic between the ports of Morocco and Portugal and Spain, passing through such ports as Lisbon, Tangiers, Madeira and the ports of the Canary Islands.

In 1972, they were still living in the villa while the ship was in drydock in Lisbon for repairs.

Sometime after they had established themselves in the villa, LRH received a written proposal from Richard Wrigley. He suggested that he be given approval to find some way to get an audience with King Hassan II and win him over, so that LRH and his crew would have a safe haven in Morocco without further fear of expulsion.

It was an offer LRH couldn't refuse, and Richard and Liz Gablehouse were sent off to carry the day. Specifically, they were to make contacts within the palace of Hassan II, preferably with the king himself.

In reply to his proposal LRH had written not only his approval, but also a note stating that Richard would have "unlimited backing" (any amount of money) and the missionaire of his choice to join him.

Liz and Richard spent a lot of time around bars and meeting people, and did make friends with a French girl named Bidea who had married into the royal family.

Despite this connection, nothing developed until Richard was withdrawn from that project to go hob-nob with Black African diplomats on the Ivory Coast, (undoubtedly another country to win over).

Bidea at that point confided in Liz that she had been uncooperative because she didn't trust Richard.

From that time onwards progress began to be made. Liz was introduced to the king's top people and later invited for dinner by a palace representative.

LRH was very excited and said, "Bidea is the key to Morocco," and we formed the Rabat office and recruited Bidea and her husband to work for it.

Subsequently at a party, Colonel Allam, (who was a personal friend of Bidea's) began to become very friendly with me and another missionaire from the *Apollo*. Bidea told us not to pursue anything with him because he was military.

This overture by Colonel Allam was reported to LRH, who was keeping very close tabs on the project. He directed that they pursue the Allam connection.

Liz protested that this would be violating the guidelines about meddling with the military, but to no avail. LRH was very excited about the turn of events and would hear of nothing but compliance with his orders.

Colonel Allam was encouraged to invite a few crew members to a party. At that party he told them about General Oufkir, who was a Berber. He said that the King kept Oufkir close to him because this was useful in keeping peace between the Berbers and the Arabs. (The King is an Arab, while a large proportion of the population is Berber. The Berbers are a group of non-Arab tribes who have their own native language.)

A later party by Colonel Allam was also attended by Liz and an escort from the ship.

General Oufkir had come back from America and arrived for the party accompanied by this dumb blonde who had worked in the consulate's office in New York. They couriered a baby horse for the king's son, which had been given them by the U.S. government.

Calhoun (my escort) and I played dumb American tourists and this blonde spilled the beans after she had had a few drinks. The beans were that General Oufkir had been at Port Holibert, which I knew was a CIA training center because I had lived near there when I was in my teens, and that he had been there secretly seeing the CIA. This was kept secret from the king.

Basically, I decided that Oufkir must have been taken over by the CIA to operate for them.

Next Liz and some of the crew were personal guests for the war games, an annual display of all the latest weaponry attended by the chiefs of staff and heads of government.

During the performance a jet plane swooped down and collapsed some of the tents.

The whole object, it turned out, was to kill the king.

The generals, who had been seated near the Scientologists, were interviewed on TV at gunpoint, where they admitted to conspiracy against the king. They were then shot and killed right there in front of the cameras.

Later LRH sent Peter Warren and Amos Jessup to Rabat to see if they could get a proposed security checking* project approved that

*Essentially interrogation done on an E-meter.

would aid the loyalists in finding out who were the leaders of those plotting against him.

This was intended by LRH to be a back-up for the king.

LRH decided to use this security checking project as a way to get close to the king—because, of course, by now the king feared for his life and would presumably be grateful for the help with security.

The proposal was to security check all the officers in the Moroccan Army to find out who was involved in the coup.

Amos Jessup and Peter Warren were actually able to approach General Oufkir (the king's friend and most trusted adviser and head of the military) with a project designed by LRH to train the military officers to use the E-meter to security check. Oufkir said, "Very interesting. I'll get back with you."

The King flew off to safe ground (France) while his loyal staff claimed to be organizing a clean-up operation to root out the remaining rebel conspirators.

Meanwhile the sec checking project did get approved by the officer below the general.

A team from Hubbard's headquarters were sent to train the selected members of the military on the techniques of Security checking on the E-meter.

****

The King was flying back from France a week or two after the sec checking project started.

As the return flight from his visit to Paris was descending to begin the approach to Rabat airport, three American-made F-5 Freedom Fighters of the Moroccan Air Force came out to meet Hassan's Boeing 727. Suddenly, the aerial escort opened fire on the royal plane. After two passes they had damaged the cockpit, cut hydraulic lines, smashed instruments and blown out the rear door.

Hassan ran to the cockpit and held the pilot at gun-point while he called the attacking pilots on the airliner's radio and, disguising his voice, told them he was the flight engineer. "*Ce Majestè est mortè. Cesez la fusillade!*" (The king is dead," he said. "Cease fire." He also told them that the airliner's two pilots were dead.) The plane landed safely.

Shortly before the crippled plane had landed, General Oufkir had been summoned to the telephone at the airport control tower. What was said over the phone was not revealed. But shortly after the king, with three of his four children, had sped away to his summer palace in a small black Renault-16, a Moroccan Airforce jet made four passes at the field, shooting up cars, scattering the honor guard, killing eight people and wounding 47. The king got away unscathed.

The next morning it was announced that, eight hours after the attack on the king's plane, Oufkir had shot himself in the head at the king's palace. The word from the palace was that Oufkir was the mastermind behind the coup. The king's plane was to have been shot down over water, thus appearing to be an accident.

The phone call from the tower made by Oufkir was presumably to order the jets to strafe the king on the ground, after he had realized that he had not been killed in the air.

Subsequent to these events Hubbard pushed the sec checking project even more heavily. Now, surely, the Moroccan government would realize the high necessity to utilize any and all methods to root out the remaining plotters against the King.

The students in the course were taught to sec check each other and the work sheets were turned over to the supervisor of the course. One day, among these worksheets, evidence turned up that the very people who had approved the security checking were involved with the coup attempt.

Elena Lorrel:

It's a puzzle as to why they had approved the sec checking project, except to say that they feared that someone loyal to the king might be approached by us, and decide sec checking was a good idea. It would then have been out of his [Oufkir's] hands.

At least this way it was under his control. But I don't think he really expected anything to come of it. He didn't expect the real dirt to be dug up. Boy was he wrong!

Well, needless to say, the sec checking was terminated, and we were given twelve hours to vacate Morocco.

All the people who connected to General Oufkir were later put on a boat that was sunk, as a result of the fact they "somehow" were in the area during the seven day war between Israel and Egypt. They all died, including Colonel Allam, whom we had gotten to know so well.

7

Fear in the Master's Eye

One of the maxims which Hubbard often cited in one form or another, and which he actually lived by, was: "Knowledge is power." He saw in this maxim, however, something quite different from what is seen by most people.

Collecting data about groups and individuals was one of his most cherished passions. He worked incessantly to find out the secrets of his followers and enemies alike. He built up detailed dossiers on them. This was one of his key techniques for maintaining power.

In order to gain first-rate intelligence information, he not only utilized the full theory he had gained from what courses in naval intelligence he attended during the early part of the Second World War, but also implemented much from readings of Nazi spymasters. He also developed creative techniques of his own. All this constituted what he called "intel tech" and was part and parcel of his constant efforts to gain and maintain power.

An example of this tech:

"When you move off a point of power," he wrote in 1967, "pay all your obligations on the nail, empower your friends completely and move off with your pockets full of artillery, *potential blackmail on every erstwhile rival* [emphasis added], unlimited funds in your private account and the addresses of experienced assassins and go live in Bulgravia and bribe the police."

While he absolutely denied anyone the right to have *any* secrets from him, any person who discovered too much about the real L. Ron Hubbard was on his or her way out!

RON JR.:

Dad's business was his business. Very few even got a hint of his steel-lined, soundproof, compartmented mind.

Occasionally there would seem to be a threat to this state of affairs. Someone would probe. Someone would appear to have the ability to break through this fortress of secrecy. Dad would at such times go on full alert, mobilizing all his resources to ensure he preserved the status quo. . . .

Hubbard organized a secret service over the years and mobilized it effectively. This was his answer to investigations by various establishments—the American Medical Association in the 1950s, the Food and Drug Administration, and the Australian Government in the mid- and early sixties, the British Government beginning in 1967, and Interpol and the French and U.S. governments during the 1970s (along with an assortment of Mediterranean and North African Governments).

****

In 1971 the French initiated legal action against Hubbard and his Paris organization for fraud and customs violations. He was advised by one of his agents that he was in danger of being extradited to France.

In December of 1972, he flew from northern Africa to New York with a bodyguard and a "medical officer." Besides his legal problems, he was also having health problems.

The three moved into an apartment in Queens, New York. Hubbard disguised himself with a wig whenever venturing outside. During this time he conceived the project to retrieve confidential information from the U.S. government. He wanted desperately to know what the government had in their files on him and Scientology.

He called this project "Operation Snow White" (the seizing of confidential government files containing "false" reports in the U.S. Government's files on Hubbard, Scientology and Scientology's perceived enemies).

Hubbard's claim was that Scientology's troubles stemmed from lies being distributed to agencies all over the world by the World Federation of Mental Health. The WFMH had "been isolated" by the intelligence arm of Hubbard's church as being Scientology's prime enemy on the planet.

This operation (see Chapter 13) was destined to have a profound effect on his life, his family and the Scientology movement.

****

Having achieved some success in alleviating his physical travails, using the nutritional writings of Adelle Davis along with some innovations of his own, Hubbard returned to the *Apollo* after almost a year's stay in the Big Apple.

His concerns regarding extradition had been quieted, and he looked forward to the smell of the ocean, the feel of the warm tropical sun and balmy breezes of the Canary Islands.

Back in the Canary Islands in early 1974, Hubbard was confronted with a skyrocketing price of oil. As a result, the price of operating the *Apollo* also soared.

He decided to offset the extra expense by opening up the ship for visits from wealthy Scientologists. They were to receive auditing aboard, paying rates much higher than those charged ashore.

Among those drawn by this offer, were some of the more successful Scientology "franchise holders."

I was by this time one of those franchise holders, and the events that followed constitute only a small drama when compared with Hubbard's undercover battles with governments. However, it illustrates the fact that Hubbard was concerned with even the smallest potential threat to his fortress of secrecy.

The story also introduces a major source of Hubbard's income and flow of new converts (the "franchise" program). Being separated from the tightly cloistered environment of the Sea Org and being exposed to regular public, these franchise holders were, however, a source of irritation as well as funds and people for Hubbard.

Hubbard, since the beginnings of Scientology, had granted franchise rights to various people, enabling them to set up shop as a franchise of the Church of Scientology. The franchise holder would pay 10 percent of the franchise's income to the Church.

In return for this "tithe," the franchise holder was promised financial independence, and freedom from interference in the form of heavy disciplinary actions by the Church. Scientology franchises were a sort of religious non-profit McDonald's, where the franchise holder and his staff were able to pursue their ideals while having the opportunity to reach a middle-class standard of living, as opposed to the abject poverty and virtual slavery of most Sea Org members.

This system was a hangover from days when Hubbard had not enjoyed the financial clout which he now wielded; days when he wasn't able to get away with being militaristic and dictatorial.

The franchise program had borne fruit for him, being the vehicle that supplied him with over 90 percent of the new converts (or "customers" as he sometimes called them).

Franchises brought in "raw meat" (people new to Scientology), and delivered basic courses and lower-level auditing to them. They then sent these people on to official Scientology organizations for the higher and much more costly services.

Franchises also sold Hubbard's books. He had written many science-fiction stories, adventure stories, and numerous magazine articles under various pen names, prior to the advent of Scientology. Since the enormous success of his first book on the mind, *Dianetics, the Modern Science of Mental Health* in 1950, he had written over 20 books on the subjects of Dianetics and Scientology. He set up his own publishing company to produce these books and constantly exhorted all Scientologists to sell, sell, sell them. Churches and franchises set aside large numbers of staff, and healthy advertising budgets, for this purpose. All orgs and franchises were ordered to maintain large stocks of all titles.

****

In 1970 I was twenty-eight and, with my wife Mary, had taken out a franchise in Riverside, California. By late 1974, the franchise was booming.

Having missed a few key chances to meet with Ron, since entering Scientology in 1961, and having read the promotion enticing me to come to the *Apollo*, I decided my time had finally come—to meet the Old Man face-to-face.

The location of the *Apollo* had been kept secret from the time she had left England back in 1967; thus, while leaving on my pilgrimage to the sacred ship, I had little idea where I was headed. I was given the name of an agent who would meet me in New York and put me on a plane.

In New York I was found by the agent, and was told that my next destination would be Lisbon, where another Church representative would meet me. This rendezvous also occurred and, after a short trip through the streets of Lisbon, I was taken to an apartment where I was greeted by the agent's wife. I did a double-take when I saw three telex machines clattering away. "These machines receive and send messages to and from the ship," the agent explained. "This location, and these machines are to be kept strictly confidential."

I showered, ate some particularly sweet-sauced shrimp, and then continued my journey via Madrid, to the Island of Tenerife, one of the Canary Islands owned by Spain, off the Northwest coast of Africa.

There, I climbed into a taxi and requested, "Apollo, *por favor.*"

The driver's face lit up in recognition and, 20 minutes later (at 3:00 in the morning) I was dropped off on the opposite side of the island.

The ship was a hive of activity. On deck, Israeli singer Tsura and a band were practicing. Her husky voice and foreign-language song were spellbinding. The waters of the harbor provided perfect acoustics.

After a routine check for any contagious disease, I was cleared for boarding.

Cabin space on the *Apollo* was at a premium. Only the highest ranking officers, and now the high paying visitors, were assigned shared cabins. I would be sharing one with an officer. "Great news!" exclaimed a young steward, who had introduced himself as "the host." "An officer, who says he knows you, Barry Watson, happens to have the bunk above him vacated by a fellow officer, who has just been sent on mission. He'll let you use that bunk. You'll love this cabin. It's really luxurious!"

It turned out to be a tiny, two-bunk cabin which, admittedly, did have a beautifully varnished door. I pushed my way through the narrow doorway, squeezing my luggage under the bottom bunk, and slurped some bad-tasting water from a tap atop the tiny sink. "Perhaps that sink could have other uses?" I wondered, having searched in vain for facilities one takes for granted in the U.S. I climbed into the narrow, upper bunk, carefully, so as not to bang my head.

Sleep was quick to come, bordering on coma. It had been a long and tiring trip.

The following day, the standard briefing was delivered to me by a public relations officer—a very pretty, smartly uniformed woman, in her early twenties. The sounds of seagulls fighting for food blended with the balmy breezes and workaday sounds and sights of Tenerife's busy harbor as she invited me to come sit on the promenade deck and began the briefing:

"You never mention the word 'Scientology' when you're off the ship," she explained. "You tell anyone who asks that you are an executive who has come for training on how to improve your business. Now, just as general information, should it come up, the *Apollo* is a

Panamanian-registered vessel and she is owned by Operation Transport Corporation. Operation Transport Corporation consults large corporations all over the world by telex and correspondence, and sometimes executives fly in to receive briefings and training. This is our shore story.

"The British consulates have been especially bad in telling all sorts of terrible lies to the locals wherever we go. In Corfu, Greece, for instance, they told the locals that we had poisoned their water wells. So, it's important that we have an acceptable story as to who we are and what we are doing. . . ."

As she continued her canned speech, my attention was drawn to a barrel-chested man with red hair, dressed in a freshly laundered, fashionable, tropical outfit. He had walked onto the deck and was conversing, in an easy, friendly manner with a teenage girl. As I looked over towards them, both Hubbard and the girl smiled and said, "Hi."

"Is this the first time you've ever met Ron?" asked the PR girl.

"Yes," I answered. "I've been close a few times and I've met Mary Sue on a few occasions, and I did a course at Saint Hill with the older children, Quentin and Diane."

"Ron is really very impressive, isn't he?" she said. "He has tremendous presence. I sure wish I could be as thoroughly in present time, the way he is. He is really *there*, isn't he?"

Ron had passed the presence test in my mind. Very impressive indeed!

"Boy, what I'll be able to tell my group when I get home!" I enthused.

The course hours were liberal, and I had plenty of time to explore the island and enjoy long conversations with another franchise holder, a friend of mine, J.C. Hughes.

I was talking to J.C. on the poop deck when Hubbard, surrounded by an entourage of messengers, walked up and struck up a conversation. "I'm having a hell of a time getting that drummer of mine to get the rhythm the way I want it," he said, referring to the drummer of the "*Apollo* All Stars." He was on his way to an all-night recording session in the island's township.

As J.C. and Hubbard kidded each other and exchanged anecdotes, I noticed that Ron was nursing his right arm. The arm was in a sling inside his coat, while the sleeve hung loose. But other than this, everything I saw and heard harmonized with the preconceived image of my hero. This was obviously one of the high points of my life, and I took it all in with great zest.

It was explained to me later that Hubbard had come off his motorcycle at high speed and had broken his arm. There seemed to be no good reason to disbelieve this, although I found myself ill at ease that Hubbard could be vulnerable enough to have an accident. To my mind, that kind of travail was generally reserved for lesser beings.

During the days that followed, I busied myself with the course I was taking, and it wasn't until a couple of days before I was due to leave the ship that I saw him again.

Before dinner, I had noticed that Hubbard's Ford Cortina rental car was being meticulously prepared on the dock. I decided to forego the meal in the hope of catching one last glimpse of The Founder before returning to the States. I placed myself on a section of the deck where he would have to pass by.

There was only myself and one of Mary Sue Hubbard's aides on the deck when Hubbard descended the stairs, alone, towards us. He passed the aide who bade him, "Good evening, sir." He nodded, without saying anything, and proceeded to walk in my direction.

Hubbard studiously avoided looking at me and there was a distinct air of tension. As he came up to me and began to pass, I ventured a "Good evening, sir." I felt I could say this with some sense of security, since the other guy just got away with it. Hubbard didn't answer, but instead looked at me, for a brief instant, with an unmistakable mixture of fear and antagonism in his eyes. He then sped up his pace so that he virtually scuttled off.

I felt stunned, and had considerable difficulty sleeping that night as I kept asking myself: "What did that look in his eyes mean? How come *he* was frightened of *me*?"

Interviewed at great length the following day, with the tin can electrodes of the E-Meter clutched in my hands, I was asked: "What were your intentions in coming to the ship? How do you feel about L. Ron Hubbard? Why have you taken photographs? Do you have any evil intentions towards L. Ron Hubbard? Mary Sue Hubbard? Any Scientologist in good standing? Are you a member of the FBI? The CIA? The KGB?", and many more questions in a similar vein.

I was then escorted to another interview with a security guard, who demanded my camera and removed the film. I was told I would be given my camera back (minus the film), along with my passport, just prior to leaving the ship, when returning to the States.

It wasn't until four years later that I came across a note written in Hubbard's hand, over his distinctive signature that read:

"Re. Bent Corydon: Check this guy out *thoroughly*! I am informed that he has been a reporter."

It was dated coincident with my visit to the *Apollo*.

I had been a reporter for an 18-month period, working for a weekly newspaper in Auckland, New Zealand, where one of my most notable stories was about a pig who had escaped and was running through a grocery store. I was a teenager during that time. I was now 32. Hubbard had apparently been alerted to my background by the intelligence section of his "Guardian Office."

I told no one, except for my wife and my auditor, about this last meeting with Hubbard. But it left a deep impression, along with the same, haunting, unanswered question:

What had that look in Ron's eyes meant?

The answer to that question took years to appear.

At the time, I dared not consider the idea that perhaps Hubbard had something to hide.

My mood was sober as I flew back to California. "Why," I asked myself, "do I feel that I have been put under a microscope? Why this foreboding of danger? The feeling that from now on my life is somehow going to be fundamentally meddled with?" I tried hard to shrug off these thoughts and take a nap. Failing to sleep, I tried to read. The thoughts and feelings kept coming back.

It was a few months after I returned to the States that the "Rock Concert" occurred and the *Apollo* sailed across the Atlantic.

8

Crucifying the Evil Out!

THE INCEPTION OF THE
REHABILITATION PROJECT FORCE

"Offenders against us get ill because they can never truly justify it. It is mercy to put a padlock on such a person's activities. Every word he says or writes against us, every plot he enters into, alike push him further and further down. . . .

"It's a relief to a bad case to be punished . . . Axe him—but rehabilitate him too."—L. RON HUBBARD

It was not until early 1974 that blatant breaking of another person's will—"break 'em down, build 'em back up"—became full blown and implemented as official dogma: The Rehabilitation Project Force.

The RPF was essentially a slave labor prison project, where inmates ate scraps from the table after other crew had finished, and where they were not allowed to speak to any non-RPFers unless spoken to. Even then they were only to briefly answer, while addressing their betters always as "sir." RPFers were dressed in blue overalls and had to run wherever they went. (I shouldn't be describing this in the past tense. The RPF continues to this day, very much a part of the Church of Scientology.)

At its inception in 1974, the RPF, aboard the *Apollo*, was located in lower hold number 1. "Meals"—consisting of plate scrapings—would be lowered in a large bucket down into the hold. The RPFers were not permitted any eating utensils and had to scoop this "food" by hand.

While the flagship was at sea, escape, of course, was impossible.

According to Scientology "think," putting someone on the RPF is actually a benevolent act. RPFers are considered to be, for all practical purposes, insane, loaded with "evil purposes" which have caused them to commit many harmful actions (overts). This, in turn, caused them to have many secrets (withholds).

The RPF is their last shot at "redemption."

****

Some who have been on the RPF, but have since managed to leave Scientology, tell of fabricating "overts," which they then wrote up in long lists. This was to appease the "ethics" officer, and prove that they were, indeed, becoming rehabilitated, since it was firmly believed that they must have *lots* of overts.

A common reason for putting someone on the RPF was the decision to leave.

According to Hubbard:

> People leave because of their own overts and withholds.·
> The only reason anyone has ever left Scientology is because people failed to find out about them.

This became one of the basic doctrines, firmly believed by Scientology staff and crew. That there might be some other factor such as "choice" or "preference" was overlooked. (After all, it would be pretty ridiculous to claim the Jews were escaping Nazi Germany because of their offenses against Hitler, and there's no doubt that Hubbard was aware of that.)

****

Laurel Sullivan testified in 1985 at the Cristofferson trial, and was questioned about the RPF:

> I had several discussions. L. Ron Hubbard was increasingly upset with some of the personnel that were on the ship and he thought that their actions were deliberately against him . . . and he was frustrated. Also, he had suffered an accident . . . had got in a motorcycle accident, so he was recovering and in some pain, and he was increasingly upset with his own household staff, saying they had not cared for him and so on. And he said this kind of thing was manifest amongst the staff and the crew and that they had evil or unworthy intentions towards him or Scientology. . . .

There was a period of probably a week where discussions went on on this in his office, and he said he wanted certain people segregated. . . . And he asked that these people be detected. And so I had one of my staff, Barry Watson and a few other part-time staff members in the PR bureau, go over various lists of people. Some of the lists were made up of people's reads in their PC folders where they had had certain meter reads during their private counselling sessions.

Q: You would look at PC folders on auditing?

A: Yes. There was what was called the "Rock slam read," which was an agitated movement of the needle, indicating discomfort or bad or evil intention—that's how it's supposed to be—against the subject being discussed, which would be weeded out of their folders. And these names were put on lists.

Hubbard had decided that this particular movement of the needle of the E-meter was proof of psychosis. (Oddly enough "rock slams" were found liberally scattered throughout his own auditing folders when, in 1972, while he was very ill, a review of all his past auditing was done. Enraged, he had the folders confiscated. The person in charge of the project was declared a "Suppressive Person." See Part II, Chapter 14.)

****

John Ausley, one of Hubbard's top executives for 10 years, who left in 1978, says this on the origins of the RPF:

Hubbard went out one morning in the Portuguese island of Madeira in early '74, shortly after his return from New York. He had sort of a rowdy physical side to him that he liked to bring out from time to time.

It was sort of like, "I'm old but I'm still zesty!"

I don't remember which bike it was. It was either his Harley Electroglyde or his Triumph 750. But cobblestone streets don't offer a lot of traction, and there's a lot of bump.

He went out one morning and decided to challenge the universe. A zesty 63-year-old biker: Mr. Harley Bad Ass!

Anyway, when you start going around corners on cobblestones you better start paying real attention to what your bike can and cannot do.

Now you add a lot of zest—or what they used to call lunacy—on top of that. And add some morning dew so that it's all super slippery. And crank your bike up to about seventy or eighty and start cookin' through turns.

And just challenge the Whole Universe to take you out.

And the Universe goes, "Crunch!!! Got ya!"

And he had strawberries all over his body. He went down at seventy or eighty! It didn't have to break him up. It just skinned his ass alive!

When you do that you're gonna be a hurtin' little puppy. You got skin your knee trips as big as pancakes all over your body, and bone chips.

Well, he wouldn't get off international lines when he was in that shape. He still wanted to run the group, day to day.

That was when he invented the RPF.

While he was healin' up he was being Jimbo bad ass: "I can run the group and be unbalanced, defile the group, but still be momentarily brilliant while I'm in pain."

He began to really go out of his way to scream at people at the top of his lungs for ten or fifteen minutes.

He used to blow up at his wife. He would scream at her in front of his little nubile messengers. I mean that's seriously rude.

There are two old boys I know who hunt. And they hunt bear and wild boar back in the swamps. One of 'em's named Eugene and one's named Booger. And Booger said, "That's something you'd sic your dogs on."

In a technical bulletin dated 1 November 1974, Hubbard wrote of what was to be expected of "Rock Slammers" who were "finished products" or "successful completions" of the RPF:

A handled R/Ser [rockslammer] can be expected to eventually wind up in the same category as a cleared cannibal. His experiential track is too educated in evil and too uneducated in anything else. So even when cleaned up will need lots of living.

The degree of degradation experienced by someone on the RPF is difficult to describe. To Scientologists, Hubbard is the *ultimate* authority on affairs of the mind and spirit, and he tells RPFers that they are sub-human, incredibly degraded, evil, and wretched beyond belief.

It was the ultimate evaluation; the ultimate invalidation.

GERRY ARMSTRONG:

There is no way to really describe the RPF experience, the hopelessness, the humiliation, the horror. It seemed to go on forever, the days all identical, no time to oneself, the same blue boiler suits like prison garb, day after day, the same questions in the same endless security checks.

Hubbard's purpose in creating the RPF, and running it as a prison with assignees considered criminals, was the breaking of people's wills, the total subjugation of anyone he considered exhibited "counter intention" to his goals.

He achieved his purpose with me so well that I thanked him for the opportunity of doing the RPF, much like prisoners of war, who are broken emotionally and spiritually, through deprivation and mind control techniques, thank their captors.

Graduates of the RPF routinely wrote (and to this day write) "Success Stories," where they thank Hubbard for "giving them their sanity." That "sanity" being the "product" of having successfully completed the RPF—very much a "gift" from L. Ron Hubbard.

Los Angeles Church President Ken Hoden is a graduate of the RPF. When questioned on the subject by the *L.A. Weekly*, he responded, "I was RPFed for nine months in 1982. . . . I liked the RPF."

"Who wants to scrub floors and cart trash for a year?" responded one former Church staffer after hearing of Hoden's comments. "The idea is to make you think twice before doing or saying anything that church officials will RPF you for."

****

Hubbard had begun the Rehabilitation Project Force shortly before I had arrived on the Flagship in mid-1974. I saw crew members in dark boiler suits working on separate decks and eating food in small groups at irregular times.

They looked to me like they were in some state of shock, and when once I spoke to one of them he seemed not to know how to react. He apparently wondered what a "paying public" was doing talking to an RPFer? He had the look of a pursued animal. The pain in his eyes told of very long hours, heavy work, bad food, and emotional trauma.

I felt odd about the RPF. It nagged at me. What in hell was going on?

At the time I put such thoughts into the background for the same reason I had ignored the previous abuses I had come across in Scientology: People were obviously excited about the dreams that

Hubbard had outlined, and there were such good feelings that usually blossomed during and following auditing sessions; a warm glow; *hope* and *positive expectation* of a better world.

I still believed that the survival of the human race, a sane planet, and the glorious freedom of "Operating Thetan," were possible "only through Scientology."

And a fellow can do a lot of selective forgetting and "unlooking" when he believes that such things are at stake.

9

The Brainwashing Manual

"The Church of Scientology is truly a fulfillment of Orwell's 1984. That it has gained such support among Americans is testimony to the unawareness of so many who don't want to hear about the accounts of Soviet dissidents such as Solzhenitzyn and others.

"Life in the Sea Organization is parallel to living behind the iron curtain. The types of censorship that are imposed on Sea Org members, the selective truth, the priorities and the emphasis on 'the group above all.'

"In 1976 I was ordered to go to Paris to receive an honor on behalf of LRH as a writer.

"At the same place there was a showing of some paintings by a Soviet dissident, who had recently come over to the West. I had a series of meetings with him and some other dissidents. That was the first time I realized the degree to which I was intellectually disaffected with the Sea Org, yet for various reasons I stayed on for some time.

"I began to understand this man's life and why he was exiled to Siberia. It all sounded so similar to LRH's Rehabilitation Project Force. And I really realized the degree to which my lifestyle was parallel to what theirs had been in Russia."

Elena Lorrel, formerly Personal
Public Relations Officer for L.
Ron Hubbard

The *Brainwashing Manual* is one of Scientology's most revealing Documents. Secretly authored by L. Ron Hubbard in 1955, he incorporated its methods into his organization in the mid 1960s and beyond.

"The art and science of asserting and maintaining dominion over the thoughts and loyalties of individuals through . . . mental healing," is the *Brainwashing Manual's* sub-title.

The original purpose of the Manual was to discredit psychiatry. This was to be accomplished by presenting psychiatry as a "tool" of a communist conspiracy to take over the West by means of deception and "brain-washing."

John Sanborne, the editor of Hubbard's books in the nineteen-fifties, was there in 1955 at the *Manual's* inception:

> I suggested it. Just kidding around on his front porch. Slygo Avenue in Silver Spring, Maryland. Talking about how are we going to get these psychiatrists. I said, "What we need to do is take over their subject. What we need to put out is a manual of psych-military something or other . . . as coming from the communists, and then put a lot of psychiatry in it."
>
> And we're sitting there, with our chairs tipped back on the front porch, tipped against the house, with our feet up on the railing, and all of a sudden he came down on his chair and he grabs me.
>
> And I thought, "I've had it!"
>
> And he said, "That's it!"
>
> Then he disappeared into this little front room which was sort of a bedroom and study, and you could hear him in there dictating this book.

****

According to its forward the *Manual* was "A synthesis of the Russian textbook on Psycho-politics," originally designed for use as a course on how to wage psychological warfare on Western Democracies.

Hubbard had long wanted control of the field of "mental health," and anything he could do to spoil the image of a competitor (in this case psychiatry) was a worthwhile action. (The *Manual* was later actually being distributed by such groups as the John Birch Society, who believed wrongly that it was a genuine Russian document.)*

RON JR.:
Dad wrote every word of it. Barbara Bryan and my wife typed the

---

* The "Psychiatric establishment" has—over-all—a bad reputation, as does the Scientology organization. Both have more in common than either can tolerate thinking about. Scientology's borrowings from Behaviorism and Pavlov are glaringly obvious, yet absolutely denied by Scientology.

manuscript off his dictation. And we took it up to New York and tried to get them to do a program with Charles Collingwood at CBS. Dad also tried to sell it to the FBI.

Later they snuck it into the Library of Congress, and somebody else came by and said, "Oh lookie, it was found in the Library of Congress!" which was a lot of baloney.

****

Hubbard even included in the *Brainwashing Manual* a plug for Dianetics, by mentioning Dianetics as a key target of "Russian Psycho-politics.":

> The psychopolitical operative should also spare no expense in smashing out of existence, by whatever means, any actual healing group, such as that of acupuncture of China, such as Christian Science and Dianetics in the United States, such as Catholicism in Italy and Spain, and the practical psychology groups of England.

Hubbard briefly mentioned the *Manual* to his followers in *"Operational Bulletin No. 8,"* of 13 December 1955:

> The Brainwashing Manual which came into our possession so mysteriously is being released, not with any intent to unmock psychiatry, but as a necessary piece of information . . . Some of the mystery concerning the manuscript which came into our hands in Phoenix was resolved when it was discovered that the book called Psychopolitics (spelled with a K) is in the Library of Congress.

****

Most of today's membership have never seen the *Manual*, yet it touches their lives daily.

RON JR.:
If you want to see how Dad worked things Org[anization]-wise, especially from the mid-sixties on, you just have to read the Brainwashing Manual.

****

The following excerpts from the *Brainwashing Manual* illustrate the parallels between its contents and "Modern Scientology." All bracketed words and quotes have been inserted to further illustrate those parallels.

THE BRAINWASHING MANUAL:

The populace [Scientologists] must be brought into the belief that every individual within it who rebels in any way, shape, or form against efforts or activities to enslave [Scientologize] the whole, must be considered to be a deranged person whose eccentricities are neurotic or insane . . .

[Labelling any dissident "psychotic" is commonplace in Scientology. This is mandated by Hubbard's written policies. For instance in his *Introduction to Scientology Ethics,* written in 1966, Hubbard states under the category of "suppressive acts," i.e., "high crimes" against Scientology:

DISAVOWAL, SPLINTERING, DIVERGENCE
    1. Public disavowal of Scientology or Scientologists in good standing with Scientology Organizations.
    2. Announcing departure from Scientology . . .
    3. Seeking to resign or leave courses or sessions and refusing to return despite normal efforts . . .
    8. Dependency on mental or philosophic procedures other than Scientology . . .

To commit any of the above—or dozens of other similar—"high crimes" is to be, per Scientology "ethics," a "suppressive person," and to officially be "announced" in a "declare" as such.

Of these "suppressive persons" Hubbard wrote in the book *Science of Survival*: "Such people should be taken from society as rapidly as possible and uniformly institutionalized . . ."]

THE BRAINWASHING MANUAL:

Entirely by bringing about a public conviction that the sanity of a person is in question, it is possible to discount and eradicate all the goals and activities of that person.

It is important to know that the entire subject of loyalty is thus as easily handled as it is. One of the first and foremost missions of the psycho-politician ["Ethics" Officer, Church of Scientology] is to make an attack upon communism [Scientology] and insanity synonymous.*

* Categorizing critics as being either "psychotic" or "criminal" is not only a means of "maintaining dominion over the thoughts" of the membership; it's also a "public relations" gimmick. Critics are, per policy, to be reduced in the public's mind to "beasts" by the use of "standard wartime propaganda." "Know the mores of your public opinion, what they hate. That's the enemy. What they love. That's you." See *Update section* Chapter 25.

No laymen [Scientologists] would dare adventure to place judgment upon the state of sanity of an individual whom the psychiatrist [Church of Scientology] has already declared insane [S.P.].

Should any whisper, or pamphlets, against psychopolitical activities [Scientology] be published, it should be laughed into scorn, branded an immediate hoax, and its perpetrator or publisher should be, at the first opportunity, branded as insane . . .

[See Paulette Cooper in chapter 14. After she wrote a book critical of Scientology, Hubbard's Guardian's Office initiated a near successful frame-up to have her institutionalized.]

The idea that anyone who doesn't see eye to eye with Hubbard is insane goes back, really, to the very earliest days of Dianetics and Scientology. However, it wasn't made official written policy and the "standard ethics action" until one day in 1965.

John Sanborne recalls the first "S.P. Declare":

Hubbard had Marilyn Routsong, who was the World Wide Ethics Officer at St. Hill Manor, deliver the first Suppressive Person Declare. He had written this system up and now he was going to use it.

Hubbard said declare so and so. And she put out the order. Boy, in those days being declared was like a death sentence.*

He said, "As soon as you give him the order come back." And when she did he said, "How did he act? What did he say? Did he say anything?" And so forth. He was thrilled like a kid to see how his new dictatorial system was going to work!]

THE BRAINWASHING MANUAL:

Particularly in Capitalist countries, an insane person has no rights under law. No person who is insane may hold property. No person who is insane may testify. Thus we have an excellent road along which we can travel toward our certain goal and destiny.

[Wrote Hubbard in the book *Science of Survival*:

In any event, any person from 2.0 down on the tone scale should not have, in any thinking society, any civil rights of any kind."**

---

* It still is, Scientologists are taught that they are doomed as spiritual beings unless they remain in good graces with the Church.
** The Tone Scale is a scale of emotional states. Those chronically regarded as below "2.0" are regarded as insane. See glossary.

According to Hubbard a person's reaction to Scientology is a direct indicator of where they are on the "tone scale"—a negative reaction indicating LOW.

If this were a "Scientology planet" so yearned for by the rank-and-file of the movement, all critics of Hubbard and his Church would, by this standard, be without rights of any kind.

Perhaps, if we were not exterminated, the Church, in its benevolence, might offer us a chance to make a "reality adjustment" in some rehabilitation camp.]*

THE BRAINWASHING MANUAL:

It is not enough for the state [Sea Org/Scientology] to have goals.

These goals, once put forward, depend for their completion upon the loyalty and obedience of the workers [Sea Org crew and staff members]. These engaged for most part in hard labors, have little time for idle speculation, which is good.

Hypnosis is induced by acute fear. They discovered it could also be induced by shock of an emotional nature, and also by extreme privation, as well as by blows . . .

Belief is engendered by a certain amount of fear and terror from an authoritative level, and this will be followed by obedience.

The body is less able to resist a stimulus if it has insufficient food and is weary . . . Refusal to let them sleep over many days, denying them adequate food, then brings about an optimum state for the receipt of a stimulus.

Degradation and conquest are companions.

By lowering the endurance of a person . . . and by constant degradation and defamation, it is possible to induce, thus, a state of shock which will receive adequately any command given.

Any organization which has the spirit and courage to display inhuman-

* Manipulative-Authoritarian groups routinely engage in a "Demand For Purity." This is a radical separation between "pure" and "impure." People are either "in" or "out." If they are "out," then they are either "anti" or simply "in a fog." Before the collapse of communism in Eastern Europe it was standard procedure to issue "I.D." cards to dissidents designating them as "Anti-Social Personalities"—that is to those not already jailed or held in mental institutions. Demand For Purity, and Milieux Control, ie., Environmental (group) control over the communication and where-abouts of the individual, and the imposition of a degrading system of "rewards and penalties," is the main focus of the Brainwashing Manual. Steven Hassan's excellent book, *Combatting Cult Mind Control* examines in detail the various characteristics of manipulative-authoritarian groups.

ity; savageness, brutality, and uncompromising lack of humanity, will be obeyed. Such a use of force is, itself, an essential ingredient of greatness . . .

The psychopolitical dupe [ideal Scientologist] is a well-trained individual who serves in complete obedience to the psychopolitical operative [L. Ron Hubbard or the Church hierarchy] . . .

The cleverness of our attack in the field of psychopolitics [the human mind and spirit] is adequate to avoid the understanding of the layman and the usual stupid official [Scientologist], and by operating entirely under the banner of authority, with the oft repeated statement that the principles of psychotherapy [the ever present next mysterious level of auditing] are too devious for common understanding, an entire revolution can be affected [the creation of obedient converts] . . .

In rearranging loyalties we must have command over their values. In the animal the first loyalty is to himself. This is destroyed by demonstrating errors in him . . . The second loyalty is to the family unit . . . This is destroyed . . . by lessening the value of marriage, by making an easiness of divorce and by raising the children whenever possible by the State [the Church of Scientology]. The next loyalty is to friends and the local environment. This is destroyed by lowering his trust and bringing about reporting upon him allegedly by his fellows . . . The next is to the State [Church of Scientology] and this, for the purposes of Communism* [Scientology] is the **only loyalty** [sic] which should exist . . .*

[In Scientology Organizations "Parent time" is a short period of an hour or so per day for the parents to visit with their children, if their "statistics are up." Children are otherwise watched as a group by full-time sitters. The child-care conditions in the past have been described as scandalous.

Marriages among staff in Scientology, especially the Sea Org, have a very high incident of failure. Strong sexual and family loyalties— such as that developing between Hana Eltringham and John O'Keefe—are routinely undermined, in one way or another.

To not report a fellow Scientologist who is seen violating one of Hubbard's numerous rules is a major "crime."

This policy gives a strong incentive to report even on close friends

* Please keep in mind that it is not being implied that the Church of Scientology is a communist operation. The IRS case against the Church would appear to indicate that it has been a "capitalistic" money-making operation, while at the same time utilizing practices with which any 1960s fanatical Chinese Red Guard would feel quite at home.

and family. Stories of Scientologists "writing up" their husbands or wives, with regard to intimate conversations, are not uncommon. Laurel Sullivan, Hubbard's personal public relations officer, who left Scientology in 1980, burst into tears in court upon recounting such an incident.]

THE BRAINWASHING MANUAL:

The field of the mind must be sufficiently dominated by the psycho-political operative [Scientology], so that whatever tenets of the mind are taught they will be hypnotically received.

[From "Hubbard Communication Office Policy Letter" of 14 January 1969:

Thus in the case of Scientology Orgs one should attack with the end of view of taking over the whole field of mental health.

Could it be that Hubbard wanted to become the authority on the mind and spirit so that whole populations would hypnotically follow what he said?

According to Ron Jr., his father "believed he would achieve enormous personal power from taking over the field of mental health."

Certainly, for the membership, he is the final authority; speaking from on high, his infallibility never doubted].

THE BRAINWASHING MANUAL:

The tenets of rugged individualism, personal determinism, self-will, imagination, and personal creativeness are alike in the masses [staff and Sea Org personnel] antipathetic to the good of the Greater State [the Church of Scientology]. Those willful and unaligned are no more than illnesses which will bring about disaffection, disunity, and at length the collapse of the group to which the individual is attached.

The constitution of man lends itself easily and thoroughly to certain and positive regulation from without of all its functions, including those of thinkingness [sic],* obedience, and loyalty, and these things must be controlled if the Greater State [Church of Scientology] is to ensue.

* Hubbard often added "ness" to the end of verbs transforming them into nouns. For example, "beingness," "doingness' " "havingness," "eatingness," "sexingness," etc.

The end thoroughly justifies the means.

****

THE FIVE CARD SYSTEM

While the basics of the *Brainwashing Manual* were incorporated into "Scientology tech" in the mid-1960s, the years since have produced many other "innovations" on its methods and "philosophy." One of the most recent is the "Five Card System."

In 1986 the "5 Card System" was adopted to further ensure that staff members remain "cooperative." Apparently the relentless pressure to "keep stats up" so as not to be placed in a "lowered ethics condition" was not enough. So, short of being sentenced to the RPF, staff members are daily subjected to the "5 Card System."

Sea Org Executive Directive 3490 International introduces the new system:

"A brilliant system is being put into your org which heavily validates those staff who are actively working on contributing to and achieving your org's purpose of 5.4X statistics.*

"At the same time, this system penalizes "downstat" staff who are not actively contributing.

"There are five team shares and you, as a team member of the group, will be issued five cards representing each share.

"1. Social Card (blue)
"2. Bonus card (green)
"3. Allowance care (orange)
"4. Berthing Card (yellow)
"5. Chow Card (red)"

The social card entitles the staff members to "participate in any social activity such as liberty**, parties, sport events, special meals, outings, and the like"

The Bonus Card entitles the staff member to a "bonus in addition to the regular Sea Org allowance"***

* Meaning increasing one's production by 5.4 times before Hubbard's birthdate.
** "Liberty" is time off.
*** Approximately $7 to $12 a week.

The Berthing Card grants space in which to berth (a bed).

The Chow Card entitles the staff member to receive food at meal times from the Org.

Here's the good news:

A staff member who "is pulling his weight and taking responsibility for the org as a whole" is entitled to all five cards. He is also awarded a "Silver Star." He is to wear this star at all times.

Here's the bad news:

If a staff member is "being downstat or generally unproductive, or uncooperative" he starts losing his cards one at a time.

Lose one card and you lose your silver star.

Loss of all cards means the person "goes on rice and beans while living in pig's berthing . . ." The Directive goes on to explain:

"The Sea Organization is the most ethical group this planet has ever known or will know. Star high standards are enforced . . . Those who have other fish to fry show up fast on the Team System and can be quickly handled."

****

Quoting from Brian Ambry's *Critique on Scientology:*

> Scientologists can be counted on to snarl and snicker at assertions that the Scientology organization incorporates a combination of deceptive, manipulative, and coercive methods—ie., "Brain-Washing"—in (and around) its administrative and counseling "tech."
>
> "White Scientology" (techniques and data which have the potential to assist an individual to become more independent and self-determined) is promoted by the "Church" as the entirety of the subject. But there is a **dark side.** A dark side which makes the individual permanently dependent upon the "Church," and instead of self-determined, "Ron-determined."
>
> The marriage of potentially liberating methodologies with enslaving ones, the mixing of truth with lies, and love with hate: This is the strange story of L. Ron Hubbard and his Church.*
>
> Hubbard was a "user." He used freedom. He used goodness. Helping others feel better, understand more, communicate better—this was all fine, so long that he considered that it **aided in the attainment of his primary objective: Power and Fame.**

* For a more detailed look at this bizarre state of affairs, see Part One Chapters 12, **Souls turned Inside Out,** and Part Two Chapter Nine **Clay in the Master's Hands.**

He helped others so as to own them; to create gratitude and trust and give himself authority or "altitude." He "set up" people to be manipulated by first assisting them to feel better, have "wins" and so forth.

There are those who insist that every "gain" or "win" in Scientology is delusory. That all aspects of the counseling are brainwashing. That's nonsense. The trap is much more sophisticated than that.

He was a man of many methods.*

****

The *Brainwashing Manual* of 1955 reveals Hubbard's knowledge of methods aimed at, "asserting and maintaining dominion over the thoughts and loyalties of individuals, officers, bureaus, and masses, and the effecting of conquest of enemy nations through mental healing."

Ten years later, he began to vigorously apply these methods on his own followers. He soon added other methods to "assert and maintain dominion."

****

The idealistic, yet naive individuals who've been lured into Scientology, have no idea of the true nature of the organization to which they have given their unquestioning loyalty.

Hubbard's beguiling Introduction to the *Brainwashing Manual*— viewed many years later—presents a frightening parallel to the dilemma of "Today's Modern Scientologist":

"Unfortunately a large number of well-meaning people are being used to further the attack on the mind without realizing the significance of what they are doing . . . under the guise of creating some World Utopia."

---

* A particular counseling procedure that might be helpful in an honest and non-authoritarian situation, can be harmful in a manipulative one.

"Going through changes" or "changing one's mind" in a manipulative environment—even if the counseling procedure itself seems harmless—is very unwise.

10

The Sea Org Goes Ashore—
Dirty Tricks and Secret Codes

The "rock concert" and the numerous UNWELCOME mats had left
Hubbard frustrated with the Eastern Atlantic. So on October 10,
1974, he steamed towards the Americas.

Elena Lorrel tells the story of the final stages of the crossing of the
Atlantic:

> The night we were coming in to America (South Carolina) from Ma-
> deira, somebody picked up the frantic call from Jane, [Jane Kember—
> head of the Guardian's Office] on the pier saying, "Don't come in,
> there are 140 IRS agents waiting on the dock."
> So we took off for the Bahamas.
> We berthed at several ports during what was to be almost a year's
> cruise around the Caribbean. The intention had been to land in
> America, but since those plans had been foiled, we had to make the
> best of a difficult situation.
> In late 1974, in the Caribbean, LRH went ashore and we went to a
> movie with him. It was a real landmark because it was one of the first
> times he had been ashore for well over a year.
> He would get reports from his intelligence people that it was unsafe
> to go places. He didn't like to hear that, and, when he did, he could get
> really nasty to be around. . . .
> Cathy Cariataki and I knew that the only way to get him in a good
> humour was to get him off the ship. So we mocked up these dumb
> photo shoots. And he went ashore and he loved it. He wanted more
> and more and more.
> Well, after the Dominican Republic (where we had done a lot of
> photo shooting) we went to Jamaica. He told me he wanted to shoot
> stuff to do with the buccaneers. So I had to go off and do research on

Henry Morgan the pirate. And one of the pictures that are peddled, of LRH sitting in the open Pontiac with the messengers, is the one we shot at the fort there in Jamaica.

Well, I tell you, I almost got knifed trying to get that car. He wouldn't go anywhere unless he had a convertible.

I had to go into the ghetto section and play footsie with Kingfish, who was the local head of the organized crime there. The only convertible on the island was also the fanciest car on the island. It also happened to be his car!

None of the taxi drivers would take me there. They told me that this guy would kill me for sport. That's how motivated I was. I "made it go right" just so I wouldn't get in horrible trouble with the Old Man.

And I don't know how I kept from getting knifed but we came back with the big red convertible.

Anyway we did a ghetto photo shoot where, I swear to God: he was sitting up snapping pictures of these destitute children; and there were hungry, angry people with broken bottles and knives coming at us.

He'd yell at Liz Gablehouse, "You're the PR, handle them." And he wouldn't even bat an eye, he'd just keep shooting and expect her to handle these huge guys who were coming at us, trying to knife us.

There we were in a convertible, in all our glory, sitting on top of this thing like it was a parade. And there were three or four messengers sitting there in their little white tooty fruit outfits handing him equipment back and forth—lenses and camera backs—and Liz was the PR, and he'd yell at her to handle this guy who'd be there running along the side of the car with a rusty machette trying to whack at us. All she could try to do is say things to them in Spanish or their local lingo, of which she'd learned a few words, in order to try and buy us a few seconds while I got Cathy to speed up the car.

After that there were more photo shoots and he was going to publish this whole journal. Then Cathy and I sat down and reviewed our situation and said, "God we're really on a roll. The man hasn't been in a sour mood in two weeks and he's constantly asking, "What's the next thing planned ashore?" So now we were at sea headed to Curaçao and decided that we would have to mock up as many shoots and get him off the ship.

And the people on international management lines realized what a successful action this was because he was being kind to them and the orders of the day were real cheerful and he was not meddling with them and so on.

Then we went to this synagogue where, for some reason known only to the Devil, he was just being a spoiled brat. He so alienated the orthodox Rabbi there that he tried to throw LRH out of the sanctuary surrounding the synagogue. Here was LRH cursing the Rabbi and using God's name in vain to such an extent that the Rabbi was holding his ears and just screaming!

We placated the poor man after LRH left.

The photographs he took there really were spectacular, however. He got some extraordinary shots and we put together a brochure that they still use at that synagogue to this day, as a souvenir.

****

The pleasure Hubbard was deriving from these photo shoots did not prevent him from having another heart attack. Since he refused to go to a hospital, X-ray equipment and other medical gear had to be located and brought aboard.

Finally the condition got very serious and Kima Douglas, who was medical officer at the time, with the assistance of others took him off the ship, driving him to a hospital on the island of Curaçao where he received treatment.

For three months following his treatment, Hubbard stayed at a Cabana-type bungalow, which is part of the Hilton Hotel there, recovering.

As he began to regain mobility and strength, more photo shoot missions were undertaken on the island. As it had been in the Mediterranean, however, so it was to be in the Caribbean: the ship was being expelled from the various ports where it sought refuge. Finally the decision was made to attempt to relocate on the mainland.

Homer Shomer, a successful businessman attracted to the lofty stated ideals of the Sea Org, says:

> The actual moving to Florida was the best kept secret that I knew of. One of the last places we were in was Curaçao and we were there for a number of months. The shore story was that we were refitting the forward lower hold for berthing. We'd actually spent 20 to 25 thousand dollars getting it refitted and painting it and chipping it, and welding the air shafts. And we really had no intention of ever using it!

In October of 1975, the ship sailed to Freeport in the Bahamas and the crew was divided into three groups: The management group was flown to New York City, where they established a management unit called RONY (Relay Office New York). It was located on the fifth floor of the N.Y. org. A second group went to Miami, and a third to Washington, D.C. The remaining crew travelled by bus from wherever they landed to Daytona. Here they gathered in a motel on the beach.

Hubbard flew in from the Bahamas to Miami airport with three aides. One carried a million dollars in cash. They all carried passports giving false names.

He took up residence in another hotel on the beach, next door to the one his crew were occupying. Mary Sue Hubbard and her entourage arrived a short while later.

****

Soon thereafter, my wife Mary arrived in Daytona Beach to take a Scientology course. While there she observed Quentin Hubbard, Hubbard's oldest son by Mary Sue.

She described an incident where Quentin was running away from his father, who was coming down on an elevator: "He paled dramatically and exclaimed, 'Oh shit, it's Dad, I've got to get out of here!" He sprinted up several flights of stairs.

He had previously confided in her that he was in desperate need of help regarding his problems with his father. She said his emotion was "terror."

She observed him again in early 1977, in Florida at the "Flag Land Base," looking devastated, having again been placed in a "lowered ethics condition."

Several months later Quentin Hubbard committed suicide.

****

Wrote Tonja Burden:

The boat was sold sometime in October 1975. Approximately 500 people moved to Daytona Beach. We rented several hotels in Daytona.

After several months we moved to the hotel in Clearwater. At first, LRH called it the United Churches. I heard LRH scheme this cover. He said it would be called United Churches, although no other churches were involved.

At Fort Harrison, I remained LRH's personal messenger. I observed LRH control the operation of Scientology throughout the various "orgs" worldwide from Fort Harrison.

I coded and decoded messages to, and directly from, Hubbard. He used approximately 15 codes at this time to conceal his operations, programs and policies, which he disseminated worldwide. I personally delivered messages concerning Operation Snow White, and Operation Freakout, Operation Goldmine, and other Scientology secret and illegal operations to frame people, steal, infiltrate private and government offices, and break into buildings.

At this time I was only 15 years old and did what I was told, and although I knew the names of the operations I did not know the exact nature of those operations. I also filed these operations in Hubbard's personal filing cabinets.*

"Operation Goldmine" was a local Clearwater operation. She describes it as a "conspiracy to use Scientology funds to, in effect, take over the city of Clearwater."

TONJA:

All telex communications were processed through his messengers. Telexes were sent to all Guardian Offices Worldwide. One telex from LRH questioned Mayor Cazares' background. He discovered this information through a private investigator.

In just one of the operations conducted against the mayor, the Guardian's office faked a hit-and-run accident implicating Cazares. Then they leaked the incident to his political opponents.

Following this "hit and run accident" a church memo gleefully crowed: "I should think the mayor's political days are at an end." The operation did in fact cause considerable havoc for the mayor, but was eventually resolved as part of a subsequent F.B.I. investigation.

****

About this same time, Hubbard was being fitted for several suits of clothes when the tailor, who happened to be a science fiction fan, rec-

---

*Amongst the documents seized by the FBI during their July 1977 raids, was one entitled, "General Categories of Data Needing Coding."
  It states:
"1. Secret PR Front Groups
    a. APRL Alliance for the Preservation of Religious Liberty.
    b. ACCRA–American Committee For Civil Religious Actions.
    c. PAC Parents group
    d. Any others developed.
"2. PR Traffic on B-1 [covert operations] Flubs
    a. Strategic handlings
    b. Evidence of C of S involvement
"3. Anything we do not want connected to LRH or MSH.
    a. Such as #1 or #2 above. For this situation we code their names.
"4. Words or actions that would tend to dispute the fact that the C of S's motives are humanitarian: harass, eradicate, attack, destroy, annihilate, cave in, third party, spreading rumors, entrapment . . .
  5. Admission to Unpunished Crimes and/or Incriminating Data. . . .

ognized him and asked him if he was in fact *the* L. Ron Hubbard. He fessed up. The man was ecstatic and very proud to have shaken his hand.

The tailor then went back to Tarpon Springs and told everyone he knew about his exciting afternoon.

This story was soon picked up by the *St. Petersburg Times*, and staff reporter Betty Orsini discovered that Hubbard was indeed living in Dunedin. She blew the Scientology cover and exposed the fact that they were the real group behind the "United Churches" purchase of the Fort Harrison and various other buildings in Clearwater.

The deception was not appreciated by Mayor Cazares, who initiated hearings regarding the Church's activities.

Hubbard took off in the middle of the night. Jim Dincali and Mike Douglas accompanied him on a trip to Washington, D.C., by car. They took out an apartment and occupied it for the next five or six months.

****

Being located on land, as opposed to the ship, posed certain problems. Actions had to be taken to maintain the kind of control over the crew that a ship's environment had previously provided.

The Rehabilitation Project Force was reinstated with some novel adaptations to the new environment. One such adaptation was the "RPF's RPF."

This was for those who would not "comply" or do the RPF.

Those on the RPF's RPF in Fort Harrison in Clearwater report being locked in the lower boiler rooms to live among the piping, to have to clean the filthiest areas of the property, and to being guarded against "blowing" (trying to escape).

According to eyewitness reports, the RPF's RPF in the lower boiler rooms was a nightmare. Dimly lit, with hot steam pipes running everywhere, the subject slept on the floor on a blanket. The boilers ran day and night, clanking and rumbling.

After a few days, one looked like an animal, depraved and degraded. Soot, dirt, grease and grime were everywhere. Inmates were instilled with a deep fear of violating a senior's orders. These staff were programmed to be machine-like producers whose function is not to think, only to comply . . . to carry out orders.

Tonja Burden wrote:

> At the Fort Harrison, security guards were stationed outside to pre-

vent people from "blowing." To "blow" meant to leave Scientology. People were not allowed to just leave Scientology. Approximately 30 or 40 people tried to escape. These people were caught and placed in the RPF (Rehabilitation Project Force). The RPF was a Scientology "concentration camp," where people who were "security threats" were kept under guard. The RPF at Fort Harrison was in a storage area.

LRH declared the people suppressive persons if they escaped from Scientology. He sent telexes to the Guardian's Office listing the SPs. I have seen the names of people declared by LRH. I continued to decode and code messages from Hubbard to the Guardian's Office seven days a week until August of 1977.

In August of 1977, I refused to perform a certain order and was sent to the galley, where I performed menial labor until I broke apart emotionally and was sent to the RPF on direct orders of Hubbard.

Finally, in November 1977, I decided I had to escape. At approximately 4:30 A.M., I stole the keys from a guard who was sleeping at the door to the storage area where we slept. I crawled through an air duct on my stomach, where I observed the telephone in the lobby. I saw no one, ran to the telephone, and called my father and told him about my situation. He told me he would send my uncle to come and get me and take me to Fort Lauderdale. I convinced the officers in the RPF that my uncle was a VIP for the Miami Dolphins (which was not true), and that if they refused his request to visit, that might cause bad public relations. Finally, with my uncle's assistance, I escaped and flew back to Vegas.

Approximately two weeks after I returned to Vegas, two of Hubbard's agents came to my house and told me that Hubbard wanted to see me. I told them that I would never return. They then asked if I would go for a cup of coffee with them, which after a short while I agreed to do. I got into the car in the front seat and sat between the two agents. After driving a few minutes, I noticed we were driving to the highway, and I asked where we were going. They told me I was being taken to Los Angeles to see Hubbard.

In Los Angeles, I was locked in a room and forced to undergo a "security check" on the E-meter. I was very scared and crying, and told them that I had a family reunion to go to during the holidays. I told them I had relatives in the police department in Las Vegas, and that I would come back after the holidays. I convinced them to release me, and I returned home by bus. For weeks after I returned home, they constantly called me to find out when I'd return. I said never!

****

Tonja tells of how she got involved with Hubbard and of the events leading up to her sentence to the RPF:

I was in Scientology from the age of 13 to age of 18 and was paid between $2.50 a week and $17.50 a week. I received no education, and in fact phony classrooms were set up in Florida to demonstrate to educational officials that education was taking place. I have been sent a bill for the amount of $58,000.00 for auditing given me while I was working for them.

I [had] signed my billion-year contract on or about March 3, 1973.

My parents joined the "American Saint Hill Organization" while I was placed in the "Cadet Organization."

The Cadet Organization consisted of two three story buildings that housed approximately 400 children. It was designed to teach children about Scientology.

I was assigned to care, clean and feed the children, since I and another girl my age were the oldest there.

The living conditions were squalid. Glass from broken windows lay strewn over the floors and, in some places where children played, live electrical wires were exposed.

We received little food. On several occasions spoiled milk with maggots were served to the children. (The maggots were removed by hand before the milk was served.) In addition to caring for the children, I cleaned the toilets daily.

I wrote to L. Ron Hubbard explaining the conditions. Nothing improved.

The children were not allowed to live with their parents. Scientology permitted one visit every other week, and only for 45 minutes during mealtimes.

One day, after about three months, a man arrived at the Cadet Organization from the flagship *Apollo.* He spoke of the "Source," L. Ron Hubbard. He told us that Ron needed "messengers" to work for him aboard his ship.

After much security checking, Tonja was eventually placed on a plane which took her to the island of Madiera, off the coast of Portugal.

Once aboard, I was assigned a "buddy" and given two days to learn about the ship. I was given a berth in the women's dorm and placed in the EPF (The Estates Project Force).

I was told the EPF was going to transform me into an "able bodied seaman."

In the EPF, my day began at six A.M., I scrubbed clothes from six A.M. until noon without breakfast or any breaks. The clothes were scrubbed by hand in a bucket, and I was directed to rinse each article in 13 separate buckets. Then I hung the clothes on the deck to dry.

After a half-hour lunch, I was assigned to clean six cabins. These had to meet white-glove inspection. This meant a white glove or Q-tip was used to check corners and shelves of each cabin for dust. If the cabins were not cleaned to white-glove perfection, I had to run a lap around the boat before recleaning the rooms (the equivalent of 1/5 of a mile). My day ended about midnight.

On rainy days I ironed the clothes dry. This required ironing during the evening hours and into the morning hours. On many occasions I ironed through the night and finished at six A.M. I then started washing the next morning's clothing. On occasion, I worked three or four days without sleep. I sometimes fell asleep at the ironing board with a hot iron in my hand. My senior, "Doreen" Gillam, "caught" me sleeping and yanked my head off the board. She ordered me to run laps and assigned me a condition of "Doubt." A condition of "Doubt" required 15 hours of "amends" work. This additional work had to be performed during my sleep or meal time.

Until I completed my amends work I was ordered not to communicate with anyone. I ate lunch alone. I finally spoke up, telling them I had enough. I was sent to the Commanding Messenger, and she assigned me one month in the galley, washing pots and pans. I washed pots and pans for a month and went back into the EPF. EPF was like prison. I had to say "sir" to everyone and was generally allowed 15 minutes for meals. They would not let me out of the EPF until I proved myself. I was totally brainwashed to receive and take orders. I was paid $2.90 a week for this work.

While in the EPF, I never heard from my parents. No phone calls or letters. Aboard the ship, I received a telex from Peter Albert who was the Continental Justice Chief at FOLO at the Flag Liaison Office. The telex informed me that my father had been declared an SP. They said he was a "plant"; a spy within Scientology. I began crying and asked to leave, telling them I could convince my father to return to Scientology. I was not allowed to leave. I then explained that I wanted to leave and reunite with my mom and dad but this was not permitted. Instead I was told to disconnect from my parents because they were SPs. This meant no more communication with them.

Tony Armstrong, the Commanding Officer, assigned me a condition of Doubt and ordered me back to the EPF. So I returned to the six A.M. to midnight schedule again, occasionally working 24 hours a day.

Approximately one month after this, I was put on training routines.

During the training routines, myself and others practiced carrying messages to LRH. We had to listen to a message, repeat it in the same tone, and practice salutes.

"Ghosting" was on-the-job training where I learned how to serve LRH. I followed another messenger around and observed her carry his hat, light his cigarettes, carry his ashtray, and prepare his toiletries. I eventually performed those duties.

As his servant, I would sit outside his room and help him out of bed when he called "messenger." I responded by assisting him out of bed, lighting his cigarette, running his shower, preparing his toiletries and helping him dress.

After that I ran to his office to check it, hoping it would pass white-glove inspection. He frequently exploded if he found dust or dirt or smelled soap in his clothes.

****

Gerald Armstrong and Tonja were both "insignificant" people as far as Hubbard was concerned. But they were to play very significant roles in his life.

Gerry Armstrong joined Scientology in 1969 in British Columbia, Canada, and in 1971 joined the Sea Organization.

He met up with the *Apollo* in Tangiers, Morocco, a week after he joined the Sea Org. In late 1974 he became the ship's intelligence officer, a position he held until he left the *Apollo*.

When the crew moved to Daytona Beach he worked there in the intelligence unit of the Guardian's Office.

At the end of May of 1976 he was sent to Culver City, California, to set up a communications office for Hubbard.

In Culver City he got into an argument with Mary Sue Hubbard's communicator (secretary) after which Hubbard deemed him a "security risk" and had him removed from the property and locked up and guarded for three weeks in the Scientology intelligence office in Los Angeles.

Gerry Armstrong wrote in a legal affidavit:

After that, he ordered me and my wife Terri back to Florida, to the Clearwater base.

There a telex from him awaited us ordering us to the RPF. I spent a total of 17 months on the RPF and was put in charge of it for some 12 months. Tonja Burden was also assigned there.

An RPF assignment was an unbelievably traumatic experience. When it happened to me—and I was a grown man—I was so devastated that I went into shock that lasted several days, during which time I could eat hardly anything. . . . I was in such heavy grief, my body convulsed uncontrollably. . . .

Shortly after "graduating" I was transferred to the Commodore's Messenger Organization unit in Los Angeles.

There I was ordered to retrieve Tonja from her parent's home in Las Vegas after she escaped from the RPF in Clearwater. . . .

On December 14, 1977, my wife and I went to get Tonja back.

She was shocked that we had tracked her down so quickly and she was terrified by us. Terri had been her senior for some years in the CMO, and I had been her senior in the RPF, and we both intimidated her.

She said over and over that she did not want to go back. Tears welled up in her eyes. But Terri and I would not be swayed from our purpose. We talked to her mother and father, and intimidated them with veiled threats of what might happen, how it would be better for all if Tonja came back. We also insisted that Tonja coming back and "routing out properly" was the most ethical thing to do.

The truth was that our purpose was to get Tonja back, have her sec checked and get her to sign waivers, releases and promissory notes, so she would be rendered harmless to Hubbard and the organization. Tonja was, in fact, considered a significant threat because she had worked so closely with Hubbard and potentially knew a great deal about his control of the organization and G.O. intelligence operations.

After several hours, and still against her will, Tonja succumbed to our tactics, and we drove with her to Los Angeles. There we turned her over to the Los Angeles RPF where she would be sec checked and made to sign the required documents.

What I did to Tonja, coercing her back to Los Angeles to subject her to sec checks and forcing her to sign documents and signing myself a false statement against her, was cruel and shameful and only shows the desensitization I had gone through.

Tonja was herself brutalized by Hubbard and his organization, yet I perceived her as a "suppressive person" and "fair game," [and so] any act against her, any trick, anything to destroy her, [was] laudable.

****

To the reader of Tonja's story and of the horrors of the RPF, it might seem inconceivable that there was a luxury hotel being serviced by the RPF and crew of the Flag Land Base.

The occupants of the hotel, mostly well-to-do Scientologists, saw little of the RPFers, and were usually completely unaware of the degrading conditions to which the staff and their children were being subjected.

The "public pcs" would fly in from Los Angeles, Zurich, Frankfurt or Mexico City. They would pay the huge fees, play backgammon, swim, sunbathe, listen to tapes by Hubbard, and be given special PR briefings by a smartly uniformed host or attractive PR girls.

Diners in the Hour Glass Restaurant, which is part of the Fort Harrison Hotel, were, and are to this day, served by waiters with black suits, bow ties, and crisp white shirts. The talk would usually drift to the great wins each was having in his auditing.

The Fort Harrison "Land Base" was a roaring success as the "Mecca for Technical Perfection."

Celebrities and well-to-do Scientologists (and those who sold houses, blew their life savings or inheritance, or who borrowed the necessary dollars) began arriving in large numbers.

11

"I Let Him Undress Me Without Resisting"

In 1975, while Hubbard was staying in Washington, D.C., another location was found for him in California and he moved there. It was known as ASTRA, and was located in Culver City, California, which is part of the Los Angeles metropolitan area near the Airport.

This location of Hubbard's was part of a three-part telex network designed to disguise the fact that Hubbard was very much in communication with the Church.

It was during this time that he possibly made visits to the seventh floor of the Fifield Manor in Los Angeles, also called the "Chateau Elise." This building was constructed in accordance with the architectural style preferred by French royalty when building castles for their stays in the country. It was in its day a favorite hotel of many of Hollywood's great personalities.

The seventh floor was cordoned off and secured as private premises to which only L. Ron Hubbard and his wife had access.

According to a sworn affidavit the following events occurred during this period.

Heidi Forrester (not her real name) joined The Church of Scientology in July of 1974, just after having completed her senior year of college. She had read a science fiction book by L. Ron Hubbard, and had become curious about a book called *Dianetics, the Modern Science of Mental Health* advertised in the back of the book. She wrote for the book and received it shortly afterwards.

Fascinated by the claims made by Hubbard about enhancing creative and perceptive talents, she responded positively to a call by a Sea Org recruiter who mentioned he had received the card she had sent in for more information.

As she tells it:

> The next day, July 16, 1974, I went to the Columbus Airport and caught a flight to L.A. I arrived at seven P.M. I took a taxi to the Hilton Hotel and waited in the lobby. Ron Noe, the recruiter, arrived shortly thereafter. Dressed in a non-formal Sea Org uniform, he appeared to me to be extremely organized and high powered.
>
> We got into his car and drove to ASHO (American Saint Hill Organization) on West Temple Street.
>
> Upon arrival, Ron Noe showed me to his desk and I noticed that on every desk was an identical color photograph of Hubbard taken on the bridge of a ship. There were also enormous posters on all the walls of Hubbard in full, formal Sea Org uniform and enormous Sea Org symbols painted in gold on many of the walls. The symbol of the Sea Org is a star surrounded by a laurel wreath. In the years ahead I would be given enormous power as a representative of that symbol, and in the end all the power would be taken away from me without explanation.
>
> At his desk, Ron Noe handed me a Sea Org contract. I had no trouble with the one billion year bit, as most new recruits did, since I had already read that Scientologists believed in past lives. I signed it. It was witnessed by Ron Noe and Gerry Larson [not his real name]. I swore in while Ron Noe stood and saluted me, and I saluted him.
>
> He read a twenty-item covenant which I repeated after him. The items consisted of promises all Sea Org members make to the group. I was basically to adhere to all orders given by Hubbard. I was to apply the technology strictly according to his standards.
>
> After the swearing in I was taken to the center of the room:
>
> "Now hear this: Heidi Forrester has just become a Sea Org member!"
>
> In seconds the entire lobby was jammed with people in uniform, cheering, clapping, yelling—it was pandemonium!
>
> The ovation lasted a full ten minutes.
>
> I was escorted to the registrar, a girl named Dawn Praeger, and signed a check for all the money I had, which was $8,500.00.
>
> I was taken to the Hollywood Inn that night by Ron Noe. It was a large red brick building located in the middle of Hollywood. It was not in good shape. I was put into a room with four other Sea Org members, none of whom I had met before.
>
> After four hours' sleep I had to go back to ASHO. I was told by Ron Noe that I would be going to the ship that night, the *Excalibur*, a fairly

large vessel in my estimation, though much smaller than the *Apollo* I was told. It was used for training Sea Org members in the basics of seamanship.

I spent some time on the ship and over the next year became fairly highly trained and audited (at my own expense). Word spread that I was on a fairly high auditing level. This fact, it appears, resulted in my being chosen for some very horrible experiences:

I was *raped* on orders that had "come down lines". . .by a person who fits the description of Hubbard. . . .

It became apparent to me that as a Sea Org member at ASHO, there was a very strong law concerning relationships. Sea Org members did not have any sexual contact with public students or preclears. At ASHO anyway, this law was observed rigidly among the staff. An interpretation of the S.O.'s feeling about sex with public persons was that the S.O. was "above" such activities. We were so "elite," that sex with the public would "spoil" our control over the public. However, there was no law preventing S.O. members from having sexual contact with other S.O. members. In fact, this was expected if one had been with the S.O. for an appreciable length of time. Marriages in the S.O. were common. . . .

I could never understand the amount and frequency of "swapping partners" in the S.O. This went on constantly.

One week two staff would be married (in a Scientology marriage ceremony) and then the woman would become pregnant. A few weeks later she would marry another Sea Org member, have the baby and then marry another S.O. member and so on. When a couple married they would obtain a marriage certificate from city hall, but it meant nothing. It was all done as part of a "shore story" to keep legal problems relating to marriage from reaching the S.O.

If a couple wanted to divorce, they just broke up. There were never formal divorces in the S.O., they didn't have to get permission from anyone to end their relationship. There was never much property to divide between them anyway.

The offspring of these "marriages" went to Pumpkin School, Apple School, and the Cadet Org to be indoctrinated with Hubbard's techniques so they didn't become problems to the Organization.

I observed all this during my first year in the S.O. It bothered me. Here were all the staff, supposedly ethical people, who were all-knowing about humanity, busting up relationships all the time.

I independently decided that I would have no sexual contact with anyone in the S.O. I totally suppressed my own sexuality, and decided I would not play that game.

****

In late 1975, I was told to report to the Hubbard Communications Office. The senior officer there at the time, informed me that I was to report to the Fifield Manor and go to the seventh floor. She gave me no other information. I did this without knowing why I was going.

At the Manor, I was directed to the elevator and went to the seventh floor. The entire floor was elaborately furnished to the point of suffocation. An S.O. member appeared and showed me to a door that was partly open.

I went into a very large living room with heavy curtains, pile carpet, overstuffed chairs and clean to the point of obsession.

Sitting on one of the chairs, drinking what looked like sherry, was a heavy-set older man. He had reddish grey hair, slightly long in the back. He was wearing a white shirt, black pants, black tie, and black shoes, highly polished.

He didn't say a word and slowly got up, motioned me to follow him into the next room.

I didn't know if it was Hubbard, and wondered if I was to have either an auditing session or an interview. I followed him.

I found myself in a lavish bedroom. This still didn't worry me as sometimes interviews and sessions were held in bedrooms at the Hollywood Inn for staff.

There was a small table set up with an E-meter on it and again I thought about a session.

Without a word he suddenly began to undress me.

I was repelled by him.

I did not want to sleep with him. Yet, I felt really chilled and cold to the bone at that moment.

I acutely sensed real fear and danger in the room. In an instant I realized the calculated power coming from this person. If I resisted I knew that my punishment would be extreme.

His eyes were so blank, no emotion, no interaction, nothing was there.

I made the decision to not resist no matter what happened. I realized it would be a bad mistake for me to do so. He seemed to be completely divorced from reality. He was so strange that I realized that if I provoked him he could be extremely dangerous.

I let him undress me without resisting.

I was totally unprepared for what happened next.

He lay on top of me.

As far as I can tell he had no erection. However, using his hand in some way he managed to get his penis inside me.

Then for the next *hour* he did absolutely nothing at all. I mean nothing!

After the first twenty-five minutes I became about as frightened as I have ever been in my life. I felt as if in some perverse way he was telling me that he hated me as a female. I then began to feel that my mind was being ripped away from me by force.

That was the worst of all. I really felt he "coveted" an aspect of my personality and he wanted it. This was weird, total control on a level I could not fathom at that time. I had no idea what was happening.*

After half an hour I really thought I was going crazy. I couldn't move my body from underneath him, and I could feel he still had no erection.

He wouldn't look at me, but instead kept his head averted to the side and just gazed into space.

I had to discipline myself to keep from screaming because I felt I was having a nervous breakdown.

Then I got the terrible thought that he was dead. He was hardly breathing. Then I thought he would kill me too. My thoughts became very morbid.

After an hour he got up and walked out.

I just lay there for ten minutes. Then mechanically I got dressed. Instantly after that I began crying hysterically. I cried and cried and cried.

I wasn't afraid of becoming pregnant. I was so afraid of whatever had been going on in this man's head.

Finally when I couldn't cry anymore, I went downstairs and took a bus back to ASHO. [American St. Hill Organization]

I didn't say a word to anyone.

****

Months went by after this. I got my period on schedule which made me feel a little gratified at least.

One night I was working late. Gerry Larson, who was now the deputy C.O., came into my area and asked if I wanted a ride back to the Inn. This seemed a little strange as he was a senior officer, OT7, Native State, class 7 auditor; but I accepted.

On the way in the car he asked me if I had ever fallen in love sexually in the S.O. I said "No."

"I think that's true," he said, "because you are much too powerful theta-wise to be controlled."

When we got to the Inn we went up in the elevator together and as I was about to get off at my floor he said he needed to talk to me.

I said "O.K." as he was an officer and I thought a friend. Also he was married. . . .

We went to the eighth floor of the Inn into a little bedroom. He sat

*This sounds like a form of "spiritual vampirism," a kind of "Black Sex-Magic."

on the bed and started talking about eight being the symbol for infinity and the highest level of OTness.

I thought that was interesting, but couldn't figure out why he was telling me this.

"Ron works in eight-year cycles," he said. "You were born in the eighth month of the year (August). Orders had come down lines that you are to conceive a child." he said.

This really shocked me.

"I can't tell you who sent the order," he said. "Your abilities are such that the Sea Org needs you to have a baby."

Without another word he pulled me up, hurriedly undressed me and threw me on the bed.

Again I felt the same feeling that I mustn't fight him.

He got undressed and for the next hour the exact same performance that had happened to me at the Manor was repeated. . . .

Afterwards I felt ripped apart mentally. As he was getting undressed I couldn't stand it anymore. I was in tears again. I said:

"Sir, I can't understand what you are doing to me."

He looked at me and said:

"Heidi, you haven't seen the OT materials for OT7 yet, but you know what you are. You are an invisible spirit operating your body. You and I actually live in a totally different universe, far away from this one. This Earth, this galaxy, our bodies are just pictures we are mocking up to play and have a game. Sex for a thetan is nothing. It's the postulates and control of mind and body that is the prize.

"If I *postulate* you will have a baby from the viewpoint of my home universe, then you will. You are under my command coming from far away. I can make your body do what I want."

Then he left.

I was so mixed up. I had been trained to believe everything he said, yet I couldn't believe he had just told me what he had.

I felt really defenseless. I cried all night.

A month later I got my period. A month after that my senior called me into his room.

"Go to ethics!" he said.

The "ethics officer" assigned me a condition of treason because I had disobeyed command intention and was not pregnant.

I had to do amends for this "crime."

After this I never had any other sexual relations in the Sea Org up to the point where I left. It was made apparent that I was a failure in this area.

Heidi did her amends. She was put on a special program. She was to eat by herself. The diet consisted of coffee for breakfast, liquid protein for lunch, and one piece of fruit for dinner. (She was at the same time put on a running program—three hours a day). This was all she got to eat for several months before finally leaving the Sea Org in 1978, yet she was an officer in uniform—granted more privileges than most.

Events that led her to finally leave the Sea Org were described by her as follows (the setting being the Cedars Sinai Hospital in Los Angeles shortly after the Scientologists had moved into it in 1978):

. . . the ASHO Ethics Officer came up to me. He said there was no door on the room where all the OT folders were and that I would have to guard the door for four hours. Silently I followed him to the very bowels of Cedars, the morgue where the folders were. I felt as if I was now dreaming. I couldn't believe what was happening. I wasn't even an OT, yet I had to guard all the OT folders.

Let me describe the morgue. It had not been cleaned out. There was the scale for weighing the bodies, the huge stone tables where the autopsies were done. Drains for blood, etc. There were no lights. I was left to sit on a milk crate in the dark, with racks and racks of OT folders all around me.

The floor was covered with trash and there was no fresh air. It smelled of death, really stank of death and chemicals and dissection.

For the first hour I just sat. Then I realized that it was very cold down here. So I walked back and forth for the second hour. My mind was blank.

I knew I could look at all the folders but I didn't care. I couldn't have cared less what was in them.

Suddenly, during the third hour I was aware of shadows in the corridor beyond me; they were people.

Slowly I realized that an entire group of people lived and worked down here. I was so tired it took me a long time to realize who they were.

Then it hit me. The Cedars RPF. They lived and worked down here in this stinkhole; this was their org.

Then I really found out what had happened to them. Filthy, tired, skeletons appeared before me and started begging to see the OT folders.

I thought I had looked bad, but I looked beautiful compared to them.

They crowded around me, pushing and shoving, then the mood turned ugly. They started hitting each other to get into the room behind me.

I realized then what had happened. They had been totally broken.

They were animals, not humans. I saw four of my friends . . . fighting to get by me. They were punching each other in the face, pulling hair, kicking. And way down in this cellar no one could hear them, no one cared.

Someone suddenly hit me hard. I realized they were turning their anger on me; they would beat me up to get to the folders. I guess in periods of deep stress we all go a little insane. Survival of the fittest.

From somewhere inside my brain, strength came. . . .

"Friends," I said, "believe me, I am your friend. By some strange fate I am not with you on the RPF. But believe me if you don't get out of here right now, I know you will be punished. Go now before it is too late."

And they ran away into the dark.

When I sat down I was trembling all over. Because the real intent of my message had been for them to get out of the hospital. Leave Cedars. But I don't think any of them got the message.

****

My last week in the Sea Org was like a dream. One night I was told to go to the basement and stuff letters. I did this in a little room with no ventilation and moisture dripping down the walls.

There was never anyone around. I was left alone most of the time at night now. That was their mistake. It gave me time to think.

This night I started stuffing my 2,000 letters. The old innocent days of the Sea Org seemed very far away. The idealistic little girl who had come here in '74 with dreams of new-found powers and increased understanding had died. . . .

Far above me the org hummed with activity. Every day someone else like me, gullible and hungry for answers, was being drawn into Scientology. Every day someone joined the Sea Org looking for security within the group, not knowing the total control of their personality they were handing over. Every day someone was sent to the RPF. These were my thoughts as I stood there.

Suddenly I flung the letters down. I needed to walk. Underneath the nine buildings were long tunnels that connected each building. Great steam pipes ran along the sides of the tunnels. It was like being in the engine room of a ship. The public didn't even know these tunnels existed.

I walked for miles, thinking.

I knew now that I was going to die: My body was completely emaciated, my mind had developed frightening blank periods when I could remember nothing at all. I had very few emotions I could feel any more. Things were breaking down.

I walked through tunnels I had never been in. Then I heard it. Inhuman screaming and ranting. It was coming from my right.

There were four doors and someone was pounding on one of them. I ran over and tried to open the door. It was locked. I yelled, "Are you all right?" I got more screams. Suddenly someone touched my shoulder.

I turned and looked at a man in clean overalls. "Hello," he said. "I'm the Ethics Officer for the RPF."

"What are you doing to her?" I said.

"Oh, she's just blowing off some charge. When someone flips out on the RPF, we lock them up for a couple of hours. They calm down after a while." He smiled.

I was stunned. "You lock them up in here?"

"Sure, you know the tech. The tech always works."*

I looked at him. Totally triumphant, with Scientology tech on his side. I felt sick to my stomach; the corridor started spinning around me. So this was it. The final answer. Cold, calculated, step by step—a progression to stamp out anyone who questioned, rebelled, criticized, disliked Scientology. Break them, all of us. You don't agree, you make a mistake, you are a staff member and you flip out. No mercy—just Scientology tech. Pure Ron Hubbard, turned insane.

He was still looking at me.

"Sure," I said, "maybe she'll drop her body and pick up a new one. She'll get regged [recruited] again and come back for another try. Death doesn't exist, does it? Suffering doesn't exist either. Only the tech sent from another galaxy."

"Wow," he said. "What OT level are you?"

"None you'd want to know about," I said. I turned and left him standing by the locked door.

*In 1974 Hubbard formulated "tech" dealing with incarceration of "psychotics."

12

Souls Turned Inside Out

Quoting from Brian Ambry's Critique on Scientology, *The Bridge to Total Freedom:*

"Few of today's membership have met L. Ron Hubbard. To the rank and file he is a huge photograph to be applauded, cheered, and saluted; a god made of ink, paper, and magnetic tape.

"They are the denizens of L. Ron Hubbard's official monogrammed universe, who day by day, year by year, strive to be the epitome of perfect mono-mindedness; content, indeed exulted to exist in an intellectual flatland, where Ron is Rightness, is Source, is Truth, is The Way.

"A place where ministers dress in military uniforms and scream profanities. A place where so much as thinking a critical thought about RON, or doubting the wisdom of the church hierarchy, is an 'ethics' offense.

"Where a dear and close friend may, at the issue of an 'ethics order,' become an evil being never to be communicated with again.

"A place of ultimate revisionist history—where forgetting those pieces of the past which conflict with today's official reality, is a key to survival.

"A 'good Scientologist' is a well-adapted cell living with enforced harmony in the body of his beloved (and feared) Church.

"He exists under conditions resembling a kind of 'spiritual marshal law.' Restrictions on thought and communication are justified, as the Church of RON works against time to free Mankind, and ultimately the universe, from the forces of evil.

"A 'good Scientologist' has little or no mind of his own, having

139

abandoned his own vastly inferior collection of ideas, information, and conclusions for the encyclopoedic MIND that manifests as the books, bulletins, policy letters, and taped lectures of L. Ron Hubbard.

"He knows that RON has 'wrapped up' the subjects of philosophy, education, organizational administration, logic, ethics, and spiritual development; it's all been figured out. Thus there is no need to look any further.

"People who continue to experiment and originate in these areas, after knowing about Scientology, are called squirrels. A 'good Scientologist' believes that squirrels are evil beings [suppressive persons] and does everything he can to stop them.*

"He knows that any doubts he may have about the rightness of Ron or his Church are caused by his own scandalous mis-deeds of this or an earlier lifetime. He learns to police his thoughts, which are always accessible to the Church authorities via the E-meter.

"A 'good Scientologist' does not question Church authority, for to be a citizen of the 'World of the Totally Free' is to obey.

"And even though he is completely subservient to the organization, he regards himself as the elite of Mankind, viewing non-Scientologists as inferior beings: 'raw meat,' 'wogs' and 'homo sap.'

"How does one become a 'good Scientologist' or, as some prefer to call it, a RONDROID?

"Usually it starts out innocently enough.

"The overriding message of the early Scientology writings and lectures is that Scientology's mission is to bring about increased awareness and ability. 'All I am trying to get you to do is look,' said Hubbard. 'The solution to any unwanted condition is to view it thoroughly.'

"The message is simple: Truth frees.

" 'Scientology is knowledge,' he said. 'That's all Scientology is. The word SCIENTOLOGY means KNOWLEDGE. That's all it means. SCIO means KNOWING IN THE FULLEST SENSE OF THE WORD . . . But this is the same word as DHARMA, which means KNOWLEDGE, TAO, which means THE WAY TO KNOWLEDGE BUDDHISM, which means THE WAY TO KNOWLEDGE.'

"In his writings he stresses that communication is the key to knowledge and, thus, is the essence of Scientology: 'When in doubt com-

---

*A common sight in Scientology organizations are posters that exclaim "Stamp out Squirrels" and "Wanted Squirrels Dead or Alive!"

municate; more communication not less is the answer'; and, 'Communication, and the simplicity of communication alone will take man from the bottom to the top. . .'

"To someone newly involved in Scientology this may seem a very enlightened message indeed. If he then reads a few of the 'basic books,' he will, among other things, come across some innovative rewordings of certain Eastern and various Western and Middle Eastern magical and mystical doctrines and practices, and rewordings of the writings of the founder of General Semantics, Count Alfred Korzybski.*

"If he reads *Dianetics* he may be impressed by a reworking of abreaction therapy** and—again—General Semantics.

"*(Whatever Hubbard's character flaws, however unbecoming his actual motives were, and regardless of the monstrosity his Church has become, he did act as a clearing house and relay point for beneficial information originated by others—which of course he claimed to have originated himself. But also he did, himself, originate or develop positive material in the fields of psychotherapy, parapsychology, and 'human potential'; material that needs to be sorted out from his negatives, falsehoods, tricks, science fiction, and hyperbole.)*

"Being unfamiliar with Korzybski's work, and in most cases knowing little of Eastern disciplines or the Western and Middle Eastern mystical and magical tradition, a new student of Scientology may begin to view with awe the man who is proclaimed the sole SOURCE of ALL this fascinating material.

AUDITING

"If you've ever sat down with someone and let him tell you his problems—get it off his chest—to a point where he felt better and, perhaps, even realized something about the situation which resulted in improved ability or willingess to deal with it, then you've been an 'auditor.'

"Auditing basically means 'to listen.' It can also involve assisting an-

---

*Probably better known than Korzybski is former California Senator S.I. Hayakawa, who initially gained public attention while a Dean at San Francisco State during the student uprisings during the sixties. Hayakawa, a student of Korzybski, has written a number of books on the subject. General semantics and Korzybski's brief biography are covered later in Part II, Chapters 2 and 9.

**Abreaction is essentially the process of bringing to the surface, or becoming conscious of, that which had been buried or "unconscious." See Chapter 2, Part II.

other to look at the external environment of the world at large, and the internal environment of his thoughts and feelings, so as to improve his communication with these things, in the direction of greater mastery and freedom.

"According to Scientology theory there are in the mind a great many outdated 'answers.' A person goes through life largely unaware of these old 'answers' while, unconsciously, being the effect of them. These 'answers' or 'solutions' might be described as 'old programming' operating not unlike hypnotic commands, imposing upon the individual undesired conditions, including pressures, fears, obsessions, and psychosomatic ills.

"In most Scientology auditing one is asked a question and invited to look for these outmoded, undesirable 'answers.' The idea being to bring to the surface and analytically examine already existing 'answers,' consisting of fixed, and uninspected, decisions, agreements, or computations.

"This is done, usually, until there is a new realization regarding the particular area being addressed at that time.

"In auditing an individual may find himself recalling incidents from early childhood long forgotten, putting past upsets into a new perspective and laughing about them, feeling brighter and lighter and more himself. In short, he may be very impressed with his newly discovered space-age religion.

"While this is happening he will be receiving approval, validation, and acceptance by the membership.

"Inevitably he'll read about Scientology's aim of 'a world without crime, insanity, or war . . . where Man is free to rise to greater heights.' He'll be told that Scientology makes available, for the first time, unimaginable spiritual power, and that the Church is the only route to immortality. It is explained to him that he is on 'The Bridge to Total Freedom.'

"He will also come to understand that without Scientology a being is doomed to what amounts to eternal damnation.

"He will, somewhere in the course of these events, make a LEAP OF FAITH: 'If what I experienced (in auditing or by reading books) was good then it all must be good . . . 'THIS MUST BE THE BRIDGE TO TOTAL FREEDOM!' (Of course there are those whose conversion is based mainly on the fear of, the threat of, Scientology's Hell.)

"Once the 'leap of faith' is made the person goes from being interested in Scientology to being IN Scientology."

A quote from *Language in Thought and Action*, by S.I. Hayakawa, describes part of this phenomenon well:

VERBAL HYPNOTISM

First, it should be pointed out again that fine sounding speeches, long words, and the general AIR of saying something important are affective in result, regardless of what is being said. Often when we are hearing or reading impressively worded sermons, speeches, political addresses, essays, or "fine writing," we stop being critical altogether, and simply allow ourselves to feel as excited, sad, joyous, or angry as the author wishes us to feel. Like snakes under the influence of a snake charmer's flute, we are swayed by the musical phrases of the verbal hypnotist. If the author is a man to be trusted, there is no reason why we should not enjoy ourselves in this way now and then. But to listen or read like this all the time is a debilitating habit.

Brian Ambry continues:

SCIENTOLOGY HAS MUCH TO HIDE—EVEN FROM ITS OWN MEMBERSHIP

"What Hubbard may have sometimes lacked in eloquence, he made up in sheer bulk; and by creating an authoritarian organization in which NOT being charmed and inspired by his words is a sign of mental illness.

"In Scientology, Hubbard's writings are everywhere. And it might be expected that Scientologists would have access to all of Hubbard's Scientology writings. But this is not so.

"The indeterminate number of 'not yet released' secret 'upper levels' of Scientology's 'grade chart,' are not available for inspection by even the most 'highly trained and audited' Scientologists. They remain a mystery until some nebulous time in the future when, 'enough people are ready for them.'

"The grotesque 'rehabilitation tech' is kept discreetly behind the scenes. 'Paying public' and **newly** recruited 'staff' see little or nothing of it.

"The vast majority of the membership have no knowledge of the existence of numerous confidential 'policy issues' and 'directives,' involving such areas as propaganda, finance, 'public relations,' and tactics for 'handling enemies.'*

*A Scientologist who dares suggest there may be a **Hidden Data Line** will likely find himself in serious "ethics" trouble. Hubbard made **very** definite in his non-hidden writings that there are **NO** Hidden Data. He also outlined penalties for rank-and-file members who might dare to think otherwise.

"Even though members are taught that 'anti-Scientologists should have no rights of any kind,' organization-sanctioned applications of the **Fair Game Doctrine** are kept undercover. These are Programs and 'Operations' (or 'OPs') designed to lie about, harass, reduce to apathy, drive insane, or, 'trick, sue, lie to, or destroy,' anyone perceived as enemy.

"Documents revealed in Federal Court in 1981, at the trial of Hubbard's wife Mary Sue, revealed extensive applications of **Fair Game**. (L. Ron Hubbard, named as an **unindicted co-conspirator was in hiding** at the time.)

"One of the most repulsive aspects of the application of the **Fair Game Policy** is the use of information 'culled' from supposedly private consultations or 'religious confessionals,' ie., auditing sessions.

"Individuals becoming involved in Scientology are **not** informed that the contents of their 'confidential counseling sessions' are subject to inspection by Scientology's version of the KGB. And that these 'confidential sessions' **may not** necessarily remain 'confidential.'

****

"As usual, Scientology is very busy in many courtrooms applying Hubbard's **Legal Harassment Policy.***

"It relays only 'good news' on the legal front to its members, and this is usually sketchy 'candy coated' propaganda designed to boost morale.

****

"And Scientology has worked diligently to conceal Hubbard's school and military records, and various revealing writings and correspondence. These have surfaced since the early 1980s, and contradict the official 'beautified' image of Hubbard.

"So while Scientologists are surrounded by Hubbard's words, they by no means have access to all of them. Scientology is **not** an 'open book.'

"The flow of information is **very** tightly controlled.

****

"Hubbard's **secret** writings affect the lives of his followers to varying degrees. However, there are some things from which no one is spared.

*The Policy of using frivolous litigation simply for purposes of harassment.

"THE HIDDEN BRIDGE"

"Even pampered celebrities and wealthy "paying public," while being spared the crude methods designed to degrade and dominate—such as the Rehabilitation Project Force—are yet subject to the more subtle 'Hidden Bridge.'

"Auditing, when utilizing the fundamental process of abreaction, can remove stale 'programming.' This is undesirable unconscious programming. The idea, it would seem, is to free the person to do his own programming, to be the boss of his own mind.

"What isn't realized is that, while the old programs are being deleted, a new Rondroid Program is being inserted. This is a gradual affair. One agrees, then agrees to a little bit more, then a little more, and so on.

"(Fortunately this 'program' doesn't permanently 'take' on everyone, and that is one reason why there are former Scientologists. But it often requires many years to realize what is going on, and so snap out of it. Of course, many never do snap out of it.)

"For example:

"Joe realizes through auditing that he has been in his father's 'valence' (identity) all these years. Now he is free of it and can be himself. What a relief! He had unconsciously adopted his father's mannerisms, habits, prejudices, and general outlook on life. And since his dad happened to be an anti-semetic hypochondriac who never knew what to do with his hands and was certain that all women were no good, it's hard to argue that freeing himself of these traits is somehow bad.

"What Joe doesn't realize is that the Church of Scientology has a new 'valence,' a new identity, new habits, prejudices, and outlook waiting for him. And they are those which, for all practical purposes, will be adopted by him just as unwittingly as were his father's characteristics.

"So he gradually loses his old enforcements and inhibitions, only to have them gradually replaced by a collection of official Church of Scientology enforcements and inhibitions.

"He was told, initially, that he could become the master of his own universe; but as it ends up, he finds himself swallowed up by the universe of the Church of Scientology. Typically, and this is the great tragedy, by the time the process is complete, he doesn't know the difference.

"This is the other Bridge, the Hidden Bridge, the hypnotic Bridge.

The one that sneaks up on you bit by bit. It is the Bridge leading to Total Agreement and Total Compliance." Ambry concludes.

SOULS TURNED INSIDE OUT

While auditing is presented as the *only road to total freedom* for the individual, having "withholds" from an auditor or Church officials is presented as the *primary barrier on that road.*

Withholds are, broadly, anything one is not willing to tell someone else. The practice of withholding during auditing is seen as anti-communication and thus a barrier to "case gain."

Confiding one's withholds to a close friend or other trusted individual, such as a counselor, rabbi, minister, priest, or even the local bartender, is a time-honored tradition in society at large.

There's a flip side to this coin, however:

The disclosure of withholds under duress, to further the aims of unscrupulous individuals, can be very damaging indeed.

****

In his book *Thought Reform and The Psychology of Totalism* Dr. Robert J. Lifton describes how the Communist Chinese used certain psychological tactics to establish their control over populations and prisoners.

Three key methods were described, a: "Milieu Control" (which are environmental mechanisms for control similar to those so graphically described in the "Brainwashing Manual," Chapter 9), b: "Mandatory Confession" (dealt with in this chapter) and, c: "Loaded Language" (which was Hubbard's specialty—covered in the addendum under the "Dark Side of Scientology-Speak.")

Withholds extracted under physical torture is an extreme example of damaging "confessional" techniques.

A less dramatic example of this is confessions elicited under threat of physical pain or other harm, i.e., coercion or blackmail. The threat can be direct or very subtle.

Hubbard preferred the subtle kind of coercion, but would get openly rough at times. One example of the subtle kind: he wrote that a person who has withholds cannot achieve the state of clear. A Scientologist hearing this—with "clear" being the prerequisite to the god-like state of Operating Thetan—realizes he must tell all, whether it's anybody's business or not.

Beginning in the early sixties Hubbard put great emphasis on "pulling withholds" (getting a person to tell all).

Getting off one's withholds became an obsession among Scientologists. "He/she's got overts and withholds," is still the most common accusation heard.

While actual auditing relies for its benefits on the human communication skills and the caring of individual auditors, Hubbard was not averse to advising coercion if things got sticky.

In a 1965 bulletin, Hubbard says of the "unchanging preclear":

> We've cracked them for years and years now but not by being patty-cake or "slap my wrist."
> Takes an AUDITOR, not a lady finger.
> Mister, you've been wasting my time for three sessions. You have withholds. Give! . . . Mister, you refuse once more to answer my question and you're in for it. I've checked this meter . . . you've got withholds. Give! . . . Mister, that's it. I am asking . . . for a Comm Ev on you . . .

A "Comm Ev" (Committee of Evidence) is a Scientology "Court" which was originally presented as a fact-finding body in the tradition of British and American jurisprudence. In fact it became perverted into being mostly a rubber stamp for arbitrary executive decisions to kick staff off their posts or to declare Scientologists "Suppressive" and expel them. These committees are greatly feared.

Hubbard goes on to say:
> If skill couldn't do it, demand may. If demand couldn't do it, a Comm Ev sure will.

(An extreme in the area of forced confession is the "gang bang security check," where as many as five angry and accusative individuals interrogate someone who is attached to an E-meter.)

Hubbard knew exactly what he was doing by enforcing confessions.

He firmly believed that confession which is not absolutely volitional is damaging to an individual; that when a person's ability to hold back communication, selectivity at his own choice, is impaired, his IQ is lowered.

He understood that, when a person is coerced into confession, his ability to maintain his own viewpoint is weakened. Consequently he gradiently loses his sense of individual identity.

Yet, while being fully aware of this, he created an organization dedicated to enforcing full disclosure of all withholds; withholds to which he and his closest intelligence agents had full access.

(Kima Douglass, Hubbard's closest assistant for five years during the seventies, told of how Hubbard would often angrily order pre-clear folders of those he suspected were against him to be culled for overts and withholds, to be used against them.)

The fact that Hubbard was aware that coercion to "get withholds off" is damaging to people is revealed in a bulletin, dated 15 January, 1958. Here he asserts that the selective "ability to withhold" is a positive ability.

He wrote:

> Now the first question the minister would ask would be, "Think of something you could withhold from _____ (person)." *Now one of the discoveries that led to that question is that divulgence and confession had nothing to do with raising anybody's IQ or improving his case.* [Emphasis added] It wasn't the fact that he confessed it or divulged it but the fact that he erased it [that gave the benefit].

"Erasure" is a word used by Hubbard to denote the complete eradication of the negative influences (or "charge"*) of some traumatic event. This is achieved by viewing that event exactly and by having the person re-live it over and over in his mind, until he sees the event "as-is" and recognizes how and why the event had badly influenced his thinking and behavior.

So what he is saying here in 1958 is that it is the fact that the person confronts for himself exactly what happened that is of benefit to him, *not* the fact that he confesses.

He goes on to say,

> It is the ability to withhold communication which advances IQ and makes a person feel better, *not* the ability to divulge it. We've been told all our lives that all we had to do was go to somebody and confess. If we were to confess to our mothers and fathers that we did those dirty, nasty little things we would feel much better. It isn't true. You probably only felt better to the end of getting your pants spanked. This is an enforced communication. . . . It interrupted your self-determinism on the subject of your communication.

He clearly expresses the idea that one should be able to withhold communications and actions responsibly, at one's own choosing. On the other hand, *at one's own choosing*, one should also be free to communicate freely the full truth of something.

*The harmful energy or force accumulated in the reactive (subconscious) mind.

This advice echoes his earlier dictum, "Do not give or receive communication unless you yourself desire it."

Yet only two years after saying all this, he went on a campaign of "security checking" everyone in sight. It became a crime of some magnitude to not divulge all one's withholds to an auditor. Very much enforced communication.

Security checking involved using the E-meter as a police tool to check whether staff, students or pre-clears were "security risks." Such questions were asked as: "Have you ever accepted money for sex? Have you ever been unfaithful to your spouse? Have you ever stolen anything? Have you ever had anything to do with pornography? Have you ever been a drug addict? Have you ever been involved in an abortion? Have you ever had intercourse under the influence of drugs? Have you ever done anything you are afraid the police may find out? Have you ever done anything your mother would be ashamed to find out?" and many more such questions.

Oh, yes, he knew what he was doing. The purpose was to intimidate people, and discourage any critical examination of himself, his writings and organization.

Extensive micro-fiche files of withholds (in this case, past disreputable deeds) of Scientologists all over the world were kept at Saint Hill Manor in England.

It is probably true, as Hubbard said, that when a person feels he cannot withhold from a certain person, his IQ lowers with regard to that person. That, perhaps, explains why so many of his followers seem so unbelievably dense on the subjects of Scientology and L. Ron Hubbard.

THOUGHT CONTROL

A Scientologist is heavily indoctrinated into the idea that if he finds himself being critical of Hubbard or the Church or its executives, then the very fact of his being critical is proof positive of the fact that he himself is harboring undisclosed dirty deeds.

This is a highly effective tool to "introvert them like a bullet," as Hubbard phrased it. In other words, a person notices, for instance, something actually wrong with Hubbard and he immediately has his attention boomeranged right back at himself. So instead of pursuing his examination of Hubbard he finds himself introverting into himself, and often paying (400 dollars an hour or more) to have his withholds pulled!

Meanwhile Hubbard's errors and crimes are safe and sound, his image of infallibility intact.

THOUGHT CRIME

In George Orwell's *1984*, Big Brother watched people's facial features by means of closed circuit TV cameras and, if anyone didn't seem genuinely pleased with the propaganda announcements being made, actions were taken to brainwash them. The lack of appropriate expressions betrayed "thought crime."

In Scientology the probe for dissension goes deeper: Hubbard and his agents are able to probe the actual thoughts of their followers—via the E-meter—during confessionals. "Souls turned inside out," he told Ron Jr. in Philadelphia in 1952. He meant it.

It is noteworthy that when somebody can look into your thoughts, giving you no option for privacy of consideration and opinion, some devastating things occur. This is especially so if you are (or consider that you are) dependent upon the approval of that somebody or group for your continued well-being and very survival as a spiritual being.

It is one of the inalienable rights that one be free to think whatever one wishes. It is also one's right to choose for oneself what is true for oneself. Also, while there are exceptions (the IRS for instance, has its own ideas on this), it is generally left up to the individual in a free society to select what he or she decides to communicate to others.

When one loses these rights, the only remaining defense becomes to actually *change* one's thoughts to conform with the acceptable "think" of the individual or group which has violated the sovereign territory of one's mind. *One gets into the habit of thinking "right" thoughts and self censoring "wrong" thoughts.*

When some group, with the power to harm an individual, has full access to his thoughts, overriding his power of choice, that individual no longer has the option of rejecting any of the actions, mores, or considerations of the group.

In Scientology one can no longer have a critical thought about Hubbard. For example: "Have you had a critical thought about L. Ron Hubbard?" is a question commonly used in security checking.

If a Scientologist persists in having any critical thoughts about Hubbard, he will be penalized. As a consequence he learns to think only good thoughts about Hubbard and his Church; to never think critical thoughts about him or his Church and to censor out or "write up" (report to Church policing authorities) any criticisms he hears.

This inability to select the thoughts one chooses without fear of re-taliation causes a person to become stupid on a given subject, there no longer being any option of safe objective analysis, based on a de-tached personal appraisal of the facts involved.

This situation is similar to that existing in other dictatorships which have large spy systems and use torture and duress to get people to confess their own and other's "crimes." In these countries it is also imposed on people that they should squeal, even on their family and friends. And, like other dictatorships, the "custom" of writing re-ports, even on one's own spouse or parents, has long been enshrined in Scientology policy.

In contrast, it is one of the fundamentals of the legal systems of civ-ilized societies that thoughts, by themselves, cannot be held against an individual. A person is sovereign in his own mind. One has the right to think freely and no civilized court has jurisdiction to interfere with that right.

It is only when thoughts are translated into actions (or when they are communicated in the form of witnessed or documented plans to commit criminal actions, as in conspiracy), that legal penalties are re-sorted to.

Investigation into alleged crimes must be conducted within a cer-tain set of guidelines according to the Bill of Rights in the U.S., which proscribes "unreasonable searches and seizures." In other words, the rights of the individual are carefully balanced against the rights of so-ciety for protection against any individual's crimes against it. Evi-dence from lie detectors is inadmissible in court in most cases, and police have to gather their evidence within a severe set of guidelines.

These principles are blatantly violated by the Scientology "confes-sional," as practiced by Hubbard's Church.

In the Church's confessional an individual's mind is opened up with the aid of the E-meter and with false representations that his revela-tions will be kept strictly confidential. (To be fair, the auditors usually believe that it is confidential and are usually oblivious to the fact that their written notes may be perused by the intelligence arm of the Church.)

****

The kind of thought control described in this chapter is greatly aided by the fact that the E-meter does appear to expose to the practitioner those things which the person holding the cans (electrodes) finds difficulty facing up to. The needle of the device does appear to react when the mind's eye scans near those things. And as this occurs a competent auditor gently prompts "that," "there," "that": coaxing the submerged mental picture or idea into full view in one's mind. The same E-meter needle reaction will continue until the person fully faces up to whatever he is repressing.

It is very impressive to most people, when they first get auditing, that the auditor can apparently discover what they are thinking. They find it sheer magic that they can dredge up considerations that they have had in the distant past, but have long since forgotten.

Most who have experienced auditing will tell you that the meter assisted them in the process of bringing to light, and discarding, old false and fixed ideas which had been affecting their lives negatively.

The meter, they will say, helped them bring these ideas to the surface, thus allowing re-inspection of them, enabling them to realign their thinking in a more optimum fashion. There was, they will claim, an increase in self-confidence and newfound abilities.

The E-meter is a tool, as are the actions of basic auditing. They can be used as tools to help others. This is the positive side.

Or they can be used as bait, to lure another into a trap.

And, violating the essence of what auditing* was proclaimed to be all about, these tools can be used, in an authoritarian environment, as weapons to harm, intimidate, and subjugate.

All this was well known to Hubbard. And he used or abused these things as he saw fit, choosing to use "black" or "white" Scientology entirely at his discretion as to whether or not either aided his objectives.

"Black Scientology," whether used on individual Scientologists or an outside "enemy," is to be kept hidden. "White Scientology" is to be promoted like crazy.

This principle is similar to Hubbard's more openly stated policy about keeping intelligence and PR separated.

"PR is overt," he wrote. "Intelligence is covert.

"Threat and mystery are a lot of the power of intelligence. Publicity blows it."

Hopefully with this book, the "threat and mystery" of black Scientology will be blown.

****

*Auditing is also known as "processing," as one "runs processes," that is, asks questions, applies a procedure.

Shortly after Ron Jr. left the organization in late 1959 "because of his overts and withholds," his father made an appeal to all Scientologists in an official technical bulletin. He urged them all to assist in a new project designed to bring about a "greater group" than has ever before existed.

All Scientologists were to. . . .

"1. Get off your own overts and withholds, and

"2. Urge other people to get off theirs."

He asks that each make "a full list of present lifetime overts and withholds . . . signed and sent to HCOWW [Hubbard Communications Office World Wide]."

He continues reassuringly:

> *That these files exist in my personal possession should make it effectively impossible for anyone to try to use this information.* (Emphasis added)

(Ron Jr. was spilling the beans all over the place and Hubbard, it seems, was obsessed with knowing what others knew about his dark secrets. But that was only a small part of it. . . .)

Some time after Hubbard set up the Guardian Office in the mid-sixties, the practice of keeping extensive dossiers on people, including records of withholds from their pre-clear folders, was expanded.

On December 15, 1969, Mary Sue Hubbard put this practice into official—albeit secret—policy, addressed to "all Deputy Guardians for Intelligence." The "Guardian Order" sanctioning this practice was numbered GO 121669 MSH, and dealt with "Internal Security."

It contained a "Major Target" as follows:

> To use any and all means to detect an infiltration, double agent or disaffected staff member, Scientologist or relatives of Scientologists, and by any and all means to render null any potential harm or harm such have rendered or might render to Scientology and Scientologists.

Under the heading "Vital Targets" it states:

> To establish intelligence files on all such persons found to be infiltrators, double agents, and dissaffected staff members, Scientologists and relatives of Scientologists.

Under the heading "Operating Targets":

To make full use of all files of the organization to affect your major target. These include personnel files, Ethics files, Dead files, central files, training files, *processing files* (emphasis added), and requests for refunds.

To assemble full data by investigation of each person located for possible use in case of attack or for use in preventing any attack and to keep files of such.

There is a note in the text of this order which advises that those following the order "be effective and imaginative in your collection of data and in your actions to nullify any attack or threat of attack."

Mary Sue also notes that the program is a "continuing one regarding which projects will be issued from time to time."

This order was followed, over the years, to the letter.

****

L. Ron Hubbard had some major problems with government and various mental health groups and other private institutions during the late sixties, especially in the U.K.

Apparently his inclination was, at that time, to "pull their withholds," to find out what they knew but weren't telling.

During the latter part of the 1960s he had achieved some success with Guardian's Office intelligence agent infiltration of some of these organizations.

With these wins fresh in his mind, he wrote up his "Snow White" program in 1973, while living secretly in Queens, New York. This program was designed to handle certain U.S. Government Departments and Interpol (perceived at the time as the biggest thorns in his side), once and for all.

The title "Snow White" signified the concept that these agencies would be snow-white clean of all withholds once Scientology intelligence was done pulling them.

13

Snow White
and the Scientology 11:
The "Fair Game Law" Backfires

The first I heard of it, there was a shrill call from a friend who was on staff in Los Angeles. It was July 8, 1977.

A raid by some 134 FBI agents, armed with sledge hammers and crowbars, had been launched early that morning on the Sunset Boulevard "complex" in Los Angeles (formerly Cedars of Lebanon Hospital). Other raids were conducted simultaneously at the Manor (Chateau Elise) nearby, and at the Washington, D.C., organization.

They had carted away thousand of boxes of confidential materials, "including pre-clear folders," I was told.

We were called that night into the Fifield Manor (Chateau Elise) for a special briefing by the PR people, Heber Jentzsch and Vaughn Young. The mood was feverish when we arrived despite Heber Jentzsch's inevitable jokes equating the FBI with the Nazis.

The FBI's search warrant was going to be challenged in court and those seized documents would never be made public. They would see to that.

The press quickly responded to the raids, and were generally sympathetic to the Scientologists.

Columnist James J. Kilpatric blasted the FBI, calling the agents "klutzes": "What troubles me is the sheer crushing power that our Government can bring to bear when it chooses. Even if the Scientologist prevail in the end, they will have been put to stunning legal expenses.

155

Their normal operations will have been disrupted for months. And all for what? Is the FBI's purpose prosecution or persecution?"

I couldn't understand why the FBI would raid a church. This was especially so later, when it was explained to us by Church representatives that all that the Church could in any way be held guilty of would be stealing Xerox paper from certain government offices.

I never doubted the sincerity of Scientology's intentions behind the outpouring of anti-FBI literature, much of which was legitimately critical of abuses within that organization, which subsequently poured out of the Church Guardian's Office.

This was just another example of the abuses by this FBI gestapo organization against a church.

It took me a few years to get a fuller story of the events and personalities that had culminated in this raid, a watershed event in the history of Hubbard's adventures.

It took me even longer to learn that when the news hit, Hubbard was holed up in La Quinta, near Palm Springs, along with Mary Sue Hubbard and the top brass of his secret service elite of the Guardian's Office.

Operation Snow White had backfired.

What did Operation Snow White consist of, and why had it gone so wrong?

Interestingly enough I first learned some of the key facts from reading a book by Omar Garrison, commissioned by the Guardian's Office.

This book glorified the adventures of the "intrepid" G.O. "freedom fighters," despite the fact that it essentially admitted the illegal nature of the acts concerned.

This was after all a Church which had been subjected to extreme government attack and dirty tricks. The book was in fact titled *Playing Dirty*.

Wrote Garrison about operation Snow White:

> It was a super-secret operation that would be unimaginable to most people.
> A government official remarked in awe that it would have done credit to the intelligence service of a major country.

Hubbard's G.O. agents had pulled off an amazingly successful campaign of infiltration of numerous government and private agencies.

Besides accessing and copying voluminous government files about Hubbard and his church, they had also placed disinformation into various files. (Oddly enough, among the files stolen were those on then California governor Edmond Brown Jr., Los Angeles mayor Tom Bradley, singer Frank Sinatra, John Wayne and others.)

It was not till 1980 that I actually read the account of Michael Meisner, a key player in Operation Snow White.

I read a document prepared by the FBI. This was a thick legally worded account of events that had led to the raid. The information had obviously been compiled mainly from the testimony of Michael Meisner.

By that time Mary Sue Hubbard, and other top Guardian Office officials, had stipulated that the information in it was true.

This stipulation was part of a guilty plea, which ended the trial procedure, a procedure which could have embroiled Hubbard in the legal maelstrom. Protecting him was the prime consideration, even if it meant certain jail for the others.

Years later when Hubbard was asked in writing, by a *Rocky Mountain High* reporter, what his part had been in the Snow White Affair, he replied:

> I learned about it like everyone else, after the fact and could only shake my head in dismay. I was never involved in any of the incidents to which you refer and even governments and courts recognize the fact and actually my name has never come up in connection with it beyond the passing mention that I founded the Church.

Quite the contrary. The FBI had in fact labelled Hubbard an "Unindicted Co-conspirator."

****

Project Snow White began to be implemented in early 1974 when Jane Kember, Mary Sue Hubbard's immediate junior, titled "Guardian for Life," issued a written order (Guardian Order 1361) declaring full-scale war on the IRS in the United States.

The overt "weapons" in the war were to be litigation in the courts and a public relations campaign.

The covert "weapons" were to be the penetration of the IRS Intelligence Division, the IRS Special Services Staff, and the Chief Council's Office, by "covert G.O. operatives" (Scientology spies).

The targets of all this spy activity by the Scientologists were, initially, the IRS offices in Washington, D.C., and Los Angeles and also London, England.

MIKE MEISNER'S STORY

Mike Meisner was a 20-year-old student at the University of Illinois at Urbana in November of 1970 when he was introduced to Scientology by a friend.

During the next two months, he took several courses at the Urbana Church of Scientology franchise. In January the following year, he left the University to become a full-time course supervisor at the franchise.

In May he was sent to the Church of Scientology in St. Louis where for the next eight months he was trained to become an auditor. After returning to the franchise and continuing his duties as a supervisor for a time, he assumed the position of Executive Director of the franchise.

In mid-May of 1973 he was recruited for the Guardian's Office and moved to Washington, D.C., with his wife Patricia, who also joined the G.O.

He was taught that the intelligence bureau, which he was now a part of, deals with safeguarding the environment within which Scientology exists, by removing and rendering harmless all those perceived to be enemies of Scientology. (In other words, implementation of the Fair Game Law had been entrusted to this group.)

This was accomplished, he was taught, by infiltration, theft of documents and covert operation.

Wrote Gerry Armstrong:

> B1 [the intelligence Bureau] was created by L. Ron Hubbard who patterned it after the intelligence system developed by Nazi spymaster Reinhart Ghelen.

Following weeks of training in G.O. procedures and policies in D.C., Meisner was sent to Los Angeles for intensive on-the-job training in the "Intelligence" Bureau there.

He was taught that strict adherence to the chain of command within the organization was of paramount importance.

He was taught how to place agents in organizations targeted for infiltration, how to steal documents, and other overt and covert intelligence gathering techniques.

In November of 1973 he returned to D.C. as head of Intelligence, where his duties included obtaining personal information about and "handling" Scientologists who were dissident or disaffected.

In January of 1974, Mike Meisner was promoted by Jane Kember (Guardian World Wide) to head Bureau 1 in Washington, D.C., making him responsible for all intelligence operations in the area.

On November 21, Jane Kember wrote a letter to Henning Heldt headed: "Re Interpol Washington." In it, she informed him that the Guardian's Office had "some documents *illegally obtained*, that indicate Interpol Washington was in touch with Interpol Paris, London. . . ." (Emphasis added by the FBI) She added: "We know that Washington, D.C., has police files on LRH . . . and Interpol Washington has a file on LRH as well."

Hubbard had apparently become convinced that Interpol was being used to disseminate negative materials about him to various countries, resulting in the difficulties the ship and various Scientology Organizations were running into.

Later in the letter Jane Kember directed, "It is important that we get cracking and obtain these files and I leave you to work out how."

In late summer of 1974 Meisner was instructed to recruit a covert operative to infiltrate the IRS in D.C. Gerald Wolfe was selected. He eventually got a job at the IRS as a clerk-typist. He was code named "Silver."

While he was settling into this job, other agents were infiltrating IRS offices in Los Angeles and London.

All documents relating to Hubbard, Scientology, etc., were ordered to be photocopied.

Mike Meisner met with his superior, Don Alvarazo, who showed Mike the bugging devise he had brought with him from L.A.

The same day Mike and another G.O. operative entered the main IRS building seeking to find out where a meeting was to be held a few days later. They subsequently placed the bugging device in a wall socket of the targeted room.

Don Alvarazo and two other agents waited in a car nearby and overheard and taped the "big pow wow about what to do about us."

Duke Snider (Meisner's superior) wrote a letter shortly afterwards saying, "We must be careful with this transcript [of the meeting] as even in the distant future in the hands of the enemy the repercussions would be great. There are new laws on this federally, and a strong post-Watergate judicial climate."

Meanwhile Gerry Wolfe, as a plant in the IRS, was not an instant success. He let his superiors know that he was unable to obtain the documents he had been ordered to find and copy.

So Mike Meisner and his co-agent, Mitchell Herman, entered Gerry's workplace to demonstrate that it was possible to get the documents. They went to the seventh floor of the building and took a Scientology file from the filing cabinet there. It was taken from the building, photocopied and returned the next day without detection.

Following that "achievement" there were many others.

By December 4, 1974, Wolfe had sent off two shipments of documents to G.O. headquarters in England, each about "ten inches thick."

Gerry Wolfe continued searching the files of various offices on his own while Mike Meisner oversaw the operation and organized the Xeroxed materials mailing to his superiors.

During the first five months of 1975 alone, the documents located by Gerry Wolfe and photocopied totalled some ten feet in height.

After it was discovered that many of the files they were looking for were in the offices of Assistant U.S. Attorney Nathan Dodell, plans were made to gain entry there also.

It was deemed necessary that Meisner also obtain an IRS I.D. card such as the one Wolfe had obtained as part of his job.

In order to obtain one, Meisner and Wolfe entered the main IRS building after hours, using Wolfe's legitimate I.D. Then, using one of the tools of the burglary trade, they forced open the door to the room where the I.D. equipment was located. Using a flashlight, Wolfe picked up four blank I.D. cards (two each) and typed in fictitious names. They then took turns photographing each other's images onto the cards. Badge numbers were taken from a log they found in the room near the equipment.

Subsequently, five other Scientologists followed their example, making similar counterfeit cards.

On May 25, 1975, Mary Sue wrote a letter to Jane Kember. It states:

> Our overall strategy with the IRS shall be as follows: 1. To *use any method at our disposal* to win the battle and gain our non-profit status. . . . (Emphasis added)

Hundreds of Scientology agents were placed in a variety of government and private organizations during this period.

****

It was well known to the Scientologist G.O. hierarchy that what they were doing constituted breaking and entering and was therefore a felony. It was also known that to use the government equipment and paper constituted theft, and was a felony. A letter from a legal researcher to top executives in the G.O., which was later found during the FBI raid, spelled out the law on these matters. Meisner and Wolfe regularly briefed their seniors on their activities.

AN ORDER TO PROTECT HUBBARD AT ALL COSTS LEADS TO COMPLICATIONS

Events leading up to these complications were as follows:

On April 4, 1976, a Scientology case, in which the Church was suing for documents regarding the Church withheld from them by the government, was in progress. An apparently insignificant discussion occurred between the judge and the government attorney.

This exchange was destined to create major consequences. . . .

The judge asked Assistant U.S. Attorney Nathan Dodell if *he had considered taking Hubbard's deposition* (i.e., had he demanded Hubbard be present to testify)?

"It is an interesting thought Judge Hart. . . ." responded Dodell.

"Why don't you take his deposition?" asked Judge Hart.

"I will certainly relay that suggestion . . ." responded Dodell.

Alarm bells were set off by this exchange. Hubbard's safety was paramount, and he would have been notified immediately of the danger. Hubbard would then have immediately alerted his G.O. executives to handle "terminatedly" any threat to him!

(This panic reaction was, I believe, most likely what eventually led to the FBI's uncovering of Operation "Snow White.")

In response to this brief colloquy in court, a project was precipitated by G.O. executives: a *complete investigation was to be done regarding Judge Hart, and Dodell's office was to be penetrated to monitor his intentions regarding deposing Hubbard.*

So Mike and Gerry entered the U.S. Courthouse in Washington, D.C., at around four P.M. and went to the third floor to locate

Dodell's office. It was located in a highly secured area. Finding the door locked they unsuccessfully tried to break in.

A few days later Gerry phoned Mike from Dodell's office. "Dodell's secretary left her keys on her desk!" he enthused. He had used them to get into Dodell's office.

They met and then located a locksmith where they got duplicates of some of the keys.

At about seven P.M. on May 21, Mike and Gerry returned to the Courthouse.

They entered in the usual manner with Mike using his "John M. Forster" I.D. "We're going to the library section to do legal research," they told the security guard.

Apparently approval was given and they were issued an elevator key and proceeded to the third floor where they signed the library log, using the fake names on their I.D. cards.

At the first opportunity they left the library and went to Dodell's office where they gained entry using one of their keys. They copied all the documents they found.

A week later, Mike and Gerry again went to the Courthouse and went through the same procedure to gain entry.

This time, however, they entered the library through the back door without signing in.

They used their duplicated key and this time collected more documents relating to Scientology and also some relating to the FDA and D.C. police Department, and photocopied them nearby the office on government equipment.

As they were returning through the library to Dodell's office with originals, they were stopped by the librarian.

"Did you sign in?" he enquired.

When they said "No," he had them do so.

"You are not to return to this library unless you have specific authorization from the regular librarian," they were told.

Then they returned the originals to Dodell's office and left the building.

A few days later, the night librarian Charles Johnson and a Security Guard got around to notifying the United States Attorney's office that two individuals who had in their possession IRS I.D. cards had been seen using the photocopying machines in the U.S. Attorney's office on the previous Friday evening.

Both Johnson and the guard were instructed to immediately contact the FBI if the two returned to the Courthouse.

Meanwhile another G.O. project was begun called "Project: Target Dodell." Its purpose was stated to be to "render Dodell harmless." Hubbard wanted any threat to him stopped.

So, in line with this project, Mike Meisner was directed to return to Dodell's office to steal personal files in order to *devise and formulate a covert operation to remove him as Assistant United States Attorney for the District of Columbia.*

So, in furtherance of that operation, Mike and Gerry again went to the Courthouse on June 11, 1976.

Entering at about seven P.M., Meisner signed in and they proceeded to the library and showed the night librarian the written permission which they had earlier received from the head librarian.

When they went to Dodell's office there were cleaning ladies doing their chores there, so they returned to the library and acted like researchers while they waited for the cleaning crew to vacate.

Meanwhile the night librarian contacted the FBI.

Two FBI agents arrived while the two were still waiting in the library. They demanded to see their I.D. cards.

Mike presented his card and told them that he had since resigned from the IRS.

While one FBI agent continued to question the two, the other went off to contact a U.S. Attorney.

"We're here to do legal research," Meisner told Agent Hansen. "We used the photocopying equipment to photocopy legal books and cases."

He gave her, as his home address, an address a few doors away from his actual residence.

After fifteen minutes of questioning Mike Meisner asked, "Are we under arrest?"

No, they were not under arrest, was the response.

"Ok, let's go!" he said to Gerry.

Agent Hodges saw them leaving, and called to them.

"Agent Hansen told us we could go," Mike replied.

After leaving the Courthouse they walked a couple of blocks to make sure that they were not being followed, then caught a cab to Martin's Tavern Restaurant. From a nearby public phone they called their superior in L.A. and told him the details of their misadventure.

After another couple of calls, Mike was told to leave the next morning on a flight to Los Angeles.

THE COVER-UP

On the plane Mike wrote up a detailed report of the previous day's Courthouse incident.

When he arrived in Los Angeles, his report was turned over to Henning Heldt (Jane's junior and head of the G.O. in the U.S.), and a full description of all the events was, shortly thereafter, sent to Mary Sue Hubbard.

The crisis was analyzed and a tentative plan was adopted to contain or stop the investigation. A shore story was devised for Gerry Wolfe should he be arrested. Another story was worked out for Mike. One which would support Gerry's.

The highest priority, recognized by all parties, was to prevent the FBI from making the connection between the two and the Church of Scientology.

It was argued that if Wolfe allowed himself to be arrested, and gave the proper cover story, then the investigation could, be contained. Then following Wolfe's plea of guilty, Meisner would surrender, give the same story as Wolfe and also enter a guilty plea. This plan had a good chance, he proposed, of terminating all FBI investigation with little or no connection to Scientology being made.

Heldt approved this plan.

A cover story was devised: the whole thing was "a prank that had gone sour."

****

Gerry Wolfe, who by now had also arrived in Los Angeles, was drilled on the story and assigned an attorney to aid him through his arrest.

On June 30, 1976 Gerry Wolfe was arrested in the main IRS building by FBI agent Christine Hansen. He was charged with the use and possession of a forged official pass of the United States. He was released on his own recognizance, pending a preliminary hearing.

In a letter dated July 1, Mary Sue wrote:

> Re: Mike and the FSM" [FSM = Field Staff Member: Gerry Wolfe]
> From an investigative point of view it was really too easy for the op-

position. All they had to do was to trace back the common entry [sic] points of the log back for both Mike and the FSM [Wolfe] until they arrived at the point where the FSM used his correct I.D. card.

She urged that she be kept informed as to what happened to Wolfe.

In response to that request, she received two letters. In one she was told that the prosecutor had been informed that Gerry's I.D. was all a lark gone sour, and that Wolfe had been instructed not to go anywhere near the Church of Scientology; the writer felt it was still possible that there would be a minimal punishment for Wolfe and no connection made to the Church.

When the case came up for preliminary hearing, a U.S. Magistrate found that probable cause existed and ordered the case "bound over the action to the Grand Jury." A few days later a warrant for the arrest of Michael Meisner was issued for use of a forged official pass.

Mary Sue responded to the discovery that the FBI was onto Meisner:

> Wonder how they got onto him?
> On getting him abroad, unless you have good ID for him different from his own, it might be dangerous. He would better be "lost" in some large city where it would be difficlut [sic] to find him.
> What a shame.

Meisner was moved to a series of different motels.

Meanwhile there was a lot of communication going back and forth to and from Mary Sue regarding how best to proceed.

In late September, FBI Agent Hansen requested the Church of Scientology to provide her with examples of Meisner's handwriting. Meisner was told that it had been decided that false examples would be given.

THE FRUSTRATIONS OF MICHAEL MEISNER

A few weeks later Meisner expressed concern for his wife and parents and complained that he was being kept almost totally uninformed of G.O. actions in the ongoing cover-up.

He was assured that he would be kept informed in the future and that Mary Sue Hubbard was concerned about the situation; anything he wanted to express to her would be sent directly to her.

He wrote a letter to Mary Sue in which he said:

In my opinion, no matter what story we use, the longer we wait to implement it, the less believable it will be and the more . . . the government will be inclined to believe that the Church is behind it.

Meisner was audited three times a week after this, but despite this, towards mid-March, he began to become upset at the lengthy delays. By late March he wrote Henning Heldt demanding that he take a more active role because the delays were "becoming intolerable."

By April 27 (almost six months after he first hid out), Mike was again upset about the slowness of events and Weigand was notified that Meisner now intended to "leave for either Canada or D.C. Saturday."

The next day Mike's auditor Jim Fiducia and two G.O. executives visited him to persuade him against leaving for Canada or D.C. on his own. Mike, however, was adamant that he would leave unless the Wolfe situation was handled promptly.

"HERB" GETS ROUGHED UP

Heldt informed Mary Sue of the situation with "Herb" (Meisner) and that he was ordering the Information Bureau to "arrange to restrain Herb and prevent him from leaving, and to guard him so that he does not do so."

When Meisner was told that from that day on he would be placed under guard, he hotly responded that there was no way he would accept any guards. He also complained bitterly that the whole situation had been mishandled by the G.O. and that this fact had resulted in his becoming a fugitive.

The guards were placed there anyway.

He was next visited by a top G.O. executive who warned:

You will no longer be permitted to make demands and threats on the Church. You are to become a decent, co-operative, contributing part of the venture and nothing else will be tolerated!

He and the guard searched Meisner's apartment and removed any evidence that might have connected Meisner to the Church. The meeting concluded, according to a report, "with the guards in charge."

At six P.M. on May 1, three Info Bureau Agents and two bodyguards visited Meisner and told him he was to be moved to another apartment. He refused, and threatened to cause a commotion if forced to do so.

The two guards handcuffed him behind his back, gagged him and dragged him out of the building.

Outside they forced him onto the back floor of a waiting car. During the trip in the car one of the guards used his feet to hold him down.

At the new apartment, still in Los Angeles, three guards remained to secure him. He was prevented from leaving for the next three weeks. During this time he determined that it was best to co-operate with his captors, and he corresponded with Heldt to ask his help in having the guards removed. He also accepted auditing.

On May 13, Wolfe entered a plea of guilty to a one-count indictment charging him with the wrongful use of a Government seal.

Mike was informed of this and by the third week of May, partly due to his co-operation, his watch was relaxed and his guards began to take him out of the apartment, for short periods.

It was at that time that he was shown a written G.O. program: It had been decided that Meisner could not surrender to the FBI until the IRS had granted the Church of Scientology of California its request for tax-exempt status. This contradicted previous assurances made to him, and so alienated him further from the Church. He didn't complain, however.

By the end of May he was guarded by just one person.

One day when he was out with his guard he escaped by jumping into a taxi. He went to the bus station and caught a bus to Las Vegas. He knew of a motel there that even he could afford. He needed time to think about his predicament. He was still committed to Scientology and didn't want to leave the organization precipitately.

After a night in Las Vegas, he called Los Angeles and asked to speak to Heldt. Heldt pleaded with him to return to L.A. and the G.O.

He initially refused but agreed to meet with Info Agent Douglas the next day in Las Vegas. He was eventually persuaded to return to L.A. to speak with Henning Heldt, and they met at Canter's Restaurant. Heldt assured him that both L. Ron Hubbard and Mary Sue were working on his case and would do everything to help him.

"You will have to continue to be under guard" he was told. But he should consider the guards his friends not his enemies. He agreed to remain in the G.O.; but later described the situation as an "armed truce."

THE SENTENCING AND PERJURY OF "SILVER"

Almost exactly a year to the day after their fateful confrontation with the FBI in the Courthouse library, on June 10, Wolfe ("Silver") was sentenced to a term of probation and was required to perform one hundred hours of community service.

This was a major victory for the Scientologists.

The relief was to be brief, however: Immediately following his sentencing, Wolfe was served with a subpoena to appear that same afternoon before the U.S. Grand Jury which had been investigating the entries into the U.S. Courthouse.

It was one P.M. and the Grand Jury was attempting to identify the person or persons who had caused and conspired to perpetrate the violations. They wanted the real reasons why Mike and Gerry had penetrated the security system on June 11, 1976.

A Grand Jury member asked the question:

> When did you first come to know that the D.C. Bar Association had a library on the third floor of this building?
> A: I don't remember the exact date.
> Q: Why did you want to come to the library?
> A: To study.
> Q: To study what?
> A: To learn to do legal research.
> A: Why did you want to learn to do legal research?
> A: Well, I was planning on going back to Minneapolis to complete or further my studies in music and I thought that in addition to clerical skills that I had that if I could learn to do legal research that I could perhaps get a better paying, more interesting job to help pay for my school.
> Q: How did you propose to learn to do legal research in the D.C. Bar library?
> A: Someone was going to teach me.
> Q: Who was that someone?
> A: John Foster.
> A: You only knew him by John Foster?
> A: Right.

There were other questions, and all of Wolfe's perjured answers forwarded the shore story that had been pre-arranged.

****

After his appearance before the Grand Jury, Gerry went straight to the Church of Scientology where he was debriefed by G.O. officials.

Excerptions of that debriefing entitled "Silver Hearing and Grand Jury," went, according to the routing marked at the top left-hand corner of the document, at least as high as Mary Sue Hubbard.

On June 13, Meisner was visited by Heldt who had him read a handwritten letter from Mary Sue. In the letter she warned him that if he escaped again *he would be on his own.*

MIKE ON HIS OWN

The fact is that by this time Mike had decided that if the watch over him were ever relaxed he would immediately leave the Guardian office, surrender to federal authorities, and co-operate in the ongoing investigation.

He was feigning co-operation in the hope that the guards might be removed.

This tactic worked. By the evening, after the agent left with the positive report about Mike's state of mind, he was no longer guarded at night.

The following Monday at six A.M. he took a few clothes and left the apartment, took a couple of different buses to elude any potential tail the G.O. might have placed on him, got off the bus randomly and placed a call to United States Attorney Gary Stark in Washington, D.C., and told him that he was ready to surrender.

He was told to stay where he was and wait for the FBI agents to arrive.

After his surrender, he was sent to Washington, D.C., to meet Stark. He agreed to plead guilty to a conspiracy charge which carried a five-year prison penalty, without any condition except that he co-operate with the Grand Jury investigation. He was placed in the protective custody of the Marshal Service.

Meanwhile Heldt was informed: "Herbert was found missing today." A note had been found from him stating that he would call in a week and that he was not going anywhere he could be located, and that there was no further purpose in discussing his motivations.

It was speculated that he was hiding, probably somewhere in Los Angeles, doing legal research regarding possible defenses in his case. All documents that could connect him with Scientology were removed from his apartment and fingerprints were carefully wiped out.

Mary Sue was alerted.

All libraries in Los Angeles were ordered to be checked to find if Mike was in any of them, and all incriminating documents in the Guardian's Office were placed in the "Red Box."*

The G.O. received a letter on June 29th from "Herb" postmarked San Francisco:

> I know you don't understand what's going on, but I still need time to myself. I'm making enough money to get by on so there's no problems.
> I'll be in touch in a couple of weeks. Herb.

Unknown to them, the letter had been prepared by the FBI, to allay G.O. suspicions while they readied their raids on Washington and Los Angeles G.O. headquarters.

Mary Sue did sense something wrong, however. She wrote to Heldt:

> I frankly wld [would] not waste BurI [intelligence] resources looking for him but wld instead utilize resources to figure out a way to defuse him shld [should] he turn traitor.

On July 4th a warrant was signed by Judge Henry Kennedy. It allowed the FBI to conduct a search of the Church buildings in D.C. Another warrant was issued in Los Angeles.

So at six A.M. on the morning of July 8, 1977, FBI agents arrived at the Scientology G.O. establishment to conduct what was, according to Omar Garrison's book, the largest such raid ever in U.S. history. Another raid was conducted, almost simultaneously, in D.C.

Mike Meisner qualified for the Witness protection program.

---

*"Red Box", is explained in a document (seized during the FBI raid of the Church, precipitated by Meisner's testimony).
This document orders:
   "All the Red Box material from your areas must be centrally located together in a removable container (ideally a briefcase), locked and marked."
   Appended to that document is the "Red Box Data Information Sheet." This sheet answers the question, "What is Red Box Data?":
   "a) Proof that a Scnist [Scientologist] is involved in criminal activities.
   b) Anything illegal that implicates MSH, LRH.
   c) Large amount of non-FOI docs [Non Freedom of Information Documents illegally obtained].
   d) Operations against any government group or persons.
   e) All operations that contain illegal activities.
   f) Evidence of incriminating activities.
   g) Names and details of confidential financial accounts."

****

While they fought it off in the courts for almost five years, the fate of the 11 was sealed. They were headed for jail.

****

The documents unearthed by the FBI raids revealed a mind-boggling array of illegal activities.

Also revealed were instructions (including drills) on the use of "Front Groups"; on how to lie; how to "push buttons," ie., manipulate others; how to harass with effectiveness; and how to successfully infiltrate, and burglarize.

****

This scene, exposed by Michael Meisner, would also have enormous ramifications in Hubbard's life.

His moves to protect himself from becoming embroiled in criminal proceedings were destined to open up a Pandora's box of new problems for him.

14
Freaking Out Paulette:
A Six Year Operation to Drive a
Journalist Insane

Among the materials that the FBI seized from the Church of Scientology was a sheet of paper headed "P.C. Freakout." It detailed a program to have Paulette Cooper, a New York journalist who had written a book entitled *The Scandal of Scientology*, incarcerated in prison or a mental institution.

Her book included an interview with L. Ron Hubbard, Jr., and revealed Hubbard's connection to "Black Magic" and Aleister Crowley. This was the first time these subjects had been broached in a book. Hubbard determined—evidence indicates—to stop the book and to intimidate other writers and publishers.

Paulette Cooper had, prior to the raid, been facing charges by the FBI that she was guilty of felonies. She had been framed by Hubbard's Guardian's Office. The documents, seized by the FBI, finally proved this conclusively.

In regard to the government infiltrations of the previous chapter, Hubbard's agents might be seen by some to have been a Scientology David taking a sling shot to a government Goliath; but in this project they could be seen as a Goliath gleefully crushing a David underfoot: A sadistic bully.

Paulette Cooper testified about these events in 1981, to a hearing on Scientology by the City Council in Clearwater:

> My basic interest is as a writer; I like investigative things. . . .
> I went in and took their weekend course.
> During the time, I wandered away from the group where they were teaching the particular, well, TRs, as they call them, and I came upon a list of people, who—I don't remember for sure if it was a Fair Game

172

order, but I think it was because these people were being declared enemies of mankind.

I remember one woman's name was on there and it declared her an enemy of mankind for pushing five men down a flight of stairs. And how could she do that? It just didn't ring true.

And I decided to contact some of these people when I came home. And I think I took about five names, the five top people, and every one of them had an unlisted number, disconnected phone.

Well this was in 1968, and the people Scientology was attracting were twenty-two, twenty-three years old.

And just by chance, a whole group of people are not going to have five unlisted numbers unless there's a reason for people to unlist their number.

So, it began to bother me that, you know, was this so-called respectable Church perhaps harassing people? And in that one weekend, I had noted that they had lied about certain things, and I wondered about a church lying to people. And I decided to look in the library and see if I could get any information, any book. And I discovered that all the stories had been clipped out of every single magazine pertaining to Scientology, and I wondered whether this Church was, perhaps, possibly stealing things.

Well, I spent the next couple of years doing research into Scientology.

And my first article came out in December of 1969. That's also the month that I received my first death threat.

And then a number of mysterious events occurred, both then and during the time within the next year and a half until my book came out.

I was followed on several occasions; we found a phone tap on my phone; I was being multiply sued already at that time. Oh, people kept calling me and trying to take me out, and it seemed like people were trying to get to me.

And this went on for four unpleasant years, including four lawsuits, one of which was for somebody else's book. And when that happened, I got really annoyed. And I became the first person to sue them for harassment.

It was actually shocking to them because Hubbard had written that an enemy of—that no one would ever sue, that they had too much to hide and that people were criminals (whoever attacked the Church), and, therefore, we were going to just wither away and die. . . .

Well, about October of 1972, they started a big campaign to finally silence me or attempt to stop me. That month I received the second of what was ultimately to be five anonymous, absolutely disgusting smear letters about me. This particular one called me a part-time prostitute. . . .

During this same period of time, there were a large number of attempts to get into my apartment, which was on the ground floor of the building that I lived in at the time; it was not well guarded, and I was quite concerned. I received a tremendous number of really disgusting calls, and I remember one day counting eleven calls. . . .

I finally decided that I was going to move to a higher security apartment, even though I really could not afford to do so at the time. I moved on December 15th. The person who took over the apartment was my second cousin. We bore a physical resemblance because we're about the same age and she was very petite, and we both had short brown hair at the time.

And a series of mysterious circumstances occurred. The important thing was that she opened up the door to someone who had flowers and rang my bell. And I was no longer living there, although my name was still on the door.

When Joy opened the door to get these flowers, he unwrapped the flowers and there was a gun in it.

And he took out the gun and he put it at Joy's temple and he cocked the gun, and we don't know whether it misfired, whether it was empty and it was a scare technique, what happened, but somehow, the gun did not go off.

And he started choking her, and she was able to break away and she started to scream. And the person ran away.

And so she called a detective and he said, "It's a very wild attack because there doesn't seem to be any motive for it." There was no attempted rape, there was no attempted robbery, and why should somebody just suddenly try to kill her. . . .

About a week or two later at my apartment, I received a visit from the FBI. And they informed me that the public relations person from Scientology had claimed that she had received a couple of bomb threats and asked—and had named me as somebody likely to send bomb threats.

I didn't take the whole thing very seriously, and the FBI asked me if I would mind being fingerprinted. And I said that I would not, and I was fingerprinted.

[Later] I was called for a grand jury. . . . I didn't think this was anything very serious and did not bother to retain a lawyer, had very little money because I had used all my money to move to this more expensive, higher-security apartment.

And when I got there, they told me that I was the target of an investigation into the bomb threats. And I went and had to hire a lawyer, and every lawyer wanted—the least we could get was five-thousand dollar retainer, which, in those years, was like paying ten thousand dollars, you know, today. And to suddenly have to pay this sum of money and find out that you're in serious trouble. . . .

Finally, I went before the grand jury, and I tried to answer every question as truthfully as I could. . . .

They kept asking me again and again, "Did you ever see this letter? Did you ever touch it? Do you know who might have? And I said, incidentally, "Yes," that I suspect they might have confrontations in the press.

And they asked me to step outside the room. And when I came in, I knew I was in very serious trouble, and they asked me what my social security number was, whether I was on drugs, and did I realize what I had said so far. And again, they asked me the same series of questions.

And they said, "Well, Miss Cooper, if you've never touched this letter before, could you tell us how your fingerprints got on it?"

I felt like a grand piano had just hit me on the head. I—I fainted sitting up; the whole room just turned upside down and I didn't know what to do. And then, of course, the lawyers wanted more money.

And on May—let's see, May 19th, 1973—I was indicted on the three counts of sending bomb threats through the mail; two counts were for two letters. One was for perjury for saying before the grand jury that I hadn't done it and that I thought this public relations person might have done it. On May 29th, ten days later, I was arrested and arraigned.

The next eight months were a terrible, terrible nightmare in my life that I still feel sometimes that I suffer from to this day. I had fifteen years in jail over my head and fifteen thousand dollars in fines. I was petrified about going to jail, more so, perhaps, because of my small frame and the fact that I heard that women's federal prisons were rough places.

I risked having my career totally destroyed because—and I had been successful. And as a freelance writer, what editor is ever going to give an assignment to someone who's been indicted or convicted for sending bomb threats to someone they opposed?

I was very concerned about the indictment and the trial coming out in the newspapers. The public does not know the difference between indict and convict, and they think that if you're on trial for something, you must have done it or where there's smoke there's fire. I was left with the terrible public humiliation that every person I ever knew in New York would read the details of the trial and these accusations.

I was most concerned about my parents, who had adopted me when I was six years old, and how humiliating it would be for them and their friends to have to explain and to go through a trial like this.

During this period of time, I went through a terrible, terrible depression and a number of my friends, which I can't blame them for, did not stick by me. I was depressing to be with. I had been seeing a man for five years and had intended to marry him, and he left as a result of my depression.

I was released on my own recognizance.

I went through a period of very, very acute anxiety. . . . I couldn't sleep till about four in the morning and I'd wake up about six with my stomach just in my throat and worrying about what the next day would bring and what was going to happen at the hearing. And this went on for eight months, and I was just totally exhausted, sleeping two to four hours a day. . . .

All the money I had had gone to the lawyers, and I went into debt to try to continue to pay for them. The—in the end, just the main lawyers cost nineteen thousand dollars. . . .

I developed, for the first time in my life, acute agoraphobia; I couldn't leave the house. I think that this really started with this attempted murder that I felt had been intended for me. . . .

And meanwhile, during this period of time, there was a friend, a new friend, who I met under somewhat mysterious circumstances, but he was very, very helpful. And I obtained an apartment for him in my building, and he did some of the food shopping that I could not get out and do. And his name was Jerry Levin. . . .

The worst period of time was approximately two weeks before the trial. My lawyers informed me that, with a federal case, it was a ninety-five percent chance of conviction. They gave me the good news that, for the trial, they wanted my parents to be seated in the front row and watch the entire proceedings. And I kept saying, "You can't do that to them. It's going to be awful enough for them to read it in the paper." . . .

They felt that one circumstance that might get me acquitted was the mutually close relationship with my parents.

On top of that, going through some Scientology material I had obtained, there was the name of Jerry Levin. Now, I felt horribly betrayed, but at the same time I simply did not want to believe it. I was very naive, and his name was a very common name, especially in a city like New York.

Meanwhile, we had tried every single move possible to get the trial stopped. And—but I was in a very very nervous state and it was impossible for me to be tested correctly. And we went to some doctors who said that they felt the only thing that might work would be . . . sodium pentathol or "truth serum." . . .

So, the problem was we couldn't find a doctor who would give me a sodium pentothal test because, by this time, I weighed eighty-three pounds; I had started at about ninety-eight. And it became very, very dangerous to go and put somebody under, as if for an operation, and do that.

And I just said I didn't care if the . . . sodium pentathol killed me because, if I had to stand trial for what I didn't do and humiliate everyone and go through this humiliation, that I would just as soon be dead anyway.

And we finally did find a doctor two weeks before trial who gave me a sodium pentathol test. I was unconscious for seven hours.

I don't know what was said during that [time].

I do know that, when I came to, my mother was standing there and I said, "What happened? What did I say?"

And she just said, "It's O.K. It's all over. There won't be a trial."

The government wanted to save face because they don't like to admit that they've made a mistake. So, they said that they . . . would postpone the trial, but they would not actually drop the charges at that time.

The government did not drop the charges and, for two years after all this, I still had to worry on a daily basis whether one day there was going to be a trial and all of these things that I was afraid of, the prison and so on, was going to happen.

Paulette Cooper goes on to tell about the harassment she received over the next couple of years. She began to receive copies of a letter she had sent out in her late teens and a copy of psychiatrist's report (that had been stolen from her psychiatrist's office by a Mr. Dardano, while he was an agent for the G.O. He also testified at the Clearwater hearings, having left Scientology by that time).

By 1975, the charges had been dropped.

In the summer of 1977, the FBI raided the Scientology organizations, based on Michael Meisner's testimony.

Paulette continues:

On October 12, 1977, the FBI called me. Now, remember, this was a five-year period that I had never been able to prove my innocence; the government considered me a criminal. I had a, quote, record, end quote.

And the FBI called out of the blue and said, "We have just received evidence that you were innocent of those original charges."

I put down the phone and cried. . . .

****

Paulette Cooper learned from the FBI that the Scientologists had broken into her New York lawyer's office.

She finally saw the seized documents at the end of 1979, when a judge ruled 23,000 of them available to the public. Among them were two that made it absolutely clear that she had been criminally framed.

One document was found that indicated that there had been some consideration of using the Mafia against her, but they decided instead to frame her "so that Scientology would not look bad."

Another document proved that Jerry Levin, the fellow who had been "helping" her during her worst months, had been "calling a diary into Scientology."

This included reports as to how close she was to suicide: "She can't sleep again . . . she's talking suicide. Wouldn't this be great for Scientology!"

15

Hubbard in Hiding:
The Secret Desert
Command Post

Perhaps it could be described as locking the stable door after the horse has bolted, but since there was probably a real threat of a subsequent FBI raid at La Quinta (a high-class area near Palm Springs), that description might not be fair.

Besides later being the location for the production of "educational" or instructional Scientology films, there was, initially, at La Quinta a major project to shred, "vet" (cut out signatures with a razor blade) and burn all documents that could in any way tie Hubbard, his wife Mary Sue, or Jane Kember to the Guardian's Office activities, and Hubbard to control of the Church.

"Hubbard had resigned in 1966," was the "shore story" that had now taken on tremendous importance in the wake of the FBI raids. He was now said to be just a writer in seclusion, who sometimes consulted top Church officials. All evidence to the contrary had to be eliminated.

"If it isn't written it isn't true" was his commandment, and it was followed exactly over the years. So all his orders were in written form, as were all communications of importance between his executives and staff around the world. A great deal of this demonstrated his total dictatorial control of his Churches and the Guardian's Office.

There was a lot of paper to destroy.

"LAND BASES" IN THE DESERT

In early 1977, there were some 400 people in La Quinta, posing as the "friends of Norton Karno."

Much of the following dialogue describing that era is edited from a taped briefing by John Zegel, who is the step-father of Mark Yeager, a member of the current top "elite" rulers of the Church. John Zegel and Mark's mother resigned from the Church four years ago. Mark disconnected from them, calling them "Squirrels" and "Suppressives." His mother had proudly given him permission to "join Ron" in 1973, when he was twelve years of age.

John Zegel was in a position of knowing many of Mark's friends, who left the Sea Org concurrently with John's resigning. They related these events to him. His taped briefings became a sort of underground "news media" among ex-Scientologists in 1983–1984:

On the 15th of July, 1977, a week after the FBI raids, having spent a week conferring with Mary Sue about the matter, Hubbard made a decision to leave La Quinta. With him he took Dede Reisdorf, Claire Rousseau and Pat Broeker.

They left in a station wagon named "Beauty," in the middle of the night with their lights off. Once they were an adequate distance away they turned their lights on and made their way to Sparks, Nevada.

Hubbard was ill during the trip. He was having stomach trouble and this is not a happy time for anybody.

Pat Broeker and Claire Rousseau, under assumed names, went out and set up an apartment.

The cover story was that Pat and Claire were a young married couple, Hubbard was their elderly uncle and Dede was their cousin.

This "family" was almost completely incommunicado for nearly six months. Hubbard was spending time working on his health. He took long walks every morning and worked on the script of *Revolt in the Stars*, which he envisioned would be made into a major film. It would deal with a "catastrophic interplanetary incident that occurred 75 million years ago."

After they had been in Sparks for a short time, cash was becoming a problem, so Pat Broeker contacted Annie, his soon-to-be wife, in Clearwater.

They arranged for one million dollars in cash to be taken from the Church by Annie. Subsequently, she met Pat in the L.A. Airport where they exchanged suitcases. Each had a matching suitcase, and were disguised in some fashion.

The money arrived at Sparks, but they were still uncertain that the money had been sufficently laundered. So they took the hundred dollar bills, which was how the bulk of the money arrived, to the various casinos and broke the money down as it was needed.

They remained in Sparks until the last day of December 1977. They then headed back to the Rifle hacienda in La Quinta.

Since the filming was now to begin, more property was needed.

Two large ranches were located in Indio, California. One was 140 acres of grapefruit and date palms called "Silver," and another 10-acre plot of grapefruit and date palm, with a hacienda called "Monroe."

The film crew would eventually live at Monroe, and in the middle of Silver's grapefruit orchards, a huge barn was built, which was actually a film studio.

In September of 1978 Hubbard had another major incident with his health. It is unclear as to whether he had a heart attack or a stroke, but it is known that David Mayo, who at that time was senior case supervisor Flag, was summoned from Flag to La Quinta to audit him.

Dr. Gene Denk was in attendance when Hubbard arrived. He pronounced him "very seriously ill" with vital signs very, very low. He said that Hubbard's heart was arrhythmic, and he prepared the necessary facilities for revitalizing the heart.

Hubbard eventually recovered, but remained on heavy medication thereafter, especially blood-thinning drugs.

John Ausley tells of some of the events of the period:

Hubbard would suddenly, overnight, turn someone of his choosing into Dracula, when in fact they had been an instrumental force in building the entire group. How do you do this? You insult them to the core. And what it engenders is fear in the others.

"No matter how big you are, I can wipe you out just like that!"

There was this California surfer type. He was a Class Twelve. And he was the type of Scientologist who always wanted to work it out with two-way comm. (He wanted to discuss any disputes in order to resolve them.)

He was like one of the inner sanctum. And he was quite a good counselor. Hubbard had this rule that you weren't supposed to mess with the locals sexually, or "public on lines" (customers).

Anyway, this guy had decided to get laid. And there was some girl he was getting along with. And this was not so esoteric. This girl was in the Sea Org. It wasn't as though he was messing around with a public person or local. She was a tech groupie: she wanted to go to bed with a Class Twelve.

So he sleeps with her. Then Hubbard writes this issue and says he's been messing around with public. And makes him the garbage collector. It's like Hubbard sat down and figured out what would be the most degrading thing he could possibly do to this guy to defile him in front of his peers.

Hubbard had decided to degrade him. He just kind of *went for him*! He had to prove to everyone that he would sacrifice a Class Twelve for no reason.

****

An interesting description of the La Quinta era was one covered in the *Riverside Press Enterprise* by reporter Dick Lyneis:

A Las Vegas woman, who spent a secretive six months in the Riverside County desert in 1978 helping Scientology founder L. Ron Hubbard make movies, said she worked as "slave labor" while Hubbard lived like a king.

Mrs. Adell Hartwell said Hubbard had his own home which was surrounded by an electric fence and protected by guards. "He had his own valet," she said, "and was always in the company of his 'messengers' who were teenage girls and he had a motor home, a boat, two Cadillacs, and a Jeep and two girls who drove him everyplace."

Mrs. Hartwell, on the other hand, said she often worked long stretches without eating and—along with her husband, Ernest—lived in a "shack" which they said they had to share with a variety of desert vermin. She said they didn't get the promised Scientology counseling and were forced to work 12-hour days, with one day off every two weeks. . . .

Mrs. Hartwell was there from May until October of 1978, while her husband spent only two months there. The entire group, which authorities think arrived early in 1978, was gone by last March ['79].

Movie making was the principal activity. Location shooting was done in nearby cities, and Hubbard, who Mrs. Hartwell said was the "producer, writer, director and everything" for the movies, used his Scientology followers as actors, musicians, costume persons, set workers, and other movie jobs.

An amateur dance team, the Hartwells had been promised that once they got to the production area, which they were told would be in Florida, they would be trained to act, and their dance talents would be used.

Instead she ended up sewing costumes and her husband worked on movie soundtracks.

Mrs. Hartwell described Hubbard as being about six feet two inches, and 275 pounds. She said he "dressed very sloppily. He always had one suspender, a cowboy hat, and had a bandana around his neck. He cussed and swore all the time. He used the filthiest language I ever heard in my life."

"No one could call him by his name, Ron," she said, "because that was a breach of security. Everyone always referred to him as The Boss." She said members of the group were instructed to notify a Scientology attorney in Encino if anyone approached the property and asked questions about their identity and affiliation.

Mr. Hartwell said Hubbard got the maximum out of the group, "by controlling everyone by fear and threats of discipline."

Discipline, the Hartwells said, took strange forms.

"He (Hubbard) got mad at a messenger once," Mrs. Hartwell said, "because she overspent some money on an errand, so they took away everyone's supply of toilet paper for 10 days."

Hubbard, who is 69, was looked upon as god-like by the persons there, said Mrs. Hartwell, who admitted he had a "strong influence" on her.

"One day he touched me," she said, "and I could just feel a force there that was hard to describe."

"His messengers," she said, "were there to cater to Hubbard's every need. The girls would stick cigarettes in his mouth and light them. They had to catch his cigarette ashes. If a drop of sweat was on his forehead, they had to wipe it off. Every word he said had to be written down by the girls. You can't believe anything if it's not written down. Whenever he appeared people would clap. *If it was four in the morning, and nobody could see straight, people would clap.*"

The sense of worship that persons within the Sea Org feel for Hubbard, Mrs. Hartwell said, is "almost fanatical."

"The feeling among most people there," she said, "was that when Ron Hubbard goes (dies), we are going to go with him."

In March of 1979, with Hubbard still staying at La Quinta, a "security flap" occurred.

EDDY WALTERS:

One of the major points that put him into deep hiding was when Ernest Hartwell and I went to La Quinta to see him and he panicked.

Ernest Hartwell had left La Quinta and returned to Las Vegas where he talked to Eddy Walters, who was a counselor at the org there. He described the conditions at La Quinta and his observations and opinions of Hubbard. Eddy was a G.O. staff member who was as hard and dedicated as most of those chosen for intelligence work. But Hartwell's story, since it was messing with his illusions about the founder himself, was disturbing.

He wrote up a report of his interview with Hartwell and was almost immediately confronted with a visit from Artie Maren, a very senior G.O. official who had come all the way from Los Angeles to "handle" him.

Eddy, who was inclined not to believe Hartwell, now couldn't understand why the fuss. If what Hartwell was saying was indeed the ravings of a crazy man, what was the big deal?

Artie was obviously in a huge sweat about this report and begged Eddy not to talk about it or pursue it further.

All this made Eddy very curious and, during a subsequent conversation with Hartwell, he decided that he and Hartwell should go out and face the Old Man. "Right up to the point where I went out to La Quinta I still believed in him. I still believed that he'd somehow straighten it out. That's why I went out there," Eddy told me.

When they arrived, they were "confronted with armed guards and the paranoia was intense."

"What he did, instead of confront me, was to run," says Eddy.

Eddy couldn't figure out why Hubbard should run from him. "I'd expected that he'd stand up to me. I'd been living in Las Vegas and my motivating idea was that this man, who had so much to give the world, was headed in a certain direction. Now I was faced with the dilemma: if that was the case, why would he run from me?"

Eddy Walters was expelled and declared suppressive and the mimeographed issue, making it official, was already being handed out by the time he and Ernest Hartwell had made the five-hour return trip to Las Vegas.

Hubbard fled to a small community about 20 miles south of Riverside called Lake Elsinore. There he and his assistants lived in a motor home for approximately a month.

The next location Hubbard lived in was a place called "X." "X" was an apartment block in a small town called Hemet. Hemet is the town closest to Gilman Hot Springs. Two apartments were taken there, one in which Hubbard lived, and one for the messengers and the other people who accompanied him.

In October of 1978, another facility had been purchased. It was known as Gilman Hot Springs and included that resort and a motel known as the Massacre Canyon Inn, about 20 miles west of Palm

Springs. Gilman Hot Springs included a 27-hole golf course and a variety of other facilities.

The total purchase price for the properties was 2.7 million dollars and the Church paid for them in cash. Hubbard had huge offices that were renovated and constructed for him at Gilman. He also had a house that was renovated for his use, called "Bonnie View." However, neither of these was ever put to use.

****

Dick Lyneis wrote in the *Press Enterprise*:

> Church of Scientology activity in Riverside County may be more extensive than its officials acknowledge.
>
> Besides its Riverside Mission, the controversial church until early this year maintained a secret mission near Indio where its elusive founder, L. Ron Hubbard, led a group engaged in making church training and indoctrination movies.
>
> Additionally, there are strong indications that a group now occupying the former Gilman Hot Springs resort, near San Jacinto, may be a Scientology project.
>
> Although spokesmen for an individual who says he owns the old resort, and officials of the Church of Scientology deny they are connected, there are significant links between the desert mission and the Gilman Hot Springs activities.
>
> Rev. Heber Jentzsch, of Los Angeles, a Scientology spokesman, said he "has no information" that his Church has any involvement with Gilman Hot Springs.
>
> Persons at both locations have been linked to Scientology. . . .
>
> Why the group insisted on so much secrecy, while shooting Hubbard's movies, could not be determined. But the Church has a record of cloaking much of its activity, including property ownership. In addition, church members, court documents filed recently in Washington reveal, go to great lengths to keep authorities from finding Hubbard because they fear he is being sought by law enforcement authorities. . . .
>
> Security was so tight at the desert location the Hartwells said they didn't know where they were going until they got there. And when they arrived in the desert, they were instructed to tell friends and members of their family they were in Florida for advanced Scientology training. . . .
>
> While the Hartwells were in the desert, they were not allowed to make telephone calls or to send mail directly. If they had permission to

make telephone calls, they were instructed to tell the other party they were calling from Clearwater, Florida. If someone called them in Clearwater, the person answering took the name and telephone number of the caller, and forwarded the message to the Hartwells for a return call. . . .

Early this year spokesmen for the trust said the new occupants of the property were members of something they called the "Scottish Highland Quietude Club." At various times the spokesman said owners of the trust were "wealthy Eastern investors" or wealthy investors from the Palm Springs area. . . .

Riverside County sheriff's authorities became suspicious about the occupants of the two ranches at La Quinta when they learned the group was filming movies. A department source said it was feared someone was making pornography movies, but the properties were vacated before an official investigation could begin.

Captain Reid said his investigators have been trying to learn the identity of the Gilman resort owner because of inquiries made to the department by residents of the area. "We heard rumors like organized crime was taking it over," he said. "and we felt we had to look into these rumors."

A raid by the Riverside Sheriff's office on the Riverside Mission in July of 1979 and the above article's appearance in the *Press Enterprise* did nothing to make Hubbard's hiding place in Hemet more secure. Along with this unwelcome publicity there were increasing IRS legal and investigative activities into Hubbard's financial affairs.

All this, combined with Tonja Burden's going to see the FBI and anti-Scientology attorney Michael Flynn (Tonja could tie Hubbard into G.O. activities), had to have had quite an effect on Hubbard.

Hubbard's response to these events was "Operation Bulldozer Leak," the biggest of a series of shredding and vetting operations to hide his control of the Church. This was conducted mainly at Gilman Hot Springs, which was the administrative control center of Scientology International.

By February or March of 1980, Hubbard took off from Hemet with Pat and Annie Broeker, traveling to San Louis Obisbo, some four hours drive up the coast of California. Here he lived secretly in a his Bluebird motor home until his death on the 24th of January 1986.

Since the raids by the FBI, all attempts to cover up the full story seem to have created further problems.

During his reign at his desert hideout, first in La Quinta and on through his stay at the Hemet apartment block, he had initiated some major changes.

In November 1977 he had issued an LRH Directive stating that prices around the world had not been raised for over a decade and that they needed to "catch up with inflation," so they would begin being raised at a rate of 10 percent a month until they were "caught up with inflation."*

This reflected his panic reaction to the FBI raids.

The only real priority, communicated by his actions, appeared now to be his personal safety. Money became even more important.

Lawyers and private investigators, for both defense and attack purposes, are expensive.

---

*Around this time, Hubbard also made certain "discoveries" about the "state of clear." This resulted in a flood of people—and money—"up-lines." Money that was "up-lines" was more easily accessible to Hubbard.

16

The Saviour Lives Just Down the Road!

Until the first press about Hubbard's presence in La Quinta appeared in early 1980, I was unaware that Hubbard was living just down the road, some 25 minutes by car from my home. By that time my life was in a shambles, my family kept alive by a mortgage on our house.

My troubles had begun after "Source" moved into Riverside county. . . . In late 1977 the FBI raids had just happened. These raids—the result of illegal acts inspired by Hubbard—made it apparent he'd committed a major blunder, and left his ego bruised. So subsequent to the raids he was thrashing around trying to find scapegoats. Anyone and any pretext would do, so long as attention shifted from him. Franchise holders were seen to fit the bill.

The fact that he was living so close by put me high on the list of targets for attack. Most other major franchise holders in California (and subsequently the U.S. and Europe) were later subjected to similar treatment.

****

When we arrived in the U.S. eight years previously in late 1969, my wife was seven months pregnant with our first child. We were both Class VIII auditors, the highest class of auditor in Scientology at the time, and we had been hired to work for a franchise in Tustin,

California, near Disneyland. Except for our house back in New Zealand, which we had mortgaged in order to fly to England in 1967, we were poverty stricken. Two and a half years in England on Scientology staff pay does that to people.

Despite the poverty and some disillusioning experiences with high Church officials, we were—at the time—still full of enthusiasm for Hubbard and "his tech." This was partly because he and "the tech" had been so well presented by the words and example of Hubbard's key representative: John McMaster.

McMaster was the most prominent person (other than Hubbard, of course) in Scientology while we were in England (1967–1969). His work at Saint Hill Manor in England probably contributed more to the financial success of Scientology—during the mid- to late sixties—than any other individual.

When we arrived there the place was a hum of enthusiastic activity. Lectures by John McMaster were given in the chapel to overflowing crowds of enthusiastic students.

McMaster's talks were evidence to me that he had attained and experienced something paranormal, existential, or whatever words people use in a vain attempt to convey whatever is considered a true "religious experience."

John's glow of affection, and his other spiritual qualities, seemed evidence of the achievability of the most cherished dreams of Scientologists. The fact that he was Hubbard's representative and "the world's first real Clear" gave credence to Hubbard's many written claims. John's talks and "presence" reminded each listener of their own brushes with this "reality of our true godlike nature."

Besides the realm of individual spiritual abilities and the like, McMaster spoke of world peace, of creating a new civilization based on love and understanding.

He told me in a recent interview:

> I was so excited about the function of auditing and its potential for assisting individuals to become more able and aware, that I was willing to overlook Hubbard's faults, as they gradually became known to me. That was up to a point of course, the final point being my realization that his intentions were entirely self serving. I saw that he was in it for money and personal power, and his actual intentions were not as stated.
>
> The basic function of auditing is a wonderful thing, but Hubbard

perverted it. The idea of counseling has been around for an awfully long time. What is the Socratic method but a form of auditing?*

He asked me if I would go and promote the subject, and I did. I didn't know at the time what he *really* intended to do with it.

He got the technology to a point where he had a sort of assembly line as he called it. And he told me he was putting all these "square ball bearings" on the beginning of the assembly line, and then turning them into "round ball bearings" at the other end. That was his idea of "standard tech."

But there is magic in auditing. Good magic.

The important thing is not that the magic was abused—that needs to be pointed out—but that the magic should be brought to life. . . .

For a period of time, Hubbard trusted me implicitly with the technology and so on, and relied on me for the information because, although he did a lot of talking, *he couldn't audit.*

He could not audit.

He had to resort to a sort of black magic hypnosis. This was to try and convince the person that he was making gains. Then, of course, after about three weeks the person collapsed. And this was explained by Hubbard as being because there was a suppressive person around the corner, causing him to lose his "gains."

He couldn't audit, so he had to use somebody for auditing research. At this point in time, I was the one he used.

I would give him the information and then he would write the bulletins. He couldn't tell me what to do, because he didn't know himself. I had to do all the difficult cases; to go and review them, and this is where we found out so many things.

I had a wonderful sort of learning ground, if you like. This was partly because I had to learn to leave behind in Saint Hill Manor all the negative things he said about the people who I had to go out and handle. I had hundreds of students and pre-clears, and I had to be absolutely free from his ideas when I closed the door of that manor. . . .

It was the "good magic" which my wife and I had observed and experienced, and the example of John and a few others that motivated us as we crossed the Atlantic in late 1969.

Upon our arrival in the U.S. we worked in Raymond Kemp's Orange County franchise for a year, during which we managed to accumulate enough money to buy a house and put a down payment on a

*Perhaps with this in mind, Hubbard had once referred to Socrates as a "squirrel," insisting that he had merely "squirreled Buddhism." Of course Hubbard claimed to be Buddha.

car. We then commuted to nearby Riverside to set up our own franchise.

It wasn't easy. We spent the next three years struggling to stay alive. We finally sold the Tustin house and the one in New Zealand. We invested all the money into the franchise, and began to do quite well. Then we searched for new quarters and eventually came up with a 40,000-square-foot brick building (originally built in 1909 as a YMCA) and we moved there during the latter part of 1974.

It is still amazing to me how much we were able to achieve. It was accomplished as a result of a combination of our youthful idealism, hard work, and service; along with slogans, and hard sell, and the image of a god on a far-off yacht researching "the upper bands of OT." I had been to the *Apollo* by this time, and some of the Sea Org zealousness had rubbed off on me.

Franchises were extremely permissive in their operation when compared to the totalitarian Sea Org (and were tolerated by Hubbard as a necessary "PR" activity for attracting "wogs" into Scientology).

Franchises delivered the "lower" part of "the grade chart." These "lower grades" more resemble a form of psycho-therapy, as contrasted to much of what is called the "upper levels," which some have referred to as "bad science fiction."

The lower grades deal with resolving unwanted habits, fears, inhibitions and psychosomatic ills, and—generally—are aimed at helping a person straighten out his everyday life. Even some of Scientology's severest critics (such as attorney Michael Flynn) admit that these lower levels can be beneficial when they are done without the perverting control mechanisms of the Church of Scientology.

By late 1977 we had over a hundred staff and we were doing some 400 hours of auditing a week. We were sending lots of people to the Flag land base, where we ended up spending almost half a million dollars on "staff enhancement" by mid-1978.

I pushed hard for statistics, while remaining aloof from the day-to-day hustling to make it all happen.

We were the number-one single franchise in the world at this time. That crown was held tenuously, with Martin Samuels's Sacramento franchise neck and neck. It was a friendly rivalry.

We had, at Riverside by late 1977, accumulated some $840,000.00 in reserves projected to cover our future highly idealistic expansion plans. But, as was the case in most Scientology orgs and franchises, we had also put a lot of staff and public into debt.

While not approaching the severity of "discipline" that was occurring on the flagship, we nevertheless pushed the staff intensely, with a similar message of self-abnegation for the greater cause. The group's achievements was a collective source of enormous pride. We certainly had no doubts that we were helping mankind.

It was around this time, unbeknownst to me, that Hubbard had moved into Riverside County. I began to feel the heat.

****

It was difficult for me to understand the hysteria that was being generated, since I had no idea that Hubbard was endangered by the evidence uncovered by the FBI during their raids. Nor did I know that he was fearful of the potential testimony of a pretty young teenager (Tonja Burden).

Hubbard had become increasingly obsessed with the idea that the franchises were a threat to him. This belief began to override in importance even the enormous resources in people and dollars that they were generating. His paranoia probably stemmed from the fact that he couldn't control the franchises entirely: they were separate corporations, legally autonomous.

While this separation had been designed to protect him from legal liability (generated by the fact that franchises directly contacted suit-happy "raw" public), it also meant that the franchise holders had considerable independence of choice as to what to do with their own followers and financial resources. Those resources, he now feared, could be targeted at him. While it had never occurred to me that the franchise's bank accounts enabled me to afford lawyers and so to sue Hubbard, it obviously had occurred to him.

****

John Woodruff was one of the "guns" Diana Hubbard used to "shoot down" Mike Davidson, who had been the head of the franchise network for ten years. Davidson, a well-educated and intelligent Englishman, had demonstrated a sense of fair play, protecting us well from what I now know to have been Hubbard's crazed Management. On the other hand Hubbard's daughter Diana was renowned among franchise holders for mindlessly sticking to her own narrow interpretation of "Daddy's orders."

Now Woodruff was assigned to "investigate" me. In an early conversation with me he stressed that he was a company man who would ruthlessly follow orders. He had dark, dead, unfeeling eyes: blank disks.

He was very much into "finding dirt" on me, so as to discredit me in the eyes of my staff and "public." Hubbard had already decided to take my franchise, but they wanted to do so with a minimum of upheaval among the Riverside staff and "public."

In mid May of 1978, I got a call from an aide telling me that Diana wanted me to come to Florida to tell her about how I kept my statistics so high.

When I arrived at the Fort Harrison Hotel in Florida I was greeted by hugs and kisses from Diana Hubbard's aide Nancy Foster, and a pleasant smile and greeting from Diana (a beautiful woman in her twenties, with thick red hair cascading to well below her waist). I was escorted to the fourth floor and entered a room where another aide was seated with a severe-faced G.O. agent.

I sensed danger.

I was handed resignation papers. They wanted me to resign from the board of directors of my franchise, and also from its bank accounts. I wanted to know why.

"It is merely a temporary state of affairs to ensure that you are loyal and, given that you do the retraining steps and auditing that has been decided on, you will be put back on the board in two months," I was told.

They continued to assure me that I would get a full fair hearing, and that I was not in any danger as long as I did their program. If I did not cooperate they would know I was an S.P. and the appropriate penalties would be applied. Under this pressure, I signed.

There was no hearing and, after the three worst months of my life, I finally completed all the exhaustive requirements and asked to be reinstated in my franchise per the agreement. I was subsequently ushered into a meeting with Woodruff and one of Diana's aides.

"You cheated on all your courses!" lied Woodruff, obviously getting a sadistic pleasure out of my apparent pain. "You are an S.P. and you will never run another franchise."

Upon returning to my home in Riverside, I wrote up petitions; but by now I knew that Mary Sue had approved the move against me and I began to believe that Hubbard was inaccessible.

****

During the previous five years I had experienced what it was like to be a cult leader, to be Hubbard's agent. There was a seductive aspect to this which was very powerful indeed! As Hubbard's representative I had begun to be seen, in the eyes of his followers at Riverside, as similarly superhuman.

It snuck up on me by easy gradients. Anyone who has succumbed to flattery or ego-stroking has experienced the same thing, if possibly on a smaller scale.

It is somehow hard to realize that there is something seriously amiss when one is the beneficiary of this kind of adoration.

The power I was able to wield created a persona that was not me. I knew it even then, but could not—and probably did not want to— shake it off. It was like booze to an alcoholic.

Up until this removal in 1978, I had experienced a modicum of the same disease that had consumed Hubbard. Yet because of the subsequent period of absence from the madness of Hubbard and his agents, leaving me to quietly contemplate at home, I had been cured. Well, not quite completely—some powerful symptoms lingered still. . . .

In spite of everything, I still saw Scientology as the way to a better world. It had been a major part of my life for seventeen years, and in some ways I was still a zealot.

In October of 1979, I had for the second time been to England unsuccessfully appealing for the return of my franchise. There was a knock on the door of my house. I answered and the man flashed a badge. It was Sheriff Jensen and he wanted to know if I was Bent Corydon.

These guys were "the enemy," was the message that had been instilled in me by Hubbard over the years. Their presence was all "part of a plot to destroy Scientology." So I shut the door in his face and went straight to the phone to report the incident to the G.O. The agent I spoke with praised me for the way I had handled things.

I began to get very concerned because I had a series of reports and documents that I had been gathering, which were part of my attempt to have myself vindicated. I felt these documents were what the sheriff may have been looking for. After all they showed actions which might be illegal on the part of Church officials who had been disciplining me. So a few days later, I took them downtown to Xerox them, planning to send the copies off to Mary Sue Hubbard and hide the others at my brother's place.

Returning home, I drove down my driveway, which is restricted on both sides by a low brick wall. Once one has entered, there is no rational place to go except to back up onto the road.

Halfway down the driveway I looked up and noticed Sheriff Jensen and two plainclothes officers. It flashed in my mind that they must have had me under surveillance, in order to get the documents which were now lying on the seat beside me. I could be in the position of blowing it for the Church!

So I slapped the gears of my little Ford Capri into reverse and headed back up the driveway.

Jensen yelled and as he ran for his car, another officer jumped back into his and roared down the road to effectively block my exit.

As I went back down the driveway, Jensen ran right in front of me yelling. I was oblivious to what was being said; my only concern being how to get away and protect the documents. He jumped onto the flower-bed and pulled his gun. Apparently my car was aiming in his direction as I went down the driveway giving him legal rights to shoot me.

"Stop or I'll blow your fucking brains out!" He had a gun some 18 inches away from my head, but his warning meant nothing. I was obsessed with finding a way to escape, and kept telling myself I couldn't let them have the documents.*

I decided to try backing over the flower bed. So, slamming the car into reverse and revving up the engine, I sped backwards and hit the small mound causing the car to leave the ground and land at the bottom of the hillock.

In the rear view mirror I could see three officers with guns drawn and pointed at the back of my head. However, they didn't fire as I roared across the lawn and onto the street.

Escaping, I stored the papers at my brother's house.

I then called the Guardian's Office, and they provided me with a lawyer who went with me to the Riverside jail, where I spent one of the worst nights of my life. There was a later investigation into the inhumane conditions in the Riverside County jail, which did not surprise me.

My brother finally bailed me out and we walked outside into a clear sunny California day.

There were two charges of assault with a deadly weapon on a police officer, plus seven counts of conspiracy and grand theft in connection with loan applications made by public and staff at my franchise. These

---

*I had risked my life to protect Hubbard and his wife, and was praised for doing so by Scientology officials. See "Update, Part One" for Scientology's more recent perception of this incident.

loans were for services taken there. The Sheriff's officers had not
been at my house to get my documents, they had been there to arrest
me on what amounted to an invalid warrant regarding the loan fraud
charges. Had I not resisted I would have had no problem.

It turned out that the original visit to my house, where I refused to
identify myself, was an attempt to get me to turn State's evidence. It
appears that the Sheriff's Office believed that the Gilman Hot Springs
property had been bought by the Mafia. After all the name "Scottish
Highland Quietude Club," and the two-and-a-half-million cash purchase, were somewhat unusual. They did want a pretext to raid the
place, as Hubbard had feared. Since they had no pretext to do so,
they were looking for another way of gaining some leads. Loan fraud
charges were seen to fit the bill.

In late 1979 (a year after I had been removed from the franchise),
the Sheriff's Office had raided the Riverside Mission of the Church of
Scientology. Their charges had to do with loan applications and their
key witness was Riverside staff member Todd Carter. They had
hoped to add me as another witness against the Church. Failing to get
my co-operation and, regardless of the fact that they had not the
slightest evidence, they added me to the indictments.

Sheriff Jensen later confided in me that they were really not interested in the staff at Riverside, but wanted to get some leads that went
higher up.

****

There is considerable evidence that I was to be the meat Hubbard
wanted thrown to the dogs, in order to prevent the investigation from
going higher (to Gilman, near where Hubbard was living, and where
there were plenty of *real* shenanigans).

My lawyer at the time was convinced that this was the case. She
called me one morning on the phone, screaming, "What the fuck is
going on!" (She is very much a lady and it would take something outrageous to cause her to use that kind of language.)

It turned out that Terry Colvin of the Press Enterprise had called
her and asked if her client Bent Corydon was going to change his plea
to guilty. He had been paid a visit by Church President Heber
Jentzsch, he told my attorney. Jentzsch had told him that I was guilty
of all the charges against me and that the Church would co-operate
with the D.A. and the press to put me away.

Despite all this, the original charges of Conspiracy and Grand Theft *were dismissed* in preliminary hearing.   The Judge berated the deputy D.A. for having no case.

Prior to my removal from the franchise in 1978, I had been assured by my attorney that all was legal with the loan applications. I had not known of the extent of the loan application "fluffing."

"Fluffing" means to exaggerate figures such as income and leave out or lessen debts owed, in order to qualify for a loan (a practice which I'm told is common in the U.S.). In the Riverside situation, loan officers were telling our sales people ("registrars") which figures were needed for loan approval. They did this knowing fully that the information would be used to falsify a specific application. Since our people had gained an excellent reputation for loan repayment, the loan agents were anxious to make loans and collect their commissions. The judge decided that, since the banks had not *relied* on the false information, there had been no fraud.

But I had pushed *hard* for statistics. An activity, which is amoral at best.

However, *no laws had been broken.*

So, while I was cleared of the conspiracy and loan fraud charges, I did have a problem with the my outrageous cult inspired behavior in my driveway. I ended up pleading no contest to one misdemeanor charge of assault with a deadly weapon. I got a thousand-dollar fine and two years' probation, which was reduced later to one year. My record was then expunged.

Though it may seem hard to believe, I gained something positive from all this. During the legal proceedings I read a lot of law, giving me a greater understanding of what Hubbard had contemptuously labelled "wog justice." This was a major factor in my being able to free myself from Hubbard's manipulations.

I got to be good friends with Sheriff Jensen (he jokingly calls me "Killer Bent"). I appreciate the fact that he didn't shoot me that day.

My attorney had told me that, had these events occurred in Los Angeles County, I would have had a nice neat hole through my forehead. So I asked Jensen why he hadn't shot me. I get curious about things like that.

He said, "Because of the look in your eyes."

I asked, "What did you see in my eyes?" I needed to know.

He said, "You were scared shitless!"

Thank God for the look in my eyes!

17

A Reform Movement
is Derailed

During my legal battles over the loan situation and driveway offense, I followed the news as Mary Sue Hubbard and the other ten
raised large amounts of funds for their legal defense against the federal indictments resulting from the FBI raids of 1977. When later
Mary Sue's defense was seen to be futile, and the legal heat was becoming directed increasingly at Hubbard himself, Hubbard ordered a
"palace coup" by his "kids" (his youthful messengers) and the Executive Director International Bill Franks against Mary Sue Hubbard
and other top G.O. executives.

David Miscavage "handled" Mary Sue Hubbard and Bill Franks
was assigned to "handle" the head of the Guardian's Office, Jane
Kember.

With the entire old G.O. top hierarchy headed for jail, Hubbard
ordered his messengers to set up a "Watchdog Committee."

In early 1981 Hubbard also created a new post of Executive Director International. This was announced to be a resumption of the
post "vacated by L. Ron Hubbard in 1966." The new appointment to
Executive Director International was Bill Franks. By appointing him
to these posts Hubbard had ostensibly made him "Ecclesiastical
Head" of the entire Church. He was said to be the equivalent of the
Pope in the Catholic Church.

It was presented to Franks that he would be assuming all of
Hubbard's administrative functions. However, Bill told me years
later, after leaving the Church, that he had since concluded that

Hubbard set him up in order to help him rid himself of Mary Sue and Jane Kember (making them scapegoats for the break-ins).

To pull this off was tricky for Hubbard, since there was the possibility of triggering an emotional reaction from the two women. They were capable of exposing his part in the Snow White operation. Mary Sue and Jane, knowing Bill was their enemy, but not knowing Hubbard was behind their ouster, would be prone to blame him rather than Hubbard.

I knew Bill Franks well. He had helped me out of scrapes in the past and we had a common dislike for the Guardian's Office top executives. I met him by chance on the street in Los Angeles shortly after the coup against Mary Sue and Jane Kember.

"How are your attempts to get your franchise back going?" he asked. (It had been over three years since I had been defrauded of my position at the Riverside Mission.)

"I have essentially given up trying, since I keep winning appeals just to have the findings cancelled," I told him.

On his advice, I subsequently called someone in England and got a Board of Review; I was called there to appear.

By November of 1981 I was informed that the findings were positive. But I still did not have the details, when Bill Franks called a "Mission Holders' Conference" in Florida.

****

The Florida mission holders' meetings might have turned out to be a turning point for Scientology, had Hubbard been able to consider actual reform along the lines of the proposals of Bill Franks and the mission holders. That was, of course, not to be. . . .

Hubbard had never been considered to be the villain by mission holders. We mostly assigned that role to Jane Kember and her deputy, Herbie Parkhouse. These were the real bad guys, and they were gone. So now there appeared to be some hope for the first time in four years.

Even Raymond Kemp, a veteran mission holder who had been suing the Church for return of property coerced from him, was invited. Including such an "enemy" at an official meeting was unprecedented. He and his wife Pamela brought with them documents seized by the FBI during their raids. Among these were a special Training Routine called "TR L." The "L" was for "Lie." It was a secret training routine for G.O. personnel, to drill them in the art of lying!

The Kemps were in fact the first to speak. Theirs were highly emotional speeches which were followed by others by myself, Martin Samuels, Dean Stokes and Allan Walters.

We told our stories. I, for one, was pretty choked up. The crowd of over a hundred were supportive and our speeches were punctuated by applause. We were at last among friends. We could say anything; they understood. It was safe.

Many others took turns telling their stories and a revival time atmosphere pervaded the room.

Then the subject turned to Bill Franks. He was absent. A "management representative" (Jens Bogvard) was brought on stage and explained that Bill had been guilty of promiscuity and was being handled "over the rainbow" (Gilman Hot Springs, near my franchise).

So we became painfully aware that (despite his proclaimed Pope-like status) Bill was answerable to somebody. Who?

"The Watchdog Committee," was the answer.

"Who are they?" someone asked, voicing the question that was in all our minds. Nobody understood what these alphabet people were: "WDC," "CMO." Bill was one of the few people who knew and (unbeknownst to us) Hubbard had directly ordered him not to reveal their identities.

The next question for Jens was about how they had discovered about Bill's "promiscuity."

Jens, who is a genuinely likable fellow, answered candidly: "His phone was tapped."

Someone in the audience exclaimed that tapping telephones was a felony in Florida. Since this tapping had obviously occurred *after* Jane Kember and the others had been kicked out, this put a whole new complexion on things: Others besides the jailed top G.O. executives were apparently involved in violating the law.

It was decided to adjourn until a representative of the "Commodore's Messenger Org" could get to Flag to face our questions, and when Bill could also be there to give his views.

Some ten days later the meetings resumed.

Bill Franks was back, as was Annie Tasket, a representative for the Commodore's Messenger Org (C.M.O.) and a member of the Watchdog Committee.

In response to questions she explained (as Bill entered and sat near her on the podium) that Bill had *not* been locked up—imprisoned—while he was "over the rainbow." She could not see Bill's face and kept chirping out the official line. The rest of us saw his face go taut and redden.

"Don't lie to my friends!" he finally blurted out and he told us what had happened while Annie looked crushed.

Bill Franks explained under oath in 1985:

> I thought I was doing what Ron wanted me to do. No way did he want a bunch of little kids directing criminal actions to continue within the Church. So for me, I didn't even have a second thought about that. . . .
>
> I called them [the Watchdog Committee members] up and said, "Look, the game's up. You have to come down. If you are giving orders, you are going to have to be accountable for them."

Bill's action, and our support of it, so it turned out, was considered high treason so far as Hubbard was concerned. There was no turning back.

BILL FRANKS:

> It [the management of Scientology] was totally out of control. . . . And that's what I tried to change. [It was] not only myself, but . . . other people in that room really caring about the corruption in the Church and wanting to change it. And that's what was considered to be so offensive to the CMO, that we should try to change the corruption in the Church.

The incredible thing is that the Watchdog Committee eventually turned up.

Meanwhile, outside of the meeting hall while we all waited for the WDC, negotiations were going on between myself and my wife and the people who had been running my mission during the three years I had been gone.

Amazingly, during these meetings things resolved. My franchise (including the building) was returned to me and another mission was established North of Los Angeles for those leaving. The cream of the staff were taken along with $50,000.00, while I and those remaining assumed the financial liabilities.

Given the actual situation, this was hardly justice; but even some restitution was probably unique in the history of Scientology. No one else that I know of has ever had all they worked for Shanghaied by Hubbard and his mob and recovered any substantial part. I believe

that this could occur only because of a vacuum of power and the resulting confusion at the top of the Scientology hierarchy. This was the
situation surrounding the uprooting of Mary Sue and the G.O.'s top
brass while the "kids" took over.

****

Finally David Miscavige and Norman Starkey and another six or
seven executives arrived. Miscavige, the top Commodore's Messenger, was twenty-one years old. It was the first time most of us had
heard of or seen him or most of the others. Yet here were our leaders.

They lined up across the stage. They looked tense. The mood of the
room blackened.

Dean Stokes, who was M.C. at the time, saw that the chemistry
was all wrong. A confrontation between these "libertarian" mission
holders and this uptight authoritarian group was going to mean
trouble. He announced that the Watchdog Committee would be invited to discussions with Bill Franks, and a few others. He explained
that, once things had been resolved in a more closed session, the rest
of us could join in the dialogue. They filed out.

The next day an announcement was made that all was fine and that
Bill Franks would be left in charge. Bill, for his turn, spoke in glowing
terms of Miscavige, and so we all believed that truth and justice had
prevailed. I didn't realize then that it was all a charade, but Bill had
certainly begun to suspect it. If I had known that, I would have wondered why Bill was going along. He answered that recently.

BILL FRANKS:

> Messengers are considered to be emissaries of Hubbard. This is axi-
> omatic within the Church. These people are given incredible amounts
> of power based on that. And so there is no way I'm going to hold an
> emissary of Hubbard, in the frame of mind I was in at the time, up to
> public ridicule. . . .
> I was trying to relax the man [Miscavige].

What was actually happening at the time of the mission holders'
meeting was that Bill had been "put in charge" as an additional facade
for Hubbard. Bill was supposed to have "instinctively" understood that
he was merely to be window dressing. Hubbard was still in control while
operating through new additional façades, consisting of the mysterious
WDC and Franks. These fronts were designed to protect Hubbard from

the same criminal prosecution that had already consumed his previous façade, consisting of his wife and her G.O. clique.

Hubbard had not counted on Bill Franks and the mission holders' backlash reaction against what we considered "G.O. type abuses."

Franks naively believed that Hubbard had genuinely stepped down, leaving him with the top spot. Bill's reform efforts were constantly getting derailed by these "kids," however (secretly implementing Hubbard's intent), so he feared they would go on to commit crimes similar to the G.O. bunch.

His problem was that these "kids" were, to him, still "Commodore's Messengers" who were, in that role, to be treated as one would treat Hubbard himself. But now, some of them were also Watchdog Committee members. Bill was, he believed, senior to WDC members in his capacity as "Ecclesiastical Head of the Church." So, he was left with a dilemma: he never really knew if and when the "kids" spoke for Hubbard as "messengers." So he never knew if and when they were functioning in the role of his juniors or his seniors.

****

We mission holders had made our bid to reform the Church in concert with its titular head, and lost. We were to pay the price for having challenged Hubbard's top agents and (without our knowledge) Hubbard himself.

I learned much later that, following this, messages were shuttled between Hubbard and Miscavige regarding the mission holders' meetings. Pat Broeker, who represented Hubbard and carried his written messages, met secetly with Miscavige and David Mayo in a restaurant which was located just a mile from my mission.

Hubbard was livid! He wrote that the mission holders had been infiltrated by government agents in an attempt to take over Scientology.

So Bill Frank's fate was sealed. Hubbard targeted the mission holders, myself included, for a greatly accelerated program of takeover.

It was only days after the mission holders' meetings in Florida that the "Religious Technology Corporation" was officially created. Missions were now "Junior Corporations" to RTC, whose assets would be directly under Hubbard's control.

RTC articles contained, unbeknownst to us, a clause which mandated that all junior corporations to RTC would be subject to arbitrary dissolution on orders of RTC executives, and, upon such dissolution, all assets would go to RTC (Hubbard).

****

Within two weeks of the mission holder's meetings, and Miscavige's assurances to us that Bill would remain in power, twelve uniformed agents of the RTC stormed Bill's office and removed him on direct orders from Hubbard.

Other heads began to roll (unbeknownst to me on Hubbard's orders). I was stunned. Nothing had really changed. It may even have been worse since the old G.O. guard was deposed. Hubbard's part was kept secret, but for the first time it began to eat at me at some level of my consciousness that Hubbard must be involved somehow.

There was hardly a day when at least one of these expulsions didn't arrive in the mail. The top executives and personalities of Scientology, some 600 people who had given the most important youthful years of their lives to work ridiculous hours for the cause, were now officially declared to be evil psychotic beings.

18

Hubbard's "Billion Dollar Caper"

To understand this caper, some background information on Hubbard's methods of raising personal income is necessary.

In 1969 Hubbard wrote a PR article entitled "What Your Fees Buy," in which he stated:

> Even today I draw less than an org staff member, and they draw very little. . .
>
> None of the researches of Dianetics and Scientology were ever paid for out of organizational fees. With my typewriter I paid for the research myself. Occasionally orgs were supposed to but they never did. . . .
>
> So the fees you pay for your services do not go to me. . . .

He went on to explain that it "takes a lot of money to deliver Scientology services" and that it also takes an "enormous amount of money to fight the vested mental health interests," who use "their press control" and "government stooges" in an attempt to prevent Scientology from messing up their plans "for a *1984* World."

Pure PR; another shore story.

What did Scientologists' fees buy?

Howard E. Shomer, who worked for "Author Services International" (which serviced Hubbard's personal assets and income, and which was in fact the senior management of Scientology at the time) till early 1983, signed checks made out to Hubbard weekly. They were in the million-dollar range each week during the last six months before he left. At that level, Hubbard would have been receiving 52 million dollars a year in salary!

Bill Franks, while Executive Director International, kept discovering new foreign accounts the entire time he was on post. He does not know how many there were that he never discovered.

BILL FRANKS:

The problem was how were we going to get the money for Hubbard? He was not supposed to take in the money personally. So separate corporations were set up. This is RRF, Religious Research Foundation. We used to call it Ralph. That was a code name.

Money would be put into Ralph, that would be accounts [in] Liechtenstein. This is a Liberian Corporation. And he would draw from it. So in other words all of this money actually made its way over to Ralph. [It went] through these various people and various organizations, and from Ralph, then it went right to Hubbard.

In addition to all the above disguised flow lines of money to Hubbard, Franks received an order to pay money to him directly. According to Franks, the idea was formulated to bill the Church. The first was a billing of 85 million dollars for the use of the Mark VI E-meter, which Hubbard claimed to have developed. In other words, he was going to be presenting bills to the Church, and the Church was going to pay him.

Says Franks:

We had the hundred fifty million in Sea Org reserves. The problem was how were we going to get the money out to Hubbard.

In a good week, [the income of the Church of Scientology was] two million dollars a week. . . .

Scientology was able to generate such huge sums of money because of single-mindedness towards the goal of getting money to Hubbard. It was total single-mindedness. It was big-league sales, totally indoctrinated by the organization to get every last dime.

Laurel Sullivan (who served as Hubbard's personal PR) states:

In November of '73 . . . he said to find out which publics or categories of people he derived his income from and then prioritize them according to the attention I should spend on these publics. (Emphasis added)

As his public relations person, I was to stay briefed on all of his activities, all of the things that he was involved in [photography, promotional materials, management and technical writings], and his general production . . . so that appropriate billings could be done. . . .

Installments [payments to him for "backbillings"] . . . were substantial. [One billing prior to 1980] for a hundred and fifty thousand dollars was for research expenses spent apparently by him during the time he spent in New York, which was almost one year. At least that's what the trip was defined as ["research"].

That [was] the trip to New York where he was hiding out. The Snow White project came out of that. [The project that brought on the FBI raid and for which his wife took the rap.]

According to an affidavit by Gerry Armstrong, a conversation was held about September 28, 1980, in the Cedars complex, Los Angeles.

Laurel Sullivan, a top Church legal executive and an American Church attorney were the key people present.

The following exchange occurred:*

Legal executive: "The only reason it's worked so long . . . is *because everyone has effectively been bound by the authority of LRH and has ignored corporate lines.* (Emphasis added)

". . . CSC [Church of Scientology of California] has rendered much service to many foreign Scientologists and RRF has got the money. . . . *It obviously is the classic case* (loud laugh) *of inurement, if not fraud.*" (Emphasis added)

(Several laughs)

LS: "Well put."

Speaker Unidentified: "It's all privileged."

Another speaker: "The tape recorder is going here, Charles."

THE SCIENTOLOGY MISSIONS INTERNATIONAL CAPER

. . . "MONEY! REPEAT MONEY! REPEAT MONEY! REPEAT MONEY!"—L. RON HUBBARD (Stressing in a transcribed confidential taped briefing the enormous income to be made from the Scientology Missions International caper)

Some 20 months prior to the Florida mission holders' meetings, in

---

*Scientology has fought hard to suppress this tape. None-the-less, a copy is currently in the custody of federal authorities.

early 1980, Hubbard had announced to a select few aides a new caper.

It was to begin with selling mission "starter packs" to well-to-do Scientologists. Each pack would consist of "at least ten thousand dollars' worth of Hubbard's books," along with a charter for a "parish." All of this was to cost the "investor" around 35 thousand dollars per parish. Some existing mission holders were also required to buy two or three or more such purchases just to maintain what they had already been operating for many years.

Scientology Missions International was, per Hubbard's instructions, to be set up separately from the old existing "Mission (franchise) Office World Wide" network, of which (as of December 1981) I was again a member. Then at some opportune point in time, when the SMI network was in full swing, those in the old Mission Office World Wide network were to be "persuaded" to "move over" into SMI (and pay the fees necessary). SMI was a network that would, in contrast to the old MOWW, be totally dominated by Hubbard in the same way as were his "official" organizations (Churches).

Said Franks:

> I first heard of it in a taped briefing from him. He presented it as a billion dollar caper. . . . I eventually became the person responsible for establishing SMI.

SMI was financially tied in with the Liberian Corporation, called Religious Research Foundation (RRF, "Ralph").

Regarding getting the old-time mission holders to give up their autonomy as part of the MOWW network, Hubbard had said:

> "It is a very simple operation. You simply move them over. You don't make it a penalty for them to move over, you make it an advantage. . . . *This is a matter of selling. And those who don't move over, you simply start applying rules and regulations to. You lean on them.* And they'll move over. . . ." (Emphasis added.)

****

This SMI "caper" was in full swing when, just before New Year's day 1982, I walked back into my franchise after three and a half years' enforced absence. The Riverside mission was still a Mission Office World Wide (MOWW) franchise.

The legal officer lost no time getting the new "contract" sent to me to end that situation. I then called for a briefing with him and two other mission holders.

The contract he showed us gave them the power to do whatever they wanted. Now the tricks and deception were built in "legally," with cleverly worded, disguised phrases.

And I knew that if I didn't sign, my fate would be the same, only with a little extra trouble for the intel boys, who would concoct a great "fair game" project. I nevertheless put off signing.

Then the heat came: the loaded "suggestions" and innuendos. I remembered these all too well from 1978, when I was tricked into signing over my mission and its bank accounts.

This heat to sign the new "contract" was not my imagination: one mission holder actually continued to refuse to sign, and his expulsion stated this refusal to sign as the number one reason he was expelled. Finally around late September, I signed.

****

It was October when we were all invited to come to a Mission Holders' Conference in San Francisco. which was to be attended by the top brass of the Commodore's Messenger Org.

Having signed these "contracts", we were now subject to the whims of these powerful "kids."

19

The Saviour's Revenge

Hubbard's attempt to use trade-secret and industrial espionage laws to enforce "church doctrine" is probably unique in the annals of religious and legal history. Deploying "Finance Police" operating under an "International Finance Dictator" to enforce the sending of "customers" from "franchises" to the higher Church also has a bizarre ring to it: something out of Hubbard's pulp fiction.

The invitation to the Mission Holders' Conference created an air of mystery. So much brass in attendance had to mean some momentous announcement and changes.

There were a bunch of us who arrived about the same time at San Francisco International Airport and there were lots of hugs and greetings. The October air was crisp despite the sunshine as we stepped through the automatic doors to get the bus into the city.

Dean and Melanie Stokes from Texas sat with me on the bus and Dean expressed his conviction that he would lose his mission again. I disagreed and tried to be positive.

There were preliminary events, but *the* meeting did not finally happen till Sunday night at eight P.M. Between the initial Friday evening meeting and Sunday night people steadily arrived and the tension grew.

Most of these mission holders had, like my wife and me, invested their houses and ten to 30 years of their lives into their "franchises," based on Hubbard's representations in his policies that they would be "theirs." Even if they were to be run non-profit, at least one could draw a salary and expenses and live decently.

We had mostly a middle-class standard of living and families to support, and these kids who now seemingly ruled Scientology, who had never known what having to get an education for their children and pay a mortgage and insurance was like, made us nervous. My wife had just given birth to our second child, a boy. Thus, for us, this problem was particularly intense.

Discipline was to be kept light in missions, Hubbard had written. The very worst that could happen would be that we would lose our rights to call ourselves a Scientology mission. But these policies gave no one any great comfort now. Experience had demonstrated to us that policy was made to be broken where management was concerned. Any one of these kids could wipe us out on a whim.

We finally were ordered to take the elevators to the fourth floor and the room there began to fill up from the back. It was indicative of the mood that the front rows were empty while the back rows were jam-packed as the brass lined up on the stage.

There were uniformed Sea Org members around the edges and at the entrances to the room continually firing flash cameras at us, apparently to take our pictures. Later we discovered it was an attempt to intimidate and hypnotize.

Norman Starkey, with his thick guttural South African accent, began to yell at the people in the back of the room to come up to the front rows.

No one moved.

His shrill tone and the general atmosphere had everyone in an odd state. How should one react? This was outrageous. But to say anything or take action could be dangerous.

He then yelled at someone. No one was quite sure who. The tone was the same as that used by an angry master when disciplining his dog:

"YOU! COME UP TO THE FRONT ROW!"

The target of Starkey's wrath turned out to be Gary Smith, who had a franchise in Hayward, near San Francisco. Gary lived in Blackhawk, a community of multi-million-dollar houses. He had financed a classy mission because he and his wife believed in Scientology but, unlike most of the rest of us, did not need it for his livelihood. He had come to the meeting with his wife Suzy and their three-year-old blond daughter Carrie.

"Yes YOU in the red shirt. You know who I mean!" yelled Starkey at Gary, who was by this time looking around him to see who this guy might be yelling at.

Finally, realizing that he was the only one with a red shirt on, he replied, "Thank you, but I have my wife and daughter here and we're quite comfortable."

Starkey was stung by this public questioning of his ultimate authority:

"You have to the count of three, and if you don't move by then you're going to be expelled and declared suppressive!" he yelled.

"One! two!"—Gary did not move—"THREE! Get him!"

Uniformed guards ran towards him from several places in the room, and as they got near him Gary stood up and said firmly, "Don't touch!"

Gary Smith is no lightweight. He worked out regularly with weights and had a good record in college football as a quarterback.

He took his daughter's hand and they and his wife walked deliberately towards the door at which stood several guards. No one touched him.

When he had left the room it was announced that he and his wife were suppressive persons and would be declared such. They would no longer be running the Hayward franchise which they had financed and built up. Their franchise subsequently disbanded.

Then Kingsley Wimbush, an Australian who was currently running the most productive mission, was expelled. The privilege of expelling him was assumed by Miscavige himself. He announced that Kingsley was a suppressive in tones that betrayed his absolute pleasure.

Kingsley and his wife (good friends of mine: sincere and well-intentioned people) visibly froze as Starkey pointed at him and abused him as a "Squirrel."* He was ordered to leave the room and did so, leaving his wife sitting in shock with an empty seat next to her. It took her a couple of minutes to collect her wits, at which time she also stood up and walked towards the door.

"Declare her as well!' exclaimed Miscavige.

Dean Stokes had been right. He was about to lose his mission again. He was next.

His wife Melanie and I had worked very hard to get it back for him, as he had done for me after I had lost mine in 1978. For Dean, his franchise had meant his whole life for some ten years, now he took all this in stride. It was almost a relief for him, it seemed to me, as I watched his demeanor. The never knowing "if" and "when" had been driving him crazy.

---

*One who alters Scientology technology.

With these instant expulsions out of the way, Miscavige strutted. He had delivered Hubbard's retaliation for our "mutiny" 10 months previously in Florida! The Saviour's revenge was sweet.

There was more to come.

Larry Heller, a Church attorney, was introduced by Miscavige and dutifully lectured us on copyrights and trademarks. The underlying message was that we might have been bold enough to assert our views in Florida, but now that we had signed the new SMI "contract" we would be thrown in jail if we didn't respect the kids' authority and toe Hubbard's line.

Heller's suit and tie contrasted with the dark naval uniforms, with lanyards and captain's hats with scrambled eggs, the others were wearing.

HELLER:

Most of you are probably familiar with what a trademark is but perhaps, for our purposes, a small explanation might be in order.

A trademark is a symbol which is held out to the public representing to that public a certain quality of product or service which, when the public buys under that trademark, it's assured of getting.

To give you a very simple example. Some of you might have had a glass or a bottle of Coca-Cola with your lunch today. Hypothetically, one or two of you might be in Hong Kong tomorrow and have a bottle of Coca-Cola with your lunch as well. That Coke is going to taste exactly the same tomorrow when you get to Hong Kong as the bottle of Coke that you opened up today. As long as it has that Coca-Cola symbol on it, comes in that very distinctive bottle, that means that you're going to get a certain mixture of ingredients, a certain effervescence.

Scientology, as all of you know, also has trademarks. . . . Those trademarks, just like the Coca-Cola trademarks, represents a symbol which assures the public of a certain quality of *Service* which they are going to receive if they purchase something or receive services under that trademark.

He talked about how those trademarks had been owned by L. Ron Hubbard, but had been "donated" to the Religious Technology Corporation who sub-licensed them to the Church of Scientology and SMI.

Then he got closer to home: what did all this have to do with us?

RTC has a right to send a "mission" directly to the individual mission holders to determine whether the trademarks are being properly used by you. This mission may review your books, your records, and interview your personnel. . . .

If there is a determination by RTC that Scientology services being given by any of you under "Scientology" trademarks are not on Source, then RTC . . . has the right to immediately suspend any utilization by individual missions of those trademarks. The word "immediate" is the key word here. There need not be, at this point, a hearing in order for there to be a suspension. RTC will order that you no longer use the trademark and you must stop or be subject to civil penalties and ultimately criminal prosecution. . . . You will then be fined or thrown in jail.

From advice I later got from other attorneys, these assertions, to say the least, stretched the facts regarding this issue so as to make them appear much more alarming and generalized than they actually were.

There is certainly a question here as to whether the courts have any business monitoring religious doctrines and rituals.

It appeared to me, even at the time, that they were trying to have it both ways. They wanted full protection by the government as a business. Yet they demanded no interference from the government with their "religious" practices and doctrines. And, in fact, the U.S. courts were being called upon to ensure that these "religious doctrines" were not deviated from: hardly separation of Church and State!

Next—Commander Steve Marlowe, Inspector General from the Religious Technology Corporation:

The fact of the matter is you have a new breed of management in the Church. They're tough, they're *ruthless*, and they are on Source!" he announced.

Holding onto upper level students and pre-clears when they should be moving up the bridge, which is exactly what we're here for, are over. They [the actions of mission holders of denying them "customers"] are violations of long-standing policy.

They [the mission holders' actions of holding onto "org customers"] enter into such criminal or civil charges as conversion, theft, not to mention Industrial Espionage and Sabotage which will get you two years in the pokey.

I sat through all this while the cameras kept flashing at us, thinking this is so bizarre. I knew most of the mission holders in the room, and I knew how they detested what was happening, yet we all clapped at the right places. The guards were watching for anyone with disagreement showing on their faces.

Ray Mithoff, the new chief Case Supervisor was really being a zealot:

> The future can either be bright or very bad. I know for me it's going to be very bright and for someone who's out there squirreling and trying to get other people's attention off of Scientology and onto something, just to fatten their own pocket or whatever, that person's future is *black*.
>
> You hear Mr. Starkey mention a bit of how black it is. It is really *black*. It is so *black* I can't even describe it right now. I can't even find words to describe how black that person's future is. In fact it is almost as black as the future of an FBI agent. I *mean it is really black*. The depth of that blackness and the length of time that that person will be in oblivion is just immeasurable. . . .

In the same vein, Norman Starkey said of a defector:

> He will never, never, I promise you, for any lifetime, get any auditing or ever get a chance to get out of this trap. . . . That means dying and dying and dying again; forever, for eternity. . . .

Then Wendall Reynolds, was introduced as the International Finance Dictator! He said:

> Now right now you guys are Counter Intention on my lines [meaning we were getting in the way of what he was trying to do], maybe one exception in this room, but I doubt it, because you guys are sitting on public [I assumed he didn't mean it literally—but meant holding onto *their customers*], you're ripping off the orgs, you're doing all manner of crazy things. . . .
>
> Now some of these guys you see standing around here are International Finance Police and their job is to go out and find this stuff and if you guys are guilty of it, you've just had it! So, are we talking the same language here now? . . .
>
> Now this convention is costing the Church money. You're all going to sign 5 percent minimum Corrected Gross Income (income after overheads are paid) to this DMSMH Campaign.

This meant that we were to pay 5 percent of our mission's income to a TV advertising campaign for Hubbard's book, *Dianetics, The Modern Science of Mental Health*. The book was published by a *for profit* corporation and the royalties went to Hubbard, yet our *non-profit* franchises were supposed to carry part of the costs. It sounded illegal to me.

When, later that morning (the meeting ran on till 2.30 A.M.) I was told to sign the contract for 5 percent, I told the Finance Policeman that I wanted to put a proviso on the form stating that it was signed on the proviso that it was legal. He told me, "*Sign!*" When I still hesitated he said, with a sarcastic grin, that I could ask Wendall Reynolds the Finance Dictator about it. I signed knowing that any other action was dangerous in this charged atmosphere.

THE FINANCE DICTATOR:

You're going to get Dianetics and Scientology as a household word. . . .

And if you look at it *Battlefield Earth* [a science fiction book by Hubbard] has been released on the same pattern as the early 1950s, when LRH was a popular writer, with *DMSMH* released right on the heels of it and that put it right on the best-seller list!

And right now *Battlefield Earth* is selling out and selling out and selling out again. So we got a tremendous popularity thing going and you guys are getting a gift at 5 percent of CGI [Corrected Gross Income]. It's a total gift.

So if I hear one person in this room who's not coughing up 5 percent. . . . as a minimum you've got an investigation coming your way, because you got other crimes in your mission.

Questions on that? . . . .

We were pulled out one at a time to have mug shots taken by a uniformed photographer.

It was then announced by Captain Lesevre, in a heavy French accent, that teams of finance police would be coming to our missions and that we were going to be paying for them. The price would be $15,000.00 a day.

We were all finally told we could leave on the proviso that we wrote a letter to Ron thanking him for the event and acknowledging him for his contributions to us and mankind.

Guards blocked the door until we were given clearance.

****

Homer Shomer told me recently about Miscavige and company's

excitement as they returned to Author Services (on Sunset Boulevard in Hollywood) where Homer worked at the time:

> When they came back from the meeting they were laughing and joking about how they had really "socked it to those bastards." The look on Kingsley Wimbush's face when he was expelled was a source of great amusement—very *funny!* And there was much backslapping and mutual congratulations. Norm Starkey was quite a hero for his expulsion of Gary Smith. They called a special staff meeting to brag.

It was also only recently that I learned that Hubbard was the prime mover behind the actions of his messengers at the San Francisco meeting.

Homer Shomer told me that he saw a note from Hubbard which told these guys:

> Congratulations on your handling of these franchise holders. As far as I'm concerned you can get rid of all of them. We don't need them!

I believe that this revenge for the Florida "mutiny" was Hubbard's last major move as a manager of the Church as such, a move that precipitated a major schism.

Following this, according to an ex-aide, he became preoccupied with preparing for his death and with preserving the myths he had created about himself: He became obsessed with recovering his biographical and other personal documents turned over to a courtroom in nearby Los Angeles (Chapters 21 and 23).

20

Breaking Free

Not only had the mission holders been hit. Some 18 of the top messengers and executives immediately under Hubbard had been purged, accused of "working for the enemy." Among these were some of the highest "tech trained" people, including David Mayo, who had for over a decade been what is essentially the Archbishop of "Standard Technology," the Case Supervisor International.

It was Mayo who had been called to the dying Hubbard's side when he had become the victim of a stroke or heart attack in 1978 and had assisted him back to health and participated in the development of the "Nots tech."*

Also included among the 18 who were purged were the two executives who had headed the mission network, John Axel and Roger Barnes. They had been imprisoned at Gilman Hot Springs, with guards outside the doors of their locked rooms, and along with the others were then transferred to a separate property, some 15 miles away in a secluded area in the San Jacinto foothills.

Here they could not "contaminate the other crew." Their story over the next six months or so included watching David Miscavige and Steve Marlowe regularly spit in the faces of some of the inmates there. In one instance John Axel (top franchise executive) was reported to have been told to take off his glasses by Miscavige, and then punched in the face.

---

*The secret OT levels that bring in the greatest amount of money to Scientology. These are covered in Part II, Chapter 11.

****

After my return to the mission, I received constant calls for one thing or another, always accompanied by threats. One particular incident symbolized the ridiculousness of the situation: We were ordered to sell 1000 copies of Hubbard's recently released science-fiction book *Battlefield Earth* "before Thursday" or I would be kicked out as mission holder.

I was at home shaving when the phone rang. The receptionist at the mission informed me that there were three uniformed Sea Org people there, saying they were Finance Police.

Wallis Hooker was the leader of the group. He was wearing officer's regalia, and the appropriate severe "no-nonsense" expression. He briefed me on the seriousness of the situation. We had been holding on to clears and not sending them off to the orgs!

They were there to see that all "clears" (50 percent of our "public") were sent immediately, and that an astronomical quota of staff and "customers" were sent to Flag (in Florida) in less than two days, paid in full. We were to be billed for this pillage, to pay immediately at the end of each day, 15 thousand dollars a day. (By this time we had just $30,000 left, which was far below outstanding bills.)

The first day came to a close without our having met the impossible targets they had set.

"Get me a check for 15 Gs!" demanded Wallis.

I told him I needed to speak to his superior because what he was demanding was illegal. It was forcing me to do something that was not only counter to the interests of the corporation of which I was in charge, but would bring about its bankruptcy.

Wallis was terrified of questioning the orders he had received, despite the fact that I could tell he secretly sympathized with my plight. He kept mumbling about being sentenced to the Rehabilitation Project Force.

Yet I was able to get him to call a person he addressed as "Matisse." In what was genuinely an act of courage for the man, he presented my argument to him.

Then he went suddenly silent, and as he listened to the reply, I watched him blanche and almost pass out, muttering an occasional, "Yes, sir! Of course, sir! I'm sorry, Sir! Right away, sir!"

When he dropped the receiver, he had taken on a new resolve. He took a deep breath and started in on me in the manner that Matisse had obviously pounded into him.

There was to be "no more bullshit!" I was to sign the check or be expelled. I had five minutes, and he had ten to get back with Matisse and report that he had the check, signed by me for 15 Gs, in his hand. I signed and he called.

We were down to 15 thousand dollars in the bank and no prospects of further income to cover immediate urgent bills.

I called all over, everyone I knew who had not yet been kicked out. There weren't many. It quickly became clear that the orders animating poor Wallis came from *"very* high up"—which was code for Hubbard himself.

Then I received a call from Matisse, and in a strong German accent he yelled, "You will sign another check for 15 Gs tonight. If you do not have the check signed in 15 minutes you will be going to jail for a very long time!"

There was no doubt that he meant that I would be framed in the same manner as they had framed Paulette Cooper—something I was aware of by this time. I had no doubt they could pull that off. Any heroic stance of not signing would be futile, I decided, because whoever they put in after me would be happy to sign. Then the place wouldn't have a chance.

I signed, and was informed that I was to get a plane to Santa Clara in Northern California and report to Matisse for a security check.

On the way up I schemed how I would pull off lying on the sec check. The truth would obviously get me expelled and I would have no chance to figure out how to salvage my mission.

I would lie while clearly facing the truth in my own mind. For instance, if they asked me if I was communicating to any suppressive people (most my friends were "suppressive" by now and I always accepted their calls) I would say "no" while picturing in my mind talking to them.

The basic theory is that the meter reacts to those things that one resists confronting. Thus I would confront freely the truthful answer while verbally lying.

If I told the truth to these tyrants I would obviously be declared, and the mission would collapse as a working installation and all my dreams and those of my friends at the mission would be smashed.

For four hours the next afternoon, Matisse and an American Sea Org officer, whose name escapes me, interrogated me on the E-meter. I lied as much as necessary, and got away with it! They tried every trick to catch me out, but the meter constantly verified that what I was telling them was the "truth."

They were puzzled, and as I left, Matisse told me (placing his thumb and forefinger close together): "You have come this close to having your throat cut!"

I was subsequently reminded repeatedly "not to take out any loans on the building or try to sell it!"

It was coming through loud and clear. I had only a short time left and there was no way they would let us continue to keep the property, which was worth a substantial amount of money, in the name of the corporation we controlled. They obviously had plans to transfer the property out of our control.

They had their hands full with other situations, but as soon as they could muster the manpower, a caper would be pulled that would turn us into an org and, unless I signed an undated resignation, I would be replaced with someone who would.

Over the next few days there was a call from someone in the Guardian's Office. This person wanted us to go to the courthouse and xerox some papers that had to do with the L. Ron Hubbard, Jr., case against his father's estate.

I went down and read the file while it was being copied, and some of the stuff was eye-opening! For the first time I began to wonder seriously whether Hubbard himself was behind all these atrocities.

The case notes also made mention of the Armstrong case progressing in Los Angeles, so I noted down the case number. Two days later Mark Lutovski and I drove to Los Angeles County Superior Courthouse. It was during this drive that the idea was first brought up: "Were there any circumstances under which we would consider breaking away from the Church of Scientology?"

We quickly dropped any discussion of what we had been thoroughly indoctrinated was the ultimate treason, the highest of crimes!

What we read in the court records shook us both even more than had the thought of leaving. The evidence was coming through loud and clear: L. Ron Hubbard had been lying to us; he was not who he said he was, and he had undoubtedly been behind the Guardian's Office in their implementation of the "Fair Game Law" against governments and individuals.

When someone sent me an anonymous letter containing the articles and by-laws of the Religious Technology Corporation, which included what was essentially a license-to-steal-real-estate clause, I decided that some action had to be taken to protect the building. My wife and Mark agreed.

The clause stated that RTC had the power to dissolve any junior corporation (which included all SMI corporations) at will, at which point all assets (such as our building) would be distributed to RTC.

I called the lawyer and asked him for a solution to my dilemma. How would I protect the building, assets, and our beliefs (which we by now recognized as very different from those of the Church of Scientology as practiced) without alerting Church authorities?

It did not take long for events to develop, making it necessary to use contingency measures recommended by our lawyer. There was a call soon enough on a Friday night. I was ordered down to see the Master at Arms (who had disciplinary authority) at SMI in Los Angeles the next day. . . . I had no illusions about the fate of the mission: it was to become an "official org" (headed by someone who would sign an undated resignation) with or without our co-operation.

Some hundred people attended the meeting where we announced that we wanted to break away from the Church of Scientology. I gave a talk giving the reasons as best I was able, since my own mind was still in some turmoil.

There was a standing ovation at the end and people crowded around to wish us well.

****

The next day all hell broke loose!

Our staff and public were being called till three in the morning, being told that they would be damned for all eternity if they stayed with us. Many left, but few went to the Church-authorized official mission hurriedly made operational down the road.

Other missions splintered in the U.S. and Europe, but the majority of missions, over the next few weeks, just fell apart. This was devastating to Scientology's international income over the next couple of years.

The following nine months were quite hectic: I travelled to several European countries, aided by a couple from England, and "splinter groups" were springing up everywhere. It developed into a major schism reported in *The New York Times* and noted in *Time* and *People* magazines.

The central figure (the Martin Luther) consolidating much of this "independence movement" was David Mayo, who set up his group in Santa Barbara in late July—ironically, it turned out, not far from San Louis Obisbo where Hubbard lived secretly in seclusion.

The Church went utterly bonkers. There were parchment-like posters distributed with Old West criminal characters pictured and "Wanted, Squirrels, Dead or Alive" on them. ("Squirrels" had previously been defined as people who "altered the tech." Now it meant anyone who dared to help others with any aspect of "the tech" without grovelling before the Church's self-declared "ruthless managers.")

We were sued for 4.2 million dollars and private investigators were hired to spy on us and David Mayo. The suit was in line with Hubbard's writings on how to handle this kind of situation. Since we had no money, it was designed to break us with legal fees. Mayo was also sued, in an innovative legal maneuver, under federal racketeering laws (RICO) for "theft of trade secrets" (for using written "technical materials written by Hubbard—which had in actual fact been written by Mayo and then been published by Hubbard over his own name).

Hubbard had written:

> The purpose of the suit is to harass and discourage rather than to win. The law can be used very easily to harass, and enough harassment on somebody who is simply on the thin edge anyway, well knowing he is not authorized, will generally be sufficient to cause his professional decease. If possible, of course, ruin him utterly.

I discovered that L. Ron Hubbard Jr. had a listed phone number in Carson City, Nevada, so I called and spoke to him for some hours.

****

This era is rich with stories:

There was a fancy plot to get me jailed in Denmark on trumped-up charges. Denmark operates on Napoleonic law and one can be jailed until trial without bail. There were tickets paid for me waiting at the Los Angeles Airport. I had been suckered into believing that there was a businessman who would pay me twenty thousand dollars for counselling (which we needed badly for our legal defense).

Previous to this plot, an Englishman (ex-Scientology Sea Org member Robin Scott) had gone to Denmark with a couple of friends and pulled off a "caper" against the Church of Scientology there. He stole "highly confidential" upper level materials (for which Scientologists were paying hundreds of thousands of dollars to be audited on—see Chapter 13: "Are You Haunted?"). Dressed in Sea Org uniforms, his partners entered the Danish Scientology Org and announced they were from the RTC and demanded to inspect the state and security of their confidential materials. When their orders were complied with, they demanded to be left alone, and absconded with the material.

Robin Scott was later jailed and languished in prison for a month.

While I had nothing to do with this in any way, the G.O. had apparently managed to get someone to allege to the Danish Police that I had.

A couple of hours before I left for England, however, I was tipped off. My friend in Denmark went to the airport the next day to see who was there to "greet" me, had I been on the plane. Sure enough, there was a member of the Danish constabulatory and a well known member of the Danish Guardian's Office!

Another G.O. covert operation involved planting a spy in my group who was ordered to get a floor plan made of my building, especially noting the location of my office. After that there were break-ins, during one of which many pre-clear folders were stolen. He also had orders to discourage my key staff from working for me, along with a host of other destructive projects.

My friend Mark Chacon defended 23 small claims suits brought by Scientologists loyal to Hubbard (orchestrated by the G.O.). We won 21 of these cases.

The chaos was not limited to the U.S.: a shy young man in Stuttgart Germany, who had started a franchise in the mid-seventies and made it a huge success, was in trouble. When the Finance Police had arrived he went out on a limb to meet their insane financial demands. He raised nearly a hundred thousand dollars.

He was summoned to the Flag Land Base in Florida.

While there, independently from Scientology he joined up with a high stakes, high risk attempt to salvage a sunken ship off the coast of Florida.

Shortly thereafter he was dead, having drowned.

Martin Samuels, besides being expelled and removed from his four franchises and school—the school being located in a former Jesuit monastery in Sheridan, Oregon—lost his wife of 17 years (who the Finance Police turned against him) and the custody and affection of his two young children (they had been drilled to disconnect from "the S.P."). He was tricked into turning over every penny he had. Busted and emotionally devastated, he sought refuge with his parents.

He later told me:

Since the beginning of my time in Scientology there had been a bold vision of inspiring ideals. And myself and many other bright young people were attracted to that vision.

And I and they dedicated the most precious years of our lives to it.

Specifically in the mission network we sensed something was wrong. We couldn't articulate it or put our finger on it, and we worked at the perimeter away from the corruption.

When the corruption and abuses became blatant and undeniable, the better people were the first to leave, until there developed a vast exodus of all the brighter more decent people.

My time of final awakening came in November of 1982.

****

Hubbard had, in a sustained frenzy of blind fury, wiped out his most lucrative source of new customers and future income: the missions.

It would be more than two years later before a new "laissez-faire" era was proclaimed. As usual, some new Scientologists, capable but misinformed individuals, came to Hubbard's rescue.

A successful chiropractor, in San Francisco, finding himself impressed with "Hubbard's" management techniques, set up "Sterling Management Systems," targeted exclusively at professionals. This developed into a slick business-style program of seminars, some under different names, such as "The Advisory."

While the promotion for these seminars does not mention Hubbard or the Church of Scientology, a Church representative claimed that 40 percent of graduates end up "starting on The Bridge."

The seminars, along with a multi-million-dollar TV blitz ad campaign for *Dianetics: the Modern Science of Mental Health*, constituted the new program for recruiting "raw meat" into Scientology.

One claim, made by a seminar leader, was that Lee Iaccoca was a success because he used Hubbard's management techniques!

21

Hubbard's Bogus Biographies Exposed

"I have never lied to you or conned you."—L. RON HUBBARD, 1983.

Concurrent with the events starting with my "Bonnie and Clyde" confrontation with the sheriff in my driveway in late 1979, were the discovery of boxes of Hubbard's private documents at Gilman Hot Springs. A few years later, this resulted in a flood of material being revealed that changed my life and views dramatically. Another result was a widened schism within Hubbard's Church precipitated, in part, by my promotion of this material internationally.

As some background to these events, here is an excerpt from one of several short biographies circulating among Scientologists as promotional handouts or introductions to Hubbard's books during the sixties and seventies:

L. Ron Hubbard was born in Tilden, Nebraska, on the 13th of March, 1911. His father was Commander Harry Ross Hubbard of the United States Navy. His mother was Dora May Hubbard (née Waterbury de Wolfe), a thoroughly educated woman, a rarity in her time!

Ron spent his early childhood years on his grandfather's large cattle ranch in Montana. It was on this ranch that he learned to read and write by the time he was three and a half years old.

L. Ron Hubbard found the life of a young rancher very enjoyable. Long days spent riding, breaking broncos, hunting coyote and taking his first steps as an explorer.

It was in Montana that he had his first encounter with another culture—the Blackfoot (Pikuni) Indians. He became a blood brother of the Pikuni and was later to write about them in his first published novel, *Buckskin Brigades.*

Before Ron was ten years old, he had become thoroughly educated in schools as well as by his mother.

By the time he was twelve years old, young L. Ron Hubbard had already read a large number of the world's greatest classics—and his interest in philosophy and religion was born. Not that the explorer in him had been stilled. Far from it. A Montana newspaper of the period reported thusly on one of Helena's newest high school students:

Ronald Hubbard has the distinction of being the only boy in the country to secure an Eagle Scout badge at the age of twelve years. He was a Boy Scout in Washington, D.C., before coming to Helena.

In Washington, D.C., he had also become a close friend of President Coolidge's son, Calvin Jr., whose early death accelerated L. Ron Hubbard's interest in the mind and spirit of man.

The following years, from 1925 to 1929, saw the young Mr. Hubbard, between the ages of fourteen and eighteen, as a budding and enthusiastic world traveller and adventurer. His father was sent to the Far East and, having the financial support of his wealthy grandfather, L. Ron Hubbard spent these years journeying through Asia. . . .

These writings, containing numerous bogus claims, influenced many in their decision to make Scientology a "career." Some of the claims were published in *Who's Who in America* which, to many, amounted to confirmation.

One who was influenced by Hubbard's lies was Gerry Armstrong. After he left the Church in 1982, he wrote:

My research throughout 1980 and 1981, however, revealed a very different, and to me shocking, picture of Hubbard, his past, credentials, accomplishments.

[Contrary to his claims] he had not graduated in mathematics, nor was he educated in higher mathematics.

He was not educated in advanced physics.

He did not obtain a bachelor of science degree.

He was not a civil engineer.

He was not a nuclear physicist.

He was not a member of the first U.S. course in nuclear physics.

He did not excel in his subjects at university.

He attended George Washington University two years, 1931 and 1932. He was placed on probation after the first year, and in the second year his grades deteriorated. He failed both his mathematics courses his first year and got D's when he repeated them the second year. The one course he took in molecular and atomic physics he failed. He did not return to George Washington University thereafter.

Hubbard did not pursue post-graduate studies at Princeton.

During the war, he attended a less-than-four-month course in military government which was given by the Navy on the Princeton campus.

I had seen diaries Hubbard kept of his time spent in Asia, and correspondence between him and his parents and associates from the period, and was able to determine fairly accurately the truth behind his claims about this period.

He was not in China at fourteen and did not spend several years travelling thoughout Asia.

He did not study with lama priests.

He was never in India.

He attended school in the United States during the years fourteen through eighteen.

Hubbard's father, who was a naval officer, was stationed on Guam, and Hubbard travelled twice by ship to Guam to the U.S. and back, once in 1927 and once in 1928. On those trips the ships stopped briefly at various Asiatic ports in Japan, China, Hong Kong and the Philippines. The only time Hubbard travelled into the interior of China was on a tour sponsored by the YMCA given to children of U.S. service personnel stationed in the Pacific. His total time in Asia was a few weeks.

He visited a "lamasary" while on the YMCA trip and noted that the lama priests sounded like "bull frogs." His appreciation of Eastern culture was perhaps summarized when he wrote in his notes in 1929: "The trouble with China is there are too many Chinks here!"

ARMSTRONG:

I amassed approximately two thousand pages of documentation concerning Hubbard's wartime career: what he was doing, what vessels he was on, fitness reports and medical and VA disability records. The truth is far different from the public representations.

He was not crippled and blinded during the war. [Nor was he, "as a matter of medical record, twice pronounced dead."]

He did not cure himself with his discoveries.

He was not "Mister Roberts" [played by Henry Fonda]. He was removed from the U.S.S. *Algol* as "unfit" before it went into action.

He did not command escort vessels from 1941 to 1946.

He was not awarded 21 medals and palms.

At the beginning of World War II, Hubbard was assigned to Naval Intelligence in Australia. He was there briefly until ordered back to the U.S. as unsatisfactory for the duty, and after his return was transferred out of Intelligence.

He had command of two vessels: the first for a month during refit; the second for two and a half months during outfitting and shakedown.

He was removed from command of the first for exceeding orders, and from command of the second when he fired the ship's guns in Mexican waters causing an international incident.

In a diary he kept through part of the war he revealed that he had his men lie for him in the Naval Board of Investigation convened to investigate the incident.

He claimed to have sunk two Japanese submarines during the shakedown cruise during his second command, but the Commander of the Northwest Sea Frontier, Admiral Fletcher, stated in a report that "an analysis of all reports convinces me that there was no submarine in the area."

Hubbard spent the last few months of the war in a naval hospital with a duodenal ulcer. He was awarded four standard medals for his wartime service. A copy of a letter from the Department of the Navy listing his naval assignments and medals [spells this out.]

At war's end he was awarded a 10 percent disability for the ulcer. In 1946, he appealed the disability award, claiming in addition to ulcers to have "conjunctivitis" or inflammation of the eyes, and an infection in the hip joint contracted as a result of transition from the tropics to the eastern winter cold.

In October 1947 he wrote to the Veterans Administration asking for psychiatric treatment, stating, "I cannot account for no rise above long periods of moroseness and suicidal inclinations."

In 1948 he was able to get his disability award increased to 40 percent for the duodenal ulcer, infection of the eyes, bursitis of the right shoulder and arthritis of multiple joints.

In August 1951 Hubbard took another set of VA medical examinations and complained of the same conditions for which he was receiving a disability pension (and of which he would claim in his Dianetics and Scientology promotional literature he had already cured himself).

He was still receiving the 40 percent disability compensation in 1973, according to a letter from the VA.

****

In early July of 1986, I interviewed Gerry Armstrong about his discovery of Hubbard's biographical materials. Says Armstrong:

They had rented the shredder and we had 200 people and the entire property of Gilman Hot Springs dedicated to this shredding.

They had this paper shredder which was so big! This thing took them through like in quarter-inch swaths! W w w w w w w w w r r r r r r r r r r t h h h h h h h h h h h!

It was a *big big big*, giant munching shredder!

Laurel Sullivan says they called it "Jaws," but I think they also called it "Igor."

This was a bigger cover-up incident than anything that had ever happened before.

At the previous major shredding operation at La Quinta, we were ordered to shred anything which connected Hubbard to the G.O.

At Gilman each person went through his stuff that he had been assigned. There were people who did nothing else but shred, called "Shredder Operators."

This time the criteria had been expanded:

a. Any evidence of Hubbard's control of Scientology. b. Any document that showed that he had ordered anything at all. c. Any document that showed that he was intending to reside at the Gilman Hot Springs property. d. Anything that showed that he had ever been to the Gilman Hot Springs property.

Each person had to go though any documents in his area.

I was in charge at that time of the household unit at Gilman. In the household unit, we were setting up a house for Hubbard.

We tiled the floor. His bedroom tiles were dark blue and the room itself was painted dark blue. This was because he had some theory about sleeping in dark rooms and how much better he slept. . . .

Anyway, late one night I came across a box of stuff. And it was about eight inches deep, maybe 12 inches wide and 16 inches long. It was all beat up, opened, you could see that the lid had all kinds of tears. Brenda Black had found it and she handed it over to me.

I looked through it. And I knew right away that this was a whole different thing than I'd ever seen in Scientology. These papers were out of a whole different realm.

A real letter written by Hubbard? You've got to understand I knew all about Standing Order Number 1; that S.O. 1* was a lie.

These letters I was now witnessing were mainly the ones between him and his first wife.

There were also two diaries, which he had kept from [his days in]

*LRH Standing Order # 1: "All mail addressed to me shall be received by me." Replies to Scientologists' letters to Hubbard, written over Hubbard's signature, were, with few exceptions, written by someone other than himself. Neither letters nor replies were received or seen by him. Interestingly enough, the few exceptions were mostly from non-Scientologists, such as people involved in the field of science fiction writing and editing.

Asia. And then there were all sorts of other assorted papers going all
the way back, some into the 19th century.

Brenda wanted to know what to do. And I remember my Scientological mind going back and forth on whether or not to keep these documents. Did it make sense? I had to evaluate, because the whole place
was mustered into destroying documents.

We found several boxes, and Hubbard's biography had suddenly become possible, because now we had some material. All we had before
were these things written by Hubbard, and a few old science fiction
magazines. Now all of a sudden we had letters, we had diaries, and so
on. All there was known prior to that, even by the top PRs, was the
public picture that had been manufactured by Hubbard.

I wrote Hubbard a despatch proposing the biography idea.

He answered that with a couple of paragraphs. I did not have any
idea of the extent of the materials I had stumbled onto. Neither, it
turned out, did he.

I did a little bit of reading of the documents. Then I started to assemble it into some kind of sense. It was real difficult, given the time
and distractions.

In the beginning of February the messengers moved to the Complex, two and a half hours away in Los Angeles, where they were now
"The Messengers!"

They just descended on the place and had this impact on the joint.
There was DM (David Miscavage) and the WDC (Watch Dog Committee).

Laurel and I moved to L.A. also, and with us went the LRH archives.

In L.A. there are collectors and early Dianeticists, and other people
that knew Hubbard, so some research could be done there.

I got in touch with collector Virgil Wilhite and we paid him $65,000.00
for his collection of LRH memorabilia, early books and other writings
that the organization didn't have.

****

I met Omar Garrison in East Grinstead, England, in September of
1980. I had been sent there especially for the encounter.

The meeting went well and within three weeks we set up an office
for Garrison at the blue building in Los Angeles.

Garrison arrived in Los Angeles and signed a contract with the Organization, to do the biography.

He received twenty thousand dollars.

At that time, I had ready for Garrison about seven or eight binders
of material of the earliest materials that I'd found and those were

mainly the letters between Hubbard and his first wife—"the Skipper Letters," she went by "Skipper" and he was called "the Red Head."

Great letters! You should see these things. They're mind bending. But they're mainly under seal by the Court.

In those letters, you could just see an incredible battle building between him and his wife: Hubbard being so. . . . you cannot believe how ruthless he is being in those early letters!

When Omar was taking over his office I was giving him materials, and I remember thinking that I really resisted saying anything at all about what my conclusions were at the time. I had by this time some kind of confused thought of what the whole thing was about.

I remember thinking, "I'll wait and he can look at the materials. I didn't know if I could talk openly to Garrison. He was completely, up to that point, if not a died-in-the-wool advocate of Scientology, at least a firm opponent of Scientology's enemies. . . .

Between these interviews with various people from Hubbard's past, we were having meetings with Dr. Denk, in which he worked with us to get Hubbard the Nobel Prize. Hubbard said, "Unlimited funds allocated for this project." . . .

I never even said anything to Garrison until it was a little more opportune, until I was more certain that he'd looked at some of these materials. I think because I was his contact, I spent some time with him, out drinking together.

He was writing, and who does he talk to? So he talked to me. Pretty soon there was this slight conspiracy.

. It wasn't that we were conspiring to do anything, but rather it was a conspiracy of people who knew that there was something radically different from what had been presented to us before.

It took some time, but I remember Garrison commenting about having all those letters, and me sensing at that time that it was almost safe to talk to him. Inside the Church there was no one to talk to. And I didn't know if he was going to turn on me. But it was better than in there because in Scientology you can trust no one.

It was no single thing that was bothering me about Hubbard. It was that as soon as I knew the picture, I knew the picture.

It was a quantum leap. Now you know 852 thousand data and suddenly doink! a quantum leap. Suddenly all the data is different.

There was a point, for instance, where I knew that Hubbard had lied.

But I just could not attack the man. And I figured, wait a minute, this is really mind bending. I know now he lied!

I decided that in order for us to even know if there is any validity to the subject of Scientology, whatever validity there is has got to stand on its own. It can't stand on a web of lies.

As this was going on in my head I was talking more and more to Garrison.

So I knew at that time that Omar knew what was going on with Hubbard. . . .

A lot of the very early books that I gave Garrison were in Hubbard's own handwriting. And Hubbard, in his own handwriting, would introduce a book with "facts about L. Ron Hubbard".

So Omar and I would get a kick out of finding more "facts" about L. Ron Hubbard.

After a while we would dig up some more of these things written by him, and we would joke, "Oh, no, no more facts!"

We had by this time come to know that the "facts" were just so much horseshit. You could be guaranteed that if it was in the "facts about L. Ron Hubbard," it was a lie.

And Laurel Sullivan would write these PR pieces. And as I assembled more data they got it a little more accurate, but still they really couldn't change things from the way they were before. So this problem was developing—that we now knew it was all lies.

It was a shock for Omar, I think.

He became real paranoid from knowing what he knew.

I began to go through the materials and tried to separate out what truth there was, and what we just couldn't say.

I wrote a number of dispatches in an attempt to get the lies removed from the various biographical sketches in books and promotional literature; and the last dispatch was to the Master at Arms having to do with Starkey's response to a previous report of mine.

Starkey dropped into Archives, where I was working, one day. He was there to ask questions.

I had just gotten back at that time from seeing Nibs [Ron Jr.] with Omar. I said to Starkey that, in my opinion, a lot of the problems with Nibs had been created by the organization. I said that Nibs was not 100 percent wrong in this whole thing.

"He looks like he could be a decent guy," I said.

And then somehow we got up to Hubbard's lying, and I said, "Listen, we can't continue to claim that the guy's a nuclear physicist." And Starkey said, "Well *he* never said it! Just a bunch of stupid PRs said it."

So I walked over to the shelf [filled with] the books we'd bought from Virgil which contained the original *Scientology 8-80*, done in 1952, which was a manuscript edition, and there it was. . . . I showed to Starkey where Hubbard claims, in his own handwriting, to have been a nuclear physicist.

Starkey just stomped out of there.

Then a few days later I was called out to Gilman Hot Springs to talk with the Master at Arms about a report from Starkey. It was a secret report saying that he was concerned as to what documents I might have given Garrison, and he was saying things like, "Armstrong is stating that we are responsible for Nib's problems." This was a fairly accurate rendition of the way I had spoken about it, but it was apparent that it was completely unacceptable that I do such a thing. It would just be a matter of time till I was "busted."

So I was desperately trying to get Garrison everything that I could. I now knew that the whole thing was crazy, but also that I couldn't quit the job until I was through getting Garrison what he needed.

The pressure of the situation was getting to me. I was one screwed up kid in those days.

So I worked as long as I could and copied virtually everything I could for Garrison. I knew I had to do that, because I knew that I would soon be sec checked on what I'd been giving Garrison, and so I had to get it to him before that.

I knew that they were in a dilemma. They have been pumping all this stuff out for so long and all the author's sections are already published. Now what are we going to do? And one of the books they were about to republish was *All About Radiation*, which states on it's cover, "By an Atomic Physicist* and a Medical Doctor." Well wait a minute, it's copyrighted by L. Ron Hubbard and written by L. Ron Hubbard. Which one is he?

What are you going to say, "He's not the nuclear physicist, he's the medical doctor"? .

Someone in charge of the reprinting of this book wrote to Laurel. Now Laurel was faced with quite a dilemma: We've been saying for years that he's a nuclear physicist. Now are we going to change it? If we change it now, that's like saying, "Wait a minute, last time he was a nuclear physicist!"

Someone suggested a "scientific researcher." and Laurel wrote back and said, "No, I think we'd better stick with the 'atomic physicist.' I don't really like it, but you know, what exactly is an atomic physicist in any case? We can justify it; and certainly he is a physicist or something. . . ."

(The Church has recently used the fact that Laurel Sullivan said that to claim that she and not Hubbard was the source of the atomic physicist claim!)

Joycelyn [Armstrong's wife] was still working for me at that time and we were copying madly to get all we could to Garrison.

Every day I was going to Costa Mesa in Orange County, where Omar Garrison lived, and I would take down a box of materials that I

---

*Mary Sue Hubbard, in the later trial over these "Armstrong" documents, admitted Hubbard was not a nuclear physicist and that she and Hubbard used to laugh about this claim being on the cover of *All About Radiation*.

had copied. Then I'd take down a box of shirts or books or whatever, until we got down to the point where we had, box by box, totally moved the whole place out.

The last thing we had was Joycelyn's bicycle, and we made like we were going off for a ride. We were gone.

I had Garrison's truck, parked right on the corner. I went and threw the bike in it. We went to Garrison's place in Costa Mesa. The following morning we left and went to their place in Utah and stayed there for a week.

It was the great escape right under their noses.

During the next several months Gerry Armstrong and his wife were subjected to intense harassment, which included being followed by several Church-hired private eyes virtually everywhere they went; sometimes they were followed by three cars at a time.

When he turned his photos of Hubbard, which he legitimately possessed, over to collector Wilhite for a promise of six thousand dollars, Church agents subsequently got to Wilhite and "persuaded" him to hand the photos over to them.

Continues Armstrong:

So within 24 hours of that I called [attorney] Mike Flynn and, within a couple of days, flew out to Boston to see him. . . .

The more I looked, the more rotten Hubbard became. Also, the more the organization appeared more and more as nothing but illusion and evil.

Just look at the stuff they write. Just how distant it is from the truth. And the ends to which they'll go to create "truth." To make illusion appear to be something else.

The illusion, for example, of *Battlefield Earth* as a "legitimate" blockbuster bestseller. . . .

One of the wealthy Scientologists, by the name of Ellie Bolger, apparently paid a huge amount of money to the organization, which they then disbursed to staff members to go down to B. Dalton or whatever and buy the book.

(The publicity from Hubbard's science fiction "best-seller" would, in turn, get the Dianetics book selling. And this, plus a multi-million dollar TV and billboard advertising campaign, has in fact managed to get it back onto *The New York Times'* best-seller list four times in 1986. According to Hubbard's plan, "raw meat" would subsequently pour into Scientology orgs).

****

Wrote Hubbard, "The highest one can attain to truth is to attain to his own illusions." He later explained: "Reality is basically agreement."

Whether these statements are true or not, they perhaps reveal a great deal about the workings of L. Ron Hubbard's mind:

His illusions are supreme! Agree with them and voila! You have reality!

In his lectures and his writings he seldom looked back to see what he had originated. If he had bothered to listen to his own lectures, especially the early ones, he would have been flabbergasted at how much he had revealed about himself. In a Philadelphia Doctorate Course lecture he states:

> Now you say you have to be absolutely truthful. Sincerety is the main thing, and truthfulness is the main thing and don't lie to anybody . . . and you'll get ahead. Brother you sure will. You'll get ahead right on that cycle of action, right toward zero! . . . It's a trap not being able to prevaricate. . . .
>
> You say, "You know, I was downtown the other day and there's this Yellow Taxi there, and I started to step into this Yellow Taxi, and I'll be a son of a gun if there wasn't a big ape sitting in the back smoking a cigar. And I closed the door and walked on down the street."
>
> This makes life more colorful!

His prevarications about his life, certainly make him more colorful!

22

"Operation Juggernaut": Hubbard Targets Boston Lawyer

"The yapping gnats [critics of Scientology] that are trying to stop our juggernaut will be disposed of."—CAPTAIN MARK YEAGER (one of the top five elite)

An attorney from a small Boston law office, Michael Flynn, was unexpectedly thrust into an arena where, as the then number one "enemy" of L. Ron Hubbard, he was confronted with a highly organized and financed operation to "destroy" him.

Michael Flynn thought he was just handling a minor case concerning return of a small amount of money owed when he agreed to represent a young former Commodore's Messenger called La Venda Van Shaick in 1979. But because of what Ms. Van Schaik knew about L. Ron Hubbard, the fact that she had gone to an attorney would have set bells ringing and red lights flashing at Hubbard's desert hideout.

Hubbard wrote often about "the enemy" and the "war" that was being fought, which required vigilance, dedication and sacrifice on the part of his troops. Hubbard perceived Flynn as, and declared him to be, the key agent of these enemies.

"Enemy" Michael Flynn's story was told to me by Flynn himself, during lunches and dinners at the time of the Armstrong trial. He was by this time Armstrong's trial attorney.

A brief resume of these talks, and the papers for a lawsuit later filed by Flynn vs. Hubbard, will give a better idea of the battle that was culminating in the courtroom of Judge Brekenridge, on the fifth floor of the Superior Court Building in Los Angeles, in the summer of 1984. This was the scene of the Armstrong trial.

MICHAEL FLYNN VS. L. RON HUBBARD

Michael Flynn claimed in his July 1985 lawsuit that there is a *written* conspiracy by Hubbard, and his Church acting as his agents, to "destroy" him, beginning from July, 1979 to the present.

He targeted Hubbard in his lawsuit because "Hubbard executed and established an elaborate *written* plan to exercise total dictatorial control over Scientology and others."

Hubbard did this, he claimed, by ordering that each of the "Scientology" corporations be chartered, and he ordered that:

> a. Undated resignations be signed by all Corporate Officers, which he kept in his possession, and whenever any board members contested his orders he simply replaced them with others who would comply.
>
> b. He was a required signatory on all bank accounts in Scientology over $5,000.
>
> c. Hubbard supervised and controlled, in writing, an organization called the "Guardian's Office," which he placed in each of the "Scientology" Corporations for the purpose of enforcing his express daily orders, which orders he routinely called the "daily battle plan."

The G.O. was established and directed by Hubbard and was trained on manuals written by Hubbard,

****

Another organization now doing Hubbard's bidding is Religious Technology Corporation, to which he assigned all Scientology trademarks, but RTC also was fully controlled by him through the use of written advance resignations.

The policy "legitimizing" Hubbard's agent's pursuit of Flynn was this one written by Hubbard:

> This is the correct procedure.
> 1. Spot who is attacking us.
> 2. Start investigating them promptly for *felonies* or worse, using our professionals, not outside agencies.

3. Double curve our reply by saying we welcome an investigation of them.

4. *Start feeding lurid, blood, sex crimes, actual evidence on the at-tackers to the press.* (Emphasis supplied)

Don't ever submit to an investigation of us. Make it rough on our attackers all the way.

Another policy Hubbard ordered enforced:

The following is a list of the successful . . . actions used by [our] in-telligence [bureau]:

—Using . . . [sex] on someone high in government to seduce them over to our side.

—Infiltrating in every group with an end to getting documents.

—Covert third partying with forged or phony signatures.

—Anonymous third partying [stirring up trouble by a campaign of disinformation]. Particularly the Internal Revenue Service . . .

—Direct theft of documents

—Impersonating a reporter over the phone.

The following are possibilities for collecting data:

1. Infiltration
2. Bribery
3. Buying information
4. Robbery
5. Blackmail

It was pursuant to this and other secret policies laid down by Hubbard that the offenses against him had been committed, claims Flynn.

A special operation in line with the above policies and the "Fair Game policy" was designed for Michael Flynn.

It was labelled "Operation Juggernaut" and designed to "lie [about], cheat, sue and destroy" him.

Under "Juggernaut," he claims, the following acts were performed:

His offices were infiltrated and files of his were stolen. He was har-assed and some of his clients were "separated" from him. He was de-famed privately as well as in the news-media. Nine groundless law suits were brought against him, his colleagues and employees, as well as nine groundless bar complaints to get him disbarred.

Flynn further claims that water was placed in the fuel tanks of his private airplane in an attempt to murder him. There were four occu-pants in the plane at that time, including his son.

He further claims that they threatened to poison him and kidnap his clients.

False and defamatory articles were published and distributed at his law school, and false information was given to the IRS in order to initiate an investigation. Furthermore, Hubbard's agents illegally obtained his bank account information; placed dirt in his car's fuel tank; and generally engaged in a wholesale pattern of abusive and harassive behaviour.

All this began in July of 1979 when a young woman, La Venda Van Schaick, approached him for the purpose of obtaining a "refund" of monies paid by her to the Church in the amount of approximately $12,800.

Flynn sent a letter to the G.O. for the purpose of obtaining the money and thus saving the trouble of a lawsuit. They refused to pay.

Within days of that letter being sent, Hubbard, who was then in Hemet, California, ordered an immediate infiltration of Flynn's law office by G.O. agent Chuck Malone, who sought employment from Flynn posing as a private investigator. His purpose was in fact to steal records and information. He was not hired.

Van Schaick began to be followed and her apartment kept under surveillance, and numerous strange and suspicious circumstances occurred in her daily life. The same was the case with Flynn.

Yet all that had happened to cause all this fuss was one letter regarding a refund!

Then there was a reply: a letter stating that the Church would be willing to pay approximately 50 percent of the funds paid by Van Schaick. But it also suggested that Van Schaick should not sue the Church for the balance of the funds because she had an extensive drug history, and had had "three abortions," had "attempted suicide," had severe mental problems, and had signed an agreement never to sue the Church or Hubbard.

All this stuff, she told Flynn, had come from her pre-clear folder which had been divulged under the strictest of confidence.

Flynn then began getting anonymous calls suggesting that representing Van Schaick was a "dangerous matter," that no one "messes with the Church," and that if he had any doubts about this he should contact others who had "sought to interfere with Scientology."

Then at a small airport, he claims, he observed "unidentified individuals viewing his small plane and seeking information about it."

On about October 19, 1979, he was flying this plane to South Bend, Indiana, when the engine began to malfunction at approximately

8,000 feet and lost power entirely for a period of some time, and he was forced to land at an airport nearby. He claims that he subsequently discovered large amounts of water in the fuel tanks, "although prior to take-off I had gone through the normal pre-flight examination without discovering any water."

Flynn believes that water balloons, which are designed to dissolve about an hour after takeoff, were placed in the tanks by G.O. agents, on the express orders of Hubbard.

Over the next several months Van Schaick was subjected to numerous incidents, such as having her house surveilled, being run off the road in her car, numerous telephone calls to her neighbors suggesting that she was an unfit mother, calls to her employer "resulting in a loss of her job as a waitress," attempts to convince her that Flynn was engaged in harassive behavior against her in an attempt to have her fire him, and attempts to separate her from her husband.

Specifically, a G.O. agent named Gary Klinger was sent from Los Angeles to convince her that the "harassive things" that were being done to her were being done by Flynn.

During November of 1979 nine of the highest officials of the G.O. were convicted of a variety of crimes, and approximately 30,000 documents, seized by the FBI during the raids in 1977, were released to the general public.

Flynn sent an employee to the Federal Court in Washington to copy thousands of these documents.

In large part, the documents verified the allegations made by Van Schaick: namely, that Hubbard and the G.O. were responsible for the numerous inexplicable and harassive incidents that had occurred during the prior several months.

These documents revealed a 15 year pattern of infiltration, burglary, bugging, and harassment.

There were hundreds of documents showing the use of confidential information by Scientology corporations against individuals such as Van Schaick, used often for the purpose of frustrating their legal rights. Some even specified the use of extortion and blackmail.

The documents also showed extensive use of the legal system to harass with groundless lawsuits. Cases that were known to have no merit were nevertheless brought in order to break individuals financially with legal expenses.

When Flynn filed Van Schaick's lawsuit in December of 1979, the publicity regarding it swamped his office with hundreds of telephone calls over a period of weeks.

These calls were from a variety of individuals and organizations. They included parents whose children had committed suicide while in Scientology, individuals who had been hospitalized as a result of Scientology involvement, authors, reporters, individuals who had allegedly been defrauded by Scientology, and various law enforcement agencies.

Lawsuits and bar complaints by the Church against Flynn and his clients began to accumulate, and as time progressed were being dismissed as groundless, but at large expense to those concerned.

Between August 1979 and up to at least September of 1981 the G.O., pursuant to Hubbard's orders, had stolen, according to Flynn, 20,000 documents either directly from his office or from a trash dumpster. Many had been taken directly from his office files.

These were used for, among other things, blocking the legal remedies of Flynn's clients, presumably to ruin his practice. They were also used in aid of all the other tricks played on Flynn himself.

Between January and May of 1980 hundreds of former Scientology members contacted Flynn seeking legal help. Tonja Burden was one of these.

Flynn filed suit on her behalf in Federal Court.

Flynn was placed on top of the Church's "enemies list," a copy of which he received from someone who had recently left the Church.

In June of 1978, with some 50 cases being planned against them, the G.O. offered 1.6 million dollars to resolve all existing and pending litigation. Flynn accepted "in a good faith effort to resolve the entire matter," since the G.O. promised reform and the financial costs of conducting all the litigation was staggering. Flynn having "expended $200,000" of his own money already.

During the summer of 1981, however, Hubbard replaced some of his agents in the G.O. with several young members of the "Commodore's Messenger Org." They had served Hubbard personally throughout their teenage years, were approximately 21 to 22 years of age, and fanatical adherents to Hubbard. These included David Miscavage.

They were put there, according to Flynn's affidavit, to command the G.O., because Hubbard believed that Flynn had not been harassed intensively enough, and Hubbard intended to increase the level of "attack" and harassment of him.

These messengers, on Hubbard's orders, adopted a plan to broaden "Operation Juggernaut" and to conduct an all-out campaign against Flynn in order to bring him to his knees. This involved a highly secretive written plan adopted by Hubbard, Miscavige, Starkey, and others to attack Flynn "on all fronts."

A meeting of lawyers in Atlanta, Georgia, was convened by Miscavige and Starkey. Its purpose was to initiate Bar complaints, lawsuits, depositions, motions for disqualification, contempt motions and other forms of harassment making use of the judicial system.

Using the materials taken from Flynn since 1979, and some expensive legal talent, they devised various plots and put them into practice. These involved setting depositions on dates when Flynn was tied up in other hearings, and timing notices so that Flynn appeared to be in contempt.

Over the entire period of Flynn's involvement with Hubbard and the Church, Hubbard had, through the G.O., and through several attorneys retained by the G.O., systematically libelled and slandered him on hundreds of occasions, says Flynn.

All this, he claims, was in furtherance of Hubbard's policy to "manufacture" libelous evidence, to "originate a black PR campaign," and to use "covert third partying."

****

One of the most interesting accusations against Flynn is that he is part of a world-wide "Rockefeller conspiracy to destroy religion."

Apparently an offspring of one of the Rockefeller cousins (a great great granddaughter of John D.) had become involved, in some fashion, with Scientology. This seems to have precipitated a response by her parents.

Author Stewart Lamont (*Religion Inc.*) who initially planned to write a pro-Scientology book but later turned critical, has this to say:

> [The Scientologists] point to a donation of $135,000 in 1983 from the New York Community Trust to the Scientology Victims' Defense Fund, which is administered from Flynn's office. At first sight it looks peculiar. The Scientologists claim the source of the recommendation was an aide of Nelson Rockefeller who had clashed with them back in 1955 over the "Siberia Bill." Heber Jentzsch raged, "The Rockefellers backed Adolph Hitler during the Second World War and continue this tradition in present time by backing straw men who attack religious men and churches. Let it be known that we will vindicate Mr. Hubbard's good name regardless of how many Rockefeller mega-bucks are poured into the Fund." These turn out to be weasel words when the donation is measured alongside the hundreds of others of a humanitarian nature handed out by the Trust, totalling $350 million. There is

already ample evidence in this book to show that many people have
been harmed by Scientology and surely Michael Flynn, whatever his
motives, cannot be expected to go on year after year charging nothing
for his services. Until auditing is given free the Scientologists have little to complain about. Their attempts to discredit Flynn have been
shown up time and again to be sleazy and inaccurate at the very least.

23

A Fabricated Past
Revealed in a "Wog Court"

The Church side (representing Hubbard) was confident they would win the Armstrong trial.

In their view, the biographical documents clearly belonged to L. Ron Hubbard. Mary Sue Hubbard (newly out of prison, on parole) had clear claims as custodian. She claimed that her personal letters being viewed by the likes of Flynn was tantamount to "mental rape."

The documents were now in the custody of the Los Angeles Superior Court.

The Church pushed for a speedy trial, without doubt at the insistence of Hubbard, who was secretly living a couple of hours by car from the courthouse, near San Luis Obispo.

Any legal maneuvers, at any cost, were being used to ensure those documents were speedily returned "to their proper owner."

While the legal bureau fought hard for the return of "L. Ron Hubbard's" documents, Church P.R. would later make claims that key documents involved were really "forgeries" planted by Government covert agencies.

****

June of 1984 the trial began.

Gerry Armstrong was on the stand for a couple of weeks, and the trial lasted a total of almost ten weeks. There were star witnesses brought on by Flynn who had known Hubbard and his finances intimately; and the Church brought on Mary Sue and even an old sea captain called Thomas Moulton, who had served under Hubbard during World War II in the Northeast Pacific.

I was fascinated by the proceedings and disclosures on the day when I first attended, and after that I took off almost every day from my other pursuits and drove the 50 miles to L.A. to attend.

The opening arguments were presented for the Church and Mary Sue Hubbard, by Mr. Litt:

CHURCH'S OPENING ARGUMENT (excerpts):
This case is, in essence, a very simple case. . . .

Mr. Armstrong in 1980, January or February of 1980, petitioned within the church that he be appointed as an archivist to gather up materials that had been found in a building on church property in a place out in the desert called Gilman Hot Springs; it turned out to be a great deal of old material of the Hubbards which had been gathered. . . .

Now the issue, therefore, is whether or not these private materials can be used by the defendant and introduced into evidence.

They want these documents spread on the public record for use elsewhere. That is the intended objective.

It is a desire to intrude into these private materials so that they can be used in the public arena in various ways, as part of what is in reality a very intense litigation battle and public battle that exists throughout the country in which Mr. Flynn is involved with the Church. . . .

The documents themselves are private and are entitled to the privacy protections of the United States Constitution. . . .

ARMSTRONG'S OPENING ARGUMENT (by Flynn):
It was Armstrong's decision what to shred. He decided that it [the box presented to him by Brenda Black] shouldn't be shredded on an initial cursory examination of the box, and entrusted it to Laurel Sullivan.

Subsequently, after a lot of other documents in the identical location were shredded, Armstrong began to look through the box of documents and he found documents which he thought had, quote unquote, historical significance, and he wrote a petition to Hubbard asking for permission to collect more materials to complete the biography project which had actually started in 1973; and the evidence will be that Laurel Sullivan and others actually began this biography project. But at various times it got derailed because the authors, one being a fellow named Peter Thompkins, wouldn't write what Hubbard wanted him to write.

So eventually we come up to 1980. Armstrong writes to Hubbard. Hubbard approves it.

Now, there is a key fact here and that is that Hubbard is in the process of fleeing because his wife has just been convicted of a felony, [for] obstruction of justice for stealing documents.

There is a pending grand jury in New York for the frame-up of a journalist named Paulette Cooper, and there is evidence which was then coming in before the grand jury relative to Hubbard's involvement in that frame-up.

So Hubbard flees. Subsequently he is determined to be concealing himself as a fugitive, and a federal court in Tampa so found.

What happened is, because Mary Sue was on her way to jail, because L. Ron Hubbard was fleeing, the control mechanisms within the organization over the documents deteriorated, and no one really knew (and to this day, no one knows, other than Gerald Armstrong) really what is in those documents (Because he is the one—other than Omar Garrison—who has analyzed them for years).

So, even Hubbard himself did not precisely know what was in the documents.

Now, Armstrong begins to go through them. He gets the approval from Hubbard. . . .

Over a period of a year and a half Armstrong collects all these documents, turning them over to Garrison and Garrison begins to analyze them to write the book, and starts writing the book.

Well, Garrison . . . realizes that the representations that were made by L. Ron Hubbard right from his birth, right up to present . . . are false. . . .

So Garrison realizes that he can't write what Hubbard wants him to write. In fact, if he follows any journalistic ethics, he's got to write just precisely the opposite. . . .

Garrison rightfully, pursuant to the contract, has the documents.

Armstrong has no documents at this point. He's turned them over to Garrison. For the next five to six months he works intermittently with Garrison on the biography project because they are now going to write their own, and he also works for a law firm part-time, subsequently full time.

Thereafter the Church begins to harass Mr. Armstrong. . . . They do a number of things. For one thing they make him an enemy . . . and subject him to the Fair Game Doctrine.

They steal photographs from him. They are his own private materials which he actually received from a third party. . . .

They steal other materials from him, which had nothing to do with the collection of documents when he was working for Hubbard. . . .

At the same time, in light of a lot of harassive acts, he's got very paranoid. He's seen what the Church of Scientology, over the last decade, has done to other people.

He knows what they have done in the criminal cases and he is fearful . . . that they are going to kill him.

He then goes back to Garrison and tells Garrison what is happening, and Garrison then gives him the documents . . . to defend himself.

So he goes to a lawyer; namely me, and the reason he came to me is because he thought that there were very few lawyers in the United States who were willing to litigate against the organization because of what they do. . . .

Garrison, for the next year thereafter, continues to prepare the biography and, in fact, comes up with a publisher. Approximately one month after Mr. Garrison comes up with a publisher for the true biography of L. Ron Hubbard, he is approached by the Church of Scientology, attorneys for Mr. Hubbard, and they basically make a deal with Mr. Garrison. He will give them back every document he has. He will not disseminate the information. He will give them back the manuscript that he has done based upon the documents, and he will be paid some, I understand, $240,000, or something in that range . . . in the summer of 1983. . . .

There has been no conversion by Mr. Armstrong because he received the documents rightfully from Mr. Garrison . . ."

****

Regarding his examination of Mary Sue Hubbard, Michael Flynn told me he had mixed feelings about her. She had, after all, been made a scapegoat for Hubbard's crimes. On the other hand, she had done what she had done, and she did appear completely unrepentant.

In his examination of her, he did not appear to pull any punches.

During one exchange regarding Guardian's Order 121669, (covered in Chapter 11) where Mary Sue states:

". . . make full use of all files of the organization to affect your major target [prevent infiltration]. These include personnel files, Ethics files, Dead files, central files, training files, *processing files* (emphasis added), and requests for refunds."

The office headed by her, the G.O., had files that contained a great deal of information taken from "processing files"—also known as "preclear or "auditing" files:

Q (by Flynn). Let me show you a document dated 27 September, 1978, Info re_____[a woman's name omitted in respect of her right to privacy].

_____'s auditing files start with July, 1963. It goes on to state who she has been promiscuous with, and masturbating with coffee grounds, that type of thing. Do you see that Mrs. Hubbard?

A. I see that Mr. Flynn.

Later Flynn, referring to a document shown the witness, and reading:

Q. "Dear Cindy. Here is pertinent data from _____'s PC [pre-clear] files." Do you know who Cindy is?

A. She might refer to Cindy Raymond? She worked in the U.S. Guardian's Office.

Q. And there are references on the first page about the person's, for example, masturbation practices, that type of thing, Mrs. Hubbard, at the bottom.

Witness: Yes. Have you got something on masturbation? You keep asking me about it.

Q (by Flynn). Do you think your organization was interested in those types of things from a person's PC files, Mrs. Hubbard?

A. I don't know. I am looking at documents that seem to indicate that there was, yes, Mr. Flynn.

Prior to, and following, this testimony there was testimony from witnesses that pre-clear folder information was routinely "culled" for discreditable information and sent to "B-1", (the intelligence bureau).

However, one high executive, Lymon Spurlock, testified that this practice was discovered by him to have been done by Guardian's Office personnel, who had since been removed. He added that he had never done such a thing and was outraged to discover such a practice.

Later, however, Nancy Dincalsy testified that she personally culled pre-clears' folders daily and sent "overt" lists to B-1 of the Guardian's Office, per standard orders. She also said that she worked as an auditor alongside Lymon Spurlock for many months, and that she observed him also "culling" PC folders for the G.O. daily.

****

Captain Moulton was brought into the courtroom like the inevitable surprise witness in "Perry Mason." He was a handsome man in his late sixties, over six feet tall, with grey hair and a walking cane. The very image of a retired ship's captain.

Church lawyer Petersen wore an air of triumph as he marched in with Captain Moulton. With a grin, he made an aside to Flynn. I couldn't hear the words exactly. It wasn't necessary. The intent was apparent: "We got'cha now!"

It quickly became clear that Captain Moulton had served under Hubbard off the coast of Oregon, after which Hubbard was removed by Admiral Fletcher for exceeding orders.

Q [by Flynn]. He told you that he was injured by a Japanese Machine gun?

Captain Moulton affirmed that Hubbard had told him the story while they were in training together in a naval training class in Miami.

Q. Did he describe the circumstances under which he was injured by the Japanese machine gun?

A. Yes, in some detail; not entirely.

Q. What did he tell you?

A. That he had been in Soerabaja at the time the Japanese came in or in the area of Soerabaja and that he had spent some time in the hills in back of Soerabaja after the Japanese had occupied it.

Q. Now, Soerabaja was where, sir?

A. That is a port on the north part of Java in the Dutch East Indies.

Q. So you understood from Captain Hubbard that he had been in Java fighting the Japanese and was hit by machine gun fire?

A. Not quite as you put it. He had been landed, so he told me, in Java from a destroyer named the *Edsel* and had made his way across the land to Soerabaja, and that is when the place was occupied. When the Japanese came in, he took off into the hills and lived up in the jungle for some time until he made an escape from there.

Q. So you believed Captain Hubbard at the time?

A. Certainly, I had no reason not to.

Q. Did he tell you exactly where he was hit by the machine gun fire?

A. In the back, in the area of the kidneys, I believe on the right side.

Q. And did he tell you how long he remained hiding in the hills with these machine gun wounds before he was removed from the combat area?

A. I know that he told me he had made his escape eventually to Australia. I don't know just when it was. He apparently—he and another chap—sailed a life raft, I believe, to near Australia where they were picked up by a British or Australian destroyer.

Q. And that would have been late 1941, early 1942?

A. I would imagine it would have to have been early '42 because it would take some time from December 7.

Flynn proceeded to show naval documents, one stating that Hubbard was ordered to Australia on November 24, 1941; and that he left on December 8, 1941, from the United States.

Captain Moulton noted that if Hubbard had been in intelligence, the document may have been spurious. "An intelligence officer, as far as I know, has all sorts of spurious letters stating where he is sent, when he got there."*

Another document was shown to him dated 14 February 1942, by the United States Naval Attaché, Melborne, Australia (the 14th of February would have been roughly one month to six weeks after he was "shot in the back by a Japanese machine gun").

Captain Moulton, like so many others, had been completely taken in by Hubbard.

Flynn read part of it aloud:

> The subject officer arrived in Brisbane via SS *President Polk.* He reported to me that he was ordered to Manila for duty and asked for permission to leave the SS *President Polk* until a vessel offering a more direct route to his destination was available. I authorized him to remain in Brisbane for future transportation to his destination. By assuming unauthorized authority and attempting to perform duties for which he has no qualifications, he became *the source of much trouble.* [Emphasis added]
>
> On February 11, 1942, I sent him dispatch orders to report to the commanding officer USS *Chaumont* for passage to the United States, and upon arrival report to the commandant 12th Naval District for future assignment. This officer is not satisfactory for independent duty assignment. He is garrulous and tries to give impressions of his importance. He also seems to think that he has unusual ability in most lines. These characteristics indicate that he will require close supervision for satisfactory performance of any intelligence duty.

****

Witness Kima Douglass (Hubbard's "medical officer," 1976–1980).

---

*This is the essence of the Church's "sheepdipping" argument. They have an "expert" who claims that the "Armstrong" documents relating to Hubbard's military history were falsely placed there because Hubbard was in "counter-intelligence."

In fact, Hubbard spent less than two months in "intelligence" in Australia. Evidence indicates that he was engaged in the routing of ship movements.

Other documents which put Hubbard in a better light were also among the Armstrong documents, but the Church makes no claim that these were "sheepdipped." The "sheepdip" argument was apparently not given any weight by the Court.

Q. Now you have heard the name Ernest Hartwell mentioned?

A. Yes.

Q. Were you in the presence of L. Ron Hubbard when he ordered Hartwell's PC files to be culled?

A. Yes. He ordered all crimes listed and signed by the Hartwells before they left. I believe the Hartwells were incarcerated for a short while.

Q. Now did you have the opportunity to personally observe L. Ron Hubbard between 1978 and 1980 with regard to irrational or abusive behavior?

A. Yes.

Q. And what did you observe?

A. That there were times he was irrational.

Q. And was he abusive?

A. I saw him hit one person. I consider that abusive.

Q. Did you personally see L. Ron Hubbard order people to the RPF for minor infractions?

A. Yes, I was one of them.

Q. And what was the infraction?

A. I had—LRH had a kidney infection. We had taken the urine test in to be examined. The urine test came back that he had streptococci bacteria and we started treating him with an antibiotic.

Six weeks later I did another test because he wasn't getting any better. We brought the test to him and it showed different bacterial infection at that point and he was very angry and put me in the RPF.

It was not an RPF as it later became when Gerry [Armstrong] was there. I was put into Coventry for five weeks and nobody was allowed to talk to me.

Q. Are you familiar with the culling of PC files at winter headquarters and summer headquarters at the Special Unit in 1977 and 1978?

A. Yes.

Q. And what did you see with regard to the culling of PC folders?

A. I have culled PC folders myself. I have seen other staff members culling folders.

Q. For what purpose?

A. To be sent to B-1.

Q. And B-1 is what?

A. Guardian Office Intel.

Q. And were you personally familiar with his health history?

A. Yes.

Q. And because of the nature of the technology of Scientology, his health history was held out to the public as being superior?

A. Yes.

Q. And you know in fact that his health history was not what it was represented to the public as; is that correct?

A. Correct.

Q. And on at least one occasion you had saved L. Ron Hubbard's life from a pulmonary embolism?

A. I got him into hospital. That saved his life. I didn't personally save his life, but he had refused to go into a hospital and I countermanded his order, which was not a normal thing. But I countermanded his order on two occasions. That was one of them. . . .

Q. Mrs. Douglas, was one of your duties inside the organization to courier cash around the world?

A. Yes.

Q. Have you crossed the United States in excess of a hundred times with millions of dollars in cash?

A. Well, not in excess of a hundred. I have not crossed the United States in excess of a hundred. It has been under that, but I have couriered hundreds of thousands of dollars out of the United States during the period when it was actually a criminal action, as it was actually only a certain amount of money to be allowed to be taken out of the United States, and I knowingly committed that action at the time.

Q. Do you know where the money was taken at that time?

A. To the ship. I took them to the flagship myself.

Q. Did you ever take any moneys to Luxembourg or Lichtenstein bank accounts:

A. Yes, I did.

Q. And what amounts?

A. I took some from the ship. I can't give you an exact amount, but it was in excess of a million.

Q. Did he suffer from pneumonia?

A. Once in a while.

The Court: *Did he have any bullet wounds in his back?*

Witness: *No sir.*

****

Cross-examination of Howard Shomer by Mr. Harris (attorney for the Church):

Let me ask you this, Mr. Shomer: You say when Mr. Hubbard was aboard the ship, he controlled everything under all circumstances all the time; is that right?

A. That is too inclusive. I mean, I didn't have to ask him to go to the bathroom.

Q. You said he managed it all the time.

A. We are talking about—let's get down to brass tacks. We are talking about the management of the Scientology network throughout the world, and everything that had any importance to do with the running of the ship otherwise, that he was the almighty that ran everything, yes. . . .

Homer's daughter, who had been brought into the Sea Org by him with the highest of dreams and hopes for them both, had been forced to "disconnect" from him after he left.

He had escaped from Gilman Hot Springs in early 1983. There he had been left under guard after an all night "gang bang sec check." During that night he was supposed to confess that he was an agent of the FBI, CIA, IRS, KGB or whatever. When he failed to do so, David Miscavige and Steve Marlowe spat in his face. They were both chewing chaw tobacco in anticipation of the event.

****

On the 20th of June, 1984, Judge Brekenridge issued his findings. He found that the Church and Mary Sue Hubbard were not to have their documents back "at least at this time," and that they could be made public (unless specifically ordered sealed) and used as admissible evidence in current, pending and future court cases.

Armstrong was entitled to judgment and costs.

He found that neither "The Church" nor Mary Sue Hubbard had "clean hands."

He found that Armstrong had permission to have the materials and acted properly in turning them over to Garrison, and later retrieving them for his defense, and then turning them over to Flynn as his attorney.

JUDGE BREKENRIDGE (excerpts):

As indicated by its factual findings, the court finds the testimony of Gerald and Joycelyn Armstrong, Laurel Sullivan, Nancy Dincalcis, Edward Walters, Omar Garrison, Kima Douglas, and Howard Shomer to be credible, extremely persuasive, and the defense of privilege or justification established and corroborated by this evidence. . . . In all critical and important matters their testimony was precise, accurate and rang true. The picture painted by these former dedicated Scientologists, all of whom were intimately involved with LRH, or Mary Sue Hubbard, of the Scientology Organization, is on the one hand pathetic, and on the other, outrageous.

Each of these persons literally gave years of his or her respective life in support of a man, LRH, and his ideas. Each has manifested a waste and loss or frustration which is incapable of description. Each has broken with the movement for a variety of reasons, but at the same time, each is still bound by the knowledge that the Church has in its possession his or her most inner thoughts and confessions, all recorded in "pre-clear" (P.C.) folders, or other security files of the organization, and that the Church or its minions is fully capable of intimidation or other physical or psychological abuse if it suits their ends. The record is replete with evidence of such abuse.

In addition to violating and abusing its own members' civil rights, the organization over the years with its "Fair Game" doctrine has harassed and abused those persons not in the Church whom it perceives as enemies.

The organization clearly is schizophrenic and paranoid, and this bizarre combination seems to be a reflection of its founder LRH. The evidence portrays a man who has been virtually a pathological liar when it comes to his history, background and achievements.*

The writings and documents in evidence additionally reflect his egoism, greed, avarice, lust for power, and vindictiveness and aggressiveness against persons perceived by him to be disloyal or hostile.

At the same time it appears that he is charismatic and highly capable of motivating, organizing, controlling, manipulating, and inspiring his adherents.

He is referred to during the trial as a "genius," a "revered person," a man who was "viewed by his followers in awe."

Obviously, he is and has been a very complex person, and that complexity is further reflected in his alter ego, the Church of Scientology. Notwithstanding protestations to the contrary, this court is satisfied that LRH runs the Church in all ways through the Sea Organization, his role of Commodore, and the Commodore's Messengers.

He has, of course, chosen to go into "seclusion," but he maintains contact and control through his top messengers.

Seclusion has its light and dark side too. It adds to his mystique, and yet shields him from accountability and subpoena and service of summons.

LRH's wife, Mary Sue Hubbard, is also a plaintiff herein. On the one hand she certainly appeared to be a pathetic individual. She was forced from her post as Controller, convicted and imprisoned as a felon, and deserted by her husband.

---

*On "60 Minutes" Heber Jenzsch, the Church's senior public relations man, responded to the Judge's comments about Hubbard. He had, he said, investigated what was the basis of the judge's decision: "I traced back where that came from, this whole schizophrenic/paranoia concept that he has. It came from Interpol. At that time the president of Interpol was a former SS officer, Paul Dickoph. And to find that Judge Brekenridge quoted a Nazi SS officer as the authority on Scientology, I find unconscionable!"

On the other hand her credibility leaves much to be desired. She struck the familiar pose of not seeing, hearing, or knowing any evil. Yet she was the head of the Guardian's Office for years and, among other things, authored the famous order "G.O. 121669" which directed the culling of supposedly confidential P.C. files/folders for purposes of internal security.

In her testimony she expressed the feeling that defendant [Armstrong] subjected her to mental rape.

In determining whether the defendant [Armstrong] reasonably invaded Mrs. Hubbard's privacy, the court is satisfied the invasion was slight, and the reasons and justification for defendant's conduct manifest.

The court is satisfied that he did not unreasonably intrude upon Mrs. Hubbard's privacy under the circumstances by in effect simply making his knowledge that of his attorneys.

It is, of course, rather ironic that the person who authorized G.O. 121669 should complain about an invasion of privacy.

The practice of culling supposedly confidential "P.C. folders or files" to obtain information for purposes of intimidation and/or harassment is repugnant and outrageous.

The Guardian's Office, which plaintiff headed, was no respecter of anyone's civil rights, particularly that of privacy.

****

Over the years L. Ron Hubbard had called a lot of people a lot of names by public declaration. All these names: anti-social personality, rock-slammer, chaos merchant, degraded being, psychotic, 1.1., ethics bait and, most commonly, suppressive person, had been used with such devastating consequences to the people so labelled. Name calling is indeed powerful, especially when done by a person granted great authority.

When Judge Brekenridge called him a pathological liar and paranoid schizophrenic, I believe Hubbard's rage was boundless. He had tasted his own medicine and found it exceedingly bitter.

L. Ron Hubbard on his grandfather's ranch in Nebraska around 1916.

As a boy scout.

Ron the Aviator.

In his twenties, possibly in New York's Greenwich Village.

An early episode of looking for gold.

In Puerto Rico.

As a Scientology executive in the early fifties.

In his office at Saint Hill Manor in the early 1960s.

Ron the Biker: sporting a new Motorcycle at Saint Hill.

"Making breakthroughs" in horticulture.

On the grounds at Saint Hill.

The Commodore fondling his "Kools" on board the flagship *Apollo*, during the early 1970s.

Hubbard at typewriter in a hideaway apartment in Queens, New York, in 1973.

Grooms Gerry Armstrong (left foreground) and Pat Broker (right foreground) with brides (c. 1975). Hubbard (at the head of the table with package) is as ever accompanied by a group of messengers (in this instance, dressed for the occasion).

With brides.

Messengers dressed as bridesmaids. Pat Broker's future bride, Anne, is in the right foreground. She and Pat are now the new leaders of Hubbard's Church.

In disguise, doing photography
in Queens, 1973.

Ron the Movie Director.
Taken during the late 1970s near
Hemet, California.

Ron the Gambler. The most
recent available photograph,
taken around 1979 in the
Riverside County desert.

Aleister Crowley,
self-proclaimed "Beast 666."

The most displayed of Hubbard's
official photos.

"Crowley's Cross" as depicted on his
Tarot Cards.

The Scientology cross, displayed in all
Churches and worn around the neck
of their ministers.

UPDATE FOR THE SECOND EDITION

PART ONE

This section focuses on deception, manipulation, intimidation, harassment, and "financial settlement": as utilized as methods for "forwarding Scientology."

24

Shutting up the "Yapping Gnats"

One of David Miscavige's senior executives, Mark Yeager, announced in early 1986 that, "the little yapping gnats" would be "disposed of." (The "gnats" were human beings, and the "yapping" was the act of communication. Just what "disposed of" meant was yet to be seen.)

Then it happened. On December 11th, 1986 that prediction came true. It was a victory for Scientology organization. Twenty-two people—many of whom had worked personally with Hubbard—were to talk no more.

The already substantial list of those "persuaded," to shut up had grown even longer.

THE SILENCING OF ATTORNEY FLYNN
AND CLIENTS

A total sum of five and a half million dollars was paid to Michael Flynn to settle all the claims of all of his clients. (A highly questionable form of settlement since each client had a separate and specific lawsuit, and a mass or "block" settlement would place excessive pressure on the individual client to settle along with the other clients.) The monetary amounts, and terms of the agreement, were supposed to remain confidential.

258

(This "settlement"—as with other cash "settlements" with those harassed or harmed by Scientology, who had then initiated lawsuits or threatened to bring criminal charges—was kept secret from the general membership.)

GERRY ARMSTRONG TALKS DESPITE THREATS

Among Flynn's clients, of course, was Gerry Armstrong who later revealed the terms of the court settlement, citing violations of the settlement terms by Scientology, and pointing out that conditions required in the settlement amounted to violations of fundamental constitutional rights, and also would require him to participate in the obstruction of justice.

Per the settlement agreement of 11 December 1986:

"Plaintiff [Armstrong] agrees never to create or publish or attempt to publish, and/or assist another to create for publication by means of magazine, article, book or other similar form, any writing or to broadcast or to assist another to create, write, film or video tape or audio tape any show, program or movie, or to grant interviews or discuss with others, concerning their experiences with the Church of Scientology, or concerning their personal or indirectly acquired knowledge or information concerning the Church of Scientology, L. Ron Hubbard or any of the organizations . . . Plaintiff further agrees that he will maintain strict confidentiality and silence with respect to his experiences with the Church of Scientology and any knowledge or information he may have concerning the Church of Scientology, L. Ron Hubbard, or any of the organizations . . ."

Part of this settlement was the agreement to return any and all documents relating to Scientology or L. Ron Hubbard.

Scientology was especially concerned about Hubbard's handwritten hypnotic "Affirmations" [See Part One, Chapter 3, 'L. Ron and the Beast,' and Part Two, Chapter 5, 'Sara Speaks'], specifically stipulating the return of "All originals and copies of documents commonly known as the 'Affirmations' written by L. Ron Hubbard . . ."

The settlement agreement goes on to state that:

"Plaintiff agrees that he will not voluntarily assist or cooperate with any person adverse to Scientology in any proceeding against any of the Scientology organizations . . ." And that, "Plaintiff agrees not to testify or otherwise participate in any other judicial, administrative or legislative proceeding adverse to Scientology . . ." And that, "Plaintiff SHALL NOT MAKE HIMSELF AMENABLE TO SERVICE OF ANY SUCH SUBPOENA [emphasis added] in a manner which invalidates the intent of this provision."

****

Gerry Armstrong, in challenging Scientology's efforts to silence him, has demonstrated considerable courage.

It is ironic that the very same Human Spirit that Scientology gives lip-service to exalting to superman-type states, is that Human Spirit which—at its best—gives Scientology so much trouble.

25

Scientology's War on Your Right to Know

In Nazi Germany piles of books were incinerated. Since Scientology exists in a "Wog world" where book burning is currently considered bad taste, such a colorful exercise in "putting ethics in" would be very bad public relations. Other methods however have proven quite effective.

It became painfully obvious, during the early stages of the writing of 'L. Ron Hubbard, Messiah or Madman?' that publishing houses were AFRAID of Scientology. Scientology's army of "secret agents," goons in leather jackets, and well paid lawyers diligently carrying out Hubbard's policy of harassment through frivolous litigation, DO have an impact.

There were many efforts made to stop 'Messiah or Madman?' from reaching publication. (These included a bizarre attempt to have Publisher Lyle Stuart jailed for refusing to provide a pre-publication copy of the book, and an unsuccessful attempt by a private investigator to bribe the printer into providing an advance copy. An attempt for which he was later arrested by the New Jersey Police.) When all efforts failed, Scientology set into motion Hubbard's policies on the use of "black propaganda."

'CONFIDENTIAL PR Series issue 24' of 30 May 1974 states:

"If there will be a long term threat, you are to immediately evaluate and originate a black PR campaign to destroy the person's repute, and to discredit them so thoroughly that they will be ostracized."

This reflects another earlier policy issue, 'CONFIDENTIAL Issue II, Battle Tactics' of 16 February 1969, which states:

"The prize is 'public opinion' where press is concerned. The only safe public opinion to head for is they love us and are in a frenzy of hate against the enemy, this means standard wartime propaganda is what one is doing . . . Know the mores of your public opinion, what they hate. That's the enemy. What they love. That's you.

"You preserve the image or increase it of your own troops and degrade the image of the enemy to beast level."

As Hubbard explained in his Confidential 'Hubbard Communications Office Ethics Manual': **"Throw enough mud and some will stick."**

The pattern was always the same. I'd bring up a specific point or issue on a TV or radio program and then, rather than addressing that specific point or issue, the Scientology representative present would launch an attack on my character. The message was simple: I was a bad fellow and shouldn't be listened to.*

In a "pack" sent out to the media by Scientology there is an entire section describing "Bent Corydon's Criminal Mind." I have been described many times by senior PR man Heber Jentzsch as a "criminal." On one occasion a Scientology representative stated that I "tried to kill the sheriff of Riverside four times."

Of course, it takes time to respond to accusations, or to explain that Scientology—per policy—believes in "attacking the attacker" rather than discussing actual issues.

(It's noteworthy that Mr. Jentzsch was Scientology's main public spokesman before and during the time when Hubbard's wife and ten others were sent to federal prison for the commission of felonies. He actively spoke in their defense.)

****

I responded to Mr. Jentzsch's name calling, during a talk show at which we were both guests, by stating that in my opinion he was a "professional liar." (It is well documented that Scientology has drilled its agents in the art of lying effectively.) I was shortly thereafter sued for slander.

On the same show another Scientology PR man joined in, accusing

---

* These policies are very much alive and in force today. In fact they are listed on the "President of the Church of Scientology Checksheet." (In November 1988 "President" Heber Jentzsch had to "re-tread" that course.)

me of being a criminal. I responded by expressing my opinion that he too was a professional liar. You guessed it—another libel suit.

On another talk show I mentioned the incident described in the Preface of this book, where a Scientology thug arrived at my place of work looking for me. Failing to locate me he proceeded to beat up a friend of mine. On the same show I mentioned that a very large individual approached me after a radio appearance and, pointing his finger in my face, made threatening remarks. This occurred in a parking lot and was witnessed by a security guard. This person was walking with Heber Jentzsch, before coming over to me as I was about to get into my car. For describing this incident on the radio I was **again** sued for libel.

All these suits are frivolous, being applications of Hubbard's policy of using groundless lawsuits for purposes of HARASSMENT. And they are also very expensive to defend.

****

TV and radio stations, newspapers and magazines, are quite aware of Scientology's litigious inclinations. This combined with a "black propaganda campaign" against a critic or dissenter, can be effective in preventing a free public discussion of Scientology.

****

When two television stations backed off under pressure from the Scientology organization at the last minute, and agreed not to have me as a guest on their talk shows, it became the subject of a newspaper article.

The newspaper was the 'Willamette Week' and the article was entitled 'The Science of Intimidation'. Karen Hollister, a trustee of the Church of Scientology of Portland, was asked by the article's author about Scientology's approach to critics. She responded, "We're not a turn-the-other-cheek religion."

Florida's Pulitzer Prize winning St. Petersburg Times, a newspaper with more backbone than most, went forward with an article on 'Messiah or Madman?' in spite of receiving a letter from a Scientology lawyer which exclaimed:

"It has come to our attention that . . . [you] are considering publication of a review of 'L. Ron Hubbard, Messiah or Madman?' by Bent Corydon . . .

"If you forward one of his lies you will find yourself in court facing not only libel and slander charges, but also charges for conspiracy to violate civil rights. If you publish anything at all on it, you may still find yourself defending charges in court . . . We know a whole lot more about your institution and motives than you think."

The 'Times' was later awarded a 'Laurel' by the Columbia Journalism Review' for 'journalistic grace under pressure', for not buckling under to Scientology.

(Certainly, the Fair Game aspect of the Scientology is known by many in the media. For example I was provided with limousine service and body guards, when traveling to and from an interview with Mariette Hartley on CBS's 'Morning' program. Protection which I appreciated.)

Limitations on space in this Update make it impossible to detail all of Scientology's efforts to silence 'Messiah or Madman?' The following bizarre, yet so "Scientological" case will have to complete this section.

FIRE-BOMBING?

KPPC-FM of Pasadena City College was warned of the possibility of a fire-bombing of the station were I to be allowed on the air. The warning was provided by Shirley Young, the same individual who'd stated during a radio interview, that I had 'tried to kill the sheriff of Riverside four times."

Quoting from a letter from Larry Mantle, News and Public Affairs Director:

"In response to your request for a recounting of Shirley Young's statement on possible violence resulting from the broadcast, I will recall her comment to the best of my ability. Ms. Young, who is the President of the Church of Scientology of Los Angeles, warned me prior to the program over the phone, that your appearance on another station had led an angry church member to fire bomb the station. I did not ask her to elaborate and merely stated that we cannot worry about what a mentally unstable person may do in response to a given program. We did not discuss the issue any further. However, our General Manager Rod Foster told me Ms. Young had mentioned the alleged fire bombing incident to him in a conversation the following day."

To my knowledge no fire bombing ever occurred.

Scientology later denied any such statements were made.

****

It is impossible to determine the number of indirect or direct threats made to the media by agents of Scientology for the purpose of preventing discussion of Hubbard and Scientology, since those intimidated by such threats, understandably—out of fear and shame—usually say nothing.

26

Biographer Russell Miller's 'Bare Faced Messiah'

Russell Miller is no stranger to Scientology harassment. His biography of Hubbard entitled, "The Bare Faced Messiah" was initially published in England several months after the release of 'Messiah or Madman?' in America. It had to contend with a number of harassive lawsuits; however Scientology was unsuccessful in stopping the book, and it was released throughout the British Commonwealth.

Predictably, Miller became **Fair Game,** and the target of a black-propaganda campaign.

Quoting from the London Sunday Times:

"The author of a new book on the Church of Scientology cult has become the victim of a bizarre plot to link him with the murder of a communist pop singer.

". . . Miller . . . is facing the new attempt to discredit him three months after an attempt was made to frame him for the murder of a South London private detective."

Shortly afterwards (November '87) another article appeared in the 'Times' of London. It was entitled, "Cult's Private Detective Fires on Journalists":

"A private detective, employed by the Church of Scientology to investigate one of its opponents [Miller], shot at a 'Sunday Times' reporter and photographer and threatened to kill them last week."

SCIENTOLOGY COMMENTS ON
MILLER'S BIOGRAPHY

Reverend Norman Starkey, whose position of leadership in Scientology is second only to David Miscavige, had this to say about Russell Miller's biography when questioned at a legal deposition:

"That scumbag book is full of bullshit man, and you know it. It's full of bullshit. Goddamn fucking bullshit."*

Scientology's "hierarchy" may be crude, and undeveloped intellectually, but they are also very determined and have access to enormous amounts of money, and the highest-priced legal counsel.

They challenged Miller's biography in the United States on a legal technicality and won a much disputed court decision. As a result "Bare Faced Messiah" is available in Great Britain, and throughout the United Kingdom, but difficult to find in the USA (see Bibliography).

---

*David Miscavige is now firmly established as Scientology's absolute dictator. Miscavige is a high school drop-out and heavy smoker of filterless Camel cigarettes, Mirroring his Mentor, L. Ron Hubbard, he is said to have a proclivity for angry outbursts and a fondness for profane language . . . As—obviously—does his "second-in-command" Reverend Starkey.

27

The L. Ron Hubbard "22 Best Sellers and More To Come" PR Image Scam:

Or How To Be A Bestselling Author By Buying Your Own Books

I knew something was wrong when walking into a B. Daltons, the same 'Mission Earth' book (Vol. 6) that had been a "bestseller" two weeks earlier had now been drastically discounted. It was being sold for $6.95 marked down from $18.95. That seemed odd. And it happened to each "bestselling" copy of the 'Mission Earth' series.

Conversations with some bookstore managers and owners, and with a former "Bridge" executive, seemed to confirm that Scientology was living up to its "psychological profile" and was using deception to make "in-roads."

In April of 1990 a well researched article by the San Diego Union appeared. It was revealing.

The very extensive article, beginning on the front page, was entitled, 'Hubbard Hot-Author Status Called Illusion'.

The essence of the story was that, beginning with Hubbard's first recent "bestseller", 'Battlefield Earth', Scientology discovered that it could BUY bestseller status by simply dispersing funds to be used to buy L. Ron Hubbard's books, during a given week, so that a "bestseller" would be created.

And it worked. A VERY expensive PR trick, but nonetheless, TECHNICALLY SPEAKING, it made Hubbard a "best-selling author" many times over.

The 'Union' article begins:

"In 1981, St. Martin's Press was offered a sure thing.

"L. Ron Hubbard, a pulp writer turned religious leader, had written his first science-fiction novel in more than 30 years. If St. Martin's published it, Hubbard's aides promised the firm, subsidiary organizations of the Church of Scientology would buy at least 15,000 copies.

" 'Battlefield Earth,' priced at $24.95, was released the next year in hardcover, rare for a science-fiction title. Despite mixed reviews, the book quickly sold 120,000 copies—enough to place it on the 'New York Times' best-seller list.

" 'Five, six, seven people at a time would come in, with cash in hand, buying the book,' said Dave Dutton, of Dutton's Books, a group of four stores in the Los Angeles area. 'They'd blindly ask for the book. They would buy two or three copies at a time with fifty dollar bills. I had the suspicion that there was something not quite right about it.'

"Dutton only suspected what others claim to know for fact. The book's sudden success, say dozens of former Scientologists and book dealers, was the result of a church plan to create the illusion of L. Ron Hubbard as a hot author. The Church, they say, sustains the myth—15 'New York Times' best-sellers and counting—through dubious marketing tactics and the manipulation of an obedient flock of consumers . . .

"Spokeswomen for B. Dalton and Waldenbooks, the nation's two largest book chains, declined to reveal sales figures for Hubbard's books . . .

" 'Who buys his books?'' said [Waldenbooks spokeswomen] Tyson. 'We don't know.'

"A former employee of both chains offered a more detailed answer.

" 'What we used to see was the L. Ron Hubbard people coming into the chains, buying books out so we'd have to reorder them. Then they'd return them,' said Eleanor Lang, a former manager of a B.

Dalton store in the New York City area and an ex-employee of Waldenbooks.

" 'Throughout the 80s, B. Dalton had a very liberal return policy,' said Lang, now the publicist for the science-fiction publisher Tor Books. 'Once a chain store sells through a book, it's on their computer as having been sold. Once on the computer, the computer automatically reorders it.'

"That might help explain why hard-cover copies of the 'Mission Earth' series are a common sight these days on remainder shelves.

" 'This month Bridge Publications quietly offered remainder houses 237,848 'Mission Earth' hardcovers,' publisher Lyle Stuart wrote last July ['89] in his newsletter 'Hot News', under the heading 'That Scientology Scam.' 'This must be something of a record in the remainder industry.'

"Bridge's senior vice president Mark McKinstry denied that the publisher [Bridge] buys Hubbard's books to inflate sales.

"A spokeswoman for the Church of Scientology also denied that Hubbard's followers are required to purchase Hubbard's books.

" 'You can't make anyone buy anything,' said Lisa Goodman, from the L. Ron Hubbard Office of Public Relations in Los Angeles. 'People spend their money because they want to.'

"Goodman also denied any official link between the Church and Bridge Publications.

" 'We have a relationship like any client and publisher,' Goodman said. 'It's just probably closer.'

"Much closer, say former Scientologists.

"Vicki Aznaran, the former inspector general for the Religious Technology Center, said the Center controls a Scientology network of 419 subsidiary groups, including Bridge Publications. Her claim was echoed by several other former church officials.

"The Religious Technology Center is listed prominently in an internal church document, 'The Command Chart of Scientology.'

"The Religious Technology Center appears at the top of the chart. One level below, within a body called the Watchdog Committee is the office of the executive director of the Church of Scientology International. And one level below that is Bridge Publications.

"Appearing on the same level of the chart as Bridge is the church's public relations office."

****

In a 1989 issue of 'Hotline,' a Church of Scientology newsletter for its publicists, a new public relations strategy was announced:

"For the first time in the history of Dianetics and Scientology the PR [Public Relations] positioning of L. Ron Hubbard (LRH) has been established.

" 'One of The Most Acclaimed and Widely Read Authors of All Time'.

"For it is LRH's image on which all the rest of our expansion depends. To the degree that LRH is made the stable terminal in society, people will reach for his books and services and we can get them on the Bridge to Total Freedom."

That the survival of planet earth and the spiritual progress of Humankind might be dependent on "making L. Ron Hubbard look good" is absurd to the extreme.

Is there a root or origin to this priority and obsession?

****

On Sunday the 23rd of June 1990 the Los Angeles Times began its six part series of articles on Scientology. (Including one on Hubbard's bogus "best-seller" status.)

In large print atop a full page devoted entirely to the subject of L. Ron Hubbard, appeared a quote that Scientology has tried desperately to suppress. It may be revealing with regard to Hubbard's earliest and fundamental motives for creating Scientology:

"I have high hopes of smashing my name into history with such violence that it will take a legendary form . . . That goal is the real goal as far as I'm concerned."

So wrote L. Ron Hubbard to his first wife Polly, 8 years before creating the vehicle with which he intended to attain not only fantastic personal power during his lifetime, but also a kind of immortality.

PART II

"UNSCRUPULOUS WOMANIZER" TO "ASCENDED MESSIAH"

(1. Events prior to the Sea Org; 2. A different perspective of Hubbard, the Sea Org, and "the tech"; 3. Hubbard's death; 4. Update Part Two; and Addendum, with expanded glossary.)

1

Sex Magick in Pasadena

Hubbard, when he wanted to turn it on, could display a tremendous amount of charisma. One victim of that charisma was the late Jack Parsons, an acknowledged genius in the field of chemistry, and a major figure in the first stirrings of rocket research at Cal Tech, which later became the Jet Propulsion Laboratory.

He was killed in an explosion in 1952.

There is a crater on the moon named after him.

****

Parson's spiritual leader was none other than the Master Therion, the "Beast 666," Aleister Crowley.

In 1942 Crowley appointed Parsons head of the California branch of the O.T.O. (Ordo Templi Orientis). A Gnostic mass was performed each day in the lodge's temple.

Then, in fall of 1945, Parsons met L. Ron Hubbard. He was VERY impressed.

He wrote to Crowley in February 1946:

> About three months ago I met Ron . . . a writer and explorer of whom I had known for some time. . . . He is a gentleman; he has red hair, green eyes, is honest and intelligent, and we have become great friends. He moved in with me about two months ago, and although Maggy [Sara Northrup's nickname—short for magic] and I are still friendly, she has transferred her sexual affections to Ron.
>
> Although Ron has no formal training in magick, he has an extraordinary amount of experience and understanding in the field. From some of his experiences I deduce that he is in direct touch with some higher intelligence, possibly his guardian angel. Ron appears to have some

sort of highly developed astral vision. He described his angel as a beautiful winged woman with red hair, whom he calls the Empress, and who has guided him through his life, and saved him many times.

He is the most Thelemic* person I have ever met and is in complete accord with our own principles. He is also interested in establishing the New Aeon but for cogent reasons I have not introduced him to the Lodge.

We are pooling our resources in a partnership which will act as a limited company to control our business ventures. I think I have made a great gain, and as Maggy and I are the best of friends there is little loss. I cared for her deeply but I have no desire to control her emotions, and I can, I hope, control my own.

I need a magical partner. I have many experiments in mind. . . . The next time I tie up with a woman it will be on my own terms.

Parsons had, according to the account, decided to attempt an "incarnation of Babalon." By performing various rituals an ordinary human spirit would be denied access to the unborn child, and "Babalon"—which apparently was considered to be an aspect of what amounted to "the mother of the universe"—was to be invited to possess the fetus.**

In order to obtain a woman prepared to bear this magical child, Parsons and Hubbard engaged themselves for eleven days of rituals. These do not seem to have produced any marked result until January 14th when, so Parsons said, Hubbard had a candle knocked out of his hand. Parsons went on to record that Hubbard called him, "and we observed a brownish yellow light about seven feet high. I brandished a magical sword and it disappeared. Ron's right arm was paralyzed the rest of the night."

On the following night, so Parsons said, Hubbard had a vision of an enemy of the O.T.O. and, "attacked the figure and pinned it to the door with four throwing knives with which he is an expert."

All this seemed to achieve its desired result and, on January 18th, Parsons found the girl who was prepared to become the mother of Babalon, and to go through the required incantation rituals. During

---

*"Do what thou wilt," or "follow thine own true path," despite the arbitraries, mores and restrictions of society.
**From *The Rites of Modern Occult Magic*, by Francis King. Researcher Jon Atack notes that in the "Book of Babalon," attributed to Parsons by the O.T.O., it states that Hubbard participated in an attempt to create a "moonchild," and engaged in sex-magick rituals. Sex-magick, it should be noted, is part of the Crowleyan system.

these rituals, which took place on the first three days of March 1946, Parsons was High Priest and had sexual intercourse with the girl, while Hubbard who was present acted as skryer, seer, or clairvoyant and described what was supposed to be happening on the astral plane.

Parsons wrote to Crowley:

> She turned up one night after the conclusion of the operation, and has been with me since, although she may go back to New York next week. She has red hair and slant green eyes as specified. If she returns she will be dedicated as I am dedicated! All or Nothing—I have no other terms. She is an artist, strong minded and determined, with strong masculine characteristics and a fanatical independence. . . .
>
> I am under command of extreme secrecy. I have had the most important—devastating experience of my life between February second and March fourth. I believe it was the result of the ninth degree working with the girl . . . . I have been in direct touch with the One who is most Holy and Beautiful as mentioned in the Book of The Law. I cannot write the name at present. First instructions were received direct through Ron, the Seer. I have followed them to the letter. There was a desire for incarnation. I do not yet know the vehicle, but it will come to me, bringing a secret sign. I am to act as instructor guardian guide for nine months; then it will be loosed upon the world. That's all I can say now. . . .

Crowley responded:

> You have me completely puzzled by your remarks. I thought I had a most morbid imagination, as good as any man's, but it seems I have not. I cannot form the slightest idea what you can possibly mean.

To Karl Germer, the man who would assume leadership of the O.T.O. after Crowley's death the following year, he wrote:

> Apparently Parsons and Hubbard or somebody is producing a moonchild. I get fairly frantic when I contemplate the idiocy of these louts.

He added in another letter:

> It seems to me on the information of our brethren in California that—if we may assume them to be accurate—Frater 210 [Parsons] has committed . . . errors. He has got a miraculous illumination which

rhymes with nothing, and he has apparently lost all his personal independence. From our brother's account he has given away both his girl and his money—apparently it's the ordinary confidence trick.

****

On February 20, 1946, Hubbard and Parsons formally established Allied Enterprises. Hubbard contributed $1,183.91, Parsons $20,970.80. The idea was to purchase sailing vessels on the east coast of the United States and sail them to the west coast for resale at a profit.

Ron and Sara traveled to Miami and made payments toward the purchase of two boats. This, plus other expenses, depleted all the funds of Allied Enterprises.

By this time Parsons, thoroughly disenchanted with Hubbard, filed suit in an attempt to recover as much of his original investment as possible.

And, combining the forces of magick with those of the United States Coast Guard, he managed to see to it that at least a small amount of justice would be done.

Parsons wrote to Crowley in July of 1946:

> Hubbard attempted to escape me by sailing at 5 P.M., and I performed a full evocation to Bartzabel [the spirit of Mars or War] within the circle at 8 P.M. At the same time, so far as I can check, his ship was struck by a sudden squall off the coast, which ripped off his sails and forced him back to port, where I took the boat in custody. . . . Here I am in Miami pursuing the children of my folly; they cannot move without going to jail. However I am afraid that most of the money has already been dissipated.

Sara described the sea adventure to me in some detail. She and Hubbard had fought desperately to survive, drawing upon all they knew about sailing.

While she acknowledges and regrets her part in inspiring Jack Parsons' great anger at her, she denies any wrongdoing on her part regarding business and finances. She speaks of "Jack" with fondness and admiration as a "truly great man."

****

Alva Rogers was a frequent visitor to Parsons' house before and during the time Hubbard was there:

In ads placed in the local paper Jack specified that only bohemians, artists, musicians, atheists, anarchists, and other exotic types need apply for rooms—any mundane soul would be unceremoniously rejected. This ad, needless to say, caused quite a flap in Pasadena when it appeared. . . .

Betty (short for Elizabeth, Sara Northrup's middle name), who had been living with Jack for a number of years, complemented him admirably. She was young, blonde, very attractive, full of joie de vivre, thoughtful, humorous, generous. . . .

However, this tranquil relationship was soon to be exposed to pressures, from a most surprising source, that would lead to its disintegration. . . .

It all began on an otherwise undistinguished day in the late fall of '45 when we got word that L. Ron Hubbard was planning to wait out his terminal leave from the Navy at "The Parsonage." . . .

Ron arrived on a Sunday, driving an oldish Packard and hauling a house trailer which he parked on the grounds behind the house. He originally intended staying in the trailer, but within a few days someone moved out of the house and he moved in.

I liked Ron from the first. He was of medium build, red headed, wore horned rim glasses, and had a tremendously engaging personality. For several weeks he dominated the scene with his wit and inexhaustible fund of anecdotes. About the only thing he seemed to take seriously and be prideful of was his membership in the Explorers Club (of which he was the youngest member) which he had received after leading an expedition into the wilds of South America. . . . Unfortunately, Ron's reputation for spinning tall tales (both off and on the printed page) made for a certain degree of skepticism in the minds of his audience. At any rate, he told one hell of a good story. . . .

Ron was a persuasive and unscrupulous charmer, not only in a social group, but with the ladies. He was so persuasive and charmingly unscrupulous that within a matter of a few weeks he brought the entire house of Parsons down around poor Jack's ears. He did this by the simple expedient of taking over Jack's girl for extended periods of time. . . .

Ron was supposedly his best friend, and this was more than Jack was willing to tolerate. . . .

As events progressed Jack found it increasingly difficult to keep his mind on anything else . . . the atmosphere around the house became supercharged with tension; Jack began to show more and more strain, and the effort to disguise his metamorphosis from an emotionless

Crowleyite "superman" to a jealously-ridden human being became hopeless. . . .*

The final, desperate act on Jack's part to reverse events and salvage something of the past from the ruin that stared him in the face occurred in the still, early hours of a bleak morning in December. Our room was just across the hall from Jack's apartment . . . which also doubled as a temple, or whatever, of the O.T.O. We were brought out of a sound sleep by some weird and disturbing noises seemingly coming from Jack's room. . . . The noise—which, by this time, we could tell was a sort of chant—drew us inexorably to the door which we pushed open a little further in order to better see what was going on. What we saw I'll never forget, although I find it hard to describe in any detail. The room, in which I had been before, was decorated in a manner typical to an occultist's lair. . . . It was dimly lit and smokey from the pungent incense; Jack was draped in a black robe and stood with his back to us, his arms outstretched, in the center of a pentagram before some sort of altar. . . . His voice . . . rose and fell in a rhythmic chant . . . delivered with such passionate intensity that its meaning was frighteningly obvious. After this brief and uninvited glimpse into the blackest and most secret center of a tortured man's soul, we quietly withdrew and returned to our room where we spent the balance of the night discussing in whispers what we had just witnessed. . . .

A few months later when I was back in L.A. for a brief visit I had occasion to call the Parsonage to check with Betty [Sara]. . . . The phone was answered by Jack, [who] with obviously false casualness, informed me that Betty wasn't there—she and Ron had gone to Yosemite for a short vacation. . . .

They did get married and maintained this conjugal relationship until some time after Ron flipped into Dianetics, and Betty got fed up with him and precipitated a messy divorce case that made a splash on the front pages of the L.A. papers.

****

On August the 10, 1946, in Chestertown, Maryland, Hubbard married Sara Northrup (Betty), making him a bigamist. A year and four months later the divorce from his first wife Margaret became final. Just before the divorce, during the time he was living with Sara in a

---

*The Church of Scientology in 1970, in response to an article in the Sunday London *Times*, claimed that Hubbard had been sent in to break up the California O.T.O. as an agent of Naval Intelligence.

Sixteen years later, apparently in response to inquiries from author Stewart Lamont, they claimed that Hubbard was acting as a special agent for the Los Angeles police at the time!

trailer in Port Orchard, Washington, he visited Margaret and their son, Ron Jr., at Bremerton, just a few miles away. He had begun work on what was to finally become *Dianetics, the Original Thesis* and, ultimately in May of 1950, an expanded book designed to win a broad popular readership, *Dianetics, The Modern Science of Mental Health.*

Dianetics was a "new form of psycho-therapy" capable, he claimed, of "resolving the problems of the human mind" and producing the "optimum individual."

2

The Origins of Dianetics

"Man had no inkling whatever of Dianetics. None. This was a bolt from the blue."—L. RON HUBBARD

Hubbard was an experienced practitioner of hypnotism, although he lacked the credentials he often put forth to impress people, such as that he had "studied hypnotism in India."

According to Ron Jr., during the thirties and forties, his father had an obsessive interest in hypnosis, self-hypnosis, and unconscious states generally; he also claims his father had practiced drug-hypnosis on him and his mother (Hubbard's first wife).

Judging from the contents of various documents revealed in the Armstrong trial, and from my conversation with Hubbard's second wife, Sara Northrup, Hubbard appears to have grandly "discombobulated" his bodily—and perhaps his mental—health by his own indulgence in self-hypnosis: inducing physical ills to escape having to attend school or perform unpleasant assignments during his years in the Navy, and attempting to "self-implant" his way into becoming a social and sexual "superman." (See Part I, Chapter 3 and Part II, Chapter 5.)

It has been suggested by some that Hubbard's motivation for developing Dianetics, at least partially, stemmed from the hope that someone would use it to "handle his case." This view holds that Dianetics (and even Scientology) was mainly Hubbard's written account of what was wrong with himself, and attempts to resolve it.

There may be some truth to this opinion, but I think Hubbard was much too egotistical to seriously consider that a "humanoid" could ever help him in any significant way. Still, his writings about "what's wrong with the human race" appear to reflect what seems to have been wrong with him more than what was wrong with others.

I doubt, however, if he would ever have admitted this, even to himself.

Nonetheless, Hubbard was a human being, and his foibles did parallel—to some extent—those of his fellow human beings. Enough so that his description of these things—always depicted as the other fellow's—did "ring bells" for many.

****

An essential idea in Dianetics is that people, as a result of the travails of living, become, in effect, partially hypnotized. Dianetics, Hubbard explained, was here to "de-hypnotize" them.

Besides Hubbard's own experiences and, perhaps, obsessions, the main sources for what became Dianetics appear to have been psychoanalysis, abreaction therapy, and General Semantics.

In his Dianetic—and later Scientology—writings and lectures, he made a habit of lambasting any and all competition in the field of the mental therapy. In the early days, however, he did make a few positive—or at least non-denunciatory—statements about other systems and therapies.

In his "Critique on Psycho-analysis," he even acknowledges a debt to the work of Sigmund Freud:

> It is necessary to understand first that we are actually indebted to psycho-analysis and its originator, the debarred doctor, Sigmund Freud. . . .
>
> In the earliest beginnings of Dianetics, it is possible to trace a considerable psycho-analytic influence. There was the matter of ransacking the past; the matter of believing with Freud that if one could talk over his difficulties they would alleviate; and there was the matter of concentrating on early childhood. Our first improvement on psychoanalysis consisted in the abandonment of talk alone and the direct address to the incident in its own area of time as a mental image picture susceptible to erasure. But many of the things that Freud thought might exist, such as "life in the womb," "birth trauma" we . . . confirmed and for them provided an adequate alleviation.

Although Hubbard sought to create the impression that Dianetics was the first psycho-therapy to "address the [traumatic] incident in its own area of time", other therapies predating Dianetics had done so as standard procedure.

One from which Hubbard drew in his development of Dianetics, was abreaction therapy.

Abreaction is a psychiatric term defined as, "the process of bringing to consciousness and, thus, to adequate expression, material that has been unconscious. It includes not only the recollection of forgotten memories and experience, but also their reliving with appropriate emotional display and discharge of effect. This process is usually facilitated by the patient's gaining awareness of the causal relationship between the previously undischarged emotion and his symptoms."

And Dianetics *is* a form of abreaction therapy.

Bringing to the surface—becoming conscious of—previously buried "traumatic" experiences is the essence of all abreactive therapy including Dianetics.

Such input, according to Dianetics, is preserved in a kind of storehouse of "unconsciousness," pain and shock, called the "reactive mind," or "bank."

This "reactive mind" is defined, according to Hubbard, as "a portion of the person's mind that works on a totally stimulus response basis [i.e., it *REACTS*], which [thus] is not under his volitional control, and which exerts force and the power of command over his awareness, purposes, thoughts, body and actions. . . ."

This "mind" is hidden from the person's awareness. Since it consists of recordings of times of "unconsciousness," the person tends to become "unconscious"—groggy or sleepy—when attempting to recall or review any part of it.

A key concept in Dianetics is that of the "engram." This is defined by Hubbard as "a mental image picture of a moment of pain and unconsciousness." It includes shock and a condition of being "overwhelmed."

In his book *The Mneme*, published in 1923, Richard Semon used the term "engram," which he considered to be a "stimulus impression" that could be reactivated by the recurrence of "the energetic conditions which ruled at the generation of the engram."

In this connection Sara Northrup, Hubbard's second wife, married to him during the inception of Dianetics, mentioned that prior to Dianetics he was familiar with Simon's work.

Semon describes such an "engram" from his own experience:

We were once standing by the Bay of Naples . . . nearby an organ grinder played on a large barrel organ; a peculiar smell of oil reached us . . . the sun was beating pitilessly on our backs; and our boots in which we had been tramping for hours, pinched us. Many years after a similar smell of oil (reactivated) most vividly the . . . engram of Capri, and even now this smell has invariably the same effect.

From the view of Dianetic theory this would be a very "light" engram indeed. Obviously it contains some, but not much, "unconsciousness." A "heavy" engram would be one that contained much pain or shock and full "unconsciousness." The person might be able to recall before and after the occurrence of the engram, but not during—anymore than a hypnotic subject can recall receiving instructions from a hypnotist while in a deep trance.

Hubbard, apparently, decided to group all of a person's engrams into one category or "mind," which he called the "reactive mind." This was a "stimulus response mind." The engrams contained in this mind could be reactivated (or as Hubbard preferred, "restimulated" or "keyed-in") when "the perceptics of an engram were approximated."

"The reactive mind is a literal stimulus response mind. Given a certain stimulus it gives a certain response."

A "key in" is defined by Hubbard as:

. . . an analytical moment in which the perceptics of an engram are approximated, thus restimulating the engram or bringing it into action, the present time perceptics being erroneously interpreted by the reactive mind to mean that the same condition which produced the pain once before is now again at hand.

For example: A father and his five-year-old daughter are enjoying an amusement park boat ride. (Twelve years prior the father's speed boat overturned and he was severely injured in the stomach, almost drowned, and finally came to in a hospital). Now unexpectedly, their little boat stalls and tilts on a steep angle. He finds himself gasping for breath and terrified for the safety of his daughter. Within seconds an attendant corrects the mechanical problem and they are all safe. Shortly afterwards the little girl wants lunch, and Daddy agrees but eats nothing. The "key-in" is lingering. . . .

A key-in is also described by Hubbard as ". . . conscious level experiences that sort of stick and the individual doesn't quite know why."

According to Dianetic theory these "stick points" can accumulate, reducing the "aliveness" of the individual.

A fellow is walking down the street feeling moderately cheerful. Unexpectedly a car zooms by honking its horn. Suddenly, for no apparent reason, his leg muscles tense up and he feels a bit of grief. For the rest of the afternoon he feels a bit "out of it."

In the reactive mind "unexpected fast car" and "honking horn" equal tightened leg muscles and a slight feeling of loss.

Children are more likely to be "keyed-in" than adults. Witness the ease with which they cry, etc.; but they also tend to key-out easily, having yet to accumulate the array of key-ins that make life dim and joyless for many adults.

Now this whole idea of "key-in" is a manifestation of what is called "A = A thinking."

Which brings us to the works of noted Polish mathematician Count Alfred Korzybski, the founder of General Semantics.

Foremost among the subjects from which Hubbard "cut and pasted," was the General Semantics of Count Alfred Korzybski (as distinct from Semantics, the study of words and meaning). General Semantics stresses the distinction between words and objects. Most basically, it stresses the distinction between one thing, idea, or event, and another thing, idea, or event. In other words enhancing people's ability to *differentiate* as a means of improving human behavior.

Sara Hubbard told me: "In the late forties I remember reading *Science and Sanity* by Korzybski, and I became very excited. So I began reading aloud to Ron and he became very excited too. He became a big follower of Korzybski. . . .

"And much of Dianetics relates back to the works of Count Alfred Korzybski. . . ."

According to Korzybski, "non-identifying," or "non A = A thinking," is the optimum way to behave. It is the way a person who is "clear" is supposed to behave. For example, the fellow who almost drowned in a speed boat accident years earlier—now "cleared"—wouldn't involuntarily react with an inappropriate degree of alarm when the small boat he's riding in with his little daughter suddenly tilts and stalls. Nor would there by any unwanted emotions or physical discomfort following the event.

From the introduction of *Manhood of Humanity*, Korzybski's first book:

> Alfred Korzybski was born in Warsaw, Poland, in 1879 into one of the oldest families of Poland. He was trained as an engineer. . . . His

first book *Manhood of Humanity* was published in 1921, and after its publication he decided to remain in the U.S. and develop the methodology by which his new theory could be applied. These studies culminated in *Science and Sanity* in 1933. He was the Founder and Director of the Institute of General Semantics, established in 1938 as the center for training in his work, and continued to lecture and write until his death in March 1950. . . . He studied human evaluations in science and mathematics and in psychiatry, "at their best and at their worst," as he put it, from the standpoint of human predictability and human survival. . . .

He insisted that anyone who wished to could enroll for a seminar. "Because a general method of evaluation" he said, "has to work with anybody in any human activity or it's no good." Professors, doctors, psychiatrists, artists, researchers, young college students, businessmen, social workers, laborers, etc., all sat in the same classes. This may all sound chaotic; it was effective.

In 1935 Korzybski described the A = A phenomenon of a hurtful experience in much the same way as Hubbard did, many years later, in Dianetics.

HUBBARD:

[The reactive mind] is basically that area of occlusion which the [person] is unable to contact and contains within itself a total identification of all things with all things.

A = A = A, anything equals anything equals anything. This is the way the reactive mind thinks, irrationally identifying thoughts, people, objects, experiences, statements, etc.

KORZYBSKI:

We notice also that the effect of the stimulus S or A is not identical with the stimulus itself, a falling stone is not identical with the pain we feel when the stone falls on our foot.

The engram concept (roughly equivalent to "hurt"), and the idea of "reviving" (Hubbard uses the word "restimulating") "old similar hurts" (Hubbard uses "earlier similar engrams"), and "elimination of immature evaluations" (Hubbard calls it "erasure of non-optimum postulates") are also described well by Korzybski:

> . . . we begin to check this . . . process of piling up "hurts" on
> "hurts" . . . new "hurts" in practice are usually related or similar to the
> old ones; they would "revive" the older hurts. Accordingly he could
> not only "live through"* the older experiences but at once revive
> them, and after re-evaluation, eliminate the harmful effects.

Chains of incidents, earlier similar incidents, and incidents containing "hurts" (engrams), are fundamental to Dianetic processing.

Korzybski even describes the basic theory of the psycho-galvanometer (precursor of the E-meter):

> Psychogalvanic experiments show clearly that every "emotion" or
> "thought" is always connected with some electrical current.

Hubbard, in Dianetics, stressed that one needs to confront MEST
(Matter, Energy, Space and Time),** rather than just intellectualize
or "figure, figure." It is by confronting (living through again) the force
(experience) in incidents, that the non-optimum postulates (or immature evaluations) come to view and erase (eliminate), losing their
power of command over the individual.

Korzybski states essentially the same thing in *Science and Sanity*:

> It is quite remarkable that "mental" therapy . . . is only successful
> when it succeeds in making the patient not only "rationalize" his
> difficulties but also makes him "emotionalize"—live through again, so
> to say, and evaluate anew—his past experiences. This process can be
> compared with a glass of water in which some chalky sediment lies on
> the bottom . . . the different "hurts," etc., may be compared to the
> water *and* the sediment. "Rationalization" alone is like throwing away
> the clean water and letting the sediment remain. No improvement fol-
> lows. . . . But if we mix up the water *and* the chalk, then we can throw
> out both and a clearing up will follow. The "living through" of the past
> experiences is equivalent to this semantic stirring-up of meanings be-
> fore eliminating the immature evaluations.

In the early days quite a few Dianeticists had studied General Semantics. It was impossible to hide the connection between Hubbard's
work and that of Korzybski. ***   In later years, when the movement

---

*As in "running an engram."
**In Korzybski's works, this was labelled "objects, space and time."
*** It is ironic indeed that key selections of works of Korzybski should have been
revealed—without credit—to huge numbers of people through the writings of a pulp
fiction writer: L. Ron Hubbard.
   Much of the "Scientology and Dianetic" material that so deeply impressed me,
turns out to have been derived from what I consider the genius of Korzybski.

was attracting a younger and more naïve following, Hubbard could with some security assume the role of sole source.

For some reason he had to be "The Only One."

****

The idea in Dianetics is to gain access to the postulates or "think" (immature evaluations) buried in moments of pain, unconsciousness, and shock, and "erase" them from the "reactive mind," *thus refiling them in the conscious mind where they can be intelligently evaluated, used or discarded, at the individual's discretion.*

Hubbard claimed that an individual knocked unconscious recorded at a sub-awareness level *all* stimuli, including language, within the reach of his senses.

It is strongly stressed in Dianetics that one should abstain, as much as possible, from speaking in the presence of unconscious accident victims or persons undergoing surgery.

The idea seems to be slowly catching on in some medical circles.

For example, Dr. David Cheek, a fellow of the American College of Surgeons, is on record as noting that technical conversations "overheard" by the patient while he is in an "unconscious" state could cause surgical shock and changes in bodily functions:

> Anaesthetized persons are in a state resembling that of a deep hypnotic trance. They're highly suggestible. . . . Unhappily the subconscious mind operates on an infantile level and what it hears and deals with while the conscious mind is knocked out . . . can be highly disturbing.
>
> Statements which could otherwise be innocuous may become powerfully dangerous. The remark, "This thing isn't working," may apply to the suction apparatus, but may fill the anaesthetized patient with fears about his anatomy.

When the similarity between his theory and Dianetics was pointed out, Dr. Cheek responded:

Had Korzybski been as brilliant a publicist and showman as he was an innovative genius in the humanities—or had he been duly and adequately recognized and publicized by the academic community (such as being nominated for a Nobel Prize)—the injustice and insult of Hubbard's stepping in to assume full credit could never have occurred.

I am well acquainted with the work of Mr. Hubbard, and agree that there is much in his teaching that has been excellent. I do not claim that I am the first. . . . I believe James Braid (1795–1860) tried unsuccessfully to see whether anaesthetized patients could hear. Dave Elman has told me in a personal communication that he had the experience of being asked to work with a patient who was vomiting after a gall bladder operation. Accidentally, he said, he found that the patient reported verbatim a remark made by the surgeon that had been misunderstood. Correction of this misunderstanding enabled the patient to start eating and recover rapidly.

There is more, of course, to Dianetics than can be presented in these few pages. Here I have only tried to explain the essential ideas and their origins.

****

Hubbard may have had an impressive knack as a sort of "off the top of the head" psychological theoretician, though the extent to which he borrowed from others—"cut and pasted"—takes much of the luster from his claims of originality. He also had emotional problems, problems upon which all his techniques and theories apparently had little or no beneficial effect.

And his mental condition inevitably influenced his supposedly "scientific" work.

The following random example of this may serve to illustrate a point:

Dianetics, the Modern Science of Mental Health, published in 1950, contains numerous "case histories," accounts of traumatic events stored deep in the subconscious minds of various subjects to whom he had applied Dianetic techniques. Most of these had to do with physical trauma going back all the way to before birth. Indeed, the prenatal area, according to Dianetic theory at that time, was the place to look for the source of what troubles people later on in life.

RON JR.:

Reading these "case histories" made me feel very ill at ease. They seemed to reveal more about my father than the people he had supposedly studied. I quickly put the book down and repressed the thought. And I never did get around to reading it from cover to cover until 1955.

I have long since been able to face that fact that, regardless of any workability of Dianetics as a therapy, the outrageous and often bloody "case histories" were mostly embellishments of his own experiences.

In *Dianetics,* the act of a husband beating or otherwise abusing his pregnant wife is presented as a common thing. And attempted abortions are practically a way of life for the human race. He implies that virtually *no one* is conceived and comes into this world without having suffered many of them.

To quote Hubbard:

> What happens to a child in the womb? The commonest events are accidents, illnesses—and *attempted abortions!* [italics in original]
>
> Attempted abortions are very common . . . twenty or thirty abortion attempts are not uncommon. . . .
>
> For example:
>
> (Blow or bump, prenatal)
>
> FATHER: Damn it, Agnes, you've got to get rid of that goddamned baby. If you don't we'll starve to death. I can't afford it.
>
> MOTHER: Oh, no, no, no, I can't get rid of it, I can't, I can't, I can't. Honest I will take care of it. I'll work and slave to support it. Please don't make me get rid of it. If I did I'd just die. . . .

Why this seeming obsession with abortion by Hubbard?

RON JR.:

> We were living in Bremerton, Washington. The year was 1940 and I was six years old.
>
> I was in bed asleep when I was awakened by my mother's screams. I remember quietly making my way to my parents' bedroom. The door was slightly ajar and I peeked in.
>
> Their room was dimly lit and I could see my father sitting on top of my mother. She was lying on the bed naked. I remember he was wearing a robe. He was doing something to her but, of course, I had no idea what.
>
> I could see my mother wasn't resisting him, so, shaken and completely mystified, I went back to bed and tried to sleep. The next day I saw a blood-stained sheet in the garbage.
>
> Years later I realized what he must have been doing that night. When I got my courage up I mentioned it to my mother. She told me that, during the course of their marriage—they were now divorced—he had forced her to have two abortions.
>
> How many attempted abortions were done I wouldn't want to guess.

Sara, his second wife, had this to say:

> I think his obsession with abortion had to do with the fact that he
> was an unwanted child. He felt that his parents had neglected him.
> Ron spent so much time living with his grandfather. He thought they
> didn't want him. He felt he had been subjected to attempted abor-
> tions.

In *Dianetics* and also in *Science of Survival,* which was published
about a year later in June of 1951, Hubbard expresses strong anti-
abortion sentiments:

> Why people try to abort children is a problem which has its answer
> only in aberration. . . . Anyone attempting an abortion is committing
> an act against the whole society. . . .
> However many billions America spends yearly on institutions for
> the insane and jails for criminals are spent primarily because of at-
> tempted abortions done by some sex-blocked mother to whom chil-
> dren are a curse, not a blessing of God.

According to Hubbard:

> A 1.1.* mother will attempt the abortion of her child; and any

---

*The term "1.1" is a pejorative (i.e., insulting) term invented by Hubbard as part of
the "Tone Scale" which he presented in his second book on Dianetics, *Science of
Survival,* about 1952. The "tone scale" is, "a scale which plots the descending spiral
of life from full vitality and consciousness through half-vitality and half-unconscious-
ness down to death . . . from the highest to the lowest. . . ." These are, in part:

40.0	Serenity
8.0	Exhilaration
4.0	Enthusiasm
3.0	Conservatism
2.5	Boredom
2.0	Antagonism
1.5	Anger
1.1	Covert hostility
1.0	Fear
0.8	Propitiation
0.5	Grief
0.05	Apathy

Below 2.0 people are said to be no longer rational. At 1.1 they are especially dan-

woman who will abort a child, save only if the child threatens her physical life (rather than her reputation), lies in the 1.1. bracket or below. She can be expected to be unreliable, inconstant and promiscuous.
. . .

Of course, we only have Ron Jr.'s word for it that L. Ron Hubbard had a way with a coat-hanger. For, after all, in Hubbard's writings he seems consistently opposed to abortion.

Interestingly enough, he did a complete about-face on the subject only a year and a half after whole-heartedly denouncing it.

During a lecture on Scientology in Philadelphia in November of 1952, he spoke gleefully of what an "interesting place" this world might be, now that we have "venereal disease licked"* and "pregnancy termination at will."

He spoke of the ability to psycho-kinetically (mind over matter) induce an abortion:

> We mustn't mention this because, God help us all, there goes the moral code! Penicillin took out the disease level and now a girl can take a couple of beams of energy . . . and terminate a pregnancy. Nothing wild or forceful or upsetting. . . . Just make sure that the tube opens. It's very simple, there are muscles and so forth which contract and expand at a certain period every month.
>
> Pregnancies that were as much as three months advanced have been terminated this way . . . Isn't this fascinating? . . . It's just deadly. One, two, three!

Will the real L. Ron Hubbard please stand up. . . .

---

gerous, inasmuch as they are COVERTLY hostile. Those who are chronically 1.1 are considered psychotic, although, if intelligent enough, can do a convincing job of hiding their insanity. (Some claim "1.1" describes Hubbard.)

*Remember the good old days?

3

Dianetics, the Modern Science of Mental Health

About the early days of Dianetics, science fiction author A. E. van Vogt wrote in *Reflections*, his autobiography:

Early in 1950, I began to receive phone calls from L. Ron Hubbard, whom I had met in 1945. He'd call me long distance from New Jersey, every morning, and talk for an hour trying to get me interested in Dianetics. . . . [van Vogt was in California]

I said, "No, I'm a writer. I'm not interested in anything else but being a writer."

Now, surprisingly enough, people began to send me money. I can imagine that Hubbard actually wrote inquirers and told them to contact me. Anyway, I would receive checks in the mail for a hundred dollars, or more, for the course in Dianetics that was not yet in sight. I received, altogether, about five thousand dollars in the mail, and I was receiving these calls from Hubbard at the same time.

The phone would ring at seven o'clock in the morning and I would know who it was. At about ten after eight I'd be off the phone, and he would have talked the entire time. . . .

That shocked me. Finally, around the seventeenth or eighteenth day, as I recall it, my stubbornness was shattered. That kind of phone calling, long distance, was completely out of my reality. It was beyond my conception that anybody was phoning that often—and talking that long—at those rates. I had to put a stop to it, so I made an agreement and I was in Dianetics.

294

People who were associated with Hubbard told me later that his phone bills were often six thousand dollars a month. I don't doubt it because he wasn't only calling me, but dozens of other people in Europe and elsewhere.

Dianetics turned out to be a very worthwhile system, but the methods needed considerable skill and experience. . . .

Hubbard is an extremely brilliant man, but not really a research person in the ordinary meaning of the term. Yet he can integrate complex data in a flash of insight.

His basic discovery of Dianetics was made when he began to notice the non-sequitur things people said. For example, an individual would be talking animatedly and positively about something, come to the end of the thought, and add in an apathetic tone, "I don't know. You can never know about things like that."

Where did phrases like that, so different from the dynamism of moments earlier, come from? On investigation, they turned out to be phrases actually spoken by somebody during a time of illness, at the scene of an accident, or during some other physical trauma.

In the example given, it was an auto accident, "Is he badly injured?" The other person had replied, "I don't know. You can never know about things like that until a doctor examines him."

****

In April 1949 John W. Campbell, editor of *Astounding Science Fiction* magazine, became the first major convert to Dianetics. He had previously published many of Hubbard's stories and had become fascinated with his theories regarding the human mind. After Dianetic therapy had relieved him of a chronic sinus condition, he became more convinced than ever that there was something to this new form of psychotherapy.

Campbell's magazine became a kind of soap box for the broadcast of the principles and bold claims of Dianetics. By the fall of the same year, a second notable convert had been secured, Dr. J. A. Winter.

Winter had been doing experimental work in endocrinology at the University of Illinois and had contributed some medical articles to *Astounding*. Campbell wrote to him regarding Dianetics, and later Winter corresponded with Hubbard. Finally he travelled to Bayhead, New Jersey, where Hubbard lived:

I arrived in Bayhead, N.J., on October 1, 1949, and immediately became immersed in a life of Dianetics and very little else. I observed two of the patients whom Hubbard had under his treatment at the time, and spent hours each day watching him send these men "down the time-track." After some observation of the reaction of others, I concluded that my learning of this technique would be enhanced by subjecting myself to therapy. I took my place on the couch, spending an average of three hours a day trying to follow the directions for recalling "impediments" (engrams). The experience was intriguing; I found that I could remember much more than I thought I could, and I frequently experienced the discomfort which is known as "restimulation." While listening to Hubbard "running" one of his patients, or while being "run" myself, I would find myself developing unaccountable pains in various parts of my anatomy, or becoming extremely fatigued and somnolent. I had nightmares of being choked, of having my genitalia cut off, and I was convinced that Dianetics as a method could produce effects.

So impressed was Dr. Winter that he moved to Bayhead to work with Campbell and LRH on the theory, practice, and nomenclature of the subject. Collectively they came up with such terms as "reactive mind" and "anaten" (analytical cut off, or attenuation) and "valence".*

A paper giving a "resume of the principles and methodology of Dianetic therapy" was submitted by Winter to the *Journal of the American Medical Association*, but was rejected. A revised version including case histories was submitted to the *American Journal of Psychiatry*, but was again turned down.

They finally decided to direct their message to the man in the street. The article, entitled "Dianetics, a New Science," was previewed by Campbell in extremely enthusiastic terms:

> . . . in longer range view . . . the item that most interests me at the moment is an article on the most important subject conceivable. This is not a hoax article. It is an article on the science of the mind, of human thought. Its power is almost unbelievable; it proves the mind not only can but does rule the body completely; following the sharply defined basic laws Dianetics sets forth, physical ills such as ulcers, asthma and arthritis can be cured, as can all psychosomatic ills. . . . It is quite sim-

---

*A little boy, neglected by his parents, finds himself very ill and under the care of his grandfather, who gives him sympathy and encouragement. The grandfather smokes a pipe, hates cats, has a certain way of laughing, and has a tattoo of an eagle on his right hand.

Thirty years later it would not be too surprising to find this little boy a grown man who smokes a pipe, hates cats . . . etc.

Hubbard: "A valence is a substitute for self taken on, after the fact of loss of confidence in self."

ply impossible to exaggerate the importance of a true science of human thought.

Next month's issue will, I believe, cause a full scale explosion across the country. We are carrying a sixteen thousand word article entitled "Dianetics . . . An Introduction to a New Science," by L. Ron Hubbard. . . . It is, I assure you in full and absolute sincerity, one of the most important articles ever published. . . . In this article, reporting on Hubbard's own research into the engineering question of how the human mind operates, immensely basic discoveries are related. Among them:

A technique of psychotherapy has been developed which will cure any insanity not due to organic destruction of the brain.

A technique that gives a man a perfect, indelible, total memory, and a perfect errorless ability to compute his problems.

A basic answer, and a technique for curing—not alleviating—ulcers, arthritis, asthma, and many other nongerm diseases.

A totally new conception of the truly incredible ability and power of the human mind . . .

These editorial previews generated a great deal of interest, and in April of 1950 the Hubbard Dianetic Research Foundation was established in Elizabeth, New Jersey (where Campbell's magazine was headquartered), to provide services to those seeking therapy and training.

The eagerly awaited article appeared in the May issue of *Astounding*, followed almost immediately by the publication of the book, and soon to be best-seller, *Dianetics, the Modern Science of Mental Health*.

****

In April of 1950 the Hubbard Dianetic Research Foundation was established in Elizabeth, New Jersey. By the end of 1950 it had branches in New York, Washington, Chicago, Los Angeles, Honolulu and Kansas City.

Hubbard presided over the board of directors, which included John W. Campbell and Dr. Joseph Winter.

Also around this time, Aldous Huxley, author of *Brave New World*, was receiving Dianetic auditing. Wrote Sybille Bedford in her biography of Huxley:

LRH came to North Kings in person. . . . Aldous and Maria had three or four sessions with Hubbard. He and his wife came to dinner, "stiff and polite" the first time, bringing two pounds of chocolates.

(Sara, in my interview with her, insisted it was coffee and cakes rather than chocolates!)

In Huxley's words:

> Up to the present I have proved to be completely resistant—there is no way of getting me onto the time track or of making the subconscious produce engrams. . . . Maria, meanwhile, has had some success contacting and working off engrams and has been repeatedly into what the subconscious says is the pre-natal state. Whether because of Dianetics or for some other reason, she is well and very free from tension. . . .

Throughout America and England people who had read *Dianetics* were enthusiastically applying its techniques on their friends, or teaming up to co-audit. Dianetic clubs were springing up like dandelions in April.

The National Association of College Bookstores reported that *DMSMH* was top of its best-seller list. *The New York Times* list was next.

A Williams College professor, writing in *The New York Times*, said, "History has become a race between Dianetics and catastrophe. . . ."

In August of 1950 Hubbard wrote:

> There will be those who, for various reasons, do not undertake clearing and for whom no clearing is done. . . . One sees with some sadness that more than three-quarters of the world's population will become subject to the remaining quarter. . . .

In September over 300 took a course in Los Angeles which lasted for a month and cost 500 dollars. There were several such courses and these were an excellent source of income for Hubbard.

It would seem like a lot of money was being made, but somehow the financial condition of the foundation did not reflect this.

Helen O'Brian, old-time Dianeticist, in her book *Dianetics in Limbo*, states:

> I was an awed outsider with an associate membership during the boom to bust cycle of the first Dianetic Foundation. . . . One man who was an important member of the organizing group told me a few years ago that he still retained copies of the bookkeeping records that made him decide to disassociate himself from the Elizabeth Foundation fast. A month's income of $90,000 is listed, with only $20,000 accounted for. He was one of the first to resign.

By October 1950, the situation had become critical, and in the following month the combined incomes of the Foundations totalled less than one-tenth of the payroll. But Hubbard blamed the failure on the motivations of the people who had been his friends. . . . He later wrote . . . in Wichita, a bitter denunciation of his former associates, one of them his second wife Sara, who had served as executive vice-president of the corporation, saying that they, "hungry for money and power," sought to take over and control all of Dianetics.

Hubbard also blamed the American Psychiatric Association, the American Psychological Association, and the American Medical Association for inciting the many critical newspaper and magazine articles.

The Barnum and Bailey level of hype and the extreme claims made for the subject no doubt were a factor in the eventual disillusionment of many.

For those closely associated with Hubbard, his behavior and attitudes also became relevant.

In October of 1950, Dr. Winter resigned from the HDRF. In his book *A Doctor Looks at Dianetics*, published shortly afterwards, he wrote:

> It should be known . . . that Dianetics has been given careful scrutiny by numerous doctors, psychiatrists psycho-analysts and psychiatric social workers. I have corresponded with or talked to several hundred of them, and I have found that when the scientific aspects of Dianetics have been honestly examined, they present a real challenge to any serious student of the human mind. . . . I personally know of a score of psychiatrists who are using a portion of the concepts and techniques of Dianetics . . . yet these men do not feel free to admit they are doing so. . . .

He added, however:

> There was a difference between the ideals inherent in the Dianetic hypothesis and the actions of the Foundation in its ostensible efforts to carry out these ideals. The ideals . . . as I saw them, included non-authoritarianism and a flexibility of approach. . . . The ideals . . . continued to be given lip-service, but I could see a definite disparity between ideals and actualities. . . .

Winter set up private practice in New York.

In March of 1951 John Campbell resigned. Sometime later he
wrote:

> In a healthy and growing science, there are many men who are rec-
> ognized as being competent in the field, and no one man dominates
> the work . . . to the extent Dianetics is dependent on one man, it is a
> cult. To the extent that it is built by many minds and many workers it is
> a science.

4

The "Kidnapping"

Sara, Hubbard's second wife, left him early in 1951. She desperately wanted a divorce and custody of her daughter and he vehemently refused. Consequently, on April 23 she filed suit in the Superior Court of Los Angeles County, charging him with kidnapping, torture and bigamy.

The New York Times reported:

> The wife of L. Ron Hubbard, founder of the Dianetic Mental Health movement, filed suit for divorce today. Mrs. Sara Northrup Hubbard, 25 years old, said the doctors told her that her 40 year old husband was suffering from a mental ailment known as "paranoid schizophrenia." Mrs. Hubbard also charged he subjected her to "systematic torture" by beating and strangling her and denying her sleep.

Hubbard flew to Havana, Cuba, taking his daughter Alexis with him.

****

Around this time Sara received a letter from Hubbard's first wife Margaret:

> Sara—
> If I can help in any way, I'd like to—You must get Alexis in your custody—Ron is not normal. I had hoped that you could straighten him out. Your charges probably sound fantastic to the average person—but I've been through it—the beatings, threats on my life, all the sadistic traits you charge—twelve years of it. I haven't asked for anything, but with the money rolling in from "Dianetics" I had hoped to get enough

for plastic surgery for Kay's* birthmark—Please believe I do so want to help you get Alexis.

In Sara's complaint for divorce filed on April 23, 1951, at the Superior Court of California in the county of Los Angeles, it states:

COMES NOW the plaintiff and for cause of action against defendants, alleges and says:

That in the early part of 1946, plaintiff, then aged 21 and unmarried, resided with her family in Pasadena, and attended the University of Southern California, that at said time, defendant L. Ron Hubbard, hereafter referred to as "Hubbard" was a married man, age 35, he being then married to Margaret Grubb Hubbard of Bremerton, Washington, they having two children; that said Hubbard represented to plaintiff that he was single and unmarried, and plaintiff relying upon said representation, and having fallen in love, entered into a marriage ceremony with said Hubbard on the tenth day of August, 1946, at Chastertown, Maryland; that said Hubbard thereafter secured a divorce from said Margaret Grubb Hubbard on or about the 24th day of December, 1947, at Port Orchard, Washington; that plaintiff and said Hubbard ever since the said 10th day of August, 1946, have lived together as husband and wife, and on the 8th day of March, 1950, had a child born to them, Alexis Valerie Hubbard, at Point Pleasant, New Jersey. . . .

That said separation took place by reason of extreme cruelty practiced upon the plaintiff by the said Hubbard. . . .

(a) That during the marriage up until the month of October, 1950, said Hubbard, an "older man," completely dominated the youthful plaintiff, both physically, mentally and emotionally, and taking advantage of her trusting love and desire for a successful marriage, repeatedly subjected plaintiff to systematic torture, including loss of sleep, beatings, and strangulations and scientific torture experiments, including the following:

(b) That in the latter part of September, 1950, said Hubbard told plaintiff at the Chateau Marmont Apartments in Hollywood, that "I do not want to be an American husband for I can buy my friends whenever I want them," and he further said that he, Hubbard, did not want to be married, yet divorce was impossible, for a divorce would hurt his reputation, and that she, plaintiff, should kill herself if she really loves him.

(c) That at said time and place, said Hubbard systematically prevented plaintiff from sleeping continuously for a period of over four

*Ron Jr.'s sister.

days, and then in her agony, furnished her with a supply of sleeping pills, all resulting to the nearness to the shadow of death. That the foregoing was a frequent occurrence during the married life of the parties.

(d) That at said time and place, plaintiff became numb and lost consciousness, and was thereafter taken by said Hubbard to the Hollywood Leland Hospital, where she was kept under a vigilant guard from friend and family, under an assumed name, for five days.

(e) That shortly following Christmas, 1950, said Hubbard violently strangled plaintiff and sadistically ruptured the eustachian tube of her left ear, resulting in the impairment of her hearing. That such strangulation of plaintiff was a frequent practice on the part of said Hubbard.

(f) That in January, 1951, at Palm Springs, while plaintiff was getting out of an automobile operated by said Hubbard, he intentionally started the said car in gear, thus propelling plaintiff to the pavement resulting in serious personal injury.

(g) That plaintiff and her medical advisors, following the foregoing incidents, concluded that said Hubbard was hopelessly insane, and crazy, and that there was no present hope for said Hubbard, or any reason for her to endure further; that competent medical advisors recommended that said Hubbard be committed to a private sanitarium for psychiatric observation and treatment of a mental ailment known as paranoid schizophrenia; that plaintiff, on the 23rd day of February, 1951, caused the national executive officer of the Hubbard Dianetic Research Foundation at Elizabeth, New Jersey, to be advised of said preliminary diagnosis and urgent need for treatment; that said national officer immediately advised said Hubbard of said diagnosis.

(h) That at 11:00 o'clock P.M., on said 23rd day of February, 1951, said Hubbard, together with defendant Frank B. Dessler, head of the Los Angeles Dianetic Foundation, abducted the infant child of the parties, Alexis, from her crib. . . .

(i) That said Hubbard, Dessler and defendant Richard B. De Mille, having secreted said infant child, feloniously dragged plaintiff out of her bed attired only in her night gown, it then being 1:00 o'clock A.M., of the morning of the 24th day of February, 1951, and by the use of threats, strangulation, torture, and false promises to return the child to her, carried and kidnapped plaintiff to Yuma, Arizona. . . .

(j) That plaintiff has ever since sought the whereabouts of her infant child, and has consulted attorneys, police, sheriffs, Federal Bureau of Investigation agents, and courts, and has brought said habeas corpus proceedings; that said Hubbard and his attorneys refuse any information as to the whereabouts of her infant child, unless she goes back to live with said Hubbard, an alternative that means certain continued torture and possible death, a predicament no good woman, wife and mother should have to face.

(k) That through all her trials and tribulations, and up until the month of February, 1951, plaintiff bore her suffering and sorrow, in silence, and even now would not bare the truth to the world, except for the compelling advice of her attorney, Caryl Warner, that she tell the truth for the truth shall make her free, and the truth alone will bring back her baby, if alive . . .

While Hubbard was in Havana he wrote Sara:

Dear Sara—

I have been in a Cuban Military Hospital and I am being transferred to the States next week as a classified scientist immune from interference of all kinds though I will be hospitalized probably a long time. Alexis is getting excellent care. I see her every day. She is all I have to live for. My wits never gave way under all you did and let them do but my body didn't stand up. My right side is paralyzed and getting more so. I have trouble moving and I am going blind. I hope my heart lasts. . . . I may live a long time and again I may not. But Dianetics will last ten thousand years for the Army and Navy have it now. But I wanted to be well and strong and I can barely move now.

My will is all changed. Alexis will get a fortune unless she goes to you as she would then get nothing.

Get away from bad companions.

Hope to see you once more.

Goodbye—

I love you.

Ron

Shortly thereafter a divorce settlement was reached. Sara received custody and $200 a month child support and the matter was closed.

During the time of the divorce settlement Sara signed a document presented to her by Hubbard's agents in which it is stated, in effect, that all she had said about him was false.

The Church claims that Sara, herself, wrote this document in which she said:

I have not at any time believed otherwise than that L. Ron Hubbard was a fine and brilliant man. . . . I have begun to realize that what I have done may have injured the science of Dianetics, which in my studied opinion may be the only hope for sanity in future generations. . . .

The St. Petersburg Times comments:

The statement bears the subtle marks of L. Ron Hubbard's handiwork. The stilted language is similar to his writing style and the recantation includes a sentence with the word "enturbulating" which is not to be found in a dictionary but sometimes appears in Hubbard's writings.

Author Stewart Lamont adds:

If Mrs. Hubbard II is alive, she probably regards discretion as the better part of valor since she would be regarded as "Fair Game" with a vengeance.

Sara (responding to my question as to why she signed this document):

I thought by doing so he would leave me and Alexis alone. It was horrible. I just wanted to be free of him!

****

John Sanborne tells of Sara and the "kidnapping" of Alexis, their year-old daughter:

Sara was a lovely woman. She was intelligent. She was quite young. I suppose she was around 24, and Hubbard was around 40. She had an aristrocratic look.

I know very definitely that he did try to convince one person that Sara wasn't his wife and Alexi wasn't his baby. There was divorce action going between her and Hubbard so somebody must have thought they were married!

It was a great place (The Los Angeles Foundation). It had twenty auditing rooms. Some of us were living there. And Marge Hunter had a baby named Tammy the same age as Dianetics (born 1950), and the Hubbard's had a baby, Lexi, that was the same age as Dianetics.

Anyway, one night it just happened. . . . You know none of us went to the movies very much. We just did Dianetics, and fooling around, and talking and auditing and stuff. But that night there was some movie that they wanted to see, and I wasn't in the mood. I was missing my girlfriend. So I said, "Go ahead, I'll watch the kids." And there was a little room where the two kids were in their cribs. And Marge put them to bed, and they went off to the movies. The kids were totally used to me so there was no problem.

At roughly ten o'clock Lexi woke up and was upset, sobbing. So I brought her out into the main room, had her down on the bed next to me, and let her calm down.

I'm holding her. And she's sitting there looking in my eyes. She was only one year old and wasn't talking yet. Then all of a sudden I hear this hoarse whisper, she says, "Don't sleep." It was very clear. She whispered don't sleep and she meant it! Well, that sent something through me, I'm telling ya. Whoo boy! This was some kind of paranormal reality.

So she got sleepy again after that, and I put her back in bed. And I was just sitting around semi-awake feeling kind of spooked. It was a funny feeling. It went through me in a funny way. Gee, you know, the hair raising on the back of the neck type of feeling.

Then, all of a sudden, I hear a step and I look in the doorway and there's Frank Dessler in a topcoat and a felt hat, and I believe he had a gun in his hand in his pocket. He says in this very tense voice, "Mr. Hubbard is here to get his child Lexi."

Then Hubbard appeared in the door with a topcoat and a felt hat, and he had his hand in his right pocket, and I believe that he had a gun in his hand also. I said, "Hi Ron." And he said, "Hello. Where's Lexi?" I waved them in and we went into the room where they were, and they started getting Lexi up. They were looking for her clothes and blankets. . . . She had a doll or something in her hand, that she was sleeping with, and Hubbard said, "Is this hers?" And I said, "I'm not sure, I think maybe it's Tammy's." And he threw it down.

I said, "Listen, I'll give you a couple of pointers about what to do when she wakes up," and so forth. And he said, "Oh never mind about that. We've got professional care for her, don't worry about it."

So they took off.

And I was worried but not in real conflict. Nobody had ever indicated to me that he shouldn't have the child if he wanted it. And we were all pretty much on his side anyway, even though we weren't against Sara. Nevertheless, all of us were on his team really. We were all fans of his. And it was his kid. Nobody second guessed me about letting him have her. What was I going to do? say, "You'll have to kill me first!"

. . . I think Hubbard considered Lexi as a pawn in the game. Something he could deny Sara.

When asked why Sara had remained quiet all these years, Sanborne responded, "She knew what he was capable of."

5

Sara Speaks

On the twelfth of July 1986 I met with Sara and her husband at their home. It was an exclusive interview, Sara having not spoken publicly on the subject of L. Ron Hubbard for almost thirty-five years.

Although I was not permitted to tape record the conversation, I did take notes and pieced these together, forming the following narrative.*

SARA:

"*Dianetics, the Modern Science of Mental Health* took some eighteen months to write. The majority of it was written in Savannah, Georgia, then Bayhead and Elizabeth, New Jersey.

"He was the happiest I'd ever seen him when he wrote. In Savannah, where he wrote part of *Dianetics*, he was doing great. We had a wonderful time.

"I thought there was some validity to Dianetics, and that Ron had something to contribute.

"John Campbell was a very positive, and brilliant man and was a big influence on Ron and a major contributor to his success with Dianetics. He was a marvelous editor.

"After *Dianetics* the money was just pouring in, and he used to carry huge amounts of cash around in his pocket. I remember going past a Lincoln dealer and admiring one of those big Lincolns they had then. He walked right in there and bought it for me, cash!

"After the divorce he wrote me saying that Lexi would soon be asking, 'Why don't I have Lincolns?' . . .

*Interspersed throughout the narrative are several excerpts from the Armstrong trial and an account by an old-time Scientologist.

307

"Ron couldn't handle stress. He'd go insane under stress. He had an extremely violent temper.

"But he was also capable of being extremely charming. He would turn on the charm in front of someone, and when he or she left, he'd go into a vitriolic tirade about the person he had just been charming to death.

"When lecturing he was always his charming self. . . . You'd never know he had any problems at all when he was on stage. . . .

"He stood up on stage in Los Angeles and announced that I was the first 'clear.' I was so embarrassed. . . .

"Ron used a *lot* of medical drugs and vitamins, and very large doses of testosterone (male hormone). He was self-medicated and proud of it. But the vast majority of his Dianetic following never had a clue about his inclinations along this line."

Gerry Armstrong states:

It is documented that Hubbard used huge amounts of testosterone, stilbestrol (a female sex hormone).

Taking the sex hormones were his solution to an impotence problem.

Another solution was to resort to the "affirmations."

"Affirmations" were commands stated to himself as part of self-hypnosis. (Sometimes you will see a statement of fact, like, "Yeah, I'm screwed up on sex." And then he'll come back with an affirmation: "You are sexually *wonderful*! Your sexual prowess has never before been equalled on the face of the Earth!"

That kind of thing alongside his own statements of his inadequacy—which was the reality of the matter.

Clearly the impotence was a big chunk of his attitude towards women.

Impotence was on his mind a lot at that period. He wrote about it—page after page—about how he had, "after Fern," been too afraid to go to a doctor with the clap. [Fern was the girl in Miami who he claims gave gonorrhea to him.] So he dosed himself with sulphur, and then he says the sulphur depressed his libido, and his solution to that was the testosterone and stilbestrol.

"It so depressed my libido," he said, that he needed someone like Sara to stimulate him.

It was a big chunk of his mind.

From Hubbard's *Affirmations:*

"It doesn't give me displeasure to hear of a virgin being raped.
"The lot of women is to be fornicated!"

****

Sara continues:
"The fact is he was a basket case physically. He was a psycho-
somatic case. He would go blind at any moment of the day. He had
terrible fits of temper and his system was totally out of order.
"Sometimes he'd walk using a cane. It was all psycho-somatic.
There was nothing actually wrong with him."
Selected "affirmations" revealed at the Armstrong trial:

> Gerry Armstrong (reading):
> Your stomach trouble you used as an excuse to keep the Navy from
> punishing you. You are free from the Navy. You have no further reason
> to have a weak stomach.
> Your ulcers are all well and never bother you. You can eat anything.
> Your hip is a pose. You have a sound hip. It never hurts.
> Your shoulder never hurts.
> Your foot was an alibi. The injury is no longer needed. It is well. You
> have perfect and lovely feet.
> Your sinus trouble is nothing. It is not dangerous. It will vanish. The
> common cold amuses you. You are protected from further illness. Your
> cat fever has vanished forever and will never return. You do not have
> malaria.
> When you tell people you are ill, it has no effect on your health. And
> in Veterans Administration examinations you'll tell them how sick you
> are; you'll look sick when you take it; you'll return to health one hour
> after the examination and laugh at them.
> No matter what lies you may tell others, they have no physical effect
> on you of any kind. You never injure your health by saying it is bad.
> You cannot lie to yourself. . . .
> Mr. Flynn: I'd be happy to have the whole document go into evi-
> dence.
> Mr. Litt [Church attorney]: No, no, no. The words "by hypnosis"—
> The Witness: This is (g), "That my eyes (which I used as an excuse to
> get out of school) are perfect and do not pain me ever."
> Q. by Mr. Flynn: Now, were you able to date, Mr. Armstrong,
> when these documents were written by Mr. Hubbard?. . .
> A. In the period of 1946–1947 . . .

****

SARA:

"Ron was fascinated with the magick. . . .

"Jack [Parsons] was a marvelously brilliant, genuine guy. The house in Pasadena was a lovely place. Scientists, physicists, and engineers would come and stay and talk. . . .

"A lot of the scientific language Ron used in Dianetics and Scientology probably came from the courses in engineering he took in Washington in his brief college days. He flunked pretty badly in those courses. He was too erratic. He was too neurotic to sit down and study. He never went into anything in any depth.

"He would just pick up the jargon.

"He was a dilletante.

"Yet in some respects he was an extremely capable man. But he was deeply disturbed emotionally. Success put stress on him. I felt I had to stay with him despite the insanity. I had some idea that I was responsible for him. I should have left much earlier. I can't believe I stayed with him for five years! . . .

"Shortly after we first met, he told me that if I didn't marry him he'd kill himself. . . .

Regarding the Church of Scientology:

"People don't want to think. They want to hand over their lives for people to make decisions for them."

About Ron the writer:

"Ron was happy when he was writing, and fun to be with. But at times he had writer's block and could become quite distressed about it. I would often entertain him with plots so he could write. I loved to make plots. 'The Old Doc Methuselah' series was done that way."

****

Sara spoke warmly of her daughter Alexis and her other two children, and was intensely curious about the rest of Hubbard's children by Mary Sue.

She was concerned that Alexis not be harassed by the Church.

****

In June of 1986 the Church of Scientology agreed to a financial settlement with Alexis.

At that settlement conference they tried to get Alexis to write an affidavit that she was the daughter of Ron Jr.

They had her fingerprinted and video-taped and, in exchange for an unspecified sum of money, had her sign an agreement that she would not write or speak on the subject of L. Ron Hubbard and her relationship to him.

SARA:

"She got a very small settlement. But she has a husband who adores her, and life is good for her and her children. She doesn't need a lot of money, and, especially, she doesn't need the harassment.

"When we showed the photograph (of Hubbard holding Alexis as a baby) to the Scientologists representing the Church at the settlement hearings in Los Angeles, they were shocked. I think they must have really believed the stories that Alexis was just a gold digger out to get some money from Ron. They went into another room and were all huddled in intense conversation. There was quite a buzz."

****

From the Armstrong trial:

Q. By Mr. Flynn: . . . First, when you found materials relating to Alexis Holister and Sara Northrup, did those materials have particular significance for you in the biography project?

A. [Gerry Armstrong] Yes.

Q. And why is that?

A. Well, Sara Northrup was, obviously, his wife. He had been involved with Sara from 1945 through, at least, 1951.

They had gone through a pretty turbulent divorce; she was around in the beginning of all the Dianetics and Scientology organizations. She was an important part.

I had also seen the allegations made by Hubbard that she was part of SMERSH,* that she was a Soviet spy; that she was sent in to break up the Dianetics Foundation.

I had seen all these claims.

Q. So now, would you continue. What was the significance of the Sara-Alexis situation with regard to the documents that you found during the biography project?

A. Alexis tied in because she was Sara's daughter. I knew that she was Sara's daughter. I was not—I had seen the PR briefing that she was not Hubbard's daughter.

At the time I saw somewhere one of the early books (I believe *Science of Survival*, one of the very earliest books) was first dedicated to

---

*From James Bond novels. The name of an evil world wide conspiratorial organization. Used by Hubbard to designate what he considered to be a similar group in real life.

Alexis Valerie Hubbard, so I had some contradictions early on when I began to get into it. And I also interviewed several family members from Mr. Hubbard's family. There were cousins—an aunt and so on—and discussed Sara and Alexis with them.

Some time after that from the LRH Pers Sec [Personal Secretary] U.S. files I obtained this pack of materials on Alexis.

. . . it had a great deal of significance to me. It had a great deal of significance to Omar Garrison.

Q. And why is that?

A. It was the man's life, really. I think. An incredible set of events in which his daughter, after not seeing her father—the person she believed for twenty years was her father—wrote to him in 1971 . . . tried to get into communication with him.

The communication was received . . . [by] the Guardian's Office. . . . Jane Kember . . . wrote to L. Ron Hubbard because she viewed this as a threat. . . .

It was a daughter trying to get in touch with her father. . . . L. Ron Hubbard's method of handling what the Guardian's office and he . . . perceived as a threat was quite remarkable . . . he had the Guardian's office write a letter on a non-general-use typewriter.* (That had particular significance to me because I knew that that was the Guardian's office practice regarding the writing of letters which were to be used for a clandestine, secret purpose, some operation of some sort. They would write one letter on one typewriter and then get rid of the typewriter so that it was never used for any other reason, so the type faces could never be matched up, and so that the source of these kinds of letters could never be sourced). . . .

And then the letter was to be read to the girl. And it was just the most appalling letter.

She was—L. Ron Hubbard comes off like a shining knight, and her mother, who had been taking care of her through her whole life, came off like a total tramp, and then he ended up this classic document with a note to Jane Kember that,

"DECENCY IS A SUBJECT NOT WELL UNDERSTOOD." (Emphasis added)

I can vouch for that. I can't think of many more indecent acts than the one he pulled off on the girl that I conclude is his daughter. . . .

Q. On the 8th day of March, 1950, Alexis was born?

A. Yes.

Q. And what color hair did Ron Hubbard have?

A. Red.

Q. Do you know what color hair Alexis has?

A. Red. . . .

*The order to use a non-general-use typewriter was in Hubbard's own handwriting.

Q. By Mr. Flynn: Mr. Armstrong, with regard to the letter that was to be shown to Alexis on the instructions of L. Ron Hubbard, did you find representations in that letter of Mr. Hubbard that were inaccurate?

A. Yes.

Q. And what were those?

A. This is the letter to Alexis?

Q. Correct.

A. Okay. He stated to his daughter that, "Your mother was with me as a secretary in Savannah in late 1948."

Q. And she was in fact his wife then?

A. Yes. He writes here, "In July 1949 I was in Elizabeth, New Jersey writing a movie. She turned up destitute and pregnant. I do not know who she was living with in Pasadena, but she was closely associated with Jack Parsons. . . . I came up from Palm Springs, California, where I was living and found you (Alexis) abandoned. . . ."

Well actually what happened was I interviewed the person who was with him at that time by the name of Frank Dessler, and he and Frank Dessler took the child and ran off and there was a kidnapping allegation at that point in the newspapers.

Q. Against Mr. Hubbard?

A. Yes.

Q. He had taken Alexis away from Sara and run away from her?

A. Yes, went ultimately to Havana, Cuba.

Q. And was he in Havana, Cuba, with Alexis?

A. Yes. He claims that there was—

Q. This is all in his handwriting, is that correct?

A. Yes. Here he claims that there was no—her mother and Hollister, whom she later married, he said (Hubbard said), "They obtained considerable newspaper publicity, none of it true, and employed the highest priced divorce attorney in the U.S. to sue me for divorce and get the foundation in Los Angeles in settlement. This proved a puzzle, since where there is no legal marriage, there can't be any divorce."

And that was not the way it was at all. I suppose if he meant if it was a bigamous marriage, that was true. But, in fact, there was a marriage.

Q. And there was a divorce?

A. Yes. It just is a perversion of—and there is no willingness on his part to admit any responsibility for anything.

****

More from the Sara interview:

"After the marriage we went out to Port Orchard and Ron's divorce [from Jr.'s mother, Margaret Louise Grubb] started then, but I didn't know about it at that time.

"I did not discover that he was still married to her until after the divorce proceedings had begun.

"Polly [Hubbard's first wife] wrote me when she discovered that I was seeking a divorce. She was very understanding."

SARA'S HUSBAND, MILES:

"When he realized that Sara was with me, he threatened several times to kill me."

SARA:

"After the divorce from me, Ron sent people to interview me who claimed they were from the FBI. They looked like Mormons, but with bad complexions.

"They asked how I felt about him. Despite the legal resolution, he apparently had not ended it in his mind.

"I couldn't give a damn about him by that time. I was just so glad to have been able to escape!. . .

"During the divorce, he not only said I was in with the communists but also the fascists!

****

According to old-timer John Sanborne:

Earlier on (before the divorce) he made this stupid attempt to get Sara brainwashed so she'd do what he said. He kept her sitting up in a chair, denying her sleep, trying to use Black Dianetic principles on her, repeating over and over again whatever he wanted her to do. Things like, "Be his wife, have a family that looks good, not have a divorce. Or whatever."*

He had Dick De Mille reciting this sort of thing day and night to her.

Reading this Sara commented:

"Dave Williams was working on me. They always talk about Dick DeMille. They never talk about Dave Williams.

"He [Hubbard] was in Cuba for two months. The last time I saw him was in Kansas at the divorce hearings. When the divorce was over I felt like I had been freed from prison! The last year with him was particularly terrible. . . .

"I'm not a pathetic person who has suffered through the years because of my time with Ron. I can't waste my time dwelling on it. . . .

*Around this same time Hubbard was lecturing and writing on the evils of "Pain-Drug-Hypnosis," and warning about "Black Dianetics!" i.e., reverse Dianetics, used to implant hypnotic suggestions rather than "run them out."

"You show what he was in your book. You really don't need me . . .

****

In the early nineteen seventies a story was being circulated by the Guardian's Office that Sara had died. According to the story, just prior to passing away—while on her death bed—she had asked to see Hubbard.

Ron responded immediately and came to her side. She looked at him sadly and said, "Will you forgive me Ron? Everything I said was lies." And he said, soothingly, "Of course."

Then, according to the story, she added, "I had to do it Ron, I was being blackmailed." And he answered, gently, "Why didn't you tell me? I would have done something."

****

Sara, referring to the last years with Hubbard:

"It is too disgusting. I have done well keeping away from discussing it for 35 years and I don't want to talk about it now."

****

History would have been better served if the whole story came out. There is little doubt, however, that the lives of Sara and her husband and their beloved family would be badly served by the heavy-handed brutality of Scientology's "secret service" rolling out their harassment and "black propaganda machine."

Sara sat back in the chair. Her large blue eyes staring into space. "No, I'm sorry Bent, I would prefer not to continue."

6

Dianetics Abandoned

While Hubbard was in Havana, a Kansas oil man named Don Purcell offered his assistance to the struggling Foundation. An agreement was struck. The Foundation was to be moved from Elizabeth, New Jersey, to Wichita, Kansas, where Purcell would make funds and a building available. Purcell would become President of the Foundation and Hubbard its Vice-President and Chairman of the Board.

The official Church reason for the relocation of the Foundation is as follows:

> In the spring of 1951, the Hubbard Dianetic Research Foundation moved from Elizabeth, N.J., to Wichita, Kansas. Wichita, being near the geographical center of the United States, was an excellent location for the new national headquarters of Dianetics. From here the Foundation could more easily centralize and consolidate all the activities of Dianetics. . . .

During the time he was in Cuba, Hubbard completed a book in excess of 500 pages titled *Science of Survival, Prediction of Human Behaviour*.

Upon his return to the U.S. and arrival in Wichita, Hubbard began a schedule of regular weekly lectures in the building provided by Purcell.

Wrote Helen O'Brien:

> It looked like a warehouse which had been converted to Dianetic use by the erection of numerous partitions.
> On the second floor was an auditorium where classes were held and

a weekly public lecture was delivered by LRH, his only participation in foundation activities, except to sign certificates. . . . The place was always filled to overflowing for Hubbard's free public lecture.

[It] was the highlight of every week. He would arrive at the last minute, stopping briefly in his office to sign whatever professional auditor certificates were due. . . .

This pattern continued for many months, with lectures becoming more frequent. Also during this time several books were written. John Sanborne:

Purcell thought Dianetics was already wild enough, and he wanted to standardize it and make it work well for Mankind. He didn't believe in past lives. But there's nothing more you could expect from a Kansas oil man who's good hearted and wants to be famous for it. He wanted to be famous for being a benefactor of Mankind.

Around the time of the split between Purcell and himself, Hubbard started talking "whole track" and space opera and past lives. . . . He may have been putting this out just to bug Purcell. He was a prankster, a trickster. He wanted to see what he could do. And he drove Purcell a little bit berserk.

In December the Second Annual Conference of Dianetic Auditors was held. . . .
O'BRIEN:

There were none of Ron's former friends, the people who had made those [the earliest] foundations possible. He felt they had betrayed him.

By January of 1952 the popularity of Dianetics was at an all-time low, and the finances of the Foundation were a mess.

In February Hubbard resigned as Chairman and Vice-President and sold his stock in the corporation for one dollar and the agreement that he would be allowed to open up an independent school.
O'Brien continues:

I returned to Wichita (in March) but not to the Hubbard Dianetic Research Foundation (HDRF). Hubbard . . . had embarked upon what became a lengthy and well-documented feud . . . during 1952 Hubbard tried to divert people's attention from the fact that the Wichita Foundation was a financial failure by attempting to create the impression that Don Purcell, the "angel" whose money had made it a reality, was an arch villain who had plotted to seize Dianetics or, in another version, to destroy it for $500,000 from the AMA.

What apparently happened was that Purcell had been willing to subsidize the deficit operation of the Wichita Foundation, but they were constantly badgered by creditors from the early (Elizabeth based) HDRF, to whom he was forced to make payments. When the situation became grave, he told Hubbard that a declaration of voluntary bankruptcy seemed essential, and a fresh start. Hubbard refused.

Early in February the creditors became insistent and threatened a liquidating receivership. On February 12th, Hubbard called a meeting of the board of directors, of which he was chairman, and resigned completely from the HDRF. . . . He opened new offices in Wichita and called it Hubbard College, while the remaining directors took the necessary steps to enter (HDRF) into voluntary bankruptcy.

In March a restraining order was placed on Hubbard and his new right-hand man James Elliot, who'd admitted to "inadvertently" removing the Foundation's mailing lists, taped lectures, typewriters, sound-recorders and other equipment. The tapes and the mailing lists were returned although, allegedly, the tapes had been mutilated.

Shortly afterwards the assets of the Wichita Foundation were auctioned by the bankruptcy court. Purcell purchased the assets, which included the publishing rights to *Dianetics, the Modern Science of Mental Health*, the Foundation's copyrights, and the sole right to the title "Hubbard Dianetic Foundation."

Hubbard was left with two choices: give up the "save Mankind game" entirely, or start fresh, start another movement, write more books, and lecture like crazy.

Immediately, and in no uncertain terms, he chose the latter alternative. Thus Scientology poked its head out of the clouds and made itself known to the world.

"Thought is the subject matter of Scientology. It is considered a kind of 'energy' which is *not part* of the physical universe. It controls energy, but it has no wavelength. It uses matter, but it has no mass. . . . It records time but is not subject to time," wrote Hubbard in the first issue of *The Journal of Scientology*.

He says it more succinctly sometime later in the Scientology axioms:

LIFE IS BASICALLY A STATIC.
Definition: a Life Static has no mass, no motion, no wavelength, no location in space or time. It has the ability to postulate and to perceive.

THE STATIC IS CAPABLE OF CONSIDERATIONS, POSTULATES AND
OPINIONS.

SPACE, ENERGY, OBJECTS, FORM AND TIME ARE THE RESULT OF
CONSIDERATIONS MADE AND/OR AGREED UPON OR NOT BY THE
STATIC, AND ARE PERCEIVED SOLELY BECAUSE THE STATIC CONSID-
ERS THAT IT CAN PERCEIVE THEM.

This is essentially an expression of a viewpoint traceable to both
Eastern and Western mystic and occult traditions.

HUBBARD:

You can't measure this Static.

When you find something that has no mass, no motion, no wavelength—the very fact that it can't be measured tells you that you have
your hands on life itself.

You can't measure it, yet all things measurable extend from it. From
the Static all phenomena extend. . . .

Space is one of these phenomena. You could say that Life is a space-
energy-production and placement unit because that's what it does. But
when you measure these you do not measure life.

A thetan is very close to being a pure Static . . .

So you have a thetan capable of considerations, postulates and opinions . . .

Or, less technically stated:
"Spirit is the source of all. You are a spirit."

****

After he spent a little over two months in Wichita at the "Hubbard
College," where he specialized in saying things that would cause Don
Purcell to spend extended amounts of time on the toilet moaning, the
move to Phoenix, Arizona, was made.

In March of 1952, he married for the third time. Her name, Mary
Sue Whip, an attractive redhead, who had been a student in Wichita.

A little later Ron Jr. arrived and found himself suddenly on the
board of directors of the newly formed Hubbard Association of Scientologists.

Electro-psychometers or E-meters (a modified psycho-galvanometer) were now being used, having been developed by an engineer by
the name of Volney Matthison.

Aided by this device, Ron Jr. worked with his father on "researching" the "whole track"; i.e., the moment-to-moment recording

of all of one's experiences ("track") throughout all of one's past exis-
tences and lives.

According to Ron Jr., with the aid of amphetamines his father and
he came up with the booklet "What to Audit," which later became the
book entitled *History of Man*. Its foreword begins by proclaiming:

> This is a cold-blooded and factual account of your last sixty trillion
> years.

Although it contains some interesting theories about how spiritual
beings operate, the bulk of its contents are descriptions of aberrative
"whole track incidents," mainly "electronic implants." Hubbard
defines an implant as "a painful and forceful means of overwhelming a
being with artificial purposes or false concepts in a malicious attempt
to control and suppress him."

These come in a great many varieties and types, one of which is the
"Between Lives Implant." This particular type of "implant," according to Hubbard, is currently being administered in several secret locations on Earth:

> At death the theta being [the spirit] leaves the body and goes to the
> between-lives area. Here he "reports in," is given a strong forgetter
> implant and then is shot down to a body just before it is born.
> There have been many types of between lives earlier on the track,
> about ten different periods of the entire track being devoted to the
> practice of keeping a thetan in a body, working and in an area.

The *History of Man* comes equipped with its share of hype and
pretense, and its author certainly positioned himself at a place of considerable authority. For some people the book was (and still is) an in-
disputable description of what one will find on the "whole track" of an
individual, an *Evaluation* from a source on high.

"Auditing"—ideally defined as that action whereby one gradiently
increases his awareness and ability to confront and communicate—
cannot take place in the context of an overwhelming evaluation.

History of Man was one in a long series of evaluations by Hubbard
as to what another will find on his personal "time track."

The point is not that Hubbard's imaginings, opinions, or observations are valid or invalid, but only that they are *his*. And should have
been presented as such.

One of the most important points of the Auditor's Code is: *Do not
evaluate for the pre-clear.* This business of telling others what they

will see, long before they've had a chance to look, is one of the main "veer off points" of Scientology.

(When Hubbard wrote "Do not evaluate for the pre-clear," he really meant, "Nobody evaluates but me!")

****

John Sanborne has some things to say about the early days in Phoenix, Arizona:

> Hubbard led us to the idea that he'd been on destroyer-escorts in 1939/40, on convoy duty while England was at war. (The U.S. Navy would escort cargo ships across the Atlantic.) He'd also go on about his experiences in combat during the war, while he was a U.S. naval officer.
>
> I had a genuine war record and that kind of spooked him; made him uneasy in some funny kind of way that I couldn't figure out, until recently when I found he hadn't been in combat. I think he was haunted by the feeling that he'd been a coward. . . .
>
> Hubbard spent a lot of time with Nibs (Nibs is Ron Jr.'s nickname). When Nibs came to Phoenix, Hubbard just closeted himself with him and just doted on him. He gave him a lot of inside track.
>
> Nibs thought the world of his father. "Oh Dad! Oh Dad! . . . One time *Dad* was in . . ." and so forth and so on and the poor guy never had a chance. . . .
>
> Now, when someone's got a domineering pain-in-the-ass old man like that who's got a big reputation and so forth, that's tough to son under. Hemingway's kids, most kids, they have a tough time in most cases son-ing under that. . . .
>
> Hubbard's research was sloppy and "unscientific," and that's the way I liked it. I liked the way he worked in those days. Off the wall— off the top of his head.
>
> He told Dick Steves, Bud Eubank and Chet Delane to go "run effort."* And they said, "What's that?" And he said, "Never mind. Just go do it!" And so they went and "ran effort." And they were running engrams and running the efforts out of them, because they didn't know what else to do. So they fell right into past lives. And they came back and he said, "What happened?" And they said, "Hey, you have a great

---

*To counsel with Effort Processing (taken from Hubbard's "Technical Dictionary"): "The bank (subconscious mind) can be considered to have three layers, effort-emotion-thought. EFFORT buries emotion. Emotion buries thought. A physical aberration or physical disability is held in place by a COUNTER EFFORT. EFFORT PROCESSING removes the EFFORT which uncovers the PC's own EMOTION and removes the Emotion which uncovers and blows the PC's thoughts and postulates about the disability as these are the aberrative source of it."

procedure here!" And he said, "Procedure? I uh, uh . . ." He was totally aghast at the fact that this stuff happened. Because he was just
throwing it at them. . . .

At the time the emphasis was "try this and tell me what the results
are." That's how he worked in those days.

Hubbard knew how to talk stuff. The idea was to be able to talk
everything. I think he thought of it as a way to handle threats. He'd be
in some real sweaty situation and he'd be able to talk himself out of
anything.

Because he did things which were likely to get him in trouble, he
didn't much like the rewards of ordinary responsibilities. *Ordinary
decent people didn't interest him except to pose in front of them.* . . .

In a Phoenix congress . . . he talked about spooky whole track stuff.
He had a floodlight on the floor in front of this little platform shining
up, because that makes you look ghouly. And his face looked really
weird and outer space and really crazy. . . . And he talked weird. . . . I
think he was trying to drive people a little bit wacko so they'd fall into
his hand a little bit. . . .

Most of the women I audited in those days had a little place in their
hearts where they believed that he was lecturing only to them, and he
was giving signals that, "When I get a certain number of things done at
this level, then you and I can take off together."

Women from twenty to eighty were sure of this. I only had one female pre-clear, in those days, who didn't have that. She was the only
one who didn't have plans to run off with Hubbard. . . .

****

Says Old Timer Jack Horner:

He could emanate pure affinity; just engulf you in it. Of course he
wasn't sincere, but it was sure convincing to a lot of people. He had
that ability: people would go in to see him with a disagreement, and
then they'd completely forget what the hell it was.

RON JR.:

At some party or get-together people would see him sitting there,
and they'd be inclined to say, "Who in the heck would ever follow this
man?" And he'd stand up and turn around and nail them. I mean the
eyeballs, the whole thing would just change in an instant.

I've seen him when he really had it turned on. I've seen him stand
in front of an audience and just nail them to their seats. He called it his
"Cobra Eyelock." He also called it "putting the snake on 'em."

I've seen people charge into his office mad as hornets and come out a minute later pleased as punch.

According to Ron Jr., some of Hubbard's basic and most important "research" of the period was done while on drugs and/or alcohol.

RON JR.:

He'd sit at his typewriter late at night and boost up on drugs and hit way at the top, and write like crazy. He could type 97 words a minute with four fingers. That was the maximum the old IBM electric type-writer would go. When he got into one of these drug trips he'd write until the body just collapsed.

That's the way he worked. Usually what he had written in a burst would then be allowed to trickle out to the public, the classes he taught. It wouldn't just show up right away.

But it was an uneven thing. Sometimes he wouldn't write for a week, then he'd strap on the heavy duty rockets and up he'd go again.

7

"The Blood of Their Bodies, The Blood of Their Souls"

L. RON HUBBARD JR.:

"In 1951 Dad arrived in Phoenix where I was living with my grandfather. He spoke to me about the possibility of my working on Dianetics with him. It was thrilling. I was tremendously impressed with my father; with the fact that he was famous and knew other famous people. Through his involvement in science fiction he knew many well-known writers. Through Dianetics he had met many stars and starlets, and even audited a few.

"Growing up, I was constantly shuttled back and forth between my mother and grandfather; it made me feel unwanted.

"Dad wasn't home much, but when he was it was seldom dull. He used to play the ukulele and sing; he had a rich baritone voice. . . .

"It's a drag to talk about but he did have a vicious temper. . . .

"Dinner time could sometimes be memorable. He was very fussy about his food—not just right and bam! That night's dinner formed a mosaic against the wall. When it happened my mother would be in shock. She was an excellent cook and could never understand why.

"Nonetheless, he never laid a hand on me and my sister.

"He did, however, put phenobarbital in my bubble gum on several occasions.

"As a teenager I had a terrible inferiority complex. Dad's invitation for me to become, in a major way, a part of his life meant everything. And to top it all off he presented me with a fabulous gift, a '47 Buick and 100 dollars for gas. This was a particularly noteworthy event since he had forgotten so many Christmases and birthdays before that.

"That fall I returned to the Pacific Northwest with my grandparents to finish my junior year of high school. Then, in August of 1952, Dad and I were reunited in Phoenix.

"Within a few short weeks I found myself head of the newly formed "Hubbard College," as Director of Training and Chief Instructor. My life up to this point had been a grim tale of rejection and emotional turmoil. We had rarely lived at one location for any length of time. . . .

"Then, out of the blue, I'm the Great Sage's number one son."

****

The following is mainly excerpted from a piece, written by Ron Jr. in 1985, originally entitled "Philadelphia":

"We were in Philadelphia. It was November 1952. Dianetics was all but forgotten; and Scientology, a 'new Science,' had become the focus of attention.

"Every night, in the hotel, in preparation for the next day's lecture, he'd pace the floor, exhilarated by this or that passage from Aleister Crowley's writings.

"Just a month before, he had been in London, where he had finally been able to quench his thirst; to fill his cup with the true, raw, naked power of the magick. The lust of centuries at his very fingertips.

"To stroke and taste the environs of the Great Beast, to fondle Crowley's books, papers, and memorabilia had filled him with pure ecstasy!

"In London he had acquired, at last, the final keys; enabling him to take his place upon the 'Throne of the Beast,' to which He firmly believed himself to be the rightful heir.

"The tech gushed forth and resulted in the 'Philadelphia Doctorate Course Lectures.'"

[At the beginning of the very first Philadelphia Lecture Hubbard cracked a joke about the "Prince of Darkness." "Who do you think I am?" he asked. The audience chuckled. Ron's such a kidder.]

"Dad's lecture series was held upstairs in a large room. He was knocking them dead creating brilliant truths that danced in the heads of the audience. He was excelling himself. He was in hyperdrive when the U.S. Marshals showed up.

"They came bursting in like Carrie Nation attacking a saloon. Absolutely no class at all.

"We somehow distracted the Marshals from going all the way upstairs.

"It seems that all the Marshals wanted was to serve him a subpoena to appear in court over the hassle Don Purcell was kicking up over the rights to Dianetics. (He claimed he owned them).

"The subpoena was finally properly and courteously served.

"Now it was Dad's turn. When he unfolded the paper he became unglued. He hated courts; he hated Don Purcell; he hated, period. All the clicks in his head went off like a string of Chinese firecrackers.

"Well, Dad was psycho as hell, but he wasn't dumb. He took the rap. A contempt of court with a fine of $5000.00.

"One does not put a god on trial nor ridicule a god. Dad vowed never to appear in court again for any reason. He never did.

"The night after the court appearance he was still raging. When he was nervous or upset he would shout and scream. When his concrete self-confidence was shaken he would blindly attack people and furniture.

"A bottle of rum and an hour of screaming later he had cooled down a little; but the 'Power' was still translating into anger; overriding the alcohol. My whole life I've always marvelled at his capacity to consume alcohol and remain upright and coherent. A fifth of Myers dark rum was the same as two aspirin to Dad.

"After he got in the groove and plugged in his self-confidence again, he got up from the couch and retrieved several books from his suitcase. He dropped them in front of me on the hotel room coffee table.

" 'I'm going to need more help,' he says. 'More help than I'm getting. I'm going to outlive this whole damned world but I want you for back-up.'

" 'You got it Dad, you know that already,' I say.

" 'I know, I know,' Dad says impatiently, 'but you don't have much horsepower.'

" 'Hey, Dad, I'm doing O.K.'

"He flies off the handle: 'You snot-nosed kid. You don't know your ass from a hole in the ground!' He slams his hand down on the books on the coffee table. 'All you are is a fart in a hurricane, kid; now read about the Real Power!'

" 'The books and contents to be kept forever secret,' he says. 'To reveal them will cause you instant insanity: rip your mind apart; destroy you.' he says. 'Secrets, techniques and powers I alone have conquered and harnessed. I alone have refined, improved on, applied my engineering principles to. Science and logic. *The* keys! My keys to the doorway of the Magick; my magick! *The* power! *Not* Scientology power! *My* power! The real powers of Solomon,' he says, 'Caligula and Alice too. Your past is your enemy,' he says. 'the enemy of all.'

"I listen with hypnotic fascination: 'The Books; some recently published, some over 1200 years old, *The Book of the Law, The Sacred Magic of Abre-Melin,* the *Sex Magic of the Ninth Degree of the O.T.O.*' . . .

"He is excited, fearful and cautious. He is tense. Unimparted secrets, imparted for the first time.

"I open the books intending only to thumb through. I am awed and amazed; *I Know* these books! How could I?

"He answers: 'They were used to conceive you, and birth you, too. I've read them to you while you were asleep—while you were drugged and hypnotized; for years.

" 'I've made the Magick really work,' he says. 'No more foolish rituals. I've stripped the Magick to basics—access without liability.

" 'Sex by will,' he says. 'Love by will—no caring and no sharing—no feelings. None,' he says. 'Love reversed,' he says. 'Love isn't sex. Love is no good; puts you at effect. Sex is the route to power,' he says. Scarlet women! They are the secret to the doorway. Use and consume. Feast. Drink the power through them. Waste and discard them.'

" 'Scarlet?' I ask.

" 'Yes Scarlet: the blood of their bodies; the blood of their souls,' he says.

" 'Release your will from bondage. Bend their bodies; bend their minds; bend their wills; beat back the past. The present is all there is. No consequences and no guilt. Nothing is wrong in the present. The will is free—totally free; no feelings; no effort; pure thought—separated. The Will postulating the Will,' he says.

" 'Will, Sex, Love, Blood, Door, Power, Will. Logical,' he says.

" 'The doorway of Plenty. The Great Door of the Great Beast.'

"He repeats the incantation; invokes the door opening to the realm of the Beast.

"I'm nauseated. I hurt.

"He says: 'Never tell, or much worse will happen.'

"I nod."

****

"I had barely got out of my '47 Buick when Dad started me popping Rainbows. It seemed like two minutes later I was teaching Scientology, when I could barely pronounce the word."

8

Scientology in the Fifties

In my opinion, Scientology was designed by L. Ron Hubbard as a trap.

People will argue that Scientology contains some wonderful truths, and some ingenious counseling techniques. I couldn't agree more. These have been, for many, the cheese in the trap.

By the mid-fifties the cheese had become sweet indeed, and the trap, in all its insidious aspects, had not yet been adequately refined. If Scientology could be said to have had a "Golden Age," this was it.

Hubbard penned some very enlightened essays on the evils of authoritarianism, and even occasionally acknowledged that others had contributed to the subject.

During the fifties he gave over a thousand public lectures, almost all of which were taped. He also wrote over twenty books and in excess of a million words in articles and Professional Auditor Bulletins.

****

Prior to Scientology becoming a Church, Hubbard didn't seem to have much use for organized religion and often ridiculed it. In a lecture during July of 1951 he said of the Roman Catholic Church:

> What did we have when this organization was in its greatest ascendency? We had a dark age for man. By the way, I'm saying nothing against organized religion. You understand me clearly. I have nothing, absolutely nothing against organized religion. We've taken care of it. It'll go by the boards shortly. . . . I just happen to not like it.

Presaging what was to become today's Church of Scientology, he continued:

329

> Somebody jumps up and he says, "I'm the Messiah! Hurrah! Hurrah! Hurrah! I'm the Messiah!" And everybody says bonk! "Bow down to the Messiah! We're all set now . . ." And they'll do the same things and say the same things. And they're all just like puppets. Fascinating. Utterly fascinating!

****

On April 10th of 1953 he wrote to Helen O'Brian, then a franchise holder in Philadelphia:

> We don't want a clinic. We want one in operation, but not in name. Perhaps we could call it Spiritual Guidance Center . . . we could put in nice desks and our boys in neat blue, with diplomas on the walls and one, knock psychotherapy into history and, two, make enough money to shine up my operating scope and, three, keep the HAS [Hubbard Association of Scientologists] solvent. . . . I await your reaction on the *religion angle.* [emphasis added] In my opinion, we couldn't get worse public opinion than we have had or have less customers with what we've got to sell.

On December 18, 1953, the Church of Scientology, the Church of Human Engineering, and the Church of American Science were secretly incorporated in Camden, New Jersey. The incorporators were L. Ron Hubbard, Sr., L. Ron Hubbard, Jr., Ron Jr.'s wife Henrietta, John Galusha, Barbara Bryan, and Verna Greenough.

Early in 1954 the First Church of Scientology was announced.

The fact is that Hubbard had been having problems for years with the AMA and the IRS, and becoming a church was a way of avoiding these problems.

Ironically, the rank and file of today's Church, and also those who regard themselves as "Independent (separate from the main Church) Scientologists," consider quite sincerely that Scientology is their religion. It was only among the Church hierarchy (those who surrounded Hubbard) that actions and attitudes clearly betrayed a regard for it as a money-making enterprise.

In October of 1954 Don Purcell had returned the rights to *Dianetics, the Modern Science of Mental Health.* This was strictly a gift on Purcell's part. This prompted Hubbard to write the book that Scientologists know as *Dianetics 55.*

****

In the mid-1950s Hubbard wrote a series of letters to the Communist Activities Division of the FBI. These eventually earned him the title "mental" in an FBI file. One letter states:

> About two or three o'clock in the morning my apartment was entered. I was knocked out, had a needle thrust in my heart to give it a jet of air to produce a coronary thrombosis and was given an electric shock with a 110 volt current. All this is very blurred to me. I had no witnesses.

Under the letterhead, "L. Ron Hubbard D.D. Ph.D.," he later wrote:

> Gentlemen:
> Having gotten on a somewhat more even keel after the collapse of the organization in Phoenix, Arizona (the HASI), and having begun operation in the East with more public success and enthusiasm than I am used to, I have a better perspective on what occurred in Phoenix.
> The attack on the HASI, like the attacks on the 1950 Hubbard Dianetic Research Foundation, found psychiatry and Communist connected personnel very much in evidence and both active with defamation and very unreasonable—and unsuccessful—attack.
> But something has now occurred which seems strange at this juncture and entirely too pat. I have received from an unimpeachable source an invitation to go to Russia. I have been told that this would be as easy as taking a taxi to the airport.
> But the oddity of this invitation is that the person extending it, evidently on behalf of the Russian government, would not know anything about the trouble in Phoenix. He obviously has no connection with anyone or anything in Phoenix. Further, he knows little or nothing of Dianetics or Scientology and their organizational history and would not know, by any usual means, what occurred in Phoenix. Out of the blue, on an acquaintance with me from many, many years ago he locates me here, is very quiet and casual and then gradually works into the Russian situation and finally, with a burst of enthusiasm, confides in me that in view of the state of my organizations in the United States (about which he would really know nothing in fact) and in view of the U.S. public attitude toward me (which is in actuality rather good, considering) and in view of the fact that I "am a cinch to be ruined by all the people who hate me in Internal Revenue," there is "really nothing left for it but to accept this Russian offer."
> In the greatest spirit of friendship and camaraderie it seems that I can go to Russia as an advisor or consultant and have my own laboratories and receive very high fees. And it is all so easy because it has already been ascertained that I could get my passport extended and all I

had to do was go to Paris and there a Russian plane would pick me up and that would be that.

Indeed I suppose that would be that.

This is my third invitation to go to Russia. The first was extended to me by a member of Amtorg in New York in 1938 who knew of my work in the field of the mind. The second occurred less directly in 1948 after some personal difficulty. This third has come when the Phoenix organization has been collapsed and it would not be known that it did not influence my own affairs as much as it might be thought.

Hubbard goes on to list, "some of the personnel connected to the Phoenix trouble," who had "now drifted into Washington." Many of those mentioned were members in good standing and remained so for many subsequent years. One of these was Jack Horner, the first person to be awarded a "Doctor of Scientology" certificate.

Horner, when recently presented with these letters, expressed surprise. Hubbard at the time had given no indication of any hostile intention toward Horner, let alone that he was writing to the FBI implying he was a communist. But he was somewhat amused in light of the fact that he has been, for most of his life, a "Goldwater Republican."

Hubbard's letter concludes:

I suppose when the Russian-inclined "friend" finds that my desires to travel in and work in Russia do not exist, I can expect more violent measures.

I have not given you the name of this contact because it is a little too highly placed on the Hill and because it *may* be that he is acting in an entirely friendly way and it *may* be, as I sometimes learn, that the fate of Scientology and its adventures has good word of mouth. I would not submit you an irresponsible report which then might find me under the TV cameras telling one of this man's committees why I reported him as a communist because I do not know that he is—I only know that he and his influence has been quite liberal and in all the smoke of the Summit he may be carried away with enthusiasm. But he *did* know, when no possible reasonable way existed for him to know, too much about the activities of a subject about which he professes to know nothing and he has made several allusions to my possible fate in the United States, rather benign threats.

****

Around this time, Volney Matthison, whose electro-psychometer had been used by Hubbard and many Scientologists, had fallen into disfavor. He had refused to surrender the patent to his invention. It was the *Matthison* E-Meter, and Matthison was determined to keep it that way. So in late 1954 the use of the E-meter was discontinued by Hubbard.

Wrote Hubbard:

> Yesterday, we used an instrument called an E-Meter to register whether or not the process was still getting results so that the auditor would know how long to continue it. While the E-Meter is an interesting investigation instrument and has played its part in research, it is not today used by the auditor. . . . As we long ago suspected, the intervention of a mechanical gadget between the auditor and the pre-clear had a tendency to depersonalize the session. . . .

In 1958 Don Breeding and Joe Wallis developed a modified, smaller, battery operated version of Volney Matthison's device, which they presented to Hubbard. It was christened the *Hubbard* electrometer. What a difference a name makes!

As you probably guessed, E-meters were suddenly once again essential to auditing.

****

RON JR.:

> Dad believed firmly that Dianetics and Scientology were his alone: "Nobody makes any money off this but *me!*" I heard him say many times. And to do so was a fast way to be destroyed.
>
> "It's *mine!*" I heard him scream, more times than I care to recall.
>
> When he was in one of his rages he could really get profane. Sometimes he'd pick up an E-meter, "That fucking son of a bitch!" and he'd just slam the thing right off the wall. Lost a lot of E-meters that way, or whatever else was around.

****

As some old-time Scientologists have commented, "Hubbard could mock up." Meaning he could create a "beingness" for himself; an identity.

Old Timer VERN TOWNSEND:

> Yes he could "mock up." He'd be standing there lecturing, and by God if he didn't resemble a red-headed likeness of the Buddha. He seemed to be "glowing" appreciative benificence.

JOHN SANBORNE:

The guy fits the mold of the coyote and the trickster. There's a lot of lore about the coyote and the trickster. Not all bad either. There's a lot of warrior in the coyote and the trickster. It's sort of like you take a brilliant guy, who may have been sensitive. As a child he may have been hooted at. He may have been treated badly by the kids. He possibly became one of the guys that wants to "get" the world. . . .

Hubbard liked to think of himself as just naturally wonderful. He liked to think of himself as being worshipable. And he figured that if he could just keep his image up and not let us know about his girlfriends he'd be all right.

So anyway he liked to think of himself as a wonderful hero that's just as light as a feather; a guy who's dazzling and charming with red hair and sparkling blue eyes and just a winsome way about him. But a guy that can really get tough if he needs to.

****

In December of 1959 L. Ron Hubbard, Jr., walked out of the Founding Church of Scientology in Washington, D.C., never to return.

"I had grown weary of the games my father played, I wanted to live my own life. I was tired of the lies. I wanted to raise my family. I wanted to rejoin the human race . . . and I wanted my family eating regularly.*

---

*Hubbard, apparently resentful that his son had kept his wife and children out of the organization, had cut Ron Jr.'s weekly pay to almost nothing.

9

Clay in the Master's Hands —The "Lower Levels" of Scientology

In 1961 I was 18. Fine Art was one of my passions and I was doing quite well with clay sculpting. A bust I created of one of my teachers was featured in a major New Zealand magazine, with a photograph and story.

This publicity was exciting, and thereafter my art teacher Tom Morgan increasingly spent time talking with me during lunch hours and some of the after-school hours that I put in on various projects. Tom was a Scientologist, but I never heard him use the word Scientology or Dianetics until after I discovered what he was into from another source. I guess he didn't want to be hit by the school administration for promoting some strange cult.

He gave me animated and exciting one-on-one lectures about reincarnation and Eastern philosophy, in a way that appealed both to my intellect and imagination.

Sometimes he would just "run processes" on me, informally. They were delightful and just a hell of a lot of fun!

"What could you have done today?" he'd ask with a mischievous interest.

"I could have stayed at home sick and avoided that damned math test," I responded.

"O.K., what could you have done today?" he said.

"I suppose I could have hopped on my motorscooter and gone to a movie."

"O.K., what could you have done today?"

More answers by me, and the same question was repeated by Tom for some twenty or thirty minutes. It was interesting. I got more and more creative with my answers and realized that I had the potential of doing all sorts of things. This resulted in a new feeling of excitement about the possibilities and opportunities of life.

This was quite a result from a simple little question, asked repeatedly, with no advice, lecturing or prompting by Tom. Just that simple question, over and over. My admiration for what I began calling "Tom's philosophy" was enhanced.

I eventually discovered the name Scientology from a friend of Tom's and insisted that Tom give me some literature on it. He did, and I was so impressed with the material I read that I quit school to get a job to pay for a Scientology course.

I quit school six months before winning a university scholarship. This would have put me into the top five percent as far as education in New Zealand is concerned.

The Scientology course I took lasted two months full time, every week day from nine A.M. till ten P.M.

Dianetics, the Modern Science of Mental Health was the first text. It had an appendix on the "Scientific Method" by "Bell laboratories." It also had a Foreword by Dr. Winters. Both of these impressed me with their objective approach to research. Since Hubbard had included these in his book, and since he also claimed to be an engineer, I assumed that he fully supported the ideas I was reading.

Training Routines (T.R.s) were the basis of the practical training to become an auditor. These routines were done "tough."

Brian Livingston was a full-time student on these T.R.s. He was doing "T.R. O," in which the student sits facing the "coach," about three feet away, with the idea that the student does nothing but *be* there for two hours; no fidgeting or moving about, nothing else but *being there*. Among other things this drill was designed to improve an auditor's ability to listen attentively.

I noticed that Brian was turning green. He said, "I'm going to throw up!"

"Flunk, you spoke!" exclaimed his coach.

Brian stiffened and there was a determined look in his eyes, then a few seconds later, he threw up all over the coach.

"Flunk, you threw up!" said the coach stoically, while the supervisor and one of his aides scurried for a bucket and mop. The drill continued as they cleaned up the smelly mess.

Brian went on to become one of the top auditors, serving Hubbard aboard the Flagship during the later sixties and seventies.

There are "expert" witnesses who have testified as to how the T.R.s are "brainwashing." I personally have not seen that effect. On the contrary, they seem to have had beneficial effects when coached well.*

After T.R. O comes a "bullbaiting" step, where "buttons" are pushed: The coach pokes around saying all sorts of personal (even obscene) things, and cracking jokes, till he gets laughter or any other reaction, such as blushing, fidgeting, looking away, or whatever. Then he/she works that "button" over, till there is no more reaction.

The idea is that anyone who would audit another should have enough self-control to not involuntarily react—with shock, surprise, laughter, or whatever—to what his "pre-clear" tells him in session, thus the "bullbaiting" training routine.

The remaining drills teach the "Auditing Communication Cycle." This is where the auditor asks a question, the pre-clear looks into his mind for an answer, gives the answer to the auditor, and the auditor acknowledges the answer.

As a result of these drills, Scientologists have gained a reputation for looking people straight in the eye and always acknowledging whatever is said to them. Many do it to the point of obsession.

There are five more T.R. drills, all presented as having the purpose of enhancing one's ability to communicate with and direct others.

I did lots of T.R.s, and benefited quite a bit initially. I lost much of my teenage shyness and began to handle people much more positively.

These drills were originated to train Scientologists to become good auditors, but also became the basis for the introductory course to Scientology: the "communication course."

Along with the T.R.s I learned the Scientology "axioms" verbatim; one through fifty-one.

I audited all sorts of people who told me their intimate problems and considerations. Here I was 19 years old, and men and women twice or three times my age were baring their souls to me. It was quite an experience. I grew up fast.

---

*If "T.R. O" or just "being there" for extended lengths of time is "brainwashing," then so would be Zen meditation, being very similar to "T.R. O."

At the same time, looking back at it, because of the "wins" I was having, I became increasingly inclined to see nothing wrong with Hubbard and Scientology.

Hubbard and his organization, of which I really knew very little, were somehow superimposed onto the good feelings inspired by decent, caring people involved with these counseling techniques. Hubbard became equated in my mind with happiness, freedom and ability.

I began to credit Hubbard with, among other things, my feeling of being superior to virtually any challenge presented me.

Hubbard also began to become equated with my own intentions for helping Mankind. These intentions had always been there, but now they were, in my mind, increasingly being credited to Hubbard.

The natural good feelings of *esprit de corps* that evolve as a group works together for a common purpose, somehow also was credited to Hubbard. "Ron's wonderful tech" was the reason I was receiving admiration from those I assisted.

I had joined because of the anti-authoritarian message. I failed to notice at the time that the message was coming from an ultra-authoritarian source.

I did not see the similarity of what was happening to me and the clay sculpting I had done so successfully under Tom Morgan's tutelage.

I was being molded by a true master.

Obtaining a loan, and with the help of my father, who was a bricklayer, I built a house designed by Brian Livingston (who was an architect), and worked two jobs to accumulate enough money for my wife and me to travel to England and study under Hubbard.

THE "LOWER GRADES" OF THE "BRIDGE TO TOTAL FREEDOM"

The "grade chart," constituting Hubbard's "Bridge," had taken shape during the mid-1960's and consisted of a recompilation of numerous counseling procedures "developed by Ron" during the 1950s. Dianetics was again added as "a level" to the line-up in 1968.

The "Bridge" and Hubbard, its supposed "Source," are to Scientologists what the Bible, prayer, and Christ are to Christians: the central objects of worship and adoration. Any attempt to understand the phenomenon of Hubbard and the hypnotic influence he has on his followers, without some understanding of "his tech" and "the Bridge," would be a pointless exercise.

****

The first level of the "lower bridge" addressed the improvement of *memory* (in this case primarily pleasant memories). One of the processes consisted of following in sequence the commands:

Recall a time which was really real to you.

Recall a time when you felt real affinity* for someone.

Recall a time when someone was in good communication with you.

Also at this level the recalling of various "perceptics" is addressed. One is asked to recall various past experiences with particular attention to a specific perceptic or sense, such as sight, smell, touch, emotion, body position, weight, etc.

These, and the many other "recall processes," were of considerable interest, and did frequently bring about an improvement of the ability to recall.

****

The next step on "the lower Bridge" was the *communication* level.

Here the "end phenomenon" (the end result of doing these processes) was said to be that one would be able to communicate freely with anyone on any subject.

This always seemed a little bit of a tall order to me, but the processes certainly were interesting, and I did notice considerable communication skill improvements in those I audited; and I also achieved a greater ability to express myself effectively.

At the same time—true to the dual or "dichotomous" nature of the Scientology movement—I was becoming gradually less willing to communicate in certain areas. After all, *being* a Scientologist—especially with the advent of ultra-authoritarianism in the latter 1960's—meant accepting restrictions on thought and communication. But these restrictions, it was rationalized, were necessary so that Scientology could accomplish the immensely challenging and urgent task of bringing freedom and sanity to Earth. After all, when the survival of the human race is at stake, little things such as "freedom of speech" have to be put in their proper perspective.

---

*Affection or feeling of closeness.

There are many communication processes and it is possible here to present only a few.

"Communication is the universal solvent," wrote Hubbard, and indeed the mechanics of communication are the fundamentals of auditing.

An example of a communication disability might be the compulsive talker. He has an inability to receive a communication because he is compulsively subjecting others to a verbal outpouring, without ever noticing their obvious disinterest.

Of course there is also the inability to originate a communication: thus, the "wallflower" type of individual.

In order to improve communication abilities, various processes are run at the communication level (level 0) of the "Grade Chart."

One process lists identities, such as men, bosses, wives, husbands, teachers, cops, etc. (which get a reaction on the E-meter when mentioned by the auditor or the pre-clear—indicating "charge," or emotional discomfort). Providing that the pre-clear expresses interest, the following questions are asked:

Auditor: "If you could talk to a _____ (e.g., traffic cop), what would you talk about?"

The pre-clear: "Why he seems to get such pleasure hassling me for small infractions."

"O.K., if you could talk to a _____ (traffic cop) about that, what would you say exactly?"

The answer is given and acknowledged, and the questions are repeated. Usually a realization concerning the subject at hand occurs, with a resultant freeing up in the area of communication. At this point the process is ended.

(Certainly the posing of a question to another—while inviting him or her to come up with answers—culminating in a bit of enlightenment, is not original with Scientology. But Hubbard may be unique in his exploitation on this basically benign endeavor.)

Another process: "Spot [locate in the environment or in your mind] some desired communication" [e.g., someone you care for expressing affection for you, or being told, "You've got the raise you've been asking for," etc.]. "Spot some enforced communication" [e.g., having to say you're sorry when you know you're in the right]. "Spot some inhibited communication" [e.g., something you wanted to say but didn't], and so on.

Of course, if one dared reject the myriad enforced and inhibited communications that are built into the Church of Scientology—such as by not applauding Hubbard's photo during an event or muster, or by critizing some aspect of the "tech," or Church officials, or by persisting with a line of questioning about where the money goes—you'd be sent, pronto, to "ethics."

In 1965 "forbidden cognitions" (things that are not permitted for one to realize) even became an official part of Scientology—although announced by Hubbard only in a small paragraph, in a bulletin on another subject. Church pre-clears usually instinctively know better than to have such realizations. This combination of liberation and oppression, carried along far enough, tends to produce sort of half-enlightened, half-brainwashed individuals: warped little cross-eyed buddhas.

Having received much of my auditing prior to the "militarization" of Scientology, I didn't turn out as "cross-eyed" as some. But Hubbard did work his "black magic" on me. I'm still shaking it off. Interestingly enough, however, the positive results of the auditing I received largely remain.

Many former Scientologists, now more or less freed from Hubbard's "spell," still regard many of the procedures of the "lower grades" as valid and beneficial. The "upper levels" of Scientology, however, have not held up so well. (See "Through The Wall of Fire," Part II, Chapter 11.)

****

After the communication level, the *problems* level is embarked upon:

"Problems" are said to be composed of those things one has refused to confront or take responsibility for.

Of course, there are "positive problems" (consisting of challenges, goals to be attained, games to be won) and life would be very boring without them. This level of auditing deals with resolving "negative problems," which are a kind of treading water situation. One does nothing constructive about these problems, since one fails to face up to something regarding them.

Such problems often stem from false or missing information (such as, for example, "No one wants to go out with me." when—if he only asked—dozens of girls would have). They just result in useless worry and introversion.

One of the dozens of processes of this level is:

What about that problem could you confront? [alternated with the question] What about that problem would you rather not confront?

****

Areas of problems sometimes inspire bad solutions (e.g., stealing to solve the problem of lack of money; or someone "solving" the problem of frustrations at work by screaming at the kids). Such non-survival "solutions" are labelled "overts" in Scientology.

So after the problem level comes the *overts* level.

An "overt" is a harmful act.

Auditing, besides looking at harmful acts done to oneself by another, also looks at his own "overts" against others: a kind of purging of one's karma. One usually looks earlier than this life for the real juicy "overts." The idea being that one's difficulties are as much, or more, the result of what he did to others, than that which was done to him.

Reincarnation is of course hardly Hubbard's discovery, but his presentation of it was very appealing to me. The poem, "Intimations of Immortality," by Wordsworth, reflects the emotions I felt as a teen-ager contemplating reincarnation:

> Our birth is but a sleep and a forgetting:
> The Soul that rises with us, our life's Star
> Hath had elsewhere its setting,
> And cometh from afar:
> Not in entire forgetfulness
> And not in utter nakedness,
> But trailing clouds of glory do we come . . .

The idea goes that one may not only be "trailing clouds of glory," but also a few thunderclouds and perhaps some spiritual smog or acid rain.*

That one's own misdeeds are definitely a factor in one's misfortunes is very much a part of Scientology. However, to assert that at least some of the Church's troubles may have been the result of "overts" by Hubbard or his agents would be considered blasphemy.

To be a Scientologist is to live in a world full of "enemies," with Hubbard and his Church innocent and perfect, and the "enemies" totally evil. (Of course, harming "enemies" is not considered to be an "overt act.")

****

*The Church strongly adheres to the policy that any criticism of it or its founder simply means that the critic is, in effect, spiritually polluted; loaded with hidden crimes and dirty deeds. This, combined with compulsory metered confession, constitutes one of the organization's key control mechanisms. It is covered earlier, mainly in Part I, Chapters 9 and 12.

****

The next level addressed in auditing, concerns the area of *upsets*.

The basic principle of this level is that by isolating the exact "time, place, form or event" of an upset and having the person confront that, the upset resolves.

Lists of common causes of upsets are read out to the pre-clear and the E-meter is watched by the auditor for a reaction of the needle at the end of every item read on the list.

If an item "reads" (reacts), it is checked with the P.C. and he is given an opportunity to talk about it. If necessary, an "earlier similar" upset is located, and communicated until the upset is "handled."

During the *upsets* level, certain techniques are used. These have to do with locating times and places when an individual experienced severe upsets. Aiding the function of "assessing" till one locates the correct source of an upset or other "item" (person, time, place, etc.) is a basic function of the E-meter.

At this level, "assessing" includes choosing the correct source of a given upset from a series of possible sources.

Upsets often persist because of generalities such as "Everyone is against me," or "I hate women!" One hears these general phrases during everyday turmoil.

In order to resolve this, one must narrow things down to specific people, dates and places. And so "assessing" is used.

For example, mothers know how to assess instinctively:

"Who hit you?. . . . Joe, Lisa, Jonathan. . . ." and so on until the three-year-old nods, and sobbingly tells what happened (and when and where) until he ceases to be upset.

Wrote Count Alfred Korzybski, from whom Hubbard took so much:

In most cases of "insanity" or "unsanity," there is a disorientation as to "space" and "time."

So when things get irrational (insane or unsane), it is necessary to orient the person being "unsane" to the exact location and time when things went awry.

Another example of this is where a "hatred" (upset) is generalized. For example, a person might feel hatred for all mankind. He has not indexed (assessed) who he hates—and who he does not hate, and why—so he just hates generally.

It becomes necessary to differentiate whom he hates, from whom he does not hate; to discover what happened to generate the hate, and where and when the upset causing the hate first occurred.

The process of sorting this out can be highly rewarding.

Thus, tagging dates to events, (or "dating" as Hubbard calls that procedure); and sorting out *where* something occurred ("locating," Hubbard calls it) are key tools in resolving human conflicts and emotional turmoil.

Wrote Korzybski in *Science and Sanity* (first published 1935):

> In many instances serious maladjustments follow when "hate" absorbs the whole affective energy* of a given individual. . . . Thus an individual "hates" "all mothers," "all fathers," etc., in fact hates the whole fabric of human society, and becomes neurotic and even psychotic. Obviously it is useless to preach "love" for those who have hurt and done the harm. Just the opposite; as a preliminary step, by indexing [assessing] we allocate or limit the hate to the individual Smith instead of a hate for a generalization that spreads over the world. In actual cases we can watch how this allocation helps the given person. The more they "hate" the individual Smith instead of the generalization, the more positive affective energy is liberated and the more "human" and "normal" they become. . . . But even this individualized "hate" is not desirable and we eliminate it rather simply by dating. Obviously Smith 1920 is not Smith 1940 and most of the time hurt 1920 would not be a hurt in 1940.

Thirty years after the publication of Korzybski's book, Hubbard wrote:

> Great News!
> I've found the basis of ARC breaks!** [hates]
> . . . And now all is revealed: This is what makes an ARC break occur:
> An ARC break occurs on a generality . . .

Example: Little boy screaming with rage when he makes a mistake in drawing. Auditor observes little boy is upset.

Auditor: "What are you upset about?"
Little Boy: (howling) "My drawing is no good!"
Auditor: "Who said your drawing is no good?"
Little Boy: (crying) "The teachers at school" (plural).
Auditor: "What teacher?" (singular).

---

*"Affective energy" equates to Hubbard's "theta."
**Affinity, Reality, Communication, which equate to "Understanding." ARC breaks are breakdowns of Affinity or Reality or Communication or Understanding. In other words "upsets" or "hates."

Little Boy: (sobbing) "Not the teachers, the other chil-
              dren" (plural).
Auditor: "Which one of the other children?"
Little Boy: (suddenly quiet) "Sammy."
Auditor: "How do you feel now?"
Little Boy: (cheerfully) "Can I have some ice cream?"

As in Korzybski's method of resolving "hates" by indexing (assessing), this little boy (with the assistance of the auditor) isolated the
source of "hate" or upset and so ceased to be upset.*

My guess is Hubbard had just reviewed some of Korzybski's writings when he made his "discovery."

I had never read any of Korzybski's work, and was certainly not encouraged to do so. I assigned authorship of all this material to
Hubbard. It wasn't until I had left the Church of Scientology that ed-
ucator B. Robert Ross, a General Semanticist and independent Dianetic therapist, alerted me to the Korzybski connection.

****

After the "upsets" level, the next level of "the Bridge" deals with
fixed ideas.

"How blind our familiar assumptions make us," wrote Korzybski.

Giving an extreme example, Korzybski spoke of a phenomenon
(describing the insane):

> The insane have structural, conscious or unconscious, "premises"
> which are "false". . .
>   . . . these semantic disturbances and tensions make the "mentally"
> ill believe irresistibly in the "truth" of their "premises" and their in-
> ductions and deductions which they follow blindly . . . to the mentally
> ill these "premises" have the value of "the" and not "a" premise. They
> act upon them and so cannot adjust themselves to a world different
> from their own fancies.

Short of this extreme, "normal" individuals may be subject to
something similar.

For example, a fellow might be having a difficult time communicating to his wife. They have problems that don't resolve. He gets angry
and breaks her favorite teapot. She tears up his autographed picture
of Joe DiMaggio. This results in a giant argument and she moves out.

*It might be necessary to locate, and sort out, an "earlier similar upset" for the upset
to resolve. This is all pure Korzybski.

He demands she stay but she refuses. She finally insists on a divorce and, despite his impassioned pleas and protests, the marriage comes to an end. The big zinger for him is seeing her shortly thereafter with a fine-looking fellow, having a grand time—while she ignores him totally.

At that point, in order to save his self-esteem, he adopts a "fixed idea," which serves as an explanation for his failure, and makes him "right." Something like, "She's no good, all she wanted was money." This can slip into the further generality of, "Women are no good, all they want is money."

Go down to skid row sometime, and ask one of the bums what his "philosophy of life" is. He'll probably give you a very "solid" fixed idea that makes him right and another wrong. If you could find out what happened just before he adopted it, you'd find his "failure to cope."

So the "grade four" level of auditing is designed to free one of old, stupifying, fixed ideas. Of course, at the same time, if one refuses to adopt the official "fixed ideas" of the Church of Scientology, one's days are numbered. Again the dichotomy. . . . The dual nature of Scientology.

****

The next level was "*POWER.*" This is a transition level designed to prepare a person for the "upper levels." "Power" processes could only be taught at Saint Hill in England in 1967 (and are still restricted to "higher organizations"). This restriction also applies to the levels above power.

It was the first level that became confidential. Unless one had paid for the level, one could not see any of the materials regarding it. That fact, plus the surveyed title (Hubbard was keenly aware of Madison Ave techniques), was designed with marketing in mind.

Power processes constituted grade 5 and 5A. It was a big deal to be a power auditor, and my wife and I determined to learn the skills of this level after we had completed the Saint Hill Special Briefing Course.

We became "elite" class 7 power auditor interns.

The power processes were, from my observation, often effective in assisting an individual to think for himself; to become more creative; to effectively resist authoritarianism. One was strengthened in one's ability to maintain a viewpoint and to hold a position. The ability to hold a position was said to be the fundamental ingredient of power as a spiritual being.

It is interesting to me, therefore, that these procedures have been, by Hubbard's order, rarely used in Scientology since 1978.

When reading the first process, it may become apparent why this is so.

This power process deals with the ability to identify the source of things: Where do things come from? Who had the idea, who said something or who did something? On the other hand, it was also said to be important that one be able to identify who or what is *not* the source of something.

The "commands" (asked, in sequence, 1, 2, 3, 4) are extremely elementary:

> Tell me a source.
> Tell me about it.
> Tell me a no source.
> Tell me about it.

In 1978 since the FBI raids, of course, Hubbard was dedicated to disguising the fact that he was the source of management orders throughout the Guardian's Office years. He was, at the same time, heavily promoting himself as the "Source" of virtually all "valid knowledge" about the mind and spirit.

So people who could genuinely recognize true sources were not a "needed or wanted" commodity.

****

The next level, "old style" *goals* processing or "clearing," dealt with the rehabilitation of a person's own ability to create his *own* life and locate and follow his *own* current goals. It was discontinued around 1966. Apparently it was *too* effective, and sometimes made people "too free." "Too free" being defined as "free of Scientology and Hubbard's control."

Only warped little cross-eyed buddhas on this assembly line, thank you!

In its place since then is a procedure that reflects Hubbard's recurring fixation on science fiction type scenarios consisting mostly of "hypnotically implanted goals." Such goals were said to have been deliberately and maliciously installed into a person's subconscious mind throughout his travails in many lifetimes. Many of these lives were said to have been lived on other planets besides Earth. Some societies, both on Earth and on other planets, were said to have been very scientifically advanced.

Hubbard had dismissed his own idea of "implanted goals" as of no real consequence, being "1000 times less powerful," in the effect of messing someone up, than a person's own contradictory goals. That all changed after 1966.

****

I never realized the extent of Hubbard's borrowings from Korzybski until I read some of his works after leaving Scientology.

I also became aware of how many Dianeticists and early Scientologists had contributed to the creation of what is good in the "tech" (what some call "white Scientology"). Seeing Hubbard as the focal point of a thrust toward a better earth, they contributed their ideas and discoveries selflessly.

****

Until leaving the Church I had been hypnotized by "the genius" of L. Ron Hubbard, who "had singlehandedly discovered all this wonderful material!"

My gratitude had softened me up. He could mold me as he wished.

10

Lord of the Manor

Saint Hill Manor, a traditional Georgian mansion, was built in 1728. It was purchased by Hubbard in 1959 for some 14 thousand pounds (roughly 70 thousand dollars). "Mansions were going cheap then," says Reg Sharpe, Hubbard's top administrator during most of the Saint Hill years.

Prior to 1959 it was owned by the Maharajah of Jaipur, and prior to that a Mrs. Anthony Drexel Biddle.

Here L. Ron Hubbard lived in splendor. He was regularly served chilled bottles of Coke on a silver tray by his butler, Shepardson, and drove either his new American car or his vintage Jaguar, when taking a spin in the beautiful Sussex countryside.

By the time my wife Mary and I arrived in 1967 a castle had been added, along with a small cluster of brick buildings used as administrative offices and a chapel, all very quaint and blending harmoniously with the rolling English countryside. There were three tennis courts, cattle, horses and a donkey on the 40 acres adjoining the manor and an idyllic lake for fishing.

It was a disappointment when I discovered that Hubbard had not been in England for some months.

His family was still there and we saw Mary Sue Hubbard on a regular basis and Diana Hubbard and Quentin were students on the "Executive course" that we enrolled in. They were in their early teens.

The Saint Hill grounds were lush green with many old majestic trees and a small lake. They were well kept. Hubbard had set up hot houses and had been growing plants in them, and gained world-wide publicity with a photo of himself with a tomato plant hooked up to an E-meter. Even plants had emotional reactions he claimed. (I don't know if this was an original discovery—but years later others would in turn "discover" much the same thing.)

There was talk of a Sea Project that never made much sense to me. We settled down to study and work, on meager funds.

Excitement permeated Saint Hill during this period. Buses arrived each morning and unloaded students, staff and pre-clears. The parking lot was full, as were the classrooms and auditing rooms.

Much had happened prior to my arrival.

****

According to Hubbard, he came to England to promote and expand Scientology, and he liked it so much he decided to live there.

He had gone to Ireland first, prior to establishing St. Hill, to make that country a base for Scientology.

John Sanborne, who followed him to England and worked for him there, says:

> Hubbard wrote the book *Problems of Work* on the *Queen Mary*, on a trip to England in 1958. He just went into his stateroom and when he got to London he handed it to them [the Scientologists] and said, "Print it!"
>
> He wrote *Problems of Work* with the idea of becoming the Irish working man's hero. He always wanted a country, and he thought by playing on their dislike of the British and authority that he could just take over. Not become Prime Minister or anything like that, but just be the guy who pulls all the strings.

This did not work out at all well; but, undaunted, he traveled to England where he spoke, not of British tyranny, but of Britain being at the center of the bustling communication lines of the Planet (the British having established these as part of their empire over the past couple of centuries).

SANBORNE:

> He thought he was going to move up in class by buying a manor in England. That's such a queer interpretation of the system of England. . . .
>
> He put on his cowboy suit, got on his Harley-Davidson Motorcycle and, as Parade Marshal, led the annual parade in the town, And he seemed to think this was going to impress everyone.

****

John McMaster, the "world's first real clear," in a recent interview:

> I never spoke to Hubbard until I graduated from the Briefing

Course in the first week in January 1964. And he sent for me then and that's how it all started.

I said to him, "There's something I'd better tell you before somebody else does. That I'm not a Scientologist. I never have been and I never will be. I'm not even interested in Scientology. All I'm interested in is this function of auditing.

And he said, "John McMaster, that is exactly why I want you. You are not like the rest out there."

And in the years of working with him I found out that he absolutely despised people for being Scientologists. . . .

Hubbard used affinity to manipulate people.

But it was always an *apparent* affinity, really. He would say to people: "You are the *only* one." I have heard about a hundred people say that to me: "Oh well, he told me I was the only one."

And people would never destroy their allegiance to Ron because he had told them that they were "the only one."

That's the way he manipulated people with affinity. They would be told they were the only one, and then he would tell them all sorts of stories about what a difficult time he was having with Mary Sue. And how they were the only one who understood and what a difficult time he was having with the rest of the staff, and you're the *only one*. . . .

Of course, he tried this with me. "John McMaster, you are the only one," and so on. . . .

Hubbard had brought me a copy of the *Encyclopedia Britannica* and he put it next to me. And he pointed to a thing he wanted me to read, and that was where Buddha predicts that a red-headed man will appear in the West—Meitreya and so on. And that his first disciple will be a "disciple of love" (namely myself).

He got me doing all sorts of things.

For instance the "Standing Order number one" (which mandates, "All mail addressed to me [Hubbard] shall be received by me"):

He had stamps made of his various signatures and, over and above handling all the technology and so forth, I handled all his letters.

I handled the whole lot and used his stamp and so on. But I used to go over it in black ink so that people wouldn't be insulted.

But he didn't want to see the letters. He really didn't care.

So—with a few exceptions—I don't think he'd seen a letter to him in years. Because in 1964 I started handling all his mail. . . .

I was so excited and I loved the people so much that I would have done anything to keep people happy and winning. . . .

There were times when just the two of us were talking, there was sometimes something very good. Sometimes. Other times I could see that there was something very false. And then there were times when he would just denounce everyone. And he would despise everyone. He despised people for some reason. . . .

. . . I had been sending notes to him about these people and he hadn't done a thing about it, and these people were coming down to the manor, and now it had reached the stage where I had to see him.

So I said to Ken Urquart, who was his butler at the time, "You'll just have to take me up to his room. I've just got to see him."

Well it was about mid-day. He was just getting up. He was a night owl. Anyway, I got up there and he was just in his bathroom, which was attached to his bedroom. He came out and I was surprised at the color of his body. It was grey. He came out nude.

And there on a table was one of those enormous bottles of gin. . . .

He went to South Africa in '66 to find all the Kruger millions. He said he had discovered in an auditing session just exactly where he had stashed them in an earlier lifetime. He had managed to make himself quite unpopular in South Africa on a previous trip.

So, when the South African government wouldn't let him back in, he flew back to Salisbury, in Rhodesia.

And he wanted to go into South Africa and find his buried treasure. Obviously he didn't make that public. I was in America at the time doing a promotional jaunt. I was called over to Rhodesia to be briefed on a project.

In Rhodesia he was making a big thing out of what a big chap he was. He claimed to have treasure buried in Rhodesia too. He wanted to take over the whole country. He wanted a land mass . . .

****

Reg Sharpe was the number-one man prior to John McMaster's initiation to the world of staff. He had aided Hubbard with the financial side of things in England since the mid-fifties when he helped get the premises for the first London Scientology Org. He left in 1967 in protest over the Sea Org tactics.

REG SHARPE:

You've only got to look. He bought cheaply and sold expensively. I mean, what did he pay his auditors?

The Inland revenue were after him when he left England. . . .

He had ambitions of being leader of the world government. This is for real. He outlined his plans for a world government. I was to appoint the governor of the bank of England. He published that. Why I wasn't going to *be* the governor of the Bank of England I've never been quite sure!

11

Through the Wall of Fire!

"The man on the cross—there was no Christ!"—L. RON HUBBARD

In 1967, on the Canary Island of Las Palmas, Hubbard made what he claimed was *the* most important spiritual breakthrough in the history of the human race. He had unearthed, in his solo-auditing, a super traumatic ancient incident that had killed anyone else who had ever come close to uncovering it.

The resolution of, and safe passage through, this incident was "boldly explored and mapped" by him. This "map" was put into the form of his longhand writings for the highly confidential level of "Operating Thetan Level Three" (OT III).

The revelation of OT III was that virtually everyone on this planet— indeed, in "this sector of the Galaxy"—was totally overwhelmed by the effects of an incident that occurred 75 million years ago. And that underlying this cataclysmic event was another more basic cause of "human contamination": everyone without exception had been zapped and zombified by an incident that occurred four quadrillion years ago.

Human beings, he said, "*do not respond to reason, they respond only to 'R6* symbols.'* " The "R6 bank," is a part of any person's unconscious mind, according to Hubbard. This "bank" was deliberately

---

*The designation R6 derives from a process or "routine" ("R"), in this case the 6th in a series "0" to . . . (however many processes he would go through till he found the one that he felt did the trick).

He first "discovered" this "bank" (storage of damaging mental image pictures in the "reactive mind") during the early sixties, and, later in 1967, "discovered" the full incident of which these pictures were but a part. He promoted the incident as the "Wall of Fire."

created by mass implanting which occurred 75 Million years ago. This implanting was a highly "scientific" form of brainwashing, using huge movie screens as part of a program of mass hypnosis.

According to Hubbard, there was no point in reasoning with "humanoids." Instead of reasoning with "wogs," he spoke of reaching into the public and *"driving* them through your orgs."

Supposedly, "R6 bank symbols" (in the form of certain words, and pictures such as, for example, volcanoes) "key in" (in other words reconnect) people to these implants.

The result is that they become subservient and slave-like.

In 1967 all Scientology books suddenly presented a collection of images upon their covers: an exploding volcano; a woman in a monkey suit, eating what appeared to be a turkey leg; the frontal view of a speeding train; an odd-looking old man with a beard; a fellow dressed in a white spacesuit carrying a box (of "packaged beings") into a space-ship. These were R6 bank symbols.

A special "Book Mission" was sent out to promote these books, now empowered and made irresistible by the addition of these supposedly overwhelming symbols or images. Organization staff were assured that if they simply held up one of the books, revealing its cover, that any bookstore owner would immediately order crateloads of them. A customs officer, seeing any of the book covers in one's luggage, would immediately pass one on through.

The symbols of the Sea Org, which include the uniforms worn by Sea Org officers, were designed to fit Hubbard's descriptions of symbols of "R6", and were thus guaranteed to win instant respect and obedience for the person wearing them.

Hubbard had made it plain that he, and only he, had discovered and risen above the "R6 bank." Human existence is controlled utterly by it. He emphasized that, to those who had not completed the lower pre-requisite levels of Scientology, reading the materials of OT III was deadly.

He made it plain that the traumatic effects of the events of 75 million years ago had been the ultimate barrier to the attainment of "full OT." Despite the mortal dangers, however, he had braved the "Wall of Fire" and survived. He had then "taped the route" for all Mankind to follow.

Of course getting the "wogs" of planet Earth from zombiedom to godhood was going to be no easy task. Yet it must be done. And with the threat of nuclear war looming ever overhead, it must be done *fast*!

Because of this, to be in the Sea Org—or for that matter to be on staff at any Scientology org—is to be a participant in a never-ending "condensed time emergency." One never has time to pause and think about what is going on. Besides, doing so would be a form of "self-auditing"* which is strictly forbidden.

In light of all this Hubbard explained: "Anyone is entitled to have opinions and ideas and cognitions—so long as these do not bar the route out . . ." The "Route Out" being available only through Hubbard's organizations. . . . The road to "Total Freedom," it seems, was available only to those who obeyed completely.

Any newly initiated, "good Scientologist" would tell himself: "I have a reactive mind! My opinion is irrelevant, especially when compared to that of this great man who has broken free and who will eventually free me also."

Before 1967 Scientologists regarded themselves as the elite of earth. While the materials of OT III in some ways served to further enhance that feeling (many Sea Org members, for instance, were said to have been the "loyal officers," i.e., the good guys who opposed the mass implanting, when all this happened), these materials served also to greatly increase their feeling of indebtedness to their Founder.

****

While on the confidential class 8 course in Scotland, listening to Hubbard's twenty lectures—taped just weeks previously on the *Apollo* in Corfu, Greece—I was exposed to, among other things, Hubbard's opinion of Christianity:

> Somebody on this planet, about 600 B.C. found some pieces of "R6."
>
> I don't know how they found it; either by watching madmen or something. But since that time they have used it. And it became what is known as Christianity.
>
> The man on the cross. There was no Christ!
>
> The Roman Catholic Church, through watching the dramatizations of people picked up some little fragments of R6.**

Priests subsequently became objects of scorn in his writings. It is possibly this scorn which inspired Scientology agents, in 1983, to mail

---

*Self-auditing is *unsupervised*, solo auditing.
**In a bulletin of that period he states: "Also the Christian Church used (and uses) implanting. . . . They took over the Nicene Creed just before the year zero, invented Christ (who comes from the 'crucifixion' in R6, 75 million years ago) and implanted their way to power."

pornographic paraphernalia (including dildoes and an inflatable nude woman) to a Danish priest who spoke out against Scientology.

****

I have included sections of the OT III materials,* as Hubbard wrote them, in an attempt to make clear what is a very strange story indeed.

It is possible that Hubbard believed that things occurred just the way he wrote them in the OT III story. And if he had simply communicated this tale as something that he needed to say in private to an auditor, in an attempt to resolve his own problems of mind and spirit, I for one would have no objection to it.

But instead, in violation of his own "Auditor's Code" (the first clause of which states, "Don't evaluate for the pre-clear or tell him what to think about his case") he evaluates for all Scientolgoists. He is saying this same thing happened to you too! He was apparently applying another control mechanism: the overwhelming evaluation. And he also added another proven ingredient of covert control: secrecy.

In a taped lecture of 1955, presaging his later fixation on secret materials and the effect these have, Hubbard stated:

> Now if we were to sit down and try to monopolize every piece of information which we ever collected . . . and we were to take this information and carefully say, "Now look! This piece of information is absolutely sacred, and it's not to be distributed to anybody! And it's not to be given to *anybody*, and *only* those people who have a pink cross on the right shoulder will be able to read this information"—we would go into a mysterious sort of cult.

"THE WALL OF FIRE"

The following is an excerpt from his secret OT III materials. (If the reader believes it will do him harm, just skip it and go to the following chapter):

*Parts of the materials were published in the *Los Angeles Times*, when the court permitted this. The appeals court has since ruled that there is no such thing as trade secrets for a religion.

While Hubbard claimed that knowing about these materials was dangerous, he secretly wrote a script for and planned to release the key sections in a movie called *Revolt in the Stars*, which was planned for general release, and for the production of which millions of dollars were raised from investors. (Highly questionable methods of fund raising brought the project to a halt.)

The head of the Galactic Confederation (76 planets around larger stars visible from here) (founded 95,000,000 years ago, very space opera) solved overpopulation (250 billion or so per planet—178 billion on average) by mass implanting.

He caused people to be brought to Teegeeack (Earth) and put an H Bomb on the principal volcanoes (incident 2) and then the Pacific ones were taken in boxes to *Hawaii* and the Atlantic area ones to *Las Palmas* and there "packaged."

His name was Xenu. He used renegades. Various misleading data by means of circuits, etc., was placed in the implants.

When through with his crime, Loyal Officers (to the people) captured him after six years of battle and put him in an electronic mountain trap where he still is. "They" are gone. The place (Confed.) has since been a desert.

The length and brutality of it all was such that this Confederation never recovered. The implant is calculated to kill (by pneumonia, etc.) anyone who attempts to solve it. This liability has been dispensed with by my tech development.

One can *free wheel* through the implant and die unless it is approached as precisely outlined. The "free wheel" (auto running on and on) lasts too long, denies sleep, etc., and one dies. . . .

In December '67 I knew somebody had to take the plunge. I did and emerged very knocked out but alive. Probably the only one ever to do so in 75,000,000 years. I have *all* the data now but only that given here is needful. . . .

Good luck.

It turns out that Xenu was about to be deposed as leader of the Galactic Confederation, when he undertook to solve the overpopulation problem for all time.

He sent in troops and renegades who picked up the populations, froze them with an injection of alcohol-glycol solution in the lungs, and shipped them to Earth in space ships resembling DC9s. Then he blew them all up with powerful H bombs on top of all the major volcanos. (You will note the cover of Hubbard's best selling book *Dianetics, the Modern Science of Mental Health* has an exploding volcano on it, designed to ensure you feel compelled to buy it.)

As the Thetans ascended into the heavens after the explosions they were captured by electronic ribbons and force fields and pulled down to Earth to be electronically packaged into "Clusters": thousands of beings stuck together as one. There were assembly points for this packaging. One was in Las Palmas in the Canary Islands (where

Hubbard was located when he wrote this). The other was Hawaii.*

It was at the volcano locations that the Thetans were subjected to the "R6" implants, the latter part of which included pictures projected on huge screens. These include surgeons dissecting bodies right down to the skeleton which writhes in agony, the crucifixion, sex perversion, auto accidents, psychiatrists, sickness and spinning sensations, and more.

The implant was designed so that anyone recalling the sequence would start to "free wheel" through the 36 days (the heart of the implant**), would be unable to turn the pictures off, would be unable to sleep or eat, and would die of exhaustion or something like pneumonia before the 36 days were up. It was designed to be too horrible to ever escape from. After these implants, the beings, all clustered together, were let go.

Meanwhile the Loyal Officers revolted and captured Xenu. He was imprisoned in a mountain top on planet Earth (on the island of Madeira) and placed inside a wire cage with an eternal battery. In the battle between the Loyal Officers and Xenu's renegades, most of these planets were turned into billiard balls. Earth was a radioactive cinder, and became known as "The Evil Place." That's why nobody ever comes here except renegades and criminals who are dumped here.

Hubbard labelled the nuclear devastation "that occurred here," "The Wall of Fire."

In order to audit this, the pre-clear takes on the role of auditor, and directs each body thetan to relive this incident and then "blow" (leave).

"Clusters" of thetans are "broken up." This is achieved when Incident II and sometimes other incidents (which all the Thetans making up the cluster have in common) are re-experienced by the body thetans.

According to an anonymous pamphlet:

> LRH took the exorcism concept and embellished it with a huge science fiction fantasy.

*None of which existed 75 million years ago—according to Geology.
**The key part of the R6 incident is said by Hubbard to be a 36-day period of "implant." An "implant" is defined by him as "A painful and forceful means of overwhelming a being with artificial purpose or false concepts in a malicious attempt to control and suppress him."

Any geologist or archeologist can tell you that 75 million years ago the earth was over-run by dinosaurs. Many dinosaur fossils have been found from that time period, but no trace of 250,000,000 human fossils, or hundreds of billions more that were shipped here from other planets to be blown up with H bombs on volcanoes. No trace of human fossils, but dinosaur fossils all over the place!

If there is any truth or workability in exorcising BTs or demon spirits, then the story of 'Incident 2' is certainly not a part of it. It's pure science fiction, and bad science fiction at that.

Some swear by the results of having audited OT III. One person who felt this way, upon reading the above, speculated that it would have been possible for Xenu's men to have done a clean up job on all the human skeletons!

Some ex-Scientologists ridicule it. Doing so can be dangerous. One former Scientologist marched up and down in front of the Church's Los Angeles headquarters, with a sign saying, "Ron is Xenu!"

FRANK NOTARO:

Saturday, 5 Oct. '85: I went down to the Advanced Organization in Los Angeles to ask for a refund of monies paid for a level of auditing. My request was in writing.

A security guard told me to get out or I would be arrested.

"O.K. I will have to picket," I said.

The next day I picketed by myself in front of the entire Cedars of Lebanon ("Blue Building") Complex.

One sign said "Ron is Xenu!"

A Church of Scientology "Security Guard" came from the front and grabbed my signs, while three or four others jumped me from behind and threw me to the pavement in the middle of the street, where they pinned me down and handcuffed me from behind. They then took me inside the building across from the Advanced Organization.

On the way I managed to shout to a friend to call the police, as I was afraid. I was held captive for an hour or so until the police came and released me.

The police officer told me I had every right to picket and escorted me to safety.

12

Heads In Toilets

"There are men dead because they attacked us. . . ." —L. Ron Hubbard.

While my wife and I were on the Saint Hill Special Briefing course, three or four people split off from the Church and took the secret clearing course materials with them. (These were a small part of what later developed into the "Wall of Fire" materials, covered in Chapter 13.)

This was during the latter part of 1967. . . . We were still not used to seeing Scientologists in naval uniforms.

Jill Van Staden was a good looking slender brunette in her mid-twenties. She took her authority seriously and looked the part. The lanyard and the officer's hat with "scrambled eggs" all over it was carefully placed so as not to detract from her face, which was usually very easy to look at.

On this occasion, however, the eyes were cold and the face taut.

Her voice was hard as she called a "That's it!" and began slapping down a goldenrod-colored (dark yellow) mimeo sheet in front of everyone.

When she was done with the ritual, she gave us a brief announcement which had the tone of a judge pronouncing a sentence of death.

I hardly heard a word. I was reading the message on the paper.

It was typed over the name L. Ron Hubbard and essentially did order the death of the four who had "stolen" the clearing course materials.

Any Sea Org member who met up with any of these people were ordered to use "R.2—45" on them.

R.2—45 had been used as a joke in one of Hubbard's books as an "exteriorization process which is not acceptable to society at this time." The joke was that a colt .45 pistol would of course be a very effective process of getting a spirit to go exterior to its body.

This time it was no joke! (although it should be noted that, as far as I know, no one ever followed through).

Sea Org members were also ordered to run processes "wrong way to" on any of the four (meaning to reverse the processes in such a way as to cause mental damage or insanity).

This was a chilling experience for me. I had somehow been able to rationalize the "Fair Game Policy" and the various policies ordering suppressive declares and lowered conditions, but this one was hard to swallow.

This event was only the beginning.

The peaceful and beautiful environment of Saint Hill was being invaded by a team of true blue Sea Org officers with virtually total authority.

Ian Shillington (about 17 years of age) and Joe Van Staden, Jill's husband at the time, also in officers' uniforms, with daggers on the belts, had arrived on mission from the Flagship.

Irv Williams, an American, then in his late twenties, who had recently joined staff at Saint Hill, recalls:

> There were three major Sea Org missions to Saint Hill during late '67 and '68.
>
> The Van Staden mission was the third and the scariest. Ron was on the ship—somewhere—and was telexing things, and fired this mission off. I was the staff Ethics Officer at Saint Hill, and they put all ethics officers in "liability." All ethics officers and Hubbard Communications Office people (who police compliance with Hubbard's orders) were just automatically assigned "liability." (They were told they hadn't been tough enough.)
>
> And Joe Van Staden got a ladder and climbed up to the ceiling and slammed this dagger into a beam. Then he said, "This will fall on you and kill you!" Everybody was jumping to. I mean, anyone who looked cross-eyed would be declared suppressive immediately.
>
> They were just looking for heads to put on pikes. That state of siege lasted for a couple of weeks. I slept in the monkey room (a large room in the Manor, which the previous owner, the Maharajah of Jaipur, had commissioned painted with lots of monkeys). Everybody was on "battle stations" (on alert, working on a laid out plan called a "battle plan"; the terminology had turned military) 24 hours a day.

This continued until they decided that things were under control and then they went away. And things went back to normal—as normal as things were after this heavy ethics started being implemented.

By this time we began to believe that Ron meant it. We still couldn't understand why he was doing this because it was in such contradiction of all of his basic teachings and principles. With the idea that force doesn't work, with the idea that punishment is a former practice, and it's been tried for thousands of years and it doesn't help. And here are these people running around wearing Gestapo boots, and punishing and threatening.

And it was being done at his direct order.

It was very grim.

****

On the second mission, executives were removed and thrown in the dungeon. Since I was an ethics officer, I was sent down to the *Royal Scotsman* in Southhampton, before it ever sailed. I was to receive "ethics training."

Hubbard was on the ship at the time. I was picked up in the middle of the night, "You come with us now. Don't ask any questions. Just get some clothes on and come." And they took me down to Southhampton without telling me where they were taking me.

By being picked up in the middle of the night and taken to an unknown destination under conditions of great secrecy, the whole two days was kind of dream-like. It was slightly unreal. You didn't really know why you were there or what was going to happen. It was all mysterious. There was a great deal of stress. This was LRH! If he decided to have you thrown overboard you'd go! If he decided you'd never be seen again, that's probably what would happen. So you didn't want to cross him.

The Sea Org members were so gung-ho, they would have done anything, *anything*, if that had been the order.

Hubbard was on the ship for some weeks before we arrived.

He was very familiar with the ship. He knew where everything was. He was very much at home.

We arrived at this big rusty hulk of a freighter. And I was put on board and didn't see LRH for about twelve hours. They wanted me to sign this contract. And I wanted to know what I was signing. And they said, "Well, you're coming on board and you have to sign this." And I insisted on looking at the paper, and it was a Sea Org contract! And I said, "No I don't think I want to join the Sea Org for a billion years."

Anyway, they threw me in the crew quarters. And there was Fred Hare who had had "his head lobbed off " during the previous mission.

He had been a high-ranking executive. And there he was. He'd been the high and mighty who'd put me in my place when I was ethics officer and there he was miserable and degraded and coughing. God, he never stopped coughing.

And we became kind of friends at that point. I guess because we were fellow prisoners, fellow endurers of misery. . . . At one point Ron gave us a lecture on ethics in the passageway. He was resplendent in a tailored uniform with braid all over it, a jaunty naval cap, and highly polished black shoes. A couple of Sea Org people held microphones, recording the thing.

So after several days of "ethics training" we were packed up and sent back to Saint Hill.

Almost a year later, Irv Williams was sent to do the Class 8 Course on board the *Apollo* at Corfu Greece. Here the rusty hulk of the *Royal Scotsman*, which he remembered from Southhampton, England, had been transformed into the resplendent, white *Apollo*. Irv tells the story:

The original Class 8 Course . . . September to October 1968, I think. The orgs each got telexes announcing that there was now a Class 8 Course and they were to send somebody tech qualified. The telex added, "Bring real roses."

I was put on a plane and got to Athens, Greece, then over to Corfu on a commuter line. . . .

The next morning they started the class. We were given boiler suits. Everybody went to class except myself and Albert McGraw. We were brought in front of Sea Org officers who started screaming and shaking their fists in our faces because I had brought a check, and the telex had said "real roses" which meant "*cash!*"

Albert had committed a similar heinous crime. He had brought New Zealand money—which "was useless" (since they would have to go through a time-consuming procedure to be able to use it outside of that country, due to New Zealand government restrictions).

They threw him overboard on the spot with his money. And he spent the next half hour swimming around trying to grab it all. We later hung it up on a clothesline in a room. . . .

So for the next three weeks we were on course.

We didn't see LRH except each evening when he'd lecture. But he Case Supervised our auditing. And each evening we had to march in and stand at attention. And then he would come in and sit down and give a lecture, which was recorded.

It was a very grueling course. Every morning at six we arose and put on these boiler suits, and we had to wear these rough thick hemp nooses around our necks—because we weren't fit to wear a lanyard. So we wore these things, which were suggestive of a hangman's noose, around our necks.

Then we had to muster on deck. And we'd all march in formation to the deck, the lower deck, closest to the sea. About twenty feet above sea level. Then our punishments would be read out.

Those who were judged by LRH to have been non-standard in their auditing were thrown overboard on his written instructions. The Sea Org officers didn't throw us overboard. The other students had to throw the offender overboard. We had to. We would grab someone or be grabbed and tossed. And it's a long drop on a cold chilly morning.

Unfortunately nobody ever asked whether anybody could swim. And a couple of the Class 8 students could not swim and they were in trouble. The Sea Org officers didn't really care, apparently, but we cared quite a bit. And in one case someone jumped in to help the person—to keep him from drowning.

And someone would go down to a lower deck and open a hatchway. But the hatchway was about three or four feet above the water level, and when you're tired and you've got this heavy wet boiler suit hanging onto you, it's really hard to jump out of the water high enough to catch that ledge and get back in the ship.

A couple of students didn't agree about being overboarded. Most of us were resigned about it. But I remember one gal who fought tooth and nail. She was in violent disagreement about being thrown overboard.

The great feeling was at the end of that three weeks, when we graduated. When we were told that we had passed, there was this tremendous feeling of having survived. It was a great relief!

The food there, by the way, was probably the worst food I have ever eaten. It got worse every day. Burnt Brussels sprouts and other stuff, and we just couldn't eat it.

Once we were done we were patted on the back. We were the big heroes of the minute.

All during our time there we were kept away from LRH. His cabin and his working area was on an upper deck. And during the day when we were marching to lunch or dinner or whatever, we were absolutely forbidden to ever go on the deck. We were forbidden to make any noise while we were moving around because we could be disturbing him.

When he came in for lectures, we came in first. We would go in and sit. We'd wait for a while. Then he would come in preceded by a Sea Org Officer and followed by a Sea Org Officer. And we would all stand to attention. He would come in rather quickly and sit down.

He made very sure there was never any opportunity for any of us to ever ask him a question, discuss anything with him. Not even say, "Hi." It was very definite that it was one-way communication. He was going to say things to us and we were going to listen. Looking at it now, it had a hypnotic effect.

He would sit down, then we could sit down. He'd speak for an hour or so. And we would applaud for a long time. Then he would get up and leave while we all stood at attention and then we would all be marched back—and this was late at night, about ten o'clock.

After we finished the class, we all had a party on ship. And we were allowed to talk to each other and wear civilian clothes and, about halfway through the party, he came in, and actually mingled, but very briefly—five minutes at the most. He allowed each of us to say something to him. I said something like, "Thank you very much for teaching us this wonderful material." And he said, "I'm glad you like it." Then he'd go on to somebody else. It was like a little reception line thing.

And then he left. And that was it. It was very very very controlled communication. . . .

During the first lecture, he was livid, and pounding the table with his fist. But I was so in awe that I couldn't evaluate him. We were all in awe. There was such an imposed altitude. You know, when you talk to the king, he may be friendly but he's always the king. You never forget that he's the king. He doesn't let you forget that he's the king. He may be very gracious to you, but that's because he's such a wonderful person.

He was this god, this greater than life person, and he was almost unconfrontable from that perspective.

He could at a whim destroy my life.

****

When the students who had gone to the ship returned to Saint Hill, my wife and I were on the Class 7 internship. We were very excited about discovering all the new tech that these guys would be able to teach us.

The Class 8 course was being frantically promoted, on Hubbard's orders, as virtually creating these super-auditors who would quickly bring undreamed of changes in people's cases. OTs would "be coming off the line" in short order.

Shortly thereafter Mary and I drove to Edinburgh, Scotland, to take the first land based Class 8 course. The materials for this consisted mainly of the tapes from the original course on the ship.

Since we were in a hotel in the middle of winter in Scotland, a novel method had to be devised to simulate the overboarding of a ship anchored offshore on a Greek island.

The ceremonies were upstairs, where a bath was prepared with *cold* water. It was winter in *Scotland,* near the arctic circle.

With the last of my meager funds, I had bought some wool trousers to fend off the sub-zero temperatures, and it was the very next morning that I went "overboard."

Those trousers shrank half way up my ankles!

I remember particularly the "overboarding" of Joan Schnehager, a South African woman in her fifties who was an auditor in training. She was my pre-clear.

In shock, she exhaled so much air as she was immersed into the tub that it took some three or four *long* minutes, as she tried to get enough voice going, to read out the poem she had been given to read.

It was painful to hear her attempts to get some sound going. Finally it came out:

"I (gasp) _____ am _____ a _____ disciple _____ of _____ Freud _____ I _____ love _____ to _____ kill _____ Pre-clears—" (etc).

The Master at Arms was a pleasant Scottish fellow, who decided that the freezing water was not necessary. So he put in just enough hot water to take the worst chill off it. He was discovered, and was himself overboarded in freezing water the next morning.

On the plus side, being in Scotland was to me exciting and, interestingly enough, some of the auditing was quite a lot of fun and, I felt, beneficial.

The first OT level required that you went to a place where there were lots of people and note down observations of the way they carried their bodies and so on.

I have always loved to just watch people, and since Edinburgh had a festival in progress when I did this, with all the castles lit up and art wares being displayed, it was all very exciting.

These moments of pleasure contrasted with the rigors of the course room, which was locked during course hours—8 A.M. till midnight. Van Staden, the supervisor, always wore his long-laced Nazi-style boots with an attitude to match.

We ended the course before the three weeks' deadline was up, Mary and I being two of the first to graduate. We both had a knack of getting through difficult situations.

****

Shortly after I returned to England I was sent, for a couple of weeks, to Sweden to assist a small organization in Eskilstuna, near Stockholm.

It was still winter and I spent some of the coldest days of my life trying to help out this brave idealistic Swedish couple who were up against a language barrier in selling what was essentially an American subject—no books had yet been translated into Swedish.

On the way home I stopped through Copenhagen, to briefly visit with my uncle there. I also stopped by the org, where Joan Schnehager and her husband Quentin had been put in charge.

She had responded to the harsh treatment in Scotland, where she had had to read in the cold bathtub, by becoming a zealot herself.

She proudly told me how she had resolved the problem of how to throw people overboard in this building, which had no baths.

She took me into the bathroom and flushed the toilet. "See!" she said, "I have the students put their heads in here and I flush it!"

****

It was a couple of years later before I heard how things had gone for Joan Schnehager and her husband.

What had happened was that the org in Copenhagen had not been doing well under the Schnehagers. The income had begun to drop. So a Sea Org mission was sent to "handle."

Hearing about this mission, and presumably knowing what usually happened to downstats when Sea Org missions were sent in (they invariably found an S.P. and usually it was the head of the organization), Quentin Schnehager had become very depressed.

When the mission arrived, he was hanging by his neck from the rafters of his garage. Dead.

****

I was privy to a crew-only taped briefing by Hubbard, played in an organization in Los Angeles in late 1969, after we had moved to America.

Hubbard was very angry on the tape at the fact that Quentin Schnehager had hanged himself. He raved about how this had been an attempt to try to make him and the Sea Org wrong!

There was not the slightest concern or remorse—just outrage that anyone would *dare* to do such a thing to him!

That he would be talking this way, was all *too incredible* for my mind to fully grasp at the time.

I've found that the mind tends to gloss over ideas and events that depart too far from the acceptable. His attitude on this tape was in this category. I was stunned by it; but the significance of it did not really register.

****

Back in early 1969, I got back to England from Denmark and Mary and I became key personnel at the organization at Saint Hill. We were, after all, by now highly trained elite 8s.

A few months later, my wife was case supervising in her "Ivory Tower" (meaning that she must not be disturbed or see people whose cases she was supervising; a case supervisor only saw folders written during sessions by the auditor). She got a report that a man in his late twenties had arrived from London. He looked very ill. His tongue was reported to be black, and he seemed desperate that we perform a miracle right away.

In accordance with the then standard policy regarding "physically ill pre-clears," she ordered that he be sent to a doctor right away and, when he had been treated, to come back for some auditing. This person had not been audited at Saint Hill before, only in the London organization. They had not known what to do with him, so they sent him to Saint Hill.

The next day, I had been in an auditing room (designed for two people sitting at either end of a card table) auditing someone for a few hours. I ended the session and escorted the pre-clear back into the Qualifications Division room.

In the lobby was a bunch of people among whom was a young attractive woman, who was sobbing helplessly. She looked like she hadn't slept for days and was way beyond getting counseling.

I asked my immediate junior, who was in charge of handling the people waiting, what was wrong. He told me that her husband (who turned out to be the ill man from the previous night) had thrown himself in front of a train, killing himself instantly.

I suggested that she be turned over to a doctor for sedatives. He said he would get help from the Hubbard Communications Division, who were responsible for this sort of thing, and I left it in their hands.

I was called in the middle of the night and informed that the woman was on the couch of the World Wide Org executive, and that he was demanding that I come and get the girl and take care of her.

So I drove my little green Austin Mini back to Saint Hill and picked up the woman, who was still hysterical.

I got some help from a female executive, who agreed to come to my cottage and stay up and watch the woman.

I awoke after daylight the next morning to screams and the sound of broken glass and, by the time I reached the room where the woman was being watched, she was through the window and running down the roadway in this little English wood.

There were neighbors who were getting in their cars to go to work, as I chased her down the road in my bare feet and pajamas.

By the time I reached her she had torn open her dress exposing her breasts and was wailing at the top of her voice.

I tried the best I could to cover her and get her under some control, but despite her petite build, she was displaying the reputed strength of someone who is insane. I still don't know how I managed to get her back to the house. I was bruised and scratched, and the neighbors had been provided with enough for many weeks of gossip.

I got help from a couple of the others who were living there to guard her in a safer room. I had decided that, regardless of the top executive orders to the contrary, I would take her to a doctor.

As she was being escorted through the kitchen of our little cottage, she broke away from the girl who was leading her out of the house to the car, quickly opened the furnace and lunged her head towards the flames.

My friend grabbed her just in time to avert a catastrophe; the only damage was some singed hair.

It took two men and the woman executive to get her into the car and to the doctor. She fought every minute of the way.

We left her in his care after he told us that she was effectively sedated.

This whole scene was a potential threat to Guardian W.W. Jane Kember's position, as it could potentially cause press or legal action against Scientology. A scapegoat was needed, and my wife and I were the chosen ones.

A mimeographed "Ethics Order" was issued on the standard gold-enrod-colored paper approved by the highest authorities at Saint Hill (Jane's work, I believe).

Mary and I were accused of a list of "crimes" and "high crimes," among them being killing a pre-clear and causing another to attempt to commit suicide.

This was no joke. It was bizarre. We were still relatively new and naïve. My big question was, "How could clears and O.T.s be acting so insanely?"

For the next few weeks I defied the entire process and gambled on the fact that they needed us. The "Ethics Order" was eventually cancelled because of our "up statistics." Our gamble had paid off.

I fell into theories about how Jane Kember, and her assistant for finance world wide, Herbie Parkhouse, were the people causing all the crazy things that were happening.

I was reacting the way I was supposed to, suspecting anyone but Hubbard. Never think a critical thought about Hubbard. When things are really wrong, look for the S.P., but the S.P. cannot conceivably be considered to be him.

This whole thing was a soul-wrenching experience for us, and I was very much broken up about it for some time. My wife was pregnant with our first child, and suffering badly from the cold and lack of proper nutrition.

Since Americans were now banned by British law from coming to Saint Hill to do Scientology, the gross org income had drastically dropped, and we were not earning enough to pay rent and buy food. Our funds had depleted and I petitioned to L. Ron Hubbard to be allowed to go to America for a year and work for a franchise to earn enough money to get us back on our feet and take care of the baby.

"He" approved it. "He," in actual fact, being Ken Urquart at the time, who handled petitions addressed to Hubbard. I was overjoyed, and we worked hard to find replacements for ourselves and get fares together (by loans) to get to the States.

We had suffered under the rough English weather and constant poverty. These hardships were acceptable when we believed Nirvana was just around the corner. We still believed and dreamed, but the young naïve kids who had earlier arrived at Saint Hill were no more. The politics, inequities and outright madness that now pervaded those stately grounds and majestic manor house had seeped through our pores and sickened us to the core.

Soul-liberating laughter spilled out of us as we sailed across the English Channel with the white cliffs of Dover receding behind us. We sailed for France on that breezy sunny day (from where we would continue onto Luxembourg and a flight for New York).

Escaping from Saint Hill, and heading for America, was unspeakable joy!

****

Despite the negative experiences of Saint Hill, I refused to let go of the dream that something wonderful might yet come out of it all. The positives of the subject were *so* positive, that I just put the negatives in the back of my mind.

13

The Sea Org Revisited

"Hubbard may have been a genius on one level, but he was unbalanced. There was an out-of-control side to the guy. And it shows up in the auditing technology: His fixation in early Dianetics on attempted abortions; his fixation on hypnotic "implants"; his fixation on other people's "evil" intentions; his belief in Xenu and the OT III "incident 2"; his obsession with near endless "body thetans" . . . This stuff oozed out of his pores; very much *his* personal hang-ups. Most people are much simpler than that."
—JOHN AUSLEY

The entire concept of the Sea Org was said by Hubbard to be "a re-gathering of the Loyal Officers." This time he and his most trusted officers would not fail. They would "decontaminate" Earth, and later this entire sector of the Galaxy, from the devastation inflicted by Xenu and his renegades.

The early chapters of this book illustrate Hubbard's efforts to allegedly put together a "war chest" for these efforts, and to "create a safe base" from which to launch the necessary missions.

In this chapter some other views, further illustrating this bizarre scene, are presented.

First John McMaster gives a recounting of an event involving "the Commodore" on board the *Apollo* in early 1969. Typical of top executives serving Hubbard, he was doing a stint in the lowly post of galley hand (kitchen help) during the time of this anecdote. Hubbard had a habit of busting his executives to the lowest positions, often only to restore them to power at a later date, when they were more amenable to "reason" (this was prior to the RPF).

JOHN MCMASTER:

I noticed various things, that seemed to be like insanity creeping into what we were doing. Now, there is this magnificent Sea Organization which, as Hubbard told me, was to be the environment, way out on the ocean, where we were going to continue with our basic purpose of clearing the planet by doing this very high level, high frequency, almost telepathic type research; which, at that stage, he considered was necessary for us to do.

It was right on my purpose line. I was thrilled with it, and thought he had conceived of a wonderful idea.

O.K. So there's this purpose. Slap on the basic purpose to clear the planet. For me—I think this is wonderful. So we go along. I'm sitting there hoping that, one of these days, it will be announced from our Lord and Master, the Source (who had then become the Commodore of the flotilla, don't forget; you know, another medal on his chest: "Commodore"). So here we all are, waiting for the Commodore to send this message down saying, "Get all hands to clearing the planet! We are now about to start our advanced research."

But instead of this I saw more people going down the chain locker; more people climbing up the mast to stand a twelve-hour crow's nesting punishment; more people chipping the water tank; more people wandering around in grey rags with chains around their ankles and around their necks. More and more of this is going on. So this didn't, somehow, tie up with high level research.

Nevertheless, we were on this vast "safe" space, unimpinged upon by governments, where this research is supposed to be taking place.

****

So in 1969 we were rollicking around in Bizerte, in Tunisia. And I would go ashore. I was a galley hand. Occasionally we needed things, and I used to have to go into Bizerte and get what ever it was we needed for the galley. . . . Every time I went walking down the street—I didn't have any uniform or anything—I used to get a lot of smiles from children and people; and I liked it, and I'd smile back. And it was always so very friendly.

Every time I walked in the streets of Bizerte, the children and some of the people would bring me little sprigs of jasmine. We didn't speak the same language but, nevertheless, as beings, we were communicating. . . .

So I used to come back from my shopping, and go to my little space, get an empty bottle with some water in it, and put my jasmine in there. It was noticed by the messengers, and various other people that the Commodore had installed for himself, that every time that Johnny the galley hand went into Bizerte he came back with little sprigs of jasmine.

After a while, knowing about the flowers, and having sent out a lot of forward publicity about this great benevolent multi-millionaire philosopher, who gave away his technology to all these students who came eagerly on to his ships, he decided, "Well, now they must be aware of the presence of Source."

I was down in my apron one day scrubbing the steps, and I hear this voice squeaking out in a high pitched falsetto, "Now tend the rail! Now tend the rail! The Commodore's going ashore!" I drop everything, scrubbing brush, bucket, the lot, and rush to the galley and say, "Which way do we go?" And they say, "Oh, you go along here and you line up against the wall, and as soon as the Commodore comes past you've got to salute."

We're all with our backs up against the wall, and there's just enough room for the Commodore and two of his magnificently uniformed minions to walk past us together, in a threesome. Then all the others have to follow behind. So he comes past. And he stared me straight in the eye, because he wondered what I was thinking of all this, and whether or not I was taking it seriously. But I'm standing there saluting like all the rest of them. You know, oh God, it was *very* serious: The Commodore's going ashore!

He's got this magnificent practiced walk, about twenty-five medals on either side of that expanded over-fed chest, and those beginning-to-develop mammary glands. And he's strutting along with this almost goosestep-like walk, which is *definitely* going to impress those Arabs in Bizerte. So, he eventually gets to the gangplank, and he stands aside like all Commodores do, so that the rest go ashore first. . . . Then down he goes with his goosestep, down the gang plank. He gets down there and he strokes his magnificent chest, and his medals. And he extends his hands in a gesture of largesse, and walks far enough from the edge of the wharf for his minions to line up, four on each side, and there they go!

He is Source of this "flying bird" that happen to be walking along the wharf. There is he: he's in the front, and his "wings" are stretched out on both sides as he goes along.

The Arabs who were working on the dock didn't pay much attention to him; but then, of course, they were only dock hands. Of course, when he got into the city itself, then he was going to get the cream of the cream, who were going to really acknowledge a genius when they saw one.

They go through the end of the docks and they get down onto the street, and they're walking, and so far the Arabs have walked past. But still, it's not the cream of the cream. He hasn't come across any V.I.P.s yet. And these other ones didn't even look up; they just went on spitting in the street. They weren't the tiniest bit impressed by this regiment from the flotilla. So they walked a few blocks, and the Arabs just went on spitting.

All of a sudden the guest of the Commodore, a little thing called paranoia, suddenly undermined the megalomania. So the megalomania flew away. and paranoia took over. And this magnificent walk, that had been practiced and cultivated in the cabin and on the deck, disappeared altogether. And a quick little hurry-skurry rushed as fast as a fat body could go—back to the ship before the assassin came around from one of the corners . . . to shoot down the Source of this enlightenment, the Source of a clear planet.

So there he came rushing back. . . . I could see the panting and the rush, and all the minions trying to maintain some sort of dignity, while the Commodore, blustering and fat and sweaty, got eventually to the gangplank. Well, now, of course, he was correct in protocol by charging up that gangplank first. Because a commodore or a captain always boards a ship first, whether it's sinking or not. And our floating insane asylum hadn't started sinking yet.

So he charges up the gangplank first. And in the meantime we've been summoned with another one of these, "Tend the rail! Tend the rail! The Commodore's coming aboard!" So the Commodore comes aboard. And his minions come flocking up after him. And he's rushing; his petticoat was just about hanging out as he charged past us, as we were saluting against the wall. He, rushing like hell, and blustering, "There's an S.P. on board! There's an S.P. on board!" There was *definitely* an S.P. on board, because the Arabs didn't acknowledge him. There *must* be an S.P. on board.

So he locks himself up in his cabin, and writes a very quick thing, that the whole ship is put into "liability." So there he is; he's going to stay up there in safety. And he's got all his guns ready on his bed, to shoot the first of the Arabs that come charging after him. . . . And so he's locked up there, but out comes the order, and so now we're all in liability. That means more standing in the water tank, more chipping of the cattle holds and so on. . . .

****

Hubbard lived in perpetual fear of being poisoned. He wouldn't eat fresh food. Everything had to come out of a tin can. The result was that the ship was loaded with tin cans. This is true! The only other thing he would have was omelettes. He would have four meals a day. At two o'clock in the morning I would cook him a 12-egg omelette.

****

Otto Roos had been a Dutch seaman. He got involved with Scientology in his teens. When the Sea Org was formed he joined up eagerly. He was Hubbard's right-hand man for some years during the late sixties and early seventies. He is reputed to have been the one who performed the first overboarding. In fact he was the first one tossed overboard.

There is no doubt he earned his reputation as a ruthless "disciplinarian." However, his description of the situation on the ships, and Hubbard's part and motives in creating the scene as it was on the ship, is of considerable interest.

OTTO ROOS:

Things got worse as the OT III research moved on. The Flag orders at the time usually dealt with smashing "*them*" (our "enemies") and smash them we did. If not our enemies, at least ourselves and our port relations. . . .

Beaching, I have seen many times. It did not improve port relations. A "beachee" was put ashore without passport and no money (except for Sea Org pay sometimes) to make his way home. They would sometimes go to their consulate for help, at which point they had some explaining to do. . . .

To say that "LRH could not have known about this," can only be answered by "How could he not have?" on a little ship and holding all the comm[unication] lines, after *originating* the policies [that established these practices in the first place!].

Nobody ever *aared* say anything about these things and so risk losing his upper OT levels for "making the Commodore wrong." . . .

LRH was an entirely different person when dealing with, talking about, and explaining points of technology and policy; especially on a one-to-one basis. . . .

. . . [After he reinstated overboards for the Dianetics course in '69,] I started to wonder about the number of times he *acted* in a completely different fashion from what he wrote in the tech.

. . . sometimes I thought he saw "Martians." For example, on Madeira he showed several people the mountain where a famous whole track SP [Xenu] was "jailed" (and still was, to all intents and purposes). But in later Ethics Orders he suddenly said that this character had escaped some centuries back and that he had traced him and that he was so and so (name given) at present.

He was very validative of people who gave him lots of credit, especially when done in writing. . . .

As for Hubbard's habit of "engraving his initials" on other people's ideas, Roos explains:

> Originators of [technical bulletins] had to always credit him. . . .
>
> The weakness of LRH was not that he too made mistakes, but was the fact that he (1) appeared unable to admit it, and (2) invariably blamed someone else.
>
> *His* mistakes were always "another" publishing something over his name. . . .
>
> I have sent his writings back to him always stating that, "because of typing errors," it needed review as follows . . .

****

> When LRH was very sick (January 1972) he sent a note to Jim Dincalci [who was the Medical Officer at the time]. It stated: "Jim, I don't think I'm going to make it."
>
> Jim called me for help.
>
> I wrote to LRH, asking his approval. . . . I wanted to get all his folders . . . [in which was a full record of his personal auditing sessions going back many years, done mostly on himself solo—holding a special solo can; but also on occasions by various other trusted individuals, including Mary Sue Hubbard, Otto and others] to get his past auditing history corrected and handled.

Otto proposed that a council of "class XIIs" go through them, to find possible errors that could have caused him to become ill,* and to work out a series of auditing actions to handle these errors, and thus his illness.

> He sent back his approval, plus a seven-page commendation, "I'm delighted that somebody is finally going to take responsibility for my auditing."
>
> Folders came in from all over the world going back to 1948. Most of the old stuff was on scraps of paper. Solo auditing data went as high as what he called "OT level 19."
>
> It became a stack of some eight feet high, an entire filing cabinet full. [Organizing and categorizing all this material] took months.
>
> . . . one day . . . he sent a messenger down to me, stating that he wanted the folders.

---

*It is believed by most Scientologists that all illnesses are mostly, if not entirely, psychosomatic and can be handled by auditing.

Roos, using his authority as Case Supervisor, refused, citing the supporting policy.

> . . . [Hubbard] became the "Commodore" and *ordered* the folders up. sending some hefty guys down to just get them.
> A few days later I was called up to his office, and upon my entry was hit, kicked, screamed and shouted at. (Even his aides were not in sight. They were in hiding, knowing that he was really mad!)
> He just blew his stack on finding the references to the "discreditable" [meter] reads, and the contents of some of his personal folders.

This is a type of E-meter needle reaction which, according to Hubbard's own writings, indicates that someone has "evil intentions."*

> . . . He shouted that he had never had such reads.
> He screamed that I and the others had "of course talked and laughed about it" among ourselves, and had "undoubtedly told this all over the ship."
> Completely maniacal reactions, especially towards what were the best and most professional auditors in the world, who had read in some cases literally thousands of folders in which were noted down just about all that can be thought or done. . . .
> There were, in the solo folders, lots of things personal to him; but who cared. . . .
> He was very angry, but I faced him and his anger without flinching. He said, "What are you looking at me for?"
> I said, "Well, sir, you trained me personally never to break up, so you couldn't expect me to do so now."
> He then quietened down and ordered me to cabin arrest.

A few days later Otto Roos was called before a "Committee of Evidence" and declared a Suppressive Person.

> *As far as I know, no one ever saw these folders again.* . . .
> Virtually anybody close to LRH (even Mary Sue) got hit [heavily disciplined], blacklisted, and lied about. . . .

****

---

*The jerky slashing action of the needle of the E-meter called a "rock slam" is covered in the chapter "Crucifying Evil Out."

JOHN AUSLEY:

At one point—for about half an hour—he'd meet with his family once a week for a meal. This was a bit of a bother for him, but he did it.

One day, during one of these dinners, some messenger came in with talk of "tech's out" and "orgs . . ." and this and that. And he said, "That's enough of this daddy trip," and got up and walked out.

ARMSTRONG:

When Quentin, Hubbard's oldest son by his third marriage died, his response was anger. He was mad at Quentin for having committed suicide. It was bad for Hubbard's image.

TONJA AND THE BUMP

Tonja Burden's recounting of her time with Hubbard includes a story about how Ron was developing this fairly sizable bump on his forehead. This bump is visible in one of the photos taken by Jim Dincalcy in New York in 1973.

She was in her mid-teens by this time, a true believer, and that bump bothered her.

She had observed many negative things about him, but these did not bother her the way this bump did. She could somehow explain away these other things without making her feel doubtful that he was the god that the entire ship considered him to be. But this bump. . . .

One of the things that bothered her about the bump was that it obviously bothered Hubbard. He used to wear hats and would carefully position them, while examining himself in the mirror, so as to cover up the bump.

It would occur to her that if it bothered him that much, and since he was an OT, why didn't he just make it go away!

It finally did "go away," being surgically removed by Kima Douglas, his "medical officer," who opened it up and cut out the fatty deposits.

14

The Crowley Connection: L. Ron and the Beast Revisited

Origins of the "OT Data"

Hubbard had spoken admiringly about his "very good friend," the "Beast 666" Aleister Crowley, throughout his lecture series in Philadelphia in December of 1952. He had spoken words of praise about Jack Parsons, while on the topic of "real geniuses" in 1958.

In 1969 a London Sunday Times article revealed Hubbard's involvement with Crowleyan 'Magick' at Jack Parson's house in Pasadena in the late 1940s. Hubbard—now the **Commodore**—concocted a story to explain it all away.

The Sunday Times never did retract the story. It did, however, print a statement from Scientology.

Hubbard's cover-up story was that he had been sent in by Naval Intelligence to break up Jack Parsons' group. Very little research is needed before this shows up as a fabrication, pretty much in the line with Hubbard's now discredited biographical sketches. None-the-less, Scientology's PR people parrot the story whenever the issue comes up.

****

Paulette Cooper's *Scandal of Scientology*, published in 1972 contained a chapter on Hubbard's adventures in Pasadena. As a result she was harassed extensively. Also in the early 1970s, L. Ron Hub-

380

bard Jr. spoke out regarding his father's involvement with magical rites. The "silencing" of Ron Jr. rapidly became top priority.

Recent (1990s) "official" transcriptions of Hubbard's lectures delete references to either Crowley or Parsons. And Scientology even hired a "religious expert" to explain that, "Church teachings are not magical," and have "no connection" to magic.

****

I became aware of the "Crowley connection" a year or so after leaving the Church of Scientology, when Brian Ambry brought that connection to my attention. I find Crowley's work at times repulsive, but also at times of considerable interest. His works often have a familiar ring to me, since I have so often read Hubbard's restatement of them. For example:

. . . we then continue the conquest of matter; and we are getting pretty expert . . .
The world of the mind seems almost as savage and unexplored as the world of nature seemed to the Greeks. There are countless worlds unpath'd and uncomprehended—and even unguessed, we doubt not. Therefore we set out diligently to explore and map these untrodden regions of the mind.
Surely our adventures may be as exciting as those of Cortez or Cook!

—Crowley, from the **Equinox.**

. . . When all horizons are measured, all swamps mapped, all deserts charted . . . there will yet be a world of unknown frights and glooms and cheers to explore, there will yet be a universe of adventure left . . . You. The universe of You.
From the first moments of a co-auditing session the preclear begins to make discoveries—discoveries to him far more important than Balboa's glimpse of the Southern Sea or Columbus' glance at San Salvador.

—Hubbard, from **Ability** magazine, No. 6

****

Is it possible that Hubbard had more to hide than just his involvement in the **Dark Side** of Crowleyan Magick?

QUOTING FROM BRIAN AMBRY'S
CRITIQUE ON SCIENTOLOGY:

"Much of what became the 'OT data' of the 'Philadelphia Doctorate Course' tapes, and other lectures and writings by Hubbard, which Scientologists read and listen to with appreciative awe, are simply rehashings of data and techniques from the writings of Aleister Crowley.

"Crowley, in spite of his egotism and eccentricities, and regardless of the 'ultra-Nietzschean' sentiments of *The Book of the Law*, did serve as a **relay** point for a great deal of previously secret material that had been part of 'mystery schools' and the like.

"The parallels between Hubbard's work and those of Crowley could fill an entire book. These include basic concepts and practical 'technology',", to a myriad of little things.

"Even the 'Scientology Symbol', the S with the Double Triangle, is but an embodiment of Crowley's motto: Love is the Law; Love under Will.*

"Some of 'Hubbard's ideas' which were, apparently, taken from materials relayed through Crowley are:

" 'Spacation' (or the creation of 'mental space'); mental constructs of 'mock-ups' (Creative Processing); the idea of a multiplicity of infinite minds; putting the subject into 'axioms'; putting the subject into grades; various scales; the concept of OT; forms of co-auditing and solo auditing; developing past life recall; the idea of gradiently increasing one's ability to confront or experience; the idea of 'exteriorization', and drills or exercises done while out-of-body; and much much more—can be found in Crowley's works.

---

*To anyone who has studied Scientology, I recommend that they read Crowley's **Book 4,** the chapters on the "wand" (Will) and the "cup" (Understanding). It will enhance greatly their understanding of the official Scientology emblem or symbol, of "KRC/ARC" (Top triangle = Knowledge, Responsibility, Control. Bottom triangle = Affinity, Reality, Communication, which—per Scientology—equate to "Understanding."

(The concept of "ARC" appears to have been derived from the Yogic triad of **Bliss, Knowledge, Being.** Below the "Absolute"—at the level of the "dualistic" or "mundane"—"**Bliss/Joy,**" translates to "awareness of the desirability or undesirability of something"; *"Knowledge"* to "belief/agreement"; and **"Being"** to "extension of being" or "communication.")

I also recommend Crowley's **Magick in Theory and Practice,** and especially **Magick Without Tears.** (See Bibliography for other texts.)

THE KABALA

"Many have taken the 'Kabala', interpreted it in their own way, and added it to their own systems. Crowley was one of these. Indeed many serious students of the 'Kabala' are not at all happy with the fact that the subject is often identified with Crowley.

" 'Kabala' is the name used to denote a collection of ancient writings by Hebrew mystics. It is a complicated subject with a long history.

"A key concept in Kabalistic doctrine is the 'Tree of Life'. The **Tree** is—essentially—a kind of map, or diagram, depicting a progression of steps from **creator** to **created,** from **unmoved mover** to **matter,** from **full consciousness** to **unconsciousness.**

"Of course, the progression of steps leading downward, reversed, become the series of steps leading **upward.**

****

"Hubbard's 'Know to Mystery scale' and other 'scales' are simple, linear (top to bottom) descriptions of the **Tree of Life.** His 'The Factors' appears to be a re-write of a number of earlier statements, and is yet another description of the **Tree.** Hubbard's 'Four Conditions of Existence' is an interesting description of the four basic components of the **Tree.** These are known in the Kabala as the 'Four Letters of the Name (or expressions of the Will or Word) of God.'*

"The extent to which Jack Parsons contributed to Hubbard's understanding of the Kabala and other subjects, will probably never be determined. Surviving records of correspondence between Parsons and Hubbard have been vigorously suppressed by the Scientology organization.

OUT-OF-THE-BODY-EXPERIENCE

"Such things as 'out-of-the-body-experiences', 'remote viewing', 'soul travel', or as it's referred to in Scientology, 'exteriorization', or 'exteriorization with perception', are—no matter how skeptical one might be—taken quite seriously by even the likes of military and

---

*Consult the book 'Scientology 0-8' for a look at the various items listed above.

covert intelligence agencies, in both the United States and the Soviet Union.

"Certainly para-psychologists recognize that such things occur. The question is not so much **does** it but **how?** Even die-hard Soviet materialists concede that remote viewing, telekinesis, and telepathy occur, and have their own elaborate materialistic explanations for them.

"Other viewpoints expressed in the utterances of—among others— Hebrew, Persian, Indian, Tibetan, and Chinese mystics, reflect the spiritual explanation:

" 'Man is essentially a non-physical being not bound, ultimately, by physical restrictions'.

"There is a substantial and impressive background, in many disciplines, dealing with this area of capability, its development and enhancement.

"As in so many areas, Hubbard took these phenomena and claimed to be the only person who really understood them, and also to possess the only technique that would allow for their development.

SPIRITUAL EXERCISES

"Those who have read Hubbard's early Scientology writings know of his various 'OT processes'. Hubbard even claimed that these were the **first spiritual exercises** ever: Classic Hubbardian Snake-oil-salesman pitch.

"The literature of the Human Race contains a rich supply of 'spiritual exercises'. The following is one of which Hubbard was likely aware. Written by Crowley, it borrows much from earlier sources:

"0. Let the Practicus [student] study the textbooks of astronomy, travel if need be to a land where the sun and stars are visible, and observe the heavens with the best telescopes to which he may have access. Let him commit to memory the principle facts, and (at least roughly) the figures of science.

"1. Now, since the figures will leave no distinct impression with any precision upon his mind, let him adopt this practice A:

"A. Let the practicus be seated before a square table, and let an unknown number of small similar objects be thrown by his chela [teacher or trainer] from time to time upon the table, and by that chela be hastily gathered up.

"Let the Practicus declare at a glance, and the chela confirm by his count, the number of such objects . . .

"The quickness of the chela in gathering up is expected to increase with time . . . Care must be taken to detect the first symptom of fatigue, and to stop, if possible, even before it threatens. The practiced psychologist learns to recognize even minute hesitations that mark the forcing of attention.

"2. Alternating with the above, let the Practicus begin this practice B:

"B. It is assumed that he has thoroughly conquered the elementary difficulties of Dharana [concentration], and is able to prevent mental pictures from altering shape, size and color against his will.

"Seated in the open air, let him endeavor to form a complete mental picture of himself and his immediate surroundings. It is important that he should be in the center of such a picture, and able to look freely in all directions. The finished picture should be a complete consciousness of the whole, fixed, clear, and definite.

"Let him gradually add to the picture by including objects more and more distant, until he have an image of the whole field of vision.

"He will probably find that it is very difficult to increase the apparent size of the picture as he proceeds, and it should be his most earnest endeavor to do so. He should seek in particular to appreciate distances, almost to the laws of combatting perspective.

"3. These practices A and B accomplished, and his studies in astronomy, let him attempt this practice C:

"C. Let the practicus form a mental picture of the Earth, in particular striving to realize the size of the earth in comparison with himself, and let him not be content until by assiduity he has well succeeded. Let him add the Moon, keeping well in mind the relative sizes of, and distance between, the planet and its satellite.

"He will probably find the final trick of the mind to be a constant disappearance of the image, and the appearance of the same upon a smaller scale. This trick he must outwit by constancy of endeavor.

"He will then add in turn Venus, Mars, Mercury and the Sun. It is permissible at this stage to change the point of view to the center of the Sun, and to do so may add stability . . .

MIND OVER MATTER

"An old fundamental idea in Scientology is: 'Considerations take rank over mechanics of Space, Energy, Time'. In other words, thought is senior to the physical universe.

"While the glassy-eyed 'rank-and-file' of Scientology walk around terribly impressed with the idea that their considerations 'take rank over the physical universe', they overlook the fact that 'L. Ron Hubbard's considerations' (and now the 'considerations' of the 'Scientology Hierarchy') take absolute 'rank' over their 'considerations'.

****

"Hubbard defines a 'consideration' as a 'continuing postulate.'

"The idea of 'postulates', so central to Scientology, is also the very cornerstone of Crowley's Magick. A 'postulate' is a 'decision' that has the power to affect an individual or others. A postulate infers **will** and actions rather than just plain 'think'. It has a dynamic connotation.

"The subject of ceremonial magic, and related disciplines and practices, deal with 'making postulates stick' (casting spells); with making one's dynamic decisions come true; with following through on one's **will**.

"Hubbard said in 1952:

"The old magician was the great, great grandfather of your modern stage magician. The stage magician doesn't even know the old magician ever existed . . .

"And the magician was very ritualistic; and he would very carefully postulate what effect he was trying to achieve before he would be cause for that effect.

"Wrote Crowley:

"Every successful act has conformed to the postulate.

"Every failure proves that one or more of the requirements of the postulate have not been fulfilled.

"Unlike Hubbard, Crowley advocated the study of many systems and disciplines.

"Whatever one may think of Aleister Crowley and his unfortunate obsession with drugs and Satanic imagery, he gave good advice when explaining the reason behind a long 'recommended reading list' covering many subjects:

"When the mind is strongly biased towards any special theory, the result of an illumination is often to enflame that portion of the mind which is thus overdeveloped, with the result of the aspirant, instead of becoming an Adept, becoming a bigot or fanatic.

"Good advice, but odd, coming from a man who was, himself, in many respects fanatical.

ON THE UNION OF PSYCHOTHERAPY AND SPIRITUAL EXPLORATION

"In 1937 a book entitled, *The Middle Pillar* by Israel Regardie, was published. Regardie had been a student of Crowley's, yet was too independent to fit the mold of 'disciple'.

"Regardie was an advocate of the 'union of Psychology and Magical Experiment'. He favored Carl Jung's **Analytical Psychology,** and a more traditional and beneficent form of **Magic** than Crowley's version:

"Wrote Regardie:

"[Psycho-therapeutic] Analysis is the logical precursor of spiritual attainment and magical experiment . . . Not until the mind and the emotional system have been cleansed and unified by the cathartic process . . . can the full spiritual benefits of magical work be reflected into the mind of man.

". . . We should remember the parables of the archaic philosophical religions whose fundamental tenet was that within man was a spirit, a dynamic center of consciousness which, because of its contact and association with matter, had been plunged into a profound sleep, a state of somnambulism . . .

"By endeavoring to extend the horizon of consciousness, to enlarge the field of awareness so as to embrace what previously was unconscious, is obviously a logical method. To become aware of all our actions, our thoughts and emotions and unsuspected motives, to regard them in their true light as actually they are and not as we would like them to be or as we would wish an onlooker to perceive them. It requires, to take this step, an extraordinary degree of honesty and courage . . . The more of this suppressed and forgotten material stored in this at one time unknown or dormant side of our nature that can be raised to the clear light of day, by exactly so much do we awake from that inert stupor into which we have in the past been plunged.

****

"An interesting idea: An effective system of psycho-therapy, attached to a system of spiritual development in the tradition of Eastern

Meditation, Yoga, White Magic, or other disciplines—including practical applications of modern Para-Psychology.

"And some things in Hubbard's writings might be of interest to someone concerned with achieving this objective.

"Unfortunately, Hubbard's primary purpose appears to have been to build monuments to himself—and 'helping others' seems to have been simply a means to **that** end. Abundant evidence confirms that he had no problem what-so-ever with hurting people to achieve that same **end**.

****

"It would be a natural development, in a free environment, for the **actual** origins of Scientology and Dianetics to be revealed; and for the 'positives' to be freed of the 'negatives'. This would be an exercise in **real** freedom, **real** ethics, and civility.

"Unfortunately, the Scientology Organization behaves like a **machine.** It is **not** a philosophy, religion, or a 'subject' to be studied as you see fit. Its purpose is to transform you into a **perfectly round ball bearing,** so that you might roll—with the least distraction, or friction, or waste of energy, into the slot where you will be best **utilized** by it.

"Quite understandably, the Scientology organization is VERY determined that free exchange of ideas **not** prevail, and that the actual origins of the subject remain obfuscated; and that the 'positives' and the 'negatives' remain ever fused AND confused.

"Alas, a Trap lacking in Cheese is not much of a trap; and an unbaited hook catches no fish.

****

"It is ironic. If Hubbard is to have **any** positive legacy at all, it will be the result of 'heretics': Those who dare to salvage what there is of value in his vast overflow of words—'Heretics' that he spent much of his life working diligently to destroy.

EXPLOITATION OF PSYCHICAL PHENOMENA

"A portion of the **Scientological Bait-on-the-Hook** involves the belief in what is sometimes called 'psychical phenomena'.

"Efforts by deceitful-manipulative groups to monopolize and exploit the idea of psychical phenomena have not been overlooked by those actively—and credibly—involved in researching the subject. In the book, *The Mind Race,* Russell Targ, a physicist and psychical researcher from Stanford Research Institute, and by Keith Harary, an experimental psychologist, also from Stanford, explore the issue:

"In our Society, a person who is beginning to experience emerging psychic abilities, or who is interested in doing so, has almost nowhere to turn for guidance. Anyone with a purely scholarly interest in psi research can write to various laboratories or read the research reports. But this information will probably not be of much practical, personal use. . . .

"So people who think they have had psychic experiences, or who are merely interested in learning about psychic abilities, are left with very few alternatives. They can admit their interest and risk being branded as social deviants, or they can deny their interest in psychic functioning and thereby become alienated from what might be an important aspect of their own lives and experiences.

"This is the dilemma that leads many people to join cults in the first place. By accepting and exploiting psychic experiences in a society that does not readily accept them, cults have effectively monopolized the subject of psi. They have exploited many people who are interested in learning about the area, and frightened many others away from even considering the possibility of developing their own psychic potential . . .

". . . people who have what they believe to be psychic experiences are often drawn into cults that claim to offer explanations of psychic functioning, but at great personal, emotional, and financial expense to their followers. We think that giving away your mind is too high a price to pay for psychic development . . .

". . . For some people, the exposure to the possibility of developing their own psychic potential, which some cults appear to provide, may initially . . . help certain individuals to pay attention to areas of their own awareness that they might not otherwise consider exploring.

"But prolonged exposure to any cult's treatment of psychic abilities may seriously restrict the way its initiates view psychic functioning. And it may keep them from fully developing their actual psychic potential . . .

"Despite claims to the contrary by numerous factions, there is no evidence of an exclusive relationship between psychic functioning and any particular leader, doctrine, or way of life. Scientific evidence does, however, strongly suggest that the ability to function psychically is a genuine human capacity which, for many people, seems to improve with practice.

"The authors may have been thinking of Scientology's ever-growing number of secret "OT Levels," when noting:

"As recruits near what is presented as the most advanced stages, the group leader typically adds additional levels to guarantee the members' continued personal and financial involvement.*

****

INEVITABLY SCIENTOLOGY SLIMES ON WHAT IT SEEKS TO MONOPOLIZE AND EXPLOIT

"Slime? What is meant by 'slime?' This is an unpleasant word that is meant to signify the *exploitation* of a worthwhile idea or honorable intention. Unfortunately con-men tend to soil the decent things they exploit.

"Scientology has abundantly 'slimed on' the area of 'self-help', 'human potential' and 'psychical phenomena'.

****

"Despite evidence to the contrary, Scientologists believe—in their typically naive and pretentious manner—that they have some kind of monopoly on 'exteriorization' and related phenomena.

"While enticed by the idea of 'exteriorization' and 'psychic powers', Scientologists tend to be **very** 'interiorized' people—stuck inside the official Hubbard 'reality bubble'.

"For many Scientology Staffers, the idea of 'exteriorization' seems

---

*In the early 50s the Scientology **Bridge** was presented as a fairly short voyage. Many new books and new techniques flowed forth; each presented as **the** Big Breakthrough. Then, in 1965 Hubbard made all "upper levels" confidential.

From 1967 to 1978 there were eight "OT Levels." And "OT 8" was IT: "Full OT, Total Freedom, Total Power." Thousands of people attained the (then) Level of "OT 7," and the years went by. In 1978 a **new** "Grade Chart" appeared. Supposedly, **major breakthroughs** in Research had occurred. And the membership were told that, "**now** they were **really** on their way!" Only **now** "Total Freedom" was somewhere at, or above, "OT 15."

In 1986—with great fanfare—the **extremely** confidential level of "New OT 8" was "released." It finally became available in 1989. "Delivered" on the Scientology ship, **The Free Winds,** students studied "their materials" while carefully watched by "supervisors" alert to any slight twitch or indication of "non-comprehension" or "disagreement." Security guards—at a distance—surveyed the course room, and exits, through numerous cameras. The end result of this level was to be "Truth Revealed."

to be, mainly, a **hope** of escape from the daily Scientological drudgery of STATS and ETHICS CONDITIONS—and more STATS; and the never-ending fear of doing or saying the wrong thing, and not being sufficiently 'cooperative'.

"In this sense it's a form of **dissassociation:** a hoped-for, or imagined condition, that makes the miserable **actual** environment somehow tolerable. Unfortunately, this sort of thing tends to discredit the idea of 'out-of-the-body-experience', and 'psychical phenomena' generally," concludes Ambry.

****

One aspect of the "magical tradition," and also of Crowley's "magick," was the idea of exorcism or banishment.

A "magical operation" needed to be accomplished in a space freed of unwanted "influences." Crowley sometimes referred to these "influences" as "loathsome larvae".

The following chapter examines the background of this unusual subject, and traces Hubbard's outlook regarding it.

15

Are You Haunted?

"I got into Scientology because I was inhibited. Turns out I was inhabited!"—ANONYMOUS, L.A. newspaper ad

Over the past few decades some highly dramatic stories illustrating the phenomenon of "multiple personalities" have become quite well known.

Some psychiatrists and psychologists, and, in fictional accounts, novelists and scriptwriters, have given considerable attention to extreme cases where another distinctly different "personality" appears to take control over an individual for prolonged periods of time.

Less attention, however, has been given to less dramatic but, perhaps, related occurrences.

Most people have days when they are "not quite themselves." One hears comments like, "It just wasn't like Fred. He was like some kind of madman!" or "She was like a woman possessed!" or "He's a different person when he drinks," or "I don't know what came over me," or "What got into me?"

What's happening? There is no scarcity of theories. This and the following chapter examines this area, and offers various explanations concerning it.

****

Currently, the entirety of Scientology's super-secret "upper levels" deal with this type of "phenomena." But even in 1950 Hubbard was preoccupied by this sort of thing.

In *Dianetics, the Evolution of a Science*—published in 1950 and

392

aimed at a broad science fiction audience (consisting of scientifically oriented readers)—Hubbard wrote:

> . . . it was necessary to hark back to the techniques of the Kayan Shaman of Borneo, among others. Their theory is crude; they exorcise demons. . . . Provisionally, let's try to postulate that Man is good. . . . And we suppose something such as the Borneo Shaman's Toh has entered into him which directs him to do evil things.
>
> Man has believed longer that demons inhabit men than Man has believed they did not. We assume demons. We look for some demons, one way or another. And we find some!
>
> This was a discovery almost as mad as some of the patients on hand. But the thing to do was try to measure and classify demons.
>
> Strange work for an engineer and a mathematician! But it was found that the "demons" could be classified. There were several "demons" in each patient, but there were only a few classes of "demons." There were audio demons . . . visio demons, interior demons, exterior demons, ordering demons, directing demons, critical demons, apathetic demons, angry demons, bored demons and certain demons who merely occluded things. The last seemed to be most common. Looking into a few minds established soon that it was difficult to find anyone who didn't have some of these demons. . . .

Hubbard then discusses the analogy between the human mind and an electronic computer. Finally he concludes:

> There are no demons. No ghosts or ghouls or Tohs. But there are aberrative circuits.

Hubbard doesn't explain how it is that these "circuits" existed structurally. But "structure" was not his concern; his concern was *function*. He wrote:

> . . . it was not necessary to show how it is done in terms of physical mechanism if we can show that it IS done.

In 1950, a circuit was defined by Hubbard as:

> A part of the individual's bank [reactive mind] that behaves as though it were someone or something separate from him and that either talks to him or goes into action of its own accord, and may even, if severe enough, take control of him while it operates.

The jingle heard on the radio that sticks in one's mind, playing over and over; the actor who after many appearances on stage, portraying a particular character, takes a vacation and finds, to his discomfort, that he still at times possesses the qualities of that character; the obsession that grips a person causing him to do things he knows he will later regret—the materialistic viewpoint might simply say, "That's simply something the brain does."

The spiritual viewpoint on the other hand traditionally divides a human being into "body, mind, and spirit," with the spirit being the basic individual and the mind being the recordings of one's past experiences, ideas, conclusions, etc. These recordings are not necessarily considered as a part of the brain, but rather a function of the spirit.

Quoting from Joseph Krutch's *More Lives Than One*:

> The physiologists are very fond of comparing the network of our cerebral nerves with a telephone system but they overlook the significant fact that a telephone system does not function until someone talks over it. The brain does not create thought (Sir Julian Huxley has recently pointed out this fact); it is an instrument which thought finds useful.

PARACELSUS

Paracelsus von Hohenheim (1490-1541) was the outstanding medical therapist of his time and, perhaps, the greatest mystic in the history of Western medicine. He devoted his life to research in the healing arts. Paracelsus visited Constantinople to aquaint himself with the secret practices of the Dervishes and the Sufis.

The following is an excerpt from *Paracelsus—His Mystical and Medical Philosophy*, by Manly P. Hall, published by the Philosophical Research Society:

> [According to Paracelsus] . . . the elementary is an artificial being, created in the invisible worlds by man himself. In harmony with more recent findings, Paracelsus noted that most elementaries seem to be of an evil or destructive nature. They are generated from the excesses of human thought and emotion, the corruption of character, or the degeneration of faculties and powers which should be used in other, more constructive ways. . . .
>
> Man is therefore a creator, not merely in terms of the perpetuation of the species, but especially in terms of the imagination. Man is creative in the arts, sciences, and philosophies, but his creative powers are not only external, but also internal. Because he lives, man bestows life, and he can

generate creatures from his thoughts and emotions. . . . The power to create is the power of vibration, by which anything is set into a peculiar motion. . . . The invisible progeny of man include thought-forms and emotion-forms. These are like infants, especially in their beginnings, for they depend upon their creator for their nutrition and survival. Later, however, if the forces which generate continue to operate, these thought and emotion-forms gain strength, finally attaining a kind of independence. . . . Having thus become even stronger than their creator, these thought or emotion-forms will turn upon the one who fashioned them, often causing in him a terrible habit and destroying his health and happiness.

We know that the human psyche can become ridden with pressure-centers or pressure-patterns which we call fixations, complexes, phobias, and the like. We know that these negative psychic formations are nourished by the continued repetition of the attitudes which caused them. We say that negative attitudes become habitual, by degrees taking over and destroying the mental and emotional integrity of the individual. A fixation, well nourished by attitudes suitable for its perpetuation, intensifies, becoming actually avaricious and resolved to dominate or possess the entire life of its unhappy victim. . . .

Modern thinking, therefore, sheds light upon the concept of elementaries, extending beyond the basic research of Paracelsus . . . [He] used the term obsession to signify possession by an entity. Today the term is used to signify possession by an abnormal attitude. . . . Is it possible that the abnormal attitude has gradually become an entity? . . . Many persons under psychological obsession resist treatment, as though some foreign creature were fighting for its survival in them. . . .

Out of his philosophy of elementaries, Paracelsus came to the conclusion that a very large part of what we consider to be disease, results from psychic parasites generated by wrong thoughts and emotion.

GURDJIEFF

From the book *The Mystic Path to Cosmic Power*, by Vernon Howard:

Gurdjieff was probably born in Alexandropal, in Asia Minor, about 1872. This remarkable and often controversial man spent a dozen years roaming about the East in search of esoteric teachings. He returned with a tremendous wealth of wisdom for the Western world.

Gurdjieff summarized the problem: Mankind is asleep but doesn't know it. So deep is his hypnotic slumber that he does his daily walking and talking and legislating and marrying in a state of unconsciousness.

Actually, the acts are the mechanical acts of hypnotized people. And *that*, Gurdjieff declares, is the simple reason why the world goes from one disaster to another: "Would", he asks, "a *conscious* human being destroy himself through war, and crime, and quarrels? No, man simply knows not what he does to himself."

One of the basic principles explains the many and varied I's in a man. The unawakened man is not a unified person. He has dozens of selves within him, each falsely calling itself I. Many philosophers, including George Santayana and David Hume, have also observed how a person switches constantly from one I to another.

The many I's within a man explains many mysteries about human nature. For example, a man decides to give up an undesirable habit, but the next day he repeats it again. Why? Because another I has taken over, one that likes the habit and has no intention of giving it up. Or perhaps a woman decides to quit fooling around with her life; she determines to find her real self. She reads a book or two and goes to a few lectures. Then, suddenly, she loses all interest and goes back to her self-defeating behavior. What happened? An entirely different I, one that doesn't want her to wake up, took charge.

Gurdjieff provides a simple solution to this contradictory condition: Become aware of the many I's. Watch how one takes over and then another. Also, see that they do not represent the true you, but consist of borrowed opinions and imitated viewpoints. Such self-observation weakens their grip; you eventually find your real I.

LOATHSOME LARVAE

From Mouni Sadhu's *The Tarot,* * A Contemporary Course of the Quintessence of Hermetic** Occultism:

Let us imagine that a man has a common evil desire, he makes no attempt to realize it on the physical plane. He only draws a dark desire on the astral*** plane, and so creates a kind of "entity." . . . This artificial "being" does not possess a physical body. . . . Such a being can . . . act and influence only in direction as intended by its unwise creator, man, who is usually unaware of his foolishness.

Now, on whom will the influence of such a demon be exerted? Yes, firstly on the father of it himself . . . who created the astral picture of the evil deed. We call this type of ominous artificial entity a larva. Such

*A collection of cards—each representing one of the possibilities, or aspects, of consciousness or living.
**Hermes Trismegistus, alchemist and magician.
***A supposed "plane" or level of existence of a more "rarefied" nature, less tangible than the physical plane. Along this line of thought, one's mental imagery might be said to be "made of astral matter."

a larva will watch it's "father" in order to prevent him from forgetting his evil intention and desire, and to fortify the larva's life by new meditations about the same theme. But it can also attach itself to another man, who has a certain astral and mental affinity with the first one.

THOUGHT-FORMS IN TIBET

Besides the idea that "thought forms" may be inadvertently created, there is also the viewpoint that they can be deliberately brought into being.

The following excerpt is from the book *The Yoga of Sex* by Omar Garrison:*

> According to secret lore, man can develop such concentration of mind that he is able to generate psycho-mental energy (called "risal" in Tibet) and to use it for bringing about results that to the uninitiated appear to be supernatural.
>
> It has been because the Tantric* techniques employ these secret methods of concentration that Tantrism has been called the most elaborate system of auto-suggestion in the world.
>
> While such an evaluation may serve to explain the more subjective visions of the sadhaka [adept], it is hardly adequate to account for phenomena witnessed by persons other than the creator of them.
>
> For example, Tantric adepts (especially in Tibet) possess methods for projecting thought forms (called tulpas) which are materialized so completely that they are often mistaken for physical entities.
>
> Moreover, these phantoms are sometimes visualized and given a kind of autonomy, so that they may act and seemingly think without the consent or even knowledge of their creator.
>
> In this connection, Madame Alexandra David-Neel, a Frenchwoman who spent many years among the lamas of Tibet, recounts an intriguing personal experience in the creation of a tulpa.
>
> Having a sceptical turn of mind, Madame David-Neel suspected that many stories she had heard concerning such materializations might be gross exaggerations.
>
> The most common kind of Tulpa-making in Tibet is that of forming and animating the counterparts of Tibetan deities. So to avoid coming under the influence of this kind of mental suggestion—so prevalent around her—she chose for her thought-child the figure of a fat, jolly monk.

*Written by Omar Garrison long before his ill-fated association with Scientology. Garrison has written numerous books on a variety of subjects.
**From "Tantra," one of a comparatively recent class of Hindu or Buddhist religious writings concerned with mysticism and magic.

After a few months of performing the prescribed disciplines for ritual projection of thought image, Madame David-Neel relates that the form and character of her phantom monk took on the appearance of real life. He shared her apartment like a guest and, when she departed for a journey, he accompanied her entourage.

At first, the monk put in an appearance only when his creator thought of him. But after a time, he began to behave in a very independent manner and to perform various actions not directed by his maker.

So real did he become in time, that on one occasion, when a herdsman came to the Frenchwoman's encampment to bring her some butter, he mistook the chimerical monk for a live lama.

Even more alarming to the phantom's begetter, his character began to undergo a subtle change. He grew leaner and his face gradually took on a sly, malevolent look. He daily grew more importunate and bold.

"In brief," says Madame David-Neel, "he escaped my control."

Clearly, the time had come to purge herself of the unwanted companion whom she had brought to life, but who, by her own admission, had turned her existence into a day-nightmare.

It required six months of difficult practice and ritual to magically dissolve the monstrous prodigy.

"My mind-creature was tenacious in life," she declared.

How are we to explain such phenomena? Western psychology has only begun to investigate the secret and profound life of the mind. Many of their answers so far are far from adequate to account for occurrences such as that just cited.

Be that as it may, in the case of the deliberately created phantom, such as Madame David-Neel's monk, the independence and individuality of the prodigy ought to give us considerable pause. . . .

****

During the 1952 Philadelphia Doctorate Course, Hubbard said of what used to be called, in Dianetics, "demon circuits":

Each one of these things can be a thinking entity. It thinks it's alive. It can think it's a being as long as energy is fed to it.

He had also mentioned in this lecture series that someone can deliberately "mock up" (i.e., vividly imagine) something and give it a life of its own.

****

More controversial than the idea of "thought forms" created by the individual himself is the viewpoint that asserts that, while thought-forms do exist, real "demons" also exist. But not only "demons"; also many types of "disembodied beings," human and non-human, some big, some small, some good, some indifferent, some unconscious, some insane.

There are many variations of this theme. The movie *The Exorcist* illustrates one version. A powerful demonic being completely takes over a little girl.

One can also pose a less dramatic scenario. Rather than one powerful "demon," a person, theoretically, might be infested with many little "demons."

To quote again from Garrison's *Sex Yoga*:

> Tantric texts assert that the universe all about us is teeming with thought forms and with beings good and bad—deities, demons, nature spirits, discarnate human egos, phantoms, monsters.
>
> The sadhaka is not only made aware that they exist, he is taught disciplines that bring them under his control and enable him to communicate freely to them.

The tantric Yogis are not alone in their view, or the claim of ability to communicate and control this, supposed, class of beings. In fact, in various degrees of sophistication, it can be found to be part of the spiritual tradition of Man on all five continents. The witchdoctor, the magi, the medicine man, and many a modern psychic have as a commonality the view that such things exist.

On the other hand, considering oneself overly vulnerable to "invisible forces" appears to me to be one of several routes to a state of insanity.

My view is that those who decide that they are essentially responsible for their own mental state—rather than blaming some invisible entity for their foibles—tend to be far saner and happier.

****

As an aside I find it of interest that Thomas Edison wrote the following in "The Diary and Sundry observations," although it is not in the category of "unwanted psychical or spiritual influences" in one's body or "aura":

> Take our own bodies. I believe they are composed of myriads and myriads of infinitesimally small individuals, each in itself a unit of life, and that these units work in squads—or swarms, as I prefer to call

them—and these infinitesimally small units live forever. When we "die" these swarms of units, like a swarm of bees, so to speak, betake themselves elsewhere, and go on functioning in some other form or environment.

Edison not only believed in the immortality of the human spirit, but also in the immortality of that which he believed enlivens the physical body—the immortality of each cell.

"UNWHOLESOME SWARMS"

In 1978 L. Ron Hubbard, felled by his second major heart attack, lay barely conscious and helpless in bed.*

At the time Dr. Gene Denk and "Case Supervisor International" David Mayo began working with him on his health in 1978, Hubbard conceived of himself as surrounded by a swarm of confused, unconscious, or semi-conscious entities: burnt-out human souls.

"There are no demons," he had written in 1950. A couple of years later, he spoke of self-generated "thinking entities."

Then, a quarter of a century later, he was party to the development of procedures with which any medicine man or witch doctor would probably feel at home. These procedures dealt with the eviction of swarms of non-self-generated parasitic beings.

Now, any decent witch doctor "servicing a client" does his thing and a few hours later goes on his way, goat, chicken or pig in hand, in exchange for his services.

In the varied literature regarding "exorcism" and the like—whether such things are considered self-generated or not—one sees a regular reference to a relatively small number of "influences," "thought forms," "obsessions," or whatever, in need of "handling."

Hubbard operated on a much grander scale. From his hypnotic pedestal of "ultimate authority," he stated to his followers that *everyone* was engulfed in thousands upon thousands of degraded beings.

JOHN AUSLEY (ex-Flagship Class XII):

He talked about how, if you convince a person hard enough and long enough that they're at effect, you'll drive them insane. Then he turns right around and does that: He says, *"You're the effect of all these body Thetans!"* (beings attached to the body).

*It's interesting to note that a physical and emotional collapse preceded Hubbard's "discovery" of the OT III materials in 1967. This was after his failures in Southern Africa.

NEW ERA DIANETICS FOR OTs OR "NOTS"

Hubbard's theory and procedure of how to "handle" the entity "phenomenon" is highly secret. This level of auditing brings in probably a million dollars a week internationally for the Church of Scientology. The high prices charged depend upon this material's being kept tantalizingly mysterious.

"Mystery is the glue that sticks Thetans [spiritual beings] to things," Hubbard once said. He proceeded to use this principle in marketing his OT levels. The secrecy and mystery surrounding these levels pulled people in, bringing in also their wallets and check-books; a major part of it . . . just to discover the answer to the mystery.

While still in the Church, I observed something very odd: The wealthier the Scientologist, the more "body Thetans" he had. Such unfortunate people were being sold seemingly endless auditing for the eradication of their "fleas."

Such auditing costs over $400 per hour. It is quite usual for Scientologists to spend well over $100,000 for this level alone. One man, a geologist, engineer and entrepreneur, spent $450,000.

According to Hubbard, "Nots handles" are those beings or entities or "body thetans" ("BTs") that are located in the body or around the body. The auditing procedure of Nots is supposed to locate those entities, and send them off to do their own thing—picking up a body of their own or whatever—but no longer infesting the individual or his body.

The entities are *being* various things, like a body part (a bone, arm, cell, whatever) or a particular personality, or condition, such as "TV watcher," or "fear," or "worker," or "solitary angry man," and so on.

According to this line of thought, people get confused as to who they *are* and who they *are not*. A person hears these voices or feels desires, and so on, and thinks he is the source of them.

Yet, the theory goes, you are not necessarily the originator of these thoughts or impulses. Another may be.

So, by identifying *who* is the being (who is the source of these vocalizations or impulses) and spotting *where* it is located, *you* are freed to think for yourself.

So an auditor has *you* (the main guy in control) ask each BT, "What are you?" and "Who are you?"

The Body Thetans are then supposed to separate out and realize that they are in fact themselves; that they are not some body part or whatever.

At the same time, *you* realize that the BTs are different from *you*; that their mental pictures, ideas, and degraded impulses do not originate from you.

According to Hubbard, these beings are very easily overwhelmable and hypnotic. Because of this, they tend to take on the personality of whatever (or whoever) comes along that gets their attention.

HUBBARD:

> You have to actually put some life into them to activate them. They're like pebbles on a beach. . . . But listen, you're living in a universe which is crawling with this type of stuff. And planet Earth was a dumping ground to end all dumping grounds. . . . As NED for OTs is run these cats wake up and get handled. This relieves the Pre-OT of a lot of phenomena which puzzles him and can hold him down. As you go along running it you will find that the material to which NED for OTs is addressed seldom considers itself live beings. It thinks it is MEST (Matter, Energy, Space and Time), body parts, significances, conditions—anything but a live being.

That these "beings" might have been the creation of one's own mind, i.e., "thought forms" or "mock-ups endowed with life which live as long as one feeds them energy," was not considered in Hubbard's writings after 1966.

That "upper level" Scientologists may be locating all these thousands of "Body Thetans" because Hubbard told them they *are* there, and therefore *must* be there—finding them because they *know* they will—is of course not even dimly regarded as a possibility by the faithful.

No, such "beings" are the victims of what Hubbard calls the "dwindling spiral." According to him, any spiritual being in the physical universe is inevitably subject to deterioration and degradation. Beings are (without Scientology processing) *not* evolving spiritually, but rather are *devolving*—heading downward towards "Hubbardian Hell."

In "Ron's Journal 30" Hubbard explains: "But there was one discovery in 1978 that I haven't said very much about and am really not likely to since it is a sad thing. It is what really happens to a thetan who is not salvaged or processed and goes on down the chute. Man, when I saw that and knew it to be true I actually felt sorry for these guys that try to hit at us. Poor devils. Some religions talk about hell. It's an understatement of what really happens."

The message is clear. Throw yourself at the mercy of the Church of Scientology or eventually, some lifetime down the way, become somebody's big toe!

16

The Final Universe Of RON

"The starry-eyed Syndrome is . . . very hard to correct. The ancient assertion: 'If you believe what I tell you, you will be saved. If you don't you will be damned,' has been used for centuries . . . It is an integral part of the world's oldest confidence trick. It is still played today and is still profitable . . .

"The will to dominate . . . is the exact opposite of the Starry-eyed Syndrome. This is the basis for the False-Messiah Syndrome, and in those in whom it occurs are responsible for vast amounts of human misery. This error occurs in people who naturally possess some special power. They are less scattered, less divided, less lacking in unity and will than the average man. They are able to apply themselves to a single aim and pursue that aim with an emotional intensity . . .

"[The false messiah] . . . instead of becoming liberated of the self, is more tightly bound to it. He uses the power he has attained by inner discipline to further the aims of the self, these being often identified with some organization which is, in fact, the self amplified . . .

"The condition once it has developed, is hard to correct."

—from *The Master Game* by Robert S. DeRopp

Towards the end of L. Ron Hubbard's life his personal "cosmology" reached its final development and formulation.

In the last years of his life his writings often focused on the subject of "enemies," "criminals," "loathsome psychotics," and "creatures."

Psychiatrists topped the list of those "loathed."

In fact, Hubbard finally ended up attributing the degradation of all beings throughout the universe to psychiatrists. The idea is that these same "psychs"—in earlier lifetimes—have been acting out their "evil intentions" for "trillions of years."

Quoting from Hubbard Communications Office Bulletin of 26 August 1982:

> Destructive creatures who do not want people big or reaching—since they are terrified of punishment due to their crimes—invented pain and sex to shrink people and cut their alertness, knowingness, power and reach . . .
>
> They were sent on that route down through the ages by the psychs . . .
>
> These are data which emerged from recent thorough research of the whole track. This is not theory or some strange opinion. It is a provable electronic fact . . .*

****

Hubbard's embittered writings of the 1980s appear to be his final imprint on the Scientology organization. It also provides a clue as to what one might find at the organization's "upper, upper levels."

---

*It is undeniable that abuses have occurred in the field of psychiatry.

But Scientology's "war" with psychiatry has nothing to do with correcting psychiatric abuses. In fact it makes it less likely that those abuses will be corrected.

An unscrupulous and abusive organization, which utilizes many of the Behaviorist or Pavlovian methods it publicly denounces, is not likely to be a helpful ally to those **sincerely** concerned with "psychiatric abuse."

17

Typewriter in the Sky

"If the body of the King dissolve, he shall remain in pure ecstasy forever."—ALEISTER CROWLEY, *Book of The Law*

"If you see me dead I will live forever,"—L. RON HUBBARD, from "Hymn of Asia"

On the 24th of January, 1986, L. Ron Hubbard died in a $250,000 Bluebird motor home, parked near a pen of llamas and a field of grazing buffalo. The location was a 160-acre ranch in Creston, 11 miles east of Atascadero in San Luis Obispo County, California.

His personal physician, Gene Denk, cited on the death certificate that Hubbard had suffered a brain hemorrhage days before his death. Obispo Sheriff Whiting stated that blood samples taken from Hubbard's body showed acceptable levels of medication given for stroke patients.

Little is known about what happened from the time of his death and 12 hours later when Church officials asked a funeral director to pick up the body. A neighbor, Robert Whaley, a retired advertising executive, remembers seeing tremendous traffic at the ranch that Friday night.

The next morning attorney Cooley telephoned Reis Chapel in San Luis Obispo, 20 miles southwest of the ranch. "He asked if we did cremation," said Irene Reis, an owner of the Chapel. She said special arrangements for the cremation were made at the crematory, which was usually closed on weekends. Her husband Gene, picked up the body at the ranch.

Church attorney Cooley accompanied the body to the Chapel and stayed near it while other Church officials went to lunch. "Mr. Cooley insisted that we never leave the body alone."

Church officials "wanted everything private—they wanted nothing released to the press," Reis said. After Chapel officials learned the identity of the body, they called the San Luis Obispo County Deputy Coroner, Don Hines. He stopped any cremation until an independent pathologist could examine the body and tests could be performed.

Cooley presented Hines with a certificate of religious preference signed by Hubbard stating that he didn't want an autopsy at his death.

A Church spokesman said that Hubbard had lived on the ranch in Creston for the past two and a half years, writing and researching topics of the spirit and cross-breeding of animals, as well as dabbling in photography. He had lived in his motor home while his home was under renovation, a process just finished when he died.

Neighbors, and people who were hired to work on various construction projects at the ranch over the years, described him as a "Colonel Sanders" lookalike because he sported a white beard and was overweight. They said that the man they knew as "Jack" rarely emerged from his motor home and was driven around the ranch by a petite blonde woman who lived on the ranch.

According to the neighbor Whaley, Hubbard practiced an obsession with privacy. None of his neighbors knew who he was. He didn't receive mail at the ranch, and visitors often arrived in the middle of the night.

When he did come out of his motor home during the day, it was only to putter around on the estate, feeding the horses, llamas and buffaloes.

Whaley told a reporter that he invited Hubbard and "the Mitchells" (as Pat and Annie Broeker called themselves) to dinner, shortly after they moved in, but "they turned us down."

The neighbor recalled a chance eye-to-eye encounter with Hubbard.

One day Whaley went to a stable at the ranch to borrow a tool and surprised Hubbard, who was filing a piece of metal.

"This older man gave me a very dirty look and ran into the workshop and closed the door," Whaley said.

****

Hubbard's last will and testament was written the day before he died. For several years Hubbard had been frantically gathering up Church funds and placing them in accounts under his name. The new will, however, gives what is said to be the bulk of his estate "to the Church."

What exactly is meant by "the Church" is unclear. There are numerous incorporated entities set up by Hubbard's agents. Each one represents itself as being autonomous. These include the Author Services Inc. (Hubbard's private for profit corporation; headed by the top Church elite and—according to witnesses—the senior entity), The Church of Spiritual Technology, The Church of Scientology of California, etc., etc. Despite pretence to the contrary (according to former high Scientology officials) these all form one monolithic whole dominated by the same few people who were Hubbard's top agents when he died.

Attention was brought to this state of affairs recently (April, 1987) when the U.S. Supreme Court rejected pleas by the Church for relief from having to post a bond of up to 60 million dollars to guard its assets against seizure while it appeals a Los Angeles Superior Court jury award.

A front-page story in *The Los Angeles Times* explained:

> Scientology lawyers have argued the payment of the bond would plunge the church into bankruptcy. But the state court judge who presided over the jury trial contends that the controversial organization's claims of poverty are untrue. . . .
>
> In a strongly worded opinion last September [Judge] Swearinger said "the claim of relative indigency is not believed by the court, and the court has had ample opportunity to examine and consider the credibility of the defendant during five and a half months of trial and extended post-trial proceedings."
>
> Swearinger said Scientology is composed of interconnected entities, including the California Church, which form a "monolithic whole." Swearinger said the Church of California transferred "virtually all of its assets and functions" to those other entities between the time Wollersheim filed his lawsuit in 1980 and the start of the trial in February, 1986.
>
> The transfers, Swearinger said, "are seen as mere 'jiggery-pokery [deception].' The power to transfer out to a sister entity is the power to transfer back in 'when the heat is off,' so to speak."
>
> Moreover, Swearinger characterized as "pure sham" arguments by the church that the bond would deprive its parishioners of the right to practice their religion.
>
> "Proof has shown that the real estate, furnishings, fixtures and stock in trade of Scientology are in possession and control of other entities."

****

A shroud of mystery is likely to surround Hubbard's death, his will, and the amount and whereabouts of his estate for some time.

Certainly this most recent will was substantially different from that prepared in 1982.

Richard Behar of *Forbes* magazine, after interviewing Bill Franks, Homer Shomer and others concludes that Hubbard had transferred "at least $200 million" from Church accounts to his own. Chances are it was a great deal more. So any claims could be for substantial sums of money.

There are several witnesses who say that Hubbard was obsessed with the idea of returning to collect his booty (whether buried as gold or stashed in foreign banks with numbered accounts).

The idea was that, in his next life on Earth, he would recall the appropriate locations or the digits of the various numbered accounts (accounts where no I.D. is necessary), and so reclaim his riches. Apparently L. Ron Hubbard very much disagreed with the saying, "You can't take it with you."

The will's naming of "the Church" (controlled by a small elite) and family appear to be inconsistent with that intention. Unless one considers the possibility that there may be extensive hidden/buried assets unknown to anyone but Hubbard.

There are first-hand witnesses to the paper traffic regarding the "Mausoleum" Hubbard planned to build for 35 million dollars, complete with his writings etched on stainless steel and gold bullion hidden within, Pharoah style. How his new incarnation would gain access to any of this is unclear.

****

In late September of 1985, just months before Hubbard died, the IRS sent a letter to the Church.

It warned that there might be indictments against Hubbard for tax fraud. What comes to mind is that Hubbard had avoided the courts so vigorously. Being indicted would have forced him out of his seclusion, revealing his poor health.

This would have been intensely humiliating to a man who valued his image to the exclusion of all else. A man who, after his last appearance in a courtroom in 1952, vowed never again to stand before a judge.

The new leaders insist that Hubbard "causatively discarded" his body because "it had become an encumbrance." However, there are those who have speculated that Hubbard may have simply committed suicide to avoid public humiliation.

There is no evidence that I'm aware of to this effect; however, many have questions as to why the "unseemly haste" to cremate the body sans autopsy. Among these were Michael Flynn who expressed his concern to a reporter.

Cooley filed an immediate lawsuit against Flynn in regard to his comments, revealing that the top Church brass does indeed appear to be thin-skinned on this subject.

There are some who, citing a 1983 "Ron's Journal" taped message, the voice of which experts found not to be Hubbard's, and signatures of that period, which appear to have been forged, assert that Hubbard died in 1983 and was literally "kept on ice" while the youngsters consolidated their power base.

While this scenario may be an appropriate finale to a life difficult to differentiate from the novels Hubbard wrote, it is belied by neighbor Whaley's account and the coroner's report, and the statement of science fiction author and editor Ray Faraday Nelson. A long-time fan of Hubbard's science fiction works, Nelson maintained a regular epistolary exchange with him for over three decades. The last letter he received—with a postscript in Hubbard's own handwriting—arrived just a week before Hubbard's death.

Nelson, one of the few individuals with whom Hubbard maintained some kind of contact over the years, claims that Hubbard had been preoccupied with little more than his science fiction writing since prior to 1980.

This is probably true as far as avoiding direct Church management (especially following the Armstrong trial). To more correctly assess his preoccupations during his final years, one should add to this list: keeping out of courtrooms and jail cells, accumulating huge personal bank accounts, and attempting to prolong his life with the aid of medicine and nutrition. I believe he meddled with management only to the extent that it was necessary to ensure his personal safety and ever-increasing flows of money.

****

There was certainly no disgrace in a man who smoked three to four packs of cigarettes a day living to be almost seventy-five. But, to his followers, Ron was not supposed to be "just a man."

Many Scientologists thought Hubbard would never die, or at least would live to be very very old.

The news of their leader's death was lessened and for many turned into a "win"—wonderful news indeed—by the announcement, at the Los Angeles Palladium, that Ron had "causatively discarded the body," since it had become "an impediment to his research." Research that he was ("*is*") doing for all Mankind.

Yes, this was proof of Ron's "ultimate success," was the message; the ultimate victory: the conquest of the cycle of life and death!

****

In his writings and lectures Hubbard had never spoken of the body as being an "encumbrance" to heightened awareness. After all, one could "exteriorize" from it and be free of it while still being in possession of it and allowing it to live.

As I interpret it, as of January 27th—with the announcement of Hubbard's death—this was all changed. Now, beyond a certain point in "auditing," one must kill the body (an "impediment") in order to continue to greater heights. ("Discard," "kill," perhaps I'm confused. Is there a difference?)

One young Scientologist expressed her thoughts following Hubbard's death. She displayed an enthusiasm which seemed bizarre and macabre: "Once you get up to OT 14 you can go to Flag for instruction on how to drop the body and join Ron. It's really neat!"

OT 15, per the Church's "grade chart," is "Total Freedom."

Were Scientologists now nodding understandingly when they read Hubbard's words encouraging them to work diligently on getting "Across the Bridge"? For if they didn't, to quote from a piece written in 1982 (supposedly by Hubbard): "It will be very lonely in the sky," the sky where L. Ron Hubbard—wise, benevolent and powerful—awaited their arrival.

In his earlier writings Hubbard had proclaimed to the world that he had "built a bridge" which Mankind could walk, leading to total spiritual freedom in this lifetime.

This appears to have been slightly modified.

"I'll see you on the other side of the bridge." Hubbard had said. Now the "other side," where Ron is waiting, requires (so some imply) a somewhat grim passage through the local mortuary.

****

Whatever one chooses to believe, it does appear that the chain-smoking Messiah has puffed his last filterless Kool. (At least for a while, considering the possibility of reincarnation.)

Hubbard is gone.

But what of his "alter ego," the Church? It survives as *his* body, *his* hands, ready always to reach out and grope your children's minds.

The Church is, as it exists today, an enormous organizational vampire, drinking deep of the vitality of the innocent and the idealistic.

Possessing tremendous legal, financial, and public relations resources, the Church of Scientology's capacity to persuade and intimidate has been impressive. Its ability to inhibit communication, to prevent free dialogue, to terrorize, is a matter of record.

The outlook of the Church hierarchy is reflected in "aides order 210-47" of March 2, 1983. Issued by Captain Guillaume Lesevre, Executive Director International, it quotes Hubbard:

"I am not interested in wog [human] morality . . . if anyone is getting industrious trying to enturbulate or stop Scientology or its activities, I can make Captain Bligh look like a Sunday school teacher. There is probably no limit on what I would do to safeguard Man's only road to freedom."

As Omar Garrison said on CBS's "Sixty Minutes":

> I think, at the moment, that organization, the cult, is in the hands of the most fanatical followers and adherents of Mr. Hubbard, who you can equate with the followers of Ayatolla Khomeini.
>
> Everyone who has taken these courses comes out with a super ego. With a truculent, if you will, truculent view of anyone who dares to disagree. Because the person who disagrees is perceived as what they call a suppressive person, and must be dealt with as such. . . .
>
> That's the dark side of Scientology.

18

Reflections

"None are more hopelessly enslaved than those who falsely believe they are free."—J.W. VON GOETHE

L. RON HUBBARD JR.:
"My father was a cosmic outlaw. He shared his power with no one. Worshipped no one and nothing. Bowed to no one. Stood before no judges.

"But there are certain universal laws that no man is above. He considered himself to be above the truth, and in this he was very much mistaken."

****

Martin Samuels (once the world's most successful Scientology franchise holder):

Hubbard operated according to a couple of key patterns.

The first pattern involved basically decent well-intentioned people: whether you look at his personal communicator Ken Urqurt; his personal nurse Kima Douglas; David Mayo his auditor and research assistant; Reg Sharpe; John McMaster; no one has ever been able to rise in the organization or in his life to the point of any real proximity to him, without being attacked and vilified.

That's one pattern repeated over and over and over. And every time it happened to somebody Hubbard was always able to explain it away.

And of course the next person thinks that he or she is immune. Of course, now Hubbard is dead, so we won't see that pattern particularly repeated, except inasmuch as we'll see the Church hierarchy emulate and carry that pattern forward.

413

The next pattern: It's *reap and rape*. Hubbard would let the reins loose. He'd let people believe they really could get on with it. He'd let people believe that they really could prosper to the full extent of their own ability, and enjoy the fruits of their labor.

And, with that kind of freedom, prosperity does occur. Invariably though, he'd then come along and rape and pillage and rip off and take what had been produced. The most dramatic example of this was '82–'83, when he "raped" his most decent people in management along with the mission holders, and looted the entire mission network.

And look at this pattern. . . . He surrounded himself with absolute hooligans as "managers"; guys who beat the shit out of people. This man, who "is this OT, the author of *Science of Survival*, completely able to predict human behavior,". . . surrounded himself with ruthless people—like Miscavage—who got there because they emulated Hubbard's savagery. They emulated his total willingness to completely break, use, and discard another person.

And then after their hands were so bloody—and the only reason their hands were bloody is that they were doing what Hubbard wanted—when it started to finally get to the point where it couldn't be tolerated by people anymore, Hubbard wiped them out. Then he said, "My God I didn't know!" Scapegoat. He even did it to his own wife, who went to jail in his place.

We're not here talking about things that were happening five thousand miles away from him. We're talking about things that were happening fifty feet from him. But he "didn't know." . . . But the thing that's amazing, and to me terrifying, is the characteristic of the mind, my mind, your mind, and apparently many other peoples' minds, where I could buy this horseshit; where I could participate in it.

What is so hard to grasp is the inability to perceive, to exercise a sense of reality, to relate to reality in such a way that, when you look, you can go "this doesn't jive!" The fact that this horrible phenomenon of *pre-programmed blindness* occurs so commonly and so broadly is terrifying!

****

NICKY HOPKINS, musician/composer/Church member:

L. Ron Hubbard is a pioneer in the truest sense of the word. He spent a lifetime researching and developing the only workable technology ever to enable man to become free.

It was this technology that literally saved my life a few years ago when I was totally caught up in the trap of drugs and had only a short time left to live. Not only was that problem terminatedly handled, but my awareness as a spiritual being and my artistic creativity have increased beyond measure.

I can never adequately express the love, admiration, respect and gratitude that I have for this superb being, who is surely the greatest friend Mankind ever had.

Thank you, Ron, for so very, very much.

RAY FARADAY NELSON, science fiction author and fan of Hubbard's fiction works:

One of the things that Ron underestimated in the ability to do things is a certain defiance, a certain rebelliousness of character, which he himself had in spades. So the same sort of person who could be a follower of something like Scientology—especially a staff member in an organization would, by the very fact of being a follower, be cut off from the kind of creativity that Hubbard himself had.

Hubbard himself I think was very much of an outsider. Not only later on when he isolated himself but from the very beginning. I think he had a certain detachment from the entire human race: a certain feeling that he was separate. And that separateness, I think, was a very important source of his own creativity.

MICHAEL FLYNN:

The man was pure Nietzsche,—superman: "My *will* to do it gives me the right to do it!" It is will rising above conscience. I believe that "rising above the bank" was, to him, overcoming his conscience.

JEFF POMERANTZ. Actor on Broadway, television and film, and Church member:

L. Ron Hubbard and his writings have been the stabilizing influence of my life for many years now. He believed man to be basically good and proved it again and again. His discoveries and technologies ended my confusions, brightened my perceptions, increased my sense of ethics, rehabilitated me as an artist and generally made my heart sing. No man ever had a better friend. I've looked up to him for years—I guess now I just have to look a little Higher.

BOB ROSS (former Scientologist):

Well, I have met Hubbard a few times and observed him at other times. I was and remain suspicious of his intentions. I avoided him at first in order to not discover that Dianetics might be a hoax. Then I found out that auditing works. I spent over four thousand hours discovering for myself that Dianetics worked. And other things worked too in Scientology.

I told many people from 1957 onwards, after I had seen Hubbard perform in various Congresses, that he was among other things the greatest Con Man of this century. Yet he was far more than that as well. Whether or not he really and truly believed in his own set goal to "Clear the Planet," at least he made it possible for me to work toward that end with, I feel, some hope of success, in a world that needs that hope more and more. I shall continue to use what is *good* in Dianetics and Scientology to help myself and others. . . .

John Ausley (ex-Sea Org Class XII):

Hubbard had some big pluses and some big minuses. . . .

Once on the flagship he told me that his favorite person was P.T. Barnum. . . .

He could have been an actor or a director or gone on an entertainment trip. But he was a writer.

The writer in question liked gathering a whole group together under any cause, then assigning them roles as characters and watch them act out his own books. He assigned them character roles: "You're a this, or this." . . .

There is a debauchery one can get when one has one's own following and fan club. Entertainers have hit it. Elvis died at about 300 pounds. He hit debauchery and went out.

Hubbard hit a debauchery level on ego and power. . . .

The boy was paranoid.

He knew what to expect from people, because he knew what he would have been doing if he were them!

He implemented this rule that if anybody said anything bad about him, they had [performed] treacherous acts against all of Mankind.

"Introvert them like a bullet," was Hubbard's technique. They look at you, they see what's wrong. Turn them around. Why are you seeing what's wrong with me! That only means that there's something terribly wrong with you! And you better start looking at it quick!

Nothing that your average criminal doesn't know how to do naturally.

Fat redneck from Nebraska: Hubbard was a redneck. He was not a good old boy, but a redneck. A good old boy will throw his beer cans in the back of his pickup truck while he's driving. A redneck will throw 'em straight out the window.

He was a redneck. He didn't mind trashin' the Bill of Rights. . . .

He convinced others so thoroughly that he was the Messiah, that it was now their job to convince him back that what he had convinced them of was true. . . .

What did I like about him? I thought, "This guy is being up front." Turns out he wasn't.

He was some low-rent Confucius trying to sell me that he used to be Buddha. I have a lot higher nominations on who used to be Buddha. He doesn't even come close. Just another wiz kid.

CONCLUSIONS

Hubbard's *public words* were rarely a reflection of what this man was and what he fundamentally believed.

He used words to create the effect he wanted.

(He once bragged that he could write anything in any style— Shakespeare, or heartthrob love stories that Aunt Mamie would cry over, or Zane Grey cowboy tales.)

He used his gift for combining words to exploit something which is truly sacred: Man's hope and quest for values that are greater than the mundane.

His "magical incantations" were words and symbols; combinations of words like "Total Freedom," being designed to entice; and *Church of Scientology*"; and "*rehabilitation* project force," designed to deceive.

There was a huge array of symbols such as the Sea Org insignia of a star and crescent; titles such as "Finance Police" and "International Finance Dictator." All these were designed to gain a hypnotic subservience to his *will*.

It is partly his endless creation of clashing symbols (words being included as symbols)—published and dramatized by him and his followers (such as the "Creed of the Church" proclaiming "freedom of speech" on a Sea Org commander's wall)—that made this such a bizarre saga.

There were also symbols that he would wish not to be noticed, such as the *Apollo* ending up as a restaurant and the *Athena* being cut up for scrap metal. Certainly he did not wish the image of a stroke victim (possibly unable to speak clearly) known.

Even unembroidered, Hubbard's life was colorful, to say the least. But it was hardly a life which symbolized that of the reincarnated Buddha.

Yet within the teachings of Siddhartha Gautama Buddha is found wisdom that may serve to inoculate those who may be otherwise susceptible to his, and now his organization's, manipulation.

It is said that the Buddha once told a group of disciples:

> Be not led by the authority of religious texts, nor by the delight in speculative opinions, nor by seeming possibilities, nor by the idea; "This is our teacher." But . . . when you know for yourselves that certain things are unwholesome and wrong, and bad, then give them up . . . and when you know for yourselves that certain things are wholesome and good, then accept them and follow them.
>
> A disciple should examine even the teacher himself, so that he might be fully convinced of the true value of the teacher whom he followed.

****

On the 16th of September 1986, a new ship was purchased. It was christened the *Free Winds* and, at seven thousand tons and 440 feet in length, is considerably larger than the *Apollo*. It is here that OT 8 will be delivered.

At a promotional function, Mark Yaeger announced that *Free Winds* would sail on her maiden voyage before the year was out. Subsequently, a promotion featuring glossy color photos of the ship was mailed out.

It boldly invites all to:

> Help start the greatest adventure in Scientology History!

UPDATE FOR THE SECOND EDITION

PART TWO

Focusing on Scientology's abuse of the legal system; and accusations by former members of continued criminality.

19

Scientology's Abuse of the Legal System

"The law can be used very easily to harass . . . If possible of course, ruin him utterly"—L. Ron Hubbard (Level 0 Checksheet).

"Career criminals" often develop a detailed understanding of the laws of the land. Often they know more about their "rights," and the over-all legal system, than does the average law-abiding citizen.

Unscrupulous organizations follow the same pattern. While flagrantly violating the rights of others, they make **very** sure to know "their rights." And they utilize—and exploit—the "legal system" to crush their "enemies."

The term **Slap Suit** means a lawsuit initiated solely for purposes of harassment. It's a common means of crushing a "little guy" who "gets in the way of" a large and very rich organization/corporation. Simply initiate a lawsuit. And then follow it up with every expensive legal maneuver the legal system allows. This includes depositions in and out of the state, and even the country, each of which can cover days and costs several thousand dollars; not to mention the follow-up motions to compel answers not given during the depositions, and long lists of questions and demands which must be answered and satisfied within specified periods of time. One can be absolutely in the right and yet lose as a result of the crushing financial burden.

Lawyers in Los Angeles approached to take my case invariably responded with comments like "Life's too short to take Scientology cases." They all know of the Wollersheim case where Charlie O'Reilley faced every trick Scientology could maneuver, fought for years spending hundreds of thousands, and has yet to see a penny. When you are up against an organization which will gladly spend a million to see you don't get a thousand, its tough on lawyers (and there are few good ones who will risk bankruptcy to take on a cause, no matter how worthy. One who did however, is Toby Plevin who, at this writing, has fought as my counsel for almost three years. She has managed to stay in the fray on a shoestring. In her early forties, and relatively inexperienced in this type of litigation, she has nevertheless repeatedly bested some of the most experienced and expensive law-firms in the U.S. But how long can one attorney be expected to persevere in a battle which requires the kind of resources only the F.B.I. is capable of mustering?

The fact is that Charlie O' Reilley set a precedent which, once confirmed by the U.S. Supreme Court, will make suing Scientology a viable proposition for attorneys from here on out. History will show that he and Larry Wollersheim (his client) are heros in the battle for justice for the victims of Scientology. They spurned in excess of $5 million in settlement offers and endured a campaign of harassment and violence only approached by that waged against Paulette Cooper. All with no fanfare!

UNITY OF CONTROL

"Unity of Control" means a singular control-point over the finances and general operation of a number of groups. Scientology's own documents confirm that all its "groups" are totally under the control of one man and one corporation: David Miscavige who controls absolutely through the RTC, or "Religious Technology Center," which owns Hubbard's copyrights. This is an unpopular point to make with Scientology lawyers. In various court cases, they have insisted that Scientology groups are "autonomous."

A steady litany of lawsuits are created by several different Scientology corporations and executives against "enemy" individuals/organizations.* If an "enemy" does prevail then it has to collect from the organization sued. Does this corporation now have the money? Oh no! What do you know, it's another organization that has the money now and its not the one you sued. Now you've got to prove that it is really one big enterprise—and, despite the truth of this fact—that is a major legal battle all in itself. Once achieved in one case however, it can be copied in others. Whether my case against Scientology in Los Angeles (C694401) settles or goes to trial, the file has valuable information on this subject.**

"LEGAL SETTLEMENT" AND DURESS

The courts are crowded despite the fact that well over 90% of all cases settle rather than go to trial. To ease the court calendar settlement is encouraged. Scientology has exploited this fact to obtain settlements with restrictions such as the following:

1. Must not make oneself "amenable to service of subpoena" in any action against Scientology in any manner which is not in the "spirit of this agreement" [which is largely involved with covering up evidence against Scientology].

---

*In my case I was sued for libel three times in one week while on a promotional tour for the hard cover version of this book in 1987 (eg. calling Heber Jentzsch a liar on the radio) in three different jurisdictions (Washington D.C., Riverside California, San Fernando Valley, north of Los Angeles). This was additional to the ongoing litigation described earlier in this book. This litigation was easily enough to finish me off financially. And had it not been for the fact that I miraculously found an extremely competent lawyer in Washington D.C. George Driesen, who had read my book and believed in my cause enough to do over $20,000.00 worth of legal work for free to get this lawsuit thrown out, just that action would have ruined me. The other lawsuits have been coped with in another fashion and are still ongoing but are now far more frightening to Scientology than to me. If one can keep the lawsuit going towards trial, the tables are turned. Truth, presumably does win out, eventually.
**Especially the MCCS (Mission Corporate Category Sort-out) which set up the corporate structure in order to cover up the fact that Hubbard had full control of all Scientology and was to be in absolute control but be in no way accountable. And, this heritage would be passed on to his successors. This project was memorialized on a tape which the Scientologists have spent a fortune to suppress. Their legal efforts to forever bury this tape reached the U.S. Supreme Court in Scientology v. Zolin, which they lost. This tape is not immediately available and must be sought by special motion to the court in Los Angeles.

2. All documentary evidence is to be returned to them with no copies kept.
3. Must never talk about ones experiences in Scientology or the litigation concerning it with anyone but one's immediate family.
4. In the case of Michael Flynn, and the other attorneys involved in the 1986 settlements, they would never again be able to take cases against Scientology; thus eliminating the few rare attorneys willing to subject themselves to the kind of harassment depicted in chapter 22, of Part One, and virtually ensuring that victims of Scientology can not find counsel.

Gerry Armstrong signed one of these, (under immense pressure)*

Those receiving funds from Scientology, as part of a "legal settlement," usually have a clear case of **provable damages by the Scientology Organization.**

It is a sad testimony to our "system of justice" that **wealthy persons or corporations can black out publicity and cover up evidence (for use by other victims) by "financial settlement" in civil court.** Scientology can also frivolously counter-sue anyone suing them, and—in various ways—use their abundant resources to further harass those they have **already** victimized.

Those reaching the "settlement stage" are often emotionally exhausted, and under burden of enormous legal—and sometimes medical—expenses, their legal counsel are also often exhausted and eager to "settle." Scientology seeks to take advantage of these circumstances.

For example, in the case of L. Ron Hubbard Jr.'s 1986 "legal settlement" with Scientology, he had accumulated sizable hospital bills due to recent emergency surgery. This left him weakened and heavily in debt. Concerned about the welfare of his family he finally agreed to a "settlement." This included his signing various prepared documents. I don't believe for a moment that Ron Jr. ever considered these prepared statements to be accurate representations of his thoughts and beliefs. The man was under **duress.**

Scientology's use of **duress** to obtain signed "retractions" or other signed "statements" began with Sara Northrup Hubbard, Ron **Sen-**

---

*Armstrong had not only the opposing attorneys pressuring him to settle, but also all the other plaintiffs, his own lawyers and the court! All this, along with his own desperate need to achieve a period of peace in his life after his long ordeal, was a lot more than one individual can be expected to withstand.

ior's second wife. (See Chapter 4 of Part Two, the **Kidnapping**) That was way back in 1951. Since then the Organization has accumulated many "retractions" and signed "statements" of various kinds. It collects these like a little kid collects baseball cards.

20

Accusations of Continued Criminality

"I have high hopes of smashing my name into history so violently that it will take a legendary form even if all the books are destroyed. That goal is the real goal as far as I'm concerned . . .

"Psychiatrists, reaching the high of the dusty desk, tell us that Alexander, and Genghis Khan and Napoleon were madmen. I know they're maligning some very intelligent gentlemen. So anybody who dares say that maybe he's going to cut things up considerably is immediately branded as an egomaniac, or something equally ridiculous, so that little men can still save their hides in the face of possible fury.

"It's one thing to go nutty and state, 'I'm Napoleon, nobody dares touch me,' and quite another to say, 'If I watch my step and don't let anything stop me, I can make Napoleon look like a punk!' That's the difference . . ."

— L. Ron Hubbard, writing to his first wife in August 1938

"I'm not interested in Wog [Human] morality . . . I can make Captain Bligh look like a Sunday school teacher."

— Hubbard Communications Office Policy Letter, August 1967

L. Ron Hubbard was fond of pontificating on the possibility of **change.** After-all, wasn't Scientology's mission simply to change conditions and people for the better?

Strangely, Hubbard himself seemed incapable of any meaningful

425

change or improvement. He never freed himself of his deceitful ways, temper tantrums, and paranoid fantasies. He smoked heavily, drank heavily, and was a user of drugs. Ron, it seems, was incapable of responding to those potentially beneficial portions of the subject of Dianetics/Scientology. Perhaps he was too dedicated to the **dark side** to respond to the bits and pieces of wisdom and beneficence to be found in the subject he jealously owned.

Now the "hierarchy" of Scientology "owns" the subject. And Hubbard appears to have left his stamp on them. They too seem incapable of change. Incapable of reform.

Scientology PR people insist the "old" Guardian Office is long gone. In fact, the Office of Special Affairs is nothing more than a renamed G.O.

Fair Game was never canceled. The dirty tactics of Scientology's **covert** branch were never altered.

Those few rare souls in "upper management" who **do** seek to change, inevitably find they must leave the organization to do so. They also, likely, will find themselves under attack.

A MAJOR DEFECTION

Vicki Aznaran and her husband Rick left Scientology in April of 1988.

Vicki Aznaran was president of the RTC (Religious Technology Center) from 1984 to early 1987. As such she ultimately found herself caught in a power struggle between Captain David Miscavige and Pat and Annie Broeker. Miscavige is the Chairman of the Board of RTC.

Pat and Annie Broeker were described by Miscavige as "Ron's two most trusted friends and aides," during the January 1986 "Ascension of LRH" event.

Vicki Aznaran was the link between David Miscavige and Pat and Annie Broeker (who lived with Hubbard at his secret hide out). This eventually put her in a battle zone.

When Ms. Aznaran fell into disfavor with the winner of the battle— David Miscavige—she was assigned to the Rehabilitation Project Force at Gilman Hot Springs (in the Southern Californian desert) and kept under guard.

FROM DESTRUCTION OF EVIDENCE TO ORAL SEX

In a Legal Declaration of April 1988 Vicki Aznaran alleges that, during her time as a senior Scientology executive, she witnessed and—at times—participated in the destruction of evidence requested by judges for court cases; and witnessed the order by Miscavige to have his "Minutemen" (Scientology goon squads) physically harass and assault "enemies."

She states that she witnessed the "culling of pre-clear folders," (the collecting of disreputable or embarrassing material from supposedly confidential counseling sessions); attempts to blackmail judges, and applications of "TR-L," a "Training Routine" used to teach someone to "lie convincingly." In this case Scientologists who were to testify at a trial. She confirms that the "Fair Game Law" remains very much in use.

Ms. Aznaran states, "The management of Scientology consistently expressed and demonstrated a complete disdain for the court system, viewing it as nothing more than a method to harass enemies."

Vicki Aznaran: "In late 1979 and early 1980, there was a massive document destruction program undertaken to destroy any evidence showing that L. Ron Hubbard controlled Scientology. I participated in that activity in Clearwater, Florida, and am informed that there was also intensive document destruction at Gilman Hot Springs, [in Riverside county] California . . . [See Chapters 15 and 21, Part One]

"Norman Starkey [now second in command after Miscavige] ordered me to go to a computer facility and insure that all information on the computers in Los Angeles, that might show Hubbard's involvement and control of Scientology's money be destroyed, except for one copy of each document. These copies were to be saved on computer discs which were to be hidden in secure storage places. At the time I was also instructed to destroy anything that would show the control of Mr. Starkey or Mr. Miscavige over Scientology."

"During the time period of my involvement with Scientology, I also learned of various attempts to influence judges or force their removal from cases . . . [Name of private investigator] was also hired for the purpose of attempting to force the removal of a judge in Tampa, Florida. This involved what I know as the [Tonya] Burden case, which was civil litigation brought by [attorney] Michael Flynn. [The private investigator] secured a yacht and attempted to get the judge on board for the process of filming him under compromising circumstances. The judge declined to go yachting and the operation was unsuccessful. Approximately $250,000 was spent on this operation."

According to Aznaran, another attempt to "put a judge in a compromising position" was successful. It involved enticing a judge into receiving oral sex from a prostitute, all the while secretly filming the act. Aznaran states that she was witness to the video tape.

Closer to my personal situation Vicki has this to say:

"In 1985, I attended a meeting called by David Miscavige. Also present were Norman Starkey and Lymon Spurlock . . .

"Miscavige told the meeting that Scientology organizations had not been aggressive enough in combatting squirrels (individuals who had broken with Scientology but who were still using ideas similar to Scientology).

"In order to get an attack program activated, Miscavige told those at the meeting they should take the lead from Hubbard's suggestions of violence and personal attacks against squirrels both as written in the fair game policy and in Professional Auditor's Bulletin No. 53 in which Hubbard said the way to treat a squirrel is to hurt him so hard that he 'would have thought he had been hit by a Mack truck' and, Hubbard continued, 'I don't mean thought-wise.'

Miscavige's order to the assembled group was accepted and immediately put into action under the direction of McShane who directed Mike Rinder at the Office of Special Affairs U.S. Rinder did, in fact, immediately begin several actions against squirrel groups and I received reports of such completed actions. These actions included, but were not limited to burglaries, stealing records, and sending provocateurs to infiltrate squirrel events and to provoke fights. These activities were also directed against Bent Corydon, including break-ins at his office, physical attacks upon him, and the use of spies to infiltrate his group."

Vicki's husband Richard Aznaran who had for five years been in intelligence and security operations for Miscavige when he left in 1987, stated in a later sworn affidavit the following:

"Based upon his statements to me David Miscavige particularly detested Bent Corydon and ex-Scientology "Squirrel" who had defected in 1982. Corydon had previously come by the facility at Gilman Hot Springs and therefore was particularly annoying to David Miscavige . . .

"I was specifically instructed that if I could I was to hurt Corydon physically if I could arrange for it to appear justified.

"On the next occasion of Corydon visiting Gilman Hot Springs, security guards, under my direction, jostled Corydon and placed him under "Citizens' arrest" for trespassing. In actual fact Corydon never set foot on our property nor did he represent any harm or threat of harm.

"Later, Miscavige called me to his office where I was questioned as to my handling of Corydon's visit. Miscavige was enraged over the fact that the deputy Sheriffs [who had been called by Scientology to handle my "trespass"] had not taken Corydon to jail nor had he been injured. Miscavige was yelling at me and threatened me with loss of my position and with ethics conditions for not having carried out Miscavige's instructions. The bottom line was that Miscavige wanted Corydon physically and mentally punished. Miscavige perceived Corydon's visits as 'taunting' his authority."

FORMER SENIOR SCIENTOLOGY ATTORNEY
SPEAKS OUT

To the immense distress of Scientology's new youthful leadership Joseph Yanny is "getting his withholds off."

Yanny had become increasingly dismayed and disillusioned by what he had witnessed in his role as a top (full time) Scientology attorney, finally ceasing to represent Scientology in 1987.

Having represented Scientology he was bound by the attorney/client privilege. Scientology, having been a client had confided in him a great deal of "sensitive" information. And this was "privileged": it could not be revealed.

After he resigned Scientology's employ, the organization became very concerned that he might "spill the beans." And Yanny found himself being sued, and accused of a myriad of charges. This changed the situation.

Yanny—as does anyone—had a right to defend himself against charges; so he declared legal declarations in his own defense. These materials were originally "sealed." The judge in this case ordered the seal removed. The material is now public.

In a legal declaration dated 13 July 1988 Yanny makes a number of statements. These allegations include destruction of evidence, blackmail, theft, and involvement with illegal drugs.

From the Yanny Declaration:

"I also became aware of numerous "cullings" of P.C. [pre-clear confessional] folders by Cult members. I was actually given P.C. folder data to prepare for depositions of former members. Again I objected. The confidential materials were put into "prep packs." When I objected to this practice, I was told by [Scientology agents] that this was standard practice. I offered my resignation as their counsel."

Yanny states that his office thereafter was broken into three times, once with the use of a crow bar.

His declaration continues:

"There was also wholesale destruction of evidence, theft of documents from private persons, and attempts to infiltrate the court chambers of Judges Lilly and Swearinger."

"This is but the tip of the iceberg. Many of the documents in this courts Jury Room show recent attempts by this Cult to infiltrate courthouses . . .

"I was also informed of a Cult-organized group of vigilantes known as the 'minutemen' who were to go beat up dissidents and had in fact done so.

"I also became aware of a plot to obstruct justice or at least perpetuate a fraud on the Courts in the form of settlement agreements of numerous pieces of Cult litigation, which required that the lawyers never take litigation against the Cult in the future, that no one (lawyers or parties) testify against the Cult, and that all evidence and files be turned over to the Cult for destruction.

"Additionally, I became aware that witnesses . . . signed contracts to keep quiet about what they knew. In other words they were paid hush money."

Yanny concludes:

". . . The Cult—who the governments of this country have allowed to physically beat it citizens, to betray their confidences, ignore their civil rights, and use the judicial system to destroy them.

"That I had a difficult time sleeping knowing what I knew, having represented this criminal cult—I readily admit."

Addendum
—For The Second Edition—

The Dark Side of Scientology-Speak

(Manipulation Through Language)

"It is startling to realize how much unbelief is necessary to make belief possible. What we know as blind faith is sustained by innumerable unbeliefs. The fanatical Japanese in Brazil refused to believe for years the evidence of Japan's defeat. The fanatical communist refuses to believe any unfavorable report about Russia, nor will he be disillusioned by seeing with his own eyes the cruel misery inside the Soviet promised land.

"It is the true believer's ability to 'shut his eyes and stop his ears' to facts that do not deserve to be either seen or heard which is the source of unequaled fortitude and constancy . . . And it is the certitude of infallible doctrine that renders the true believer impervious to uncertainties, surprises and the unpleasant realities of the world around him."

—Eric Hoffer, **The True Believer**

"An education for freedom (and for the love and intelligence which are at once the conditions and result of freedom) must be, among other things, an education in the proper use of language."

—Aldous Huxley, **Brave New World Revisited**

Strange things such as "selective forgetting" and "unlooking," along with "non-thinking" are essential to the "total certainty" of the "true believer."

Such states of mind—or mindlessness—are encouraged and enforced by many factors. One of the more subtle ones is that of language.

****

432

THE "LOADED LANGUAGE" OF SCIENTOLOGY

Some of the nomenclature of Scientology is innovative and, in a positive sense, useful. There is also, however, a negative side. Much of the nomenclature is **loaded language.**

The first words of Scientologese learned by a new member most likely will be in the "innovative and positive" category. Or, at least, they won't qualify as manipulative "loaded language."

New words, new ideas. This is part of the "softening up" process. Once confidence is obtained, further indoctrination is possible.

States Robert J. Lifton in **Thought-Reform and the Psychology of Totalism:**

> The language of the totalist environment is characterized by the thought-limiting cliche. The most far reaching and complex of human problems are compressed into brief, highly reductive, definitive sounding phrases, easily memorized and easily expressed. These become the start and finish of any ideological analysis. In thought reform, for instance, [also known as "mind-control"] the phrase 'bourgeois mentality' is used to encompass and critically dismiss ordinarily troublesome concerns like the quest for individual expression, the exploration of alternative ideas, and the search for perspective and balance . . . [loaded language] is the language of non-thought.

By using loaded language such as "the open-minded case" as a term of abuse, and "other practices" as a term of utmost scorn, Hubbard sought to shut off (for his followers) all competitive ideas and practices in the fields of the mind and spirit.

Lifton continues:

> Also involved is an underlying assumption that language—like all other human products—can be owned and operated by the movement . . . the effect of the language . . . can be summed up in one word: constriction. The individual is, so to speak, linguistically deprived; and since language is so central to all human experience, his capacities for thinking and feeling are immensely narrowed.

****

Loaded language in Scientology takes the form of **thought-limiting cliches** presented as "maxims" or "truths," and also as single words with **thought-limiting cliches** as their definition.

Thought-limiting clichés are useful in that they serve to **instantly** explain away anything that doesn't correspond with the "party line," or official "reality."

If presented with an "alien" or "enemy" point of view, a Scientologist will usually become flustered.

In the well indoctrinated ("hatted") Scientologist this would be only for the briefest instant, as a **thought-limiting cliché** would immediately **move in** to explain why Scientology is right.

****

The most used thought-limiting cliche, of course, is "Criticizing Scientology = hidden crimes."

It's "axiomatic" that if someone **really** understood what Scientology is "all about," that person would **be** a member. If you're not a member, you're **either** an ignorant wog or a criminal.

Revealing an extensive familiarity with Hubbard's writings in a discussion with a Scientologist tells him immediately that, **since you're not a member,** you **must** be an "out-ethics" heretic, and probably psychotic.

Thus, honest and in-depth discussions on the subject of Scientology, between Scientologists and "outsiders," are difficult or impossible.

****

Additional examples of thought-limiting clichés—activated at various times—would include:

a) This person must have "Misunderstood words" or "MUs." He's misunderstood the meaning of the words in Ron's writings and is confused.

b) Scientology reveals the secrets of the universe, some people just can't **have** (tolerate, accept) that.

c) Scientology is the only hope for Mankind's survival; in that light all imagined disagreements are unimportant.

d) He's been "fed False Data" by the "enemy."

e) He's trying to "make Scientology wrong." (Being subject to irrational impulses that compel "wogs" to make others wrong.)

f) He's connected to an "SP" (Suppressive Person) and thus (under that influence) is "PTS" (a Potential Trouble Source), and probably a "DB" (Degraded Being).

g) He is an SP.

(If the above—or other—thought-limiting clichés have failed to

snap the person back into the secure mind-set of a "winning, standard Scientologist," then that **must** mean that his CASE [His yet "unhandled" aberrations and his own dark secrets] has been RESTIMU-LATED.)

Scientology and L. Ron Hubbard **must never** be "made wrong." In fact "making Ron wrong" or "making the tech wrong" is a major "high crime."

****

When **loaded language** comes in the form of a single word or term, it sometimes has a relatively simple and straight forward definition. An example would be "WOG," which is a "humanoid" too dumb and aberrated to recognize L. Ron Hubbard as "Mankind's Greatest Friend."

More often these single words or terms have double or multiple definitions: **One word** with two or more obviously **contradictory** meanings. But not obvious to the well-indoctrinated Scientologist, who is expected to see only the "harmonious" equating of one definition with another.

****

An oft used term in Scientology is **Suppressive Person.** Originally this was defined as someone mentally stuck in a past traumatic incident, which is—unbeknownst to him—superimposed over his current perceptions. He's attempting to deal with a disaster or emergency which occurred long ago, and unknowingly treats the people and situations in his current life **as though** they were the long ago people and situations.

Often he may compulsively attempt to "protect" others, to the point of nearly "smothering" them; may have inappropriate fears and doubts about friends or family; or simply view others as the "enemy," to overtly, or covertly be **stopped.** *

This image of a profoundly disturbed person has since become synonymous with **anyone who persists in being "critical" of L. Ron Hubbard or Scientology.**

Usually, someone being "routed" into the "Church" will initially be exposed to the first—possibly sensible—definition, and **then** to that which it **must equate to.**

****

*A non-cultic look at this unfortunate state of affairs can be found in a work entitled, **Sanity, Madness and the Family,** by R. D. Laing and A. Esterson.

Another example of this is the word "ENTHETA," which might simply be described as "bad vibes." Pain, emotional upsets, malicious gossip, lies—these are all in the category of "entheta."

Entheta is derived from the Scientology word **Enturbulated,** meaning **upset, or the effect of turbulence,** and **theta,** the 8th letter of the Greek alphabet. In Scientology "theta" is defined as "spirit." A "theta being" is a "spiritual being."

"Theta" also means "life energy," **elan vital,** and all "upper scale" emotions and traits such as enthusiasm, creativity, serenity, freedom, and truth.

But "Theta" **ALSO** means anything that puts L. Ron Hubbard or Scientology in a good light.

A newspaper article praising L. Ron Hubbard as the "author of 22 bestsellers," and describing him as a engineer and nuclear physicist— and saying nothing critical—would be a "theta" article. It would also be completely untrue. [See UPDATE Part One for the story behind Hubbard's "bestsellers"].

An article honestly exploring Hubbard's numerous misleading descriptions of himself and his background would be "entheta."

****

"Loaded language," is introduced gradually to new members of Scientology. This, and other forms of deception and manipulation, are an important aspect of the "cementing" of their conversion.

Glossary of Scientology Terms

(Includes a few Scientology terms that are not in the book, but represents only a small sampling of the language of Scientologists. Definitions in quotation marks are from L. Ron Hubbard's works.)

AO (Advance Organization): delivers "upper level" services.

ANCHOR POINT: "The points which mark an area of space are called anchor points, and these, with the viewpoint, alone are responsible for space." A rock star performing before ten thousand people probably has a lot of "space." A fellow introverted and "caved in," sitting in a chair with his eyes closed (his girl friend left him) has very little "space." Space equates to "beingness."

AUDITING: Counseling; asking a question that invites another to look, letting him tell you what he sees, acknowledging him, and asking another or the same question inviting him to look some more—up to a point of realization and some degree of resolution of the problem, condition, or inability being addressed. Auditing is also defined as "the application of Scientology processes and procedures." In this sense it has included more than just the posing of questions. For example an "auditor" might instruct his "pre-clear" to observe the environment:
"Look around the room and tell me something you could have," asked repeatedly until person feels good about it. Or, "Look around the room and tell me something mother can't have," or "Look around the room and tell me something you could dispense with."
Or, he might instruct him to visualize various things. For example: "What can you mock up?" (see glossary below). Then "mock up (whatever pre-clear said he could)," then "O.K., shove it in to yourself," then, "Let it remain where it is," and "Throw it away," and so on.

Also, of course, official Scientology "auditing" includes compulsory metered confession, which is one of the fundamentals of brainwashing or mind-control. So, unfortunately, "auditing" (or "counseling"), in this context, has been tainted with a rather unsavory connotation. *Any* auditing done in an authoritarian context can amount to a form of brainwashing or—at the very least—set a person up for manipulation and mind control.

B-1: Guardian's Office covert intelligence.

BRIDGE: Pathway from "unknowingness to revelation.": The Grade Chart consisting of approximately thirty major "levels".

BT (Body thetan): A degraded spirit that attaches itself to another's body or spirit.

CASE SUPERVISOR (C/S): One who supervises the auditing of pre-clears.

CHAINS: A series of incidents with similar content.

CLUSTER: a number of BTs stuck together.

CMO (Commodore's Messengers Organization): Organization consisting of L. Ron Hubbard's servants. The highest executive body. Some of its members later became the Religious Technology Corporation.

COGNITION: a realization.

CLEAR: (Used as a noun) A person who no longer has a "reactive mind."

CLEARING: A gradient process of searching out, locating, and resolving previously buried stress or trauma. Although buried, this trauma can be devitalizing or the source of various undesired physical or mental conditions. More generally, "clearing" means straightening out, or eliminating, confusion.

CREATIVE PROCESSING: "Consists of having the pre-clear make, with his own creative energies, a mock-up." Not used since the 1950s.

DB: Degraded being.

DEV-T ("Developed traffic): needless distractions that cause inefficiency.

DIANETICS: Through thought; a system of locating and resolving the causes of aberrative behavior based on the influence of subconscious trauma and "think," tracing back to "earlier similar" causes, until the point of resolution.

DMSMH: Hubbard's book, *Dianetics, the Modern Science of Mental Health.*

DWINDLING SPIRAL: According to Hubbard the path for spiritual beings—if they do not avail themselves of Scientology—is *down*. One becomes weaker and smaller and more oblivious and, eventually, lands in a hell worse than any described in any religion. One of many control mechanisms of Scientology: "Comply or you're doomed."

DYNAMIC: "The urge, thrust, and purpose of life—*survive!*" It is described as having eight primary manifestations:
    1st Dynamic: Survival as self.
    2nd Dynamic: Survival through the sex act, children and family.
    3rd Dynamic: Survival through groups.
    4th: Survival through Mankind.
    5th: Survival through animal and vegetable life.
    6th: Survival through the physical universe.
    7th: Survival through things spiritual: spiritual beings, thought, esthetics.
    8th: Survival through Infinity.

ENTURBULATE: To upset.

E-METER: "An electronic instrument for measuring change in mental state in individuals." Can be used in auditing as an aid in locating areas of buried mental stress, bringing this stress to the surface to be viewed and resolved. Also can be used as a police interrogation device as part of a system of mind-control.

ENGRAM: "A moment of greater or lesser "unconsciousness" on the part of the analytical mind which permits the reactive mind to record; the total content of the moment with all perceptics."

ENTHETA: "Enturbulated theta (thought or life); especially refers to communications, which based on lies and confusions, are slanderous, choppy or destructive in an attempt to overwhelm or suppress"; also means any criticism of L. Ron Hubbard or Scientology.

ETHICS: "Rationality toward the highest level of survival for the individual, the future race, the group, and mankind, and all other dynamics taken collectively. Also means "Doing What Ron Says.""

EXTERIORIZATION: Being outside the body as a spirit, with or without perception.

FAIR GAME: Policy initiated by Hubbard allowing enemies to be "lied to, cheated, destroyed."

FINANCE DICTATOR (International Finance Dictator): Post established in 1982 to oversee Church finances.

FINANCE POLICE: The Finance Dictator's troops.

FLAG: Headquarters of Scientology world-wide since 1968. It was aboard the Flagship *Apollo* until 1975. Since then the term has been used for the land-based service organization in Clearwater, Florida. The actual headquarters have been wherever Hubbard has been in hiding. Orders from him and his immediate aides have been relayed through Gilman Hot Springs in Riverside County, California, and more recently through the top executives on the top floor of a highrise building on Sunset Blvd. in Hollywood under the façade of Author Services Inc.

FRANCHISE HOLDER: Person chosen by Hubbard to set up shop as a branch (or mission) of the Church of Scientology, in return for 10 percent of the franchise's income paid to the Church. In return, he was promised financial independence and freedom from interference by the Church.

G.O. (Guardian's Office): A Scientology bureaucracy performing intelligence, legal, public relations, and Fair Game functions. It was renamed the Office of Special Affairs (OSA) in 1983.

HAVINGNESS: "The feeling that one owns or possesses; the concept of being able to reach or not being prevented from reaching."

IMPLANT: Fundamentally any hypnotic suggestion. Hubbard defined it in terms of "space opera": a highly technical and complex system of mass hypnosis inflicted on populations by evil rulers. He claims that these implants have been inflicted upon everyone on the planet. An example of the "most devastating" of these are in the "Wall of Fire" chapter.

INDICATES: Essentially means "rings true."

INTEL: Intelligence.

KEY-IN: To be re-connected to some part of one's reactive mind.

KEY-OUT: To be separated from—freed, at least momentarily—from the effect of the reactive mind.

LOWER GRADES: Auditing that precedes the "OT levels." Addresses psychosomatic ills, communication difficulties, fixations, upsets, and various "human level" conditions.

MEST: Matter, Energy, Space, Time.

MISSION: A Scientology franchise which delivers introductory services.

MISSIONAIRE: A member of the Sea Org sent on a mission.

MOCK-UP: (As a verb) "To get an imaginary picture of." Also to create or make something. (As a noun) "Any knowingly created mental picture." Also, "A full perceptic energy picture in three dimensions created by the thetan and located in space and time. Now, that's the ideal definition."

NATTER: Negative chatter. People who natter about Scientology or L. Ron Hubbard have, according to Hubbard, undisclosed evil deeds.

NO REPORT: Not writing up and reporting a fellow group member who is being "out-ethics."

OFF SOURCE: Not doing what Ron Says. Non-Standard.

1.1: Covert Hostility level on the emotional Tone Scale. Equates to a Suppressive Person.

ON SOURCE: Following Ron's instructions.

ORG: Organization.

OT: Operating thetan: a spiritual being who can operate, i.e., perceive, act, communicate, without need of a body.

OTC (Operation Transport Corporation): A for-profit Panamanian corporation owned mainly and controlled by Hubbard and his wife. This corporation owned the ships.

OT III: An "Operating thetan" solo auditing level which deals with the "catastrophic incident on earth of 75 million years ago."

OUT-ETHICS: Not behaving properly. Not obeying the rules of the Church of Scientology.

OVERT: A harmful action.

PDC (Philadelphia Doctorate Course): Given in December 1952.

PRE-CLEAR: P.C.: One who is not yet clear; more commonly, anyone receiving auditing.

PROCESS: "A set of questions asked by an auditor to help a person find out about himself or life."

PROCESSING: Auditing.

PSYCH: Short for psychiatrist.

PTS (Potential Trouble Source): Someone connected to an S.P. Thus this person is said to be potentially troublesome to Scientology.

REACTIVE MIND: "A portion of a persons mind which works on a totally stimulus-response basis, which is not under his volitional control, and which exerts force and the power of command over his awareness, purposes, thoughts, body and actions." Also: "Comprises an unknowing, unwanted series of aberrated computations which bring about an effect upon the individual. . . . It is an obsessive strata of unknown, unseen, uninspected data which are forcing solutions, unknown and uninspected upon the individual."

REALITY: "Is, here on earth, agreement as to what is."

ROCK SLAM: A movement of the needle on an E-meter.

ROCK SLAMMER: "R/Ser = psychosis = succumb, is trying to die (evil purpose)."

RPF (Rehabilitation Project Force): Church of Scientology "rehabilitation" program for "degraded beings" and "psychotics." Utilizes physical labor as "therapy."

RPF: Religious Research Foundation.

RTC (Religious Technology Corporation): *The* senior Scientology corporation.

SEC CHECK: Security check. Metered questioning designed to locate hidden overts, i.e., harmful acts.

SCIENTOLOGY: Described by L. Ron Hubbard as "an organized body of scientific research knowledge concerning life, life sources and the mind and includes practices that increase the intelligence, state and conduct of persons." He also defines it as, "A religious philosophy in the highest meaning as it brings man to total freedom and truth."

S.O.: Sea Organization. "Runs the advanced organizations and is the custodian of the clear and OT processing materials." Militaristic Scientology organization begun in 1967/68 to "put ethics in" on planet earth.

SPACE: "A viewpoint of dimension. It doesn't exist without a viewpoint."

SPACATION: "A process having to do with the rehabilitation of the creation of space."

SMERSH: From "James Bond"—Hubbard sometimes used this name to describe what he considered to be the conspiracy to stop Scientology.

S.M.I. (Scientology Missions International): Said to be the Mother Church for missions (franchises). It was in fact incorporated in Leichtenstein and was tied into the "Religious Research Foundation," which according to testimony was a cover for a scam to funnel money to Hubbard.

SOURCE: L. Ron Hubbard, the Source of Scientology.

SP (Suppressive Person): Someone with evil intentions. Also defined as anyone who is "anti-Scientology."

SQUIRREL: Originally meant to alter a proven workable technique because of non-comprehension or inability to apply it successfully. Has come to mean anyone who helps another with "auditing" without the permission of the Church of Scientology.

STATS: Statistics.

SAINT HILL MANOR: Between 1960 and 1968 was the headquarters for Scientology world-wide. Located in England.
THETA: Spiritual energy; also means "harmonious."
THETAN: An individual spirit.

THETA PERCEPTIONS: "That which one perceives by radiating towards an object [as a being apart from the body] and from the reflection perceiving various characteristics of the object. . . . Certainty of perception is increased by drilling. . . ." All such drills were dropped out of Scientology's "grade Chart" in 1978.

TONE SCALE: Hubbard's scale of emotional states:

40.0	Serenity of Beingness
30.0	Postulates
20.0	Action
8.0	Exhilaration
6.0	Aesthetics
4.0	Enthusiasm
3.5	Cheerfulness
3.3	Strong interest
3.0	Conservatism
2.9	Mild interest
2.8	Contented
2.6	Disinterested
2.5	Boredom
2.4	Monotony
2.0	Antagonism
1.9	Hostility
1.8	Pain
1.5	Anger
1.3	Resentment
1.2	No sympathy
1.15	Unexpressed resentment
1.1	Covert Hostility
1.02	Anxiety
1.0	Fear
.98	Despair
.96	Terror
.94	Numb
.90	Sympathy
.8	Propitition
.5	Grief
.375	Making amends
.3	Undeserving

.2   Self abasement
.1   Victim
.05   Apathy
.01   Dying

TECH: Technology.

TOTAL FREEDOM: "Existence without barriers." The elusive top state of being on Scientology's Grade Chart. It and the seven levels below it have yet to be released.

TIME: "Essentially a postulate that space and particles will persist."

TIME TRACK: "The consecutive record of mental image pictures which accumulates through the pre-clear's life or lives."

TONE 40: "Defined as 'giving a command and just knowing that it will be executed despite any contrary appearances.'" Also, "Intention without reservation." Also: "Unlimited space at will."

TRs: Training Routines: Drills designed to provide communication skills necessary for an auditor.

TR-L: Training Routines used by the intelligence wing of the Church of Scientology to teach their agents how to lie convincingly.

VALENCE: An identity assumed by a person unknowingly.

WFMH: World Federation of Mental Health.

WHOLE TRACK: "Moment to moment record of a person's experience in this universe." One's whole "time track."

WITHHOLD: "An unspoken, unannounced transgression against a moral code by which a person is bound." More commonly: Anything a person is not willing to reveal.

WOG: Racial slur used by colonial British to describe Arabs and Asians. Stands for Worthy Oriental Gentleman. Used in Scientology to describe the Human race. A wog is a non-Scientologist.

WDC (Watch Dog Committee): Senior executive body, yet subordinate to the Commodore's Messengers Org.

XENU: According to Hubbard, the evil ruler responsible for the "OT III" incident of 75 million years ago.

Non-Scientology
Terms Applicable to Scientology

ABREACTION: The process of becoming conscious of that which was previously forgotten or repressed.

Some Manipulative Groups—or more exactly **Manipulative Operations**—use the **abreactive** process in order to induce **cathartic experiences** for purposes of exploitation. There are, however, sincere counselors, ministers, and therapists who do not have a Hidden Agenda.

BIO-FEEDBACK: The E-meter is essentially a simple bio-feedback device.

BLACK SCIENTOLOGY: Deceitful, manipulative, and malevolent writings of L. Ron Hubbard, and their applications. Includes "mind-manipulation" and "brain-washing," and applications of the **Fair Game Doctrine**. The most offensive and diabolical of these writings are kept "confidential."

BLISS-KNOWLEDGE-BEING: Yogic precursor of Scientology's Affinity-Reality-Communication.

BRAINWASHING: Term relating back to Communist China (and North Korea) in the 1950s. Implies **domination** over a person's thoughts and behavior via **brutal methods,** and threats of more brutality. (Mind-Manipulation is more "subtle.") Both are used in the Church of Scientology.

CAPTAIN BLIGH MENTALITY: Ruthlessness as a virtue. The END justifies the Means. "I'm not interested in wog morality . . . I can make Captain Bligh look like a Sunday school teacher." From Hubbard Communication Office Policy Letter of 16 August 1967.

Scientology management privately prides itself on its "ruthlessness."

CARROT ON THE STICK TRICK: Gimmick used by some exploitative groups to keep the membership always yearning for the **next** level. **Exploitative "teachers" never allow their trusting students to grow up.** (It might put them out of business.)

CULLING: Use of confidential counseling session records for purposes of manipulation, threat and blackmail. Another application of Fair Game.

DIVINE DECEPTION: Term originally used by the Moonies (Unification Church) to justify the use of deception. Key tool for recruitment, for keeping the "general membership in line," and "maintaining good relations with the [wog] environment"; also used for discrediting those viewed as "enemies" or "anti." Justified as a means to an end.

DEFLATING/INFLATING: There are many aspects to this technique. "Break them down; build them back up." It usually starts with **inflation** ("You're a big being, better than most people, etc."), then follow numerous penalties for being small and stupid. Then comes "Rehabilitation." One is—in effect—inflated, deflated, then re-inflated. **A common procedure in Communist China was the demoting of high-level personnel to menial positions. This**—in many cases—was eventually **followed by re-instatement.** That is **after** Re-education or Rehabilitation had occurred. For example, Hana Eltringham-Whitfield went from highly trained auditor to high-level executive, and then to Deputy Commodore, and finally ended up on the Rehabilitation Project Force, and **then, having been "rehabilitated,"** Hana became an upper-level NOTS auditor at the FLAG Land Base in Clearwater, Florida. Hana Eltringham-Whitfield left Scientology years ago, and is now an Exit Counselor.

DESIRE FOR IMPROVEMENT: A natural and rational desire exploited by the Church of Scientology, and other manipulative groups.

DESTRUCTIVE CULT: See **Destructive Cult Defined** in **Addendum.**

DESTRUCTIVE CULT FORMAT: **A framework or context** that can be used to envelope and exploit ideas. Any good idea, or beneficent motivation, could be exploited by an unscrupulous person. Any subject is vulnerable to being **infused with** and **also encased in** a Destructive Cult Format or Pattern. Someone knowingly utilizing a Destructive Cult Format—so as to achieve a Hidden Agenda—might be said to have similarities to a virus that attaches itself to Life, and then exploits and lives off that life.

DOCTRINE OVER PERSON: deceptive-manipulative groups often preach "honesty, individual freedom, and the right to disagree" to potential recruits; a new member eventually finds that the **Doctrine** is far **senior** to any prior ideas he might have had in his **aberrated** mind.

DICTATOR'S DILEMMA: Scientology's current absolute boss, David Miscavige, has a problem. He can't go hide out as Hubbard did. Hubbard had such a high degree of control over his Organization that he could disappear, **cut all ties officially,** and still **covertly** control it.

Thus Miscavige is—ultimately—subject to lawsuits, and the dictates of the court system.

DISPENSING OF EXISTENCE: Gimmick which exploits the **will to live.** "Without us you are headed for oblivion . . . or worse."

ENFORCED CONFESSION: A perversion of the concept of trust in one's counselor, confidant, minister, priest, or rabbi. Relies on threat and coercion. Designed to induce the individual into **policing his own thoughts and excluding all "wrong thoughts."** Also would extend to dramatically influencing the individual's outward behavior. The idea is that the content of a person's mind is—essentially—the **property** of the cult.

ENFORCED GRATITUDE: Extreme gratitude and flowery praise are heavily encouraged. A new Scientologist soon learns that he is expected to be **very** grateful, and preferably in awe of "Ron and the Tech."

ENFORCED GUILT: If the **gratitude** "button" doesn't produce results right away, the **guilt** button is usually "pushed." (Scientology sales people rely on this and other "buttons.")

EXIT COUNSELING: Manipulative groups usually seek to confuse **exit counseling** with what has become known as "de-programming." The two are **very** different. **Exit counseling** is strictly **non-coercive.** It involves **only civilized communication,** and the relaying of information to another. The idea is to invite the person to **re-view** experiences and assumptions/beliefs adopted while in a Manipulative Group. Ironically, many Manipulative Groups use coercive methods—similar to the worst aspects of "de-programming" on their own "uncooperative" members. **This, however, does not deter such groups as Scientology from embarking on incredibly hypocritical PR campaigns against "de-programming," "mind-control," and "Brainwashing."**

FAIR GAME TECH: The know-how or "technology" of deception and trickery; of harassment and coercion through the use of the "legal system," ie., the courts; of harassment and destruction of opposing viewpoints through various "extra-legal" methods.

While an indoctrinated Scientologist privately considers "fair game" to be a sensible approach to dealing with Scientology's many "enemies," he does not realize that he too—in a very real sense—is "fair game" to the "greater Scientological scheme of things."

Hubbard's **secret writings** make a strong case for the idea that all Mankind, and also his own followers and friends, were always—essentially—"fair game."

FRONT GROUPS: It's not unusual for a Manipulative organization to utilize **fronts. Front groups** seek to conceal their connection to, or control by, another group.

HIDDEN BRIDGE: The pathway to unknowingly becoming the total effect of Scientology Operation. (With **"Total Freedom"** and "godlike causation" flashing in neon high above all the while.)

LOADED LANGUAGE: Language intended to be manipulative.

MILIEUX CONTROL: Environmental domination of an individual's thoughts, communication, and movement. (See the **Brainwashing Manual** and **Souls Turned Inside Out**)

NOISY INVESTIGATION: From Hubbard Communication Office Executive Letter of 5 September 1966:
"Subject: How to do a NOISY Investigation . . .
". . . You find out where he or she works or worked, doctor, dentist, friends, neighbors, **anyone,** and phone 'em up and say, 'I am investigating Mr/Mrs _____ for criminal activities . . .
"You say now and then, 'I have already got some **astounding** facts," etc. etc. (Use a generality)—It doesn't matter if you don't get much info. Just be NOISY . . ."

Such harassment is justified by the belief that all who are "anti" must have hidden crimes. Thus, making false accusations is OK, indeed, "ethical," since the person **MUST** have done such things, or worse.

THOUGHT-LIMITING CLICHÉ: "Maxims" or "truths" designed to shut off thinking.

VETTING: The cutting out with a razor blade of possible incriminating matter from documents. Another aspect of **Deception Tech.** A number of documents re. "vetting" were obtained during the FBI raids of 1977. Quoting from one:

"Now here are the details of what you VET.

"1. Mentions or the ordering of a B & E [breaking and entry]

"2. Evidence that anything was stolen by one of our guys . . .

"3. Lines similar to, 'Here are the docs we got in our usual way last night.'

"4. Evidence of casing, including keeping checks on working hours as well as locks on doors, etc.

"5. Implications of posing as a Gov't agent.

"6. Evidence of tapping phone lines or illegal taping of conversations.

"7. Mentions of harassment of an individual, although not necessarily in full operation (so not sent to **ops**).

"8. Any evidence of bribery.

"9. Any mentions of recruitments of FSM's [field staff members] to be any kind of an agent . . .

"10. Also **vet** wordings like, 'this will get him' or let's 'wipe him out' . . . or we are planning a covert **op**[eration] on him.

"11. Any mention of entrapment setting up someone to commit a crime either directly or indirectly."

WHITE SCIENTOLOGY: Term sometimes used to describe those bits and pieces of Scientology which—separated from the manipulative and malevolent, and from the Organization—can be utilized to honestly help others.

Destructive Cult Defined, and the Gradients of Deception: The Layers of the Scientological Onion

The American Heritage dictionary defines "cult" as, "1. A system or community of religious worship and ritual, especially when focusing upon a single deity or spirit. 2. a. Obsessive devotion or veneration for a person or principle, or ideal. b. The object of such devotion. 3. An exclusive group of persons sharing an esoteric interest.

None of these definitions fully describes groups such as Scientology.

The term "Destructive Cult" is a new term.

DESTRUCTIVE CULT is defined as "A closed system or group whose followers have been recruited deceptively, and retained through use of manipulative techniques of thought-reform or mind-control."

Some Destructive Cults have attempted to depict their critics as "anti-religious freedom." But having unusual ideas or beliefs, or being "out of the mainstream" does NOT qualify a group as a Destructive Cult.

Deception, followed by thought-reform, mind-control, or mind-manipulation—however one wishes to describe it—must be present.

This is a **gradual** process where an individual **unsuspectingly,** surrenders his natural—and real—freedoms, and his capacity to think for himself. What he gets in return is a promise that he will attain (fill in any desire or ideal).

And he gets more than that. He gets a group, a purpose, a new "elite" identity. **Initially, he may derive genuine benefit from his association with the group, or by reading its literature.**

Destructive Cults support "worthy causes" and offer seemingly sincere help. All they want in exchange is "your soul." "Cult-operations" want much more than money from those recruited, they ultimately seek to **own** their minds. Under "ideal" circumstances this is to be done gradually, and in a relatively "painless" manner.

The most successful Destructive Cult in the Western world today is Scientology. It is also probably the most dangerous.

Destructive Cults discreetly glorify fanaticism and ruthlessness. They revel—covertly—in hatred and destruction of "enemies." However, they sometimes have a hard time keeping their ruthlessness and hatred hidden from public view.

One characteristic of Destructive Cults is that they have **a lot** to hide, not only from "outsiders" but also from their own membership. The "inner elite" of such groups practice deception on the membership, just as the membership is expected to practice deception on the general public.*

THE SCIENTOLOGICAL ONION

Scientology is a "layers of the onion" operation.

The outermost layer of the "Scientological Onion" is not identifiable with Scientology at all, being composed of FRONT GROUPS that conceal their connection to—and control by—the Scientology organization.

These include "The Citizens' Commission on Human Rights," "The Association for Better Living Through Education" ("Able International"), the "Way to Happiness Foundation," the "Concerned Businessmen's Association of America," the "Foundation for Advancements in Science and Education," and numerous Management Consultation services using various names. There are also numerous **fronts** operating in the area of the **arts and entertainment**. While many Scientologists may be aware that these groups are part of Scientology, they are routinely presented to outsiders as independent, with no mention of Scientology.

The "Citizen's Commission on Human Rights" is one of Scientology's main fronts. In the last few years it's "cover has been blown" and it often presents itself—now—as a group loosely aligned with Scientology.

*As Steven Hassan correctly points out, a group can have "cult-like aspects" without being a **Destructive** Cult. It is vitally important to differentiate between mainly benign "cults" and malevolent Destructive Cults.

(The degree to which the connection with Scientology is concealed, varies depending on the occasion. It is usually hidden, but can be made known if it's seen as "forwarding Scientology"; or if the connection has been exposed by the "enemy," and can no longer be denied.*)

Other FRONTS that have existed at various times for various purposes include "Allied Scientists of the World," "National Academy of American Psychology," "Constitutional Administration Party," "Citizen's Press Association," the "Scottish Highland's Quietude Club," "Friends of Norton Karno," and "United Churches."**

Front groups might be said to constitute LAYER ZERO: a place where the tentacles of Scientology can grope incognito.

****

The FIRST LAYER of the Scientological Onion is meant to be VERY visible.

TV ads promoting Dianetics haunt late night TV. (And Dianetics is probably somewhere between Layer Zero and Layer One, often being used as a "front" lead-in to Scientology.)

Layer One includes Scientology's pampered clique of celebrities, and various public relations ploys, such as the "Dianetics" sponsorship of Ted Turner's "Goodwill Games." It reverberates with noble sounding sentiments about creating a better world. Scientology seeks

---

*It should be noted that the majority of the "rank-and-file" of the movement, when utilizing deception, do so to "forward Scientology" which they believe to be a wonderful thing. Unfortunately they don't realize that they have also been deceived, and the Church of Scientology is not what they believe it to be.

**In 1974 Scientology secretly moved to Clearwater, Florida, and under the name "United Churches" purchased a large amount of property. When months later it was discovered that, in fact, this was Scientology there was a public uproar, leading to an investigation by the mayor. Scientology instituted its own plan to "ruin utterly" the mayor's career and reputation. Scientology is now firmly planted in Clearwater.

In 1977 they secretly purchased a large amount of land at Gilman Hotsprings in Southern California. This time it used the name "Scottish Highland's Quietude Club." The usual uproar and commotion followed. Nonetheless, Scientology is still there.

In 1990 a group called the Association for Better Living through Education announced that it is donating 200 thousand dollars to another supposedly independent group called Narconon. Narconon was to use the money to purchase a large amount of land at Chillocco, Oklahoma. The deal was approved, and one seemingly respectable and independent group (supported by another seeming respectable and independent group) made the purchase. Both groups, of course, were Scientology. Ultimately, this became known, but it was too late.

to equate itself and its Founder with virtually anything broadly viewed as desirable or good. A little further along, this layer would include introductory courses and counseling with the stated aim of "knowing oneself" and "being free."

Here exist the potentially beneficial aspects of the vast and many-masked operation called Scientology. The tragedy of Scientology is that the "positives" are used as "window dressing" and "bait on the hook," when they should have been the core and foundation.

Thus the Scientology organization reeks of hypocrisy.

Also, at this much publicized "layer," L. Ron Hubbard is presented as an engineer, war hero, nuclear physicist, the "greatest Humanitarian of all time," and author of "22 Bestsellers With More to Come!"

This "first layer" is what Scientology wishes the outside world ("Wogs" and potential "Raw Meat") to know as Scientology. And it is essentially what new converts to the "movement" believe.

It includes most of the **what is good** in the subject: the dream of peace on earth, the desire to help, practical wisdom, civilized communication and potentially beneficial counseling procedures. The word **freedom** is used a great deal at this **layer,** and a heart-felt desire for greater personal freedom, and freedom for all Mankind, is not unusual in new recruits to Scientology.

****

(Any inconsistencies or contradictions between the publicly stated aims or claims of the movement, and actual practices or facts, become irrelevant as the individual becomes subject to the **Dark Side** of Scientology. And the deeper one descends into the "onion" the darker it gets.)

****

Descending into the "onion" it is necessary to BECOME a Scientologist. This means THINKING like a Scientologist. This is the **SECOND LAYER** where deception eases into "soft" forms of mind-control. **Love of Mankind** is modified by the awareness that human beings are mere hapless **Wogs.** The **Desire to Help** becomes the **desire to recruit.** The ideal of **practical wisdom** based on logic and science is superceded by the **belief** in the unfathomable mystery of the "tech." Indeed, one is expected to be in a state of awe regarding the "tech," much in the same manner a peasant woman might regard a piece of bone, said to have belonged to a Saint from centuries past.

The ideal of **Honesty** is modified by an awareness that **deception is**

OK as long as it serves to achieve a desired **Scientological END.** And the ideals of **civility** and **democracy** become a joke—just something that "panty-waists" and wimps fixate on.

One is slowly being "hatted" as a Scientologist.

(At this point an—unlucky—new Scientologist may be subjected to heavy handed **hard sell** tactics by a sales person or "registrar." Life savings have been lost, inheritances gobbled up, and lines of credit drained, all in a single arduous evening of "crush sell." This is really a premature taste of "Layer 4.")

****

The THIRD LAYER DOWN is composed of the never ending, very expensive, and highly confidential "upper levels." These go on and on—and on. Scientology has been selling the promise of "Total Freedom" since before most of its current membership were born. It remains the ever elusive "dangling carrot."

Well known individuals who become involved in the movement— becoming "Scientology Celebrities"—do not go any deeper into the Scientological onion than this.

They are also spared the abuses that "less valuable beings" may suffer at the hands of Scientology sales people, Sea Org recruiters, or "ethics officers."

Celebrities are highly valued for their "public relations function," and thus get the "red carpet treatment." Wealthy people, who can be expected to have friends who also are well-to-do, are also seen as a valuable resource, and can expect "special treatment." However "ordinary" people with middle-level incomes, some savings, good— but limited—credit, can become targets for heavy handed "reg cycles," and other unpleasant experiences.

****

The NEXT LAYER DOWN is the world of "Org Staff," and at the very **bottom** of LAYER FOUR can be found SEA ORG personnel.

This layer employs more pervasive and cruder forms of "persuasion" or "mind-control." Applied here are the worst aspects of Hubbard's **Brainwashing Manual.** Here also are the **Rehabilitation Project Force, the 5 Card System,** and the grim but repressed awareness that one is merely a "post" and a "stat." [i.e., statistic].

****

The FIFTH LAYER DOWN includes intimidation of the mass media, use of lawsuits purely for purposes of harassment, and applications of the policies and programs such as those revealed as the result of the FBI raids in July of 1977. These are elaborate, organized applications of the Fair Game Law and related policies, designed to harass, lie about, "sue, trick, lie to, or destroy," anyone perceived as an enemy. At this level also would be secret bank accounts and financial irregularities.

Another aspect of this level would be "blackmail." This would include threats to publicize personal information obtained during "religious confessionals" (auditing sessions); and the obtaining—by use of duress—of promises of "silence," and also the obtaining of "signed retractions" of earlier statements.

Here also can be found the handful of individuals who constitute the "Scientology hierarchy": the board of directors of the Religious Technology Center, and its current chairman David Miscavige or "DM."

****

LAYER NUMBER SIX appears to be the core of the Onion. It is a very temperamental and secret place.

Here-in lie the secrets of L. Ron Hubbard: his bad habits, bad health, bad marriages, undistinguished military service, flunked physics and engineering classes. Here-in can be found the actual motivations behind, and sources of, Dianetics and Scientology. Here can be found Mary Sue Hubbard, languishing in prison for crimes committed under her husband's direction, while her husband—in hiding—passed the time writing science fiction. Here are all the things you shouldn't know about the founder of the "Science of Knowing How to Know."

Bibliography

ANDERSON, Kevin, *Report on the Board of Inquiry*. (Government Printer, Melbourne, Australia, 1965)

ANDREWS, Lewis M., and Karlins, Marvin, *Biofeedback* (Warner, New York, 1973)

ASHBY, Robert, H., *Guidebook for Study of the Paranormal* (Samuel Weiser, Inc. York Beach, Maine, 1987)

ATACK, Jon, *A Piece of Blue Sky* (Carol Publishing, 1990)

CAMPBELL, John, W., "In Times To Come" in *Astounding Science Fiction* (December 1949, and March and April 1950)

CLEARWATER Hearings, Document Services, City of Clearwater, Florida.

COOPER, Paulette, *The Scandal of Scientology* (Tower, New York, 1971)

CROWLEY, Aleister, *The Complete Astrological Writings* (Duckworth, Dallas, Texas, 1979) This, and the majority of Crowley's writings, were originally published in the early part of this century.
—*Book 4* (Samuel Weiser, New York, 1980)
—*Book of The Law* (Thelema Publications, King-beach, California, 1976)
—*Book of Thoth* (Samuel Weiser Inc, New York, 1978)
—*Confessions of Aleister Crowley* (Bantam Books, New York, 1971)
—*Diary of a Drug Fiend* (Sphere Books, London 1979)
—*Eight Lectures on Yoga* (Falcon Press, Phoenix, Arizona, 1985)
—*Equinox*—A quarterly collection of writings by Crowley and others. *The Equinox* was first published in England 1909–1913. Copies reproduced by Samuel Weiser in 1972, and 1978.
—*Maqick in Theory and Practice* (Dover Books, 1976) Originally published in 1929.
—*Maqick Without Tears* (Falcon Press, Phoenix Arizona, 1983) Probably the most "readable" and "digestible" Crowley text.
—*Seven-Seven-Seven, and Other Qabalistic Writings* (Samuel Weiser, New York, 1973)
—*Tao Teh King*—Crowley's version that is. (Askin Publishers LTD and Samuel Weiser Inc., New York, 1976) Originally published by the OTO in 1947.

DE ROPP, Robert S., *The Master Game* (Dell Publishing, 1968)

DOUGLASS, William, O., *The Living Bill of Rights* (Doubleday and Company, New York, 1961)

EPSTEIN, Perle, *Kabbalah, The Way of the Jewish Mystic* (Doubleday & Company, New York, 1978)

ESTERSON, A and Laing, R. D., *Sanity, Madness and the Family* (Penguin Books, England)

FODOR, Nandor, *The Search for the Beloved: A Clinical Investigation of the Trauma of Birth and Pre-Natal Conditioning* (Hermitage Press, New York, 1949)

FREUD, Sigmund, *Two Short Accounts of Psycho-Analysis* (Pelican, Middlesex, England, 1984)
—*Studies in Para-Psychology* (Collier-Macmillan, New York, 1963)

FROMM, Erich, *Escape From Freedom* (Avon Books, New York, 1968)

FIRTH, Violet, *The Machinery of the Mind* (Samuel Weiser, Inc., York Beach, Maine, 1985) Originally published 1922. Violet Firth was better known as Dion Fortune.

FOSTER, Sir John G. *Inquiry into the Practice and Effects of Scientology* (HMSO, London, 1971)

GARRISON, Omar, *The Hidden Story of Scientology* (Arlington Books, London, 1974)
—*Playing Dirty* (Ralston-Pilot, Los Angeles, 1980)

GODIN, Andre, *The Pastor as Counselor* (Holt, Rinehart and Winston, New York, 1965)

HALL, Manly P., *Paracelsus—His Magical and Medical Philosophy* (The Philosophical Research Society, Los Angeles, 1977)

HARARY, Keith, and TARG, Russell, *The Mind Race* (Villard Books, New York, 1984)

HASSAN, Steven, *Combatting Cult Mind Control* (Park Street Press, Rochester, Vermont, 1988) A very valuable book for anyone seeking information or assistance in dealing with manipulative groups.

HAYAKAWA, S. T., Editor. *The Use and Misuse of Language*. Selected essays from *ETC.: A Review of General Semantics*. (Fawcett Premier Book published by arrangement with Harper and Row, 1962.) Original Copyright 1943.

HOFFER, Eric, *The True Believer* (Mentor Books, New York, 1964)

HUBBARD, L. Ron, *Creation of Human Ability* (All books published by Church of Scientology, Publications Organizations, Los Angeles) Originally published 1954.
—*Dianetics, the Evolution of a Science* (First published 1950)
—*Dianetics, the Modern Science of Mental Health* (Recently retitled, *Dianetics, Operators Manual for the Human Mind*]
—*Dianetics 55!* (1955)
—*History of Man* (early 1952)
—*Introduction to Scientology Ethics* (1965)
—*Mission into Time* (1968)
—*The Organization Executive Course ("Green") Volumes:* Consist of "management" and "organizational" policies and "tech." Does not include numerous confidential policy issues. The "Green Volumes" were originally assembled in the mid-1970s.
—*The Phoenix Lectures* (1954)
—*Scientology 0-8: The Book of Basics* (1972) Conceived and organized by John Sanborne.
—*Scientology 8-8008* (late 1952)
—*Science of Survival* (1951)
—*The Technical ("Red") Volumes*. Presented as all the "tech," but omits that which might result in "bad public relations."

HUNTER, Edward, *Brain-Washing in Red China* (Vanguard Press, New York, 1952) **A very** important early text on the subject.

HUXLEY, Aldous, *Brave New World Revisited* (Bantam Books, New York, 1958)

KAUFMAN, Robert, *Inside Scientology* (Olympia Press, London and New York, 1972)

KING, Francis, *The Magical World of Aleister Crowley* (Wiedenfield & Nicolson, London, 1977.)
—*Ritual Magick in England* (Neville Spearman, London, 1970)
—*The Secret Rituals of the OTO* (C. W. Daniel, London & New York, 1982)

KORZYBSKI, Alfred, *Manhood of Humanity: The Science and Art of Human Engineering* (Institute of General Semantics, Distributors, Lakeville, Connecticut, 1950) Originally published 1921.
—*Science and Sanity* (Institute of General Semantics. 1980) Originally published 1933.

KAPLAN, Aryeh, *In Theory and Practice—Sefer Yetzirah, the Book of Creation* (Samuel Weiser, New York, 1990) The original text is approximately two thousand years old.
—*The Bahir Illumination*—Original text attributed to Rabbi Nehunia ben haKana, master of the first century esoteric school. (Samuel Weiser, York Beach, Maine, 1979)

KROKOVSKY, Rabbi Levi Isaac, *Kabbalah. The Light of Redemption* (Research Centre of Kabbalah, New York, 1970)

KRUTCH, Joseph, *More Lives than One* (New York, Sloane Associates, 1962)

LAMONT, Stuart, *Religion Inc.* (Harrap, London, 1986)

LE Bon, *The Crowd* (Norman S. Berg, Publisher, Dunwoody, Georgia)

LEVI, Eliphas, *The Great Secret* (The Aquarian Press, Wellingborough, Northamptonshire, England, 1975)

LIFTON, Robert J., *Thought-Reform and the Psychology of Totalism* (Norton, New York, 1961)
—*The Future of Immortality and Other Essays for a Nuclear Age* (Basic Books, New York, 1987)

MALKO, George, *Scientology, the Now Religion* (Delacorte Press, New York, 1970)

MILLER, Russell, *The Bare-Faced Messiah* (Michael Joseph, London, 1987)

NIKITINE, Colonel B. V., *The Fatal Years* (William Hodge and Company, 1938)

O'BRIEN, Barbara, *Dianetics in Limbo* (Whitemore Publishing Co., Philadelphia, 1966)

OUSPENSKY, P. D., *The Psychology of Man's Possible Evolution* (Alfred A. Knopf, New York, 1971) Written in 1934.
—*Symbolism of the Tarot* (Dover, 1976)
PARSONS, John Whiteside, *Freedom is a Two Edged Sword* (Ordo Templi Orientis, New York, in association with Falcon Press, Las Vegas, 1989) Jack Parsons wrote these essays in the 1940s.
RABELAIS, Francois, *The Works of Rabelais* (Chatto Windus, 1870, London)
REGARDIE, Israel, *The Middle Pillar* (Llewellyn Publications, Saint Paul, Minnesota 1970) Original Copyright 1938 by Israel Regardie, Copyrighted in 1945 by The Aries Press.
—*Philosopher's Stone* (Llewellyn Publications, 1970) First edition 1938.
—*The Tree of Life* (Samuel Weiser, Inc., York Beach Maine, 1972) Originally published in 1932.
RIESS, Curt, *Total Espionage* (G. P. Putnam, 1975) Original copyright 1941.
SADHU, Mouni, *The Tarot, A Contemporary Course of the Quintessence of Hermetic Occultism* (Publisher unknown)
SEMON, Richard, *The Mneme* (Allen and Unwin, London, 1921)
—*Mnemic Psychology* (1923)
SPELT, David K. 'The Conditioning of the Human Foetus in Utero' in *Journal of Experimental Psychology* #38 (1948)
VAN VOGT, A. E., *Reflections* (Fictioneer Books, Lakemount, Georgia, 1975)
WALLIS, Roy, *The Road to Total Freedom* Heinemann, London, 1966)
WHITE, John: Editor, *Frontiers of Consciousness* (Avon Books, New York, 1974)
WILSON, Colin, *The Occult* (Vintage Books, New York, 1973)
WINTER, Joseph, *A Doctor's Report on Dianetics, Theory and Therapy* (Julian Press, 1951 and 1987)

Some sources of Help and Information:

BRIAN AMBRY, P.O. Box 53, Riverside, California 92501

THE FREE SPIRIT, An independent [ex-scientologist] quarterly. The Free Spirit expresses many points of view. Subscriptions $15.00 per year. Send checks or money orders to: Council for Spiritual Integrity, P.O. Box 6772, Santa Rosa, Ca. 95406.

THE ASHBY GUIDEBOOK FOR THE STORY OF THE PARANORMAL. Provides an extensive and descriptive bibliography; also provides addresses of many honest organizations working in the area. Available through Weiser's Books, Box 612, York Beach, Maine 03910.

C.A.D.A. The oldest independent dianetic organization. Incorporated 1951. 1412 Centinela Ave. #2, Inglewood, CA 90302.

The **Resources** section of Steven Hassan's COMBATTING CULT MIND CONTROL may be of value to those seeking assistance in dealing with manipulative groups. Available from Park Street Press, One Park Street, Rochester, VT 05767

CULT AWARENESS NETWORK, 2421 West Pratt Blvd., suite 1173, Chicago, 60645, Tel: 312-267-7777.

JERRY WHITFIELD AND HANA ELTRINGHAM WHITFIELD
Exit Counselors
661 N. Occidental Blvd.
Los Angeles, CA 90026

ASSISTANCE IN THE RETURN OF PAYMENTS TO SCIENTOLOGY
(818) 788-7022

TOBY PLEVIN, Attorney
10700 Santa Monica Blvd.
Suite 4-300
Los Angeles, CA 90025

COALITION OF CONCERNED CITIZENS
P.O. Box 290402
Tampa, Florida 33687

INTERNATIONAL VIEWPOINTS (Publication Representative Bob Ross)
P.O. Box 1413
Riverside, CA 92502

THE HERETIC
191 Harder Road #132
Haywood, CA 94544

THE INFORMER
1917 Hampton Lane
Glendale, CA 91201

FORD GREENE, Attorney
711 Sir Francis Drk. Blvd.
San Anselmo, CA 94960